914.38
Tor

Explore the

Nelles Guide

POLAND

Author:
Tomasz Torbus

An up-to-date travel guide
with 131 color photos
and 22 maps

PUBLIC LIBRARY, ELMHURST, IL

IMPRINT / LEGEND

Dear Reader: Being up-to-date is the main goal of the Nelles series. Our correspondents help keep us abreast of the latest developments in the travel scene, while our cartographers see to it that maps are also kept completely current. However, as the travel world is constantly changing, we cannot guarantee that all the information contained in our books is always valid. Should you come across a discrepancy, please contact us at: Nelles Verlag, Schleissheimer Str. 371 b, 80935 Munich, Germany, tel. (089) 3571940, fax: (089) 35719430, e-mail: Nelles.Verlag@t-online.de, internet: www.Nelles-Verlag.de

Note: Distances and measurements, including temperatures, used in this guide are metric. For conversion information, please see the *Guidelines* section of this book.

LEGEND

- ★★ Main Attraction (on map)
- ★★ (in text)
- ★ Worth Seeing (on map)
- ★ (in text)
- ❽ Orientation Number in Text and on Map
- ■ Public or Significant Building
- ■ Hotel
- ✝ Church
- ❈ View Point
- • Fountain

- Warszawa (Town) / Wawel (Sight) Places Highlighted in Yellow Appear in Text
- International/National Airport
- Nature Reserve
- (185) Mountain (altitude in meters)
- \ 13 / Distance in Kilometers
- 🛈 Tourist Information
- ⊖ Border crossing
- Castle
- Subway

- Motorway
- Expressway
- Principal Highway
- Provincial Road
- Secondary Road
- Pedestrian Zone
- Border
- Car Ferry
- $$$ Luxury Hotel Category
- $$ Moderate Hotel Category
- $ Budget Hotel Category
  (for price information see "Accomodation" in Guidelines section)

POLAND
© Nelles Verlag GmbH, 80935 München
All rights reserved

First Edition 2001
ISBN 3-88618-088-3
Printed in Slovenia

Publisher:	Günter Nelles	**Photo Editor:**	K. Bärmann-Thümmel
Editor-in Chief:	Berthold Schwarz	**Color Separation:**	Priegnitz, München
English Editor:	Sidaway/Sollinger	**Maps:**	Nelles Verlag GmbH
	Transwords	**Printed by:**	Gorenjski Tisk

No part of this book, not even excepts, may be reproduced in any form without the express written permission of Nelles Verlag
- S02 -

TABLE OF CONTENTS

Imprint / Legend 2
Map List 7

HISTORY AND CULTURE

Journey of Discovery 13
Geography 15
History 16
Fine Arts 34

TRAVELING IN POLAND

WARSAW 45
The Modern Center 48
Jewish Warsaw 48
Old Town (Stare Miasto) 49
New Town (Nowe Miasto) 51
The Royal Way 51
Łazienki Park 54
Wilanów Palace 55
INFO: Hotels, Restaurants, Sights 56

MASOVIA AND ŁÓDŹ 59
Kampinowski National Park 59
Płock 60
Łowicz and Environs 61
Łódź 62
INFO: Hotels, Restaurants, Sights 65

POZNAŃ AND GREAT POLAND 69
Poznań 69
The Castles of Great Poland 73
Gniezno 75
Kujawy 75
INFO: Hotels, Restaurants, Sights 76

KIELCE AND LUBLIN 81
Kielce 81
Góry Świętokrzyskie (Holy Cross Mountains) 82
Sandomierz 83
Baranów 84
Kazimierz Dolny / Lublin . . . . 84 / 85
Zamość 88
INFO: Hotels, Restaurants, Sights 90

TABLE OF CONTENTS

CRACOW 95
Main Market (Rynek Główny) 98
Wawel 105
Kazimierz 107
Auschwitz (Oświęcim) 111
Częstochowa 112
INFO: Hotels, Restaurants, Sights 115

LITTLE POLAND / GALICIA 121
Podhale and High Tatra 123
Pieniny Mountains and the Dunajec Gorge ... 128
Between Cracow and Przemyśl 130
Bieszczady 131
INFO: Hotels, Restaurants, Sights 132

SILESIA 137
Wrocław 138
En Route in Lower Silesia 146
Karzkonoze Mountains 149
Opole Country 151
INFO: Hotels, Restaurants, Sights 153

FROM GDAŃSK TO TORUŃ 159
Gdańsk 159
Kaschubia 169
Malbork 170
The Vistula Delta 174
Elbląg 175
Frombork 176
Kwidzyn 176
Chełmno Country 177
Toruń 178
INFO: Hotels, Restaurants, Sights 181

POMERANIA 187
Szczecin 188
The Island of Wolin 191
From Kołobrzeg to Słupsk 193
Łeba and the Słowiński National Park ... 195
INFO: Hotels, Restaurants, Sights 196

THE GREEN NORTHEAST 201
Olsztyn 201
Kętrzyn and Surroundings 206
Masuria 208
Suwałki 213
Biebrzański National Park / Białystok ... 215 / 216
Białowieski National Park 219
INFO: Hotels, Restaurants, Sights 221

TABLE OF CONTENTS

FEATURES

The Difficult Relationship Between Jews and Poles . . 226

Folk Art in Poland 230

Polish Cuisine 232

GUIDELINES

Travel Preparations 236
   Climate and Best Travel Times 236
   Entry Regulations 236
   Health Precautions 236
   Information 236
   Staying Safe / Customs Regulations 237

Arrival 237
   By Air 237
   By Car / By Rail 238
   By Bus / By Ferry 238

Traveling in Poland 238
   By Air 238
   By Car / By Rail 239
   By Long Distance Bus 240
   Local Transportation / Taxi 240
   Hitchhiking 240

Practical Tips from A to Z 241
   Accommodation 241
   Addresses of Diplomatic Representations 241
   Biking / Business Hours / Dangers 242
   Electricity / Emergencies 242
   Entertainment 243
   Fishing and Hunting 243
   Holidays / Information 243
   Maps / Money Exchange / Currency 244
   Photography 244
   Physicians and Pharmacies 244
   Post Office / Telephone 244
   Restaurants / Restrooms / Shopping 245
   Sports / Supplementary Reading 246
Language Guide 246

Author / Photographers 249

Index 250

POLAND

MAP LIST

MAP LIST

Poland 6/7
Poland in 1939 27
Warsaw 46/47
Warsaw's Old Town 50
Masovia 61
Poznań 70
Around Poznań 73
Around Kielce and Lublin . . . 82/83
Cracow 97
West of Cracow 109
Little Poland 122/123
Tatrzański National Park 127
Silesia 138/139
Wrocław. 140
Karkonosze National Park 149
Gdańsk 160
From Gdańsk to Toruń 171
Toruń 179
Around Szczecin 189
Masuria 202/203
Suwałki / Biebrzański
National Park 213
Białystok / Białowieski
National Park 218

7

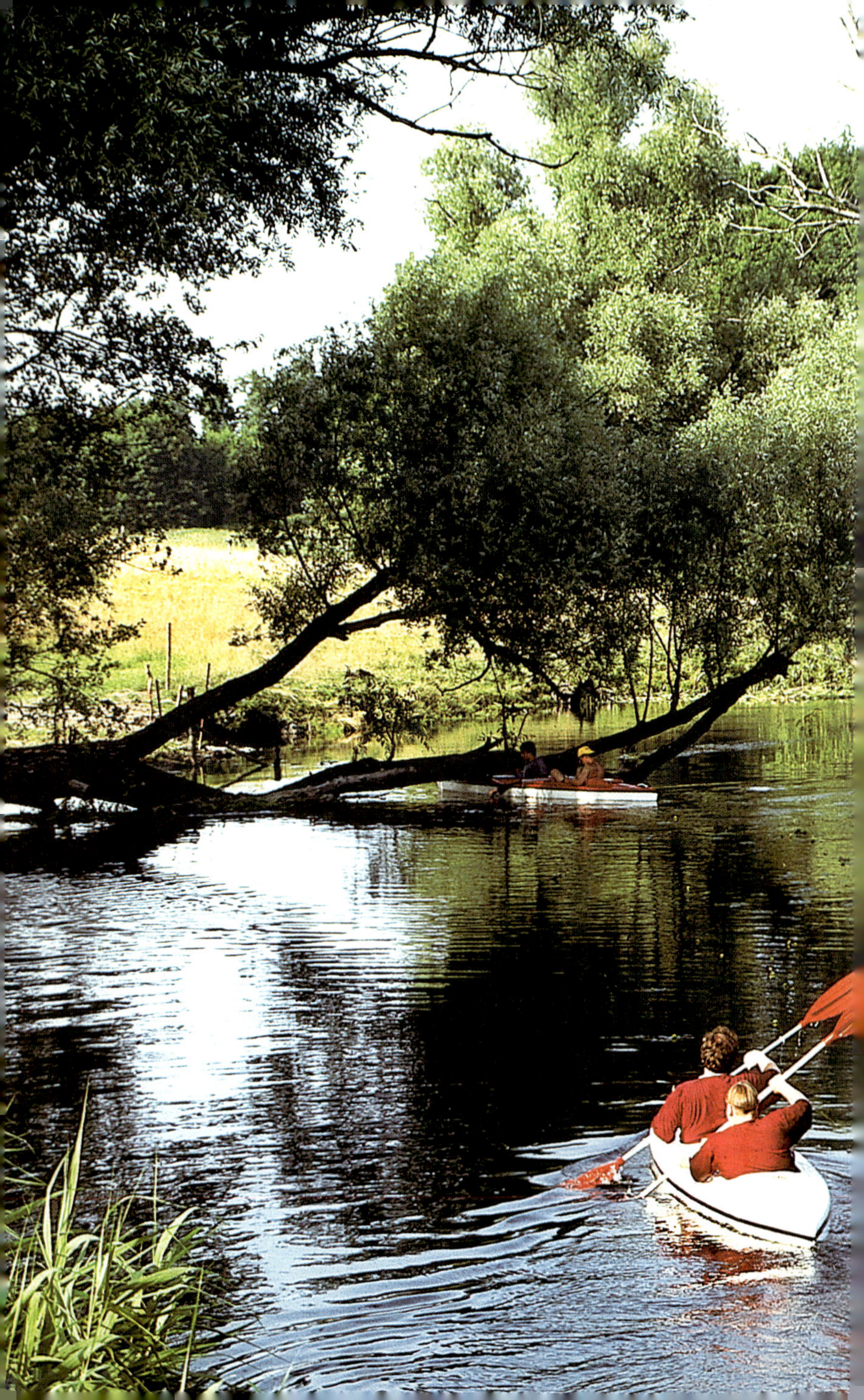

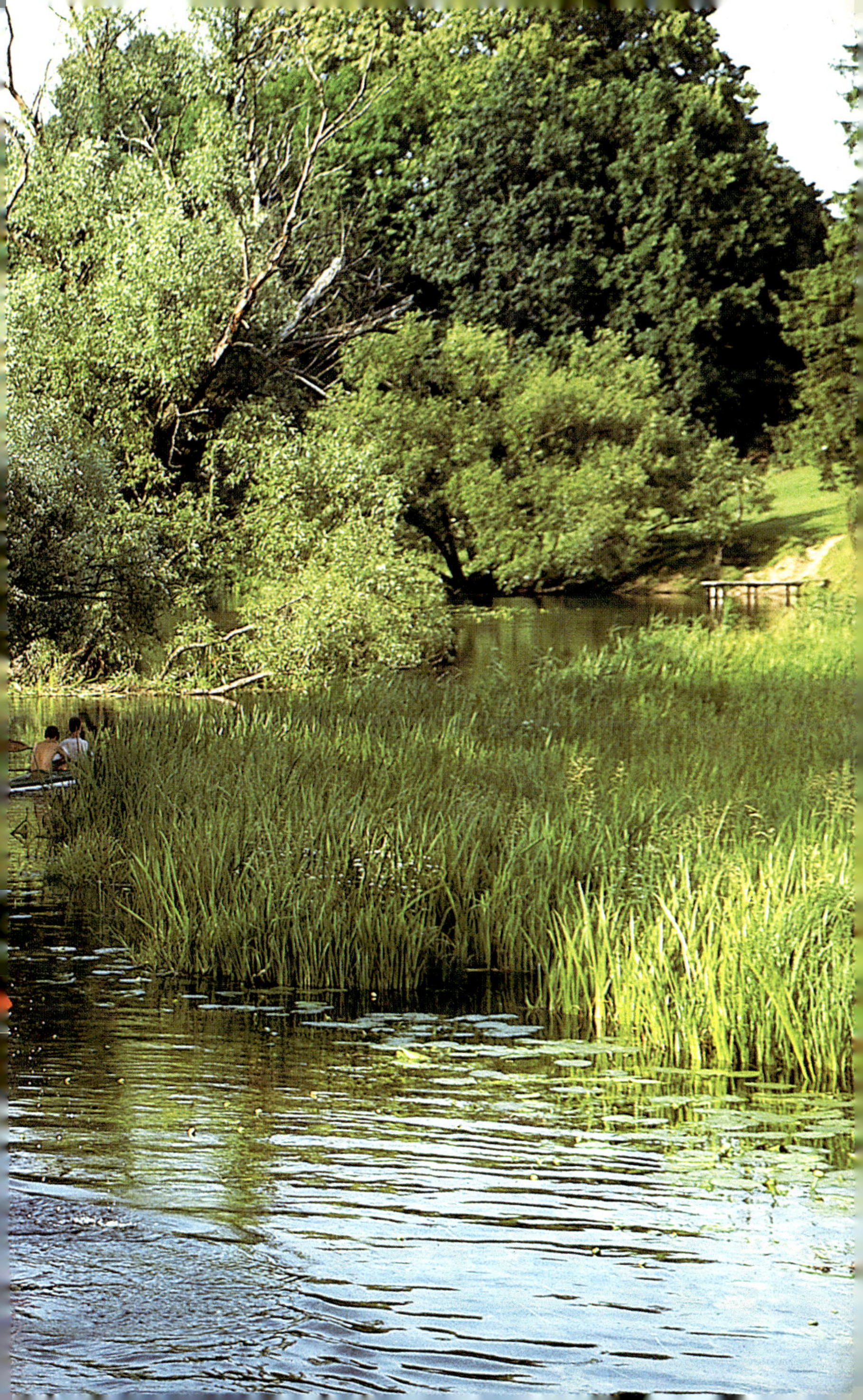

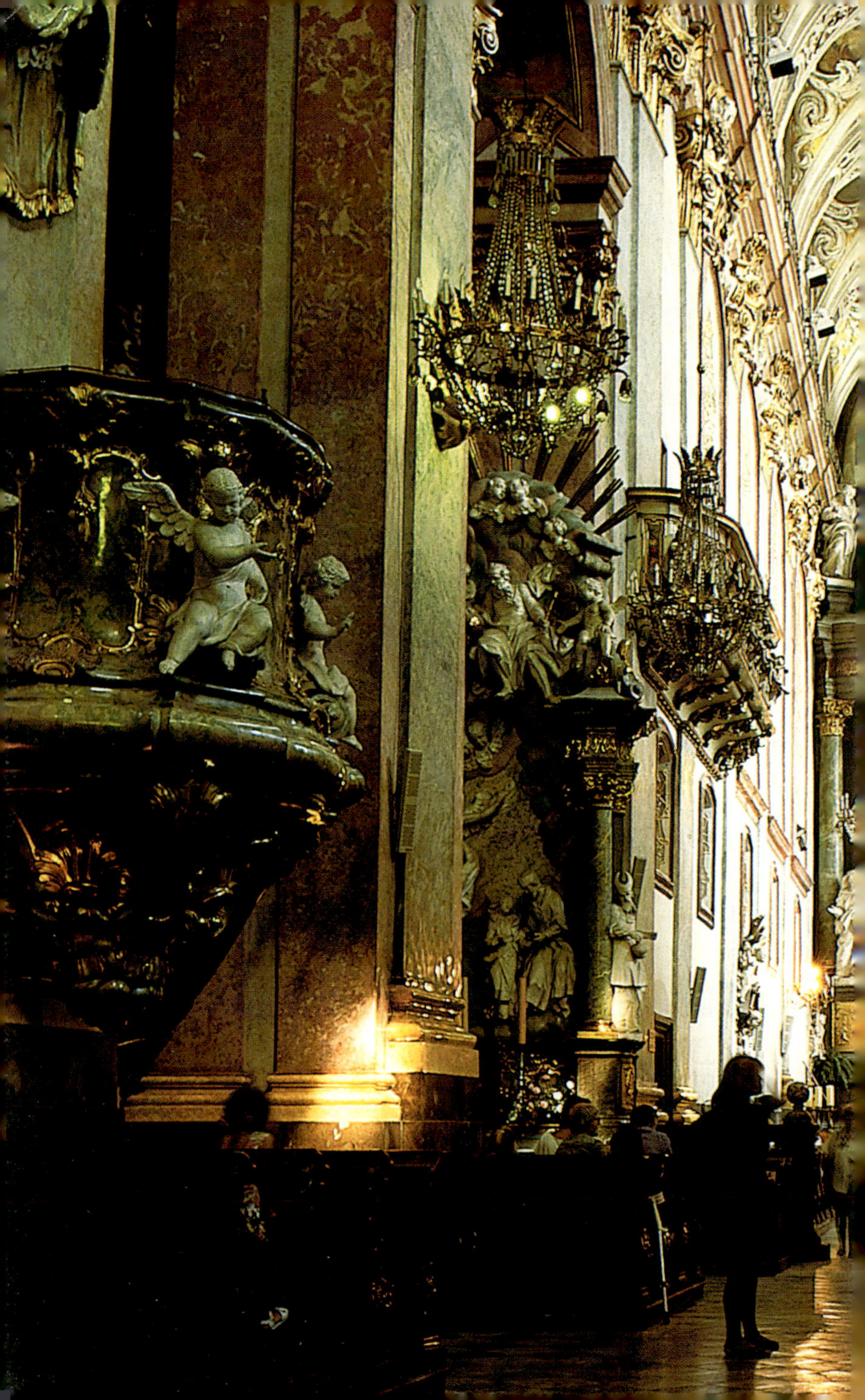

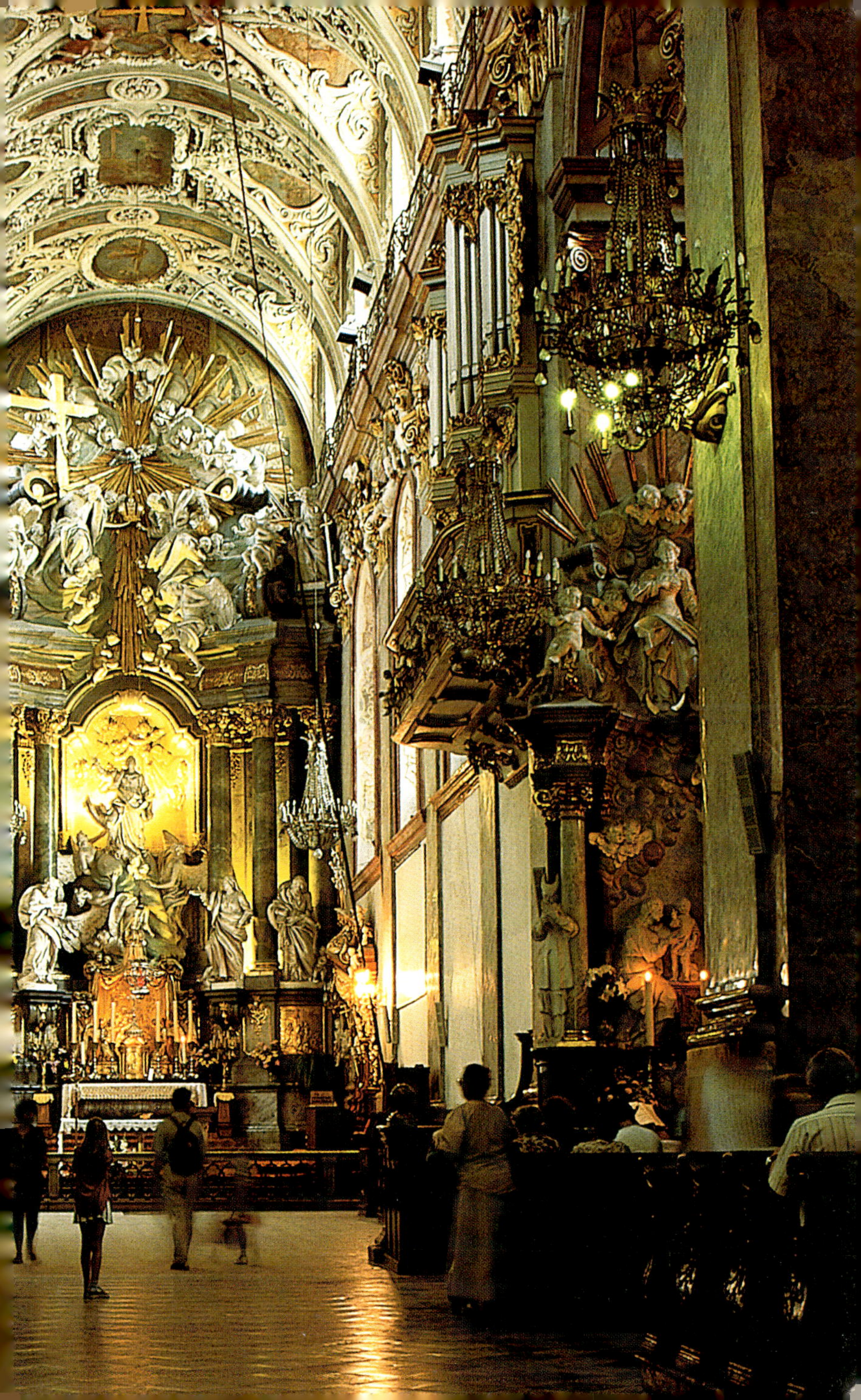

HISTORY AND CULTURE

HISTORY AND CULTURE

Journey of Discovery

Less than 100 kilometers east of Berlin is the national border of one of the largest and most densely populated countries in Europe, Poland. But with under 40 million inhabitants and an area comparable to New Mexico in the United States, it is still a country which is surprisingly unknown. Separated from the west until recently by the Iron Curtain and a difficult place to visit because of the compulsory exchange and registration regulations, it is only now starting to become a more popular destination.

Still today, scant associations spring to mind in connection with Poland, and some of those are negative. It is the land of *Solidarność* which undermined the Soviet system in Eastern Europe, but also the land of chaotic individualists, illegal workers and car thieves. Everyone knows the name of Lech Wałęsa, the electrician who became president, and Karol Wojtyła, also known as Pope John Paul II. The nation's famous emigrants often had very non-Polish sounding names such as Frédéric Chopin, Marie Curie (Maria Skłodowska) and Joseph Conrad (Teodor Józef Konrad Korzeniowski). They are thus less frequently associated with Poland than, for example, current well-known representatives of the arts such as the directors Roman Polański, Andrzej Wajda and Krzysztof Kieślowski, the playwrights Tadeusz Kantor and Jerzy Grotowski, the composers Krzysztof Penderecki and Witold Lutosławski, the writers and poets Sławomir Mrożek, Stanisław Lem and Zbigniew Herbert and recent winners of the Nobel prize for literature Czesław Miłosz and Wisława Szymborska.

Poland is a land full of contradictions, perhaps because, in the words of the poet Stanisław Jerzy Lec, in the west it is called the east and in the east it is called the west. Once a powerful empire which was allegedly brought down by an excess of democracy, it became a stateless society with a powerful sense of nationality and tragic uprisings against the superior might of its occupiers. The communist era paradoxically featured private land ownership and Catholic holidays. Today Poland is the country with the highest economic growth rate in Europe and an increasingly ordered political scene. It is preparing for EU membership, after joining NATO in March 1999.

The country has a great deal to offer its visitors. The royal city of Cracow has splendid Gothic and Renaissance architecture and a uniquely religious atmosphere which miraculously survived the turmoil of the country's history intact. Warsaw has the largest reconstructed "Old Town" center in Europe and furthermore a lively cultural scene and Gdańsk, queen of the Baltic is high on the list of attractions, with its Dutch and Hanseatic influences. Malbork with its castle (also called the Marienburg) recalls the power of the medieval Teutonic state of Prussia, and the east of Poland is full of undiscovered treasures: beautiful wooden churches, imposing ancestral castles – even, surprisingly, wooden mosques dating from the 18th century!

The cultural history of Poland is much richer than might be supposed. Cultural impulses from Germany, France, Italy, the Netherlands, the Ukraine and other countries, met in Poland. It was also in particular the country of the Jews – until the 19th century Poland had the largest

Previous pages: Canoeing on the rivers and lakes of Masuria – vacation fun in Poland. The pilgrimage church of Częstochowa, centre of religion and national identity. Left: the First Partition of Poland in 1772, the beginning of a long period of national suffering (contemporary copper engraving by J.E. Nilsson).

HISTORY AND CULTURE

concentration of Jews. Looking for the traces of their unique culture (and also of their martyrdom in the Holocaust) – whether in Cracow, Warsaw or Łódź – is part of every tour of Poland.

There is, however, a further, equally important reason for vacationing in Poland. With over 20 national and numerous country parks it is a place for nature-lovers – a place for hiking, cycling or boating. The scenery ranges from the widest sandy beaches on the continent, the rugged coast of Wolin and the unique desert landscape around Łeba to the lofty alpine peaks of the High Tatra and the more gentle but no less attractive summits of the Karkonosze or Giant Mountains or the Pieniny, where a raft ride through the Dunajec Gorge is a must on the itinerary.

Above and right: Poland's many national parks with their very varied ecology provide nature-lovers with ample opportunity to observe plants and animals (little bitterns with their young in the nest; lynx on the prowl).

Masuria is a year-round magnet for hikers and yachting enthusiasts. The land of three thousand lakes, with a charming landscape of small moraine hills and dense forest, one gets the feeling that all is still right with the world. In the villages, with their colonies of storks, you are transported into another age in which farmers drive one-horse carts and the background noises are of barking dogs and gabbling geese, which roam freely.

The last primeval forest in Europe, near Białowieża, the endless swamps of Biebrza and the empty landscape of Bieszczady are the habitat of Poland's wide range of fauna, including bison, elk, lynx, wild cats and brown bears as well as golden and sea eagles and Aesculapian snakes.

Poland's interesting cuisine, the exciting new political and economic era, and last but not least the legendary hospitality of its inhabitants, all add to the attractions of a country that seems remote but begins, as we have already said, less than 100 kilometers east of Berlin.

GEOGRAPHY

The Republic of Poland (*Rzeczpospolita Polska*) is geographically located in Central Europe, but politically and culturally often associated with Eastern Central Europe. With an area of 312,683 square kilometers, it is approximately the size of the U.S. state of New Mexico. It is the only country in the world to have had a complete change of neighbors along all of its borders since 1989, with the exception, of course, of the 524-kilometer-long natural border, the Baltic coast. The former German Democratic Republic (East Germany) became part of the Federal Republic of Germany; Czechoslovakia separated into the Czech Republic and Slovakia; and the USSR disintegrated into the CIS or Confederation of Independent States (Russia and the Kaliningrad region), Belarus, the Ukraine and Lithuania. With almost the same distance from east to west and from north to south (around 650 kilometers) Poland is roughly square in shape.

Today Poland's approximately 38.5 million inhabitants are largely ethnic Poles, although before 1939 only 69 percent of the population was actually Polish. Of the national minorities, the Germans are the largest (roughly 600,000, mostly around Opole), followed by Belorussians and Ukrainians (approximately 200,000 each). In terms of religion, 95 percent of the population is Roman Catholic; the largest minority religion is Orthodox, divided between the Autocephalous Orthodox Church and the Greek Catholic (Uniate) Church. There were three million Jews in prewar Poland, there are only around 5,000 today.

Poland's topography is characterized by almost parallel strips. In the north behind the Baltic coast is a belt of undulating glacial terrain, with the Pomeranian and Masurian lake districts (*Pojezierze Pomorskie, Pojezierze Mazurskie*), separated by the broad Vistula Valley. The center of the country – made up of Great Poland and Mazovia (*Nizina Wielkopolska, Nizina Mazowiecka*) – is flat.

HISTORY AND CULTURE

Southeast of this begin the highlands, which include the Cracow-Częstochowa Jura (*Wyżyna Krakowsko-Częstochowska*) underlain by Jura limestone, the very old Holy Cross Mountains (*Góry Świętokrzyskie*), and the Lublin Highlands (*Wyżyna Lubelska*) with their thick layer of loess.

Running along the country's southern border are the Sudeten Mountains in the West and the Carpathian Mountains in the East, separated by the Odra Valley (Moravian Gap / *Brama Morawska*). The *Karkonosze* (or Giant Mountains) with the peak *Śnieżka* (1,602 meters) in the Sudeten range, and the High Tatra (*Wysokie Tatry*) in the Carpathians are alpine with glacial trough valleys and cirque lakes. The highest mountain on the Polish side of the Tatra range, Mount Rysy (2,499 meters), is also the highest in the country.

HISTORY

Any account of the highly checkered, thousand-year history of Poland should start out by seeking a common denominator. With entry into the European Union on the agenda, the country has in any case been plunged into a discussion of its historical heritage.

Many Poles are thinking about their history and what is meant by the "Polishness" which is allegedly threatened by westernization and the advent of the consumer society. The introduction of freedom of the press after 1989 meant that at last the "gaps" in the country's history, subjects that were either banned from the official communist version of history or else presented in distorted form, could be openly discussed: the black-and-white picture of Poland as the constant victim of wicked neighbors has since acquired some shades of gray. A more objective study of its history shows that the country was not only the plaything of foreign powers: the periods of prosperity and decline were more or less evenly balanced.

Nevertheless, from the late Middle Ages to the mid-17th century Poland (together with Lithuania) was a European power on a par with the Hapsburgs that waged wars of conquest in present-day Romania and Estonia and on a number of occasions challenged Moscow. Later on in the country's history, for example in the 18th century and during the communist dictatorship, it became a society without a state, with at best only limited sovereignty.

Trapped between Germany and Russia

The Poles have always felt trapped between two great powers – Germany and

Above: Long sandy beaches on the Baltic coast attract many holiday-makers. Right: 1.5% of Poles are Orthodox – Russian Orthodox churches can be found particularly in the east of the country (Narew, East Poland).

HISTORY AND CULTURE

Russia, a reality that, in times of peace and cooperation between these two states, had devastating consequences for Poland. The boundaries of the Polish state have changed considerably over the centuries, largely due to the fact that there are no obvious natural borders either in the East or the West, and the ethnic boundaries in Eastern Central Europe have never been sure determinants of political borders. If, however, we look more closely at traditional Polish-Russian and Polish-German enmity, the picture becomes much more complex.

Antagonism against Russia began in the 16th century, since prior to this there was no Moscow-based Russia as such. Poland-Lithuania wanted to sell the "true religion" – Western European culture and the Western European social model – to the east, while Moscow's aim was to acquire the "Russian" countries, whatever these really were. In the resulting conflicts, Poles and Lithuanians were often the aggressors, until as of the 18th century the tables were turned and Russia gradually moved West, soon controlling the Polish state. Apart from two short intervals (1795-1815 and 1914-1944), Poland has essentially been a Russian protectorate since 1717. Only after 1989 did it become free to choose its own allies again – for the first time in 300 years.

Contrary to popular opinion, which is still shaped by vivid memories of the occupation of 1939-1945, the country's relationship with Germany, its neighbor immediately to the West, twice its size and economically much more powerful, was by no means dominated by armed conflict. Apart from the problems with the Teutonic State, which was not part of the Holy Roman Empire, there were no wars with the German Empire for 500 years. The western border of Poland was one of the most stable in Europe. It was also highly permeable: many Polish towns have a prominent ethnic German citizenry, which was already largely integrated into Polish society by the 16th century, and which survives today only in surnames such as Miler, Szmid, Fukier or

HISTORY AND CULTURE

Denhof. This fruitful relationship was gradually undermined with the partition of the country in 1772-1795.

Catholicism

Polish history can only be understood in the light of the country's close ties to the Catholic Church. The country has always considered itself to be the easternmost bastion of true Christendom. Poles are credited with christianizing Lithuania, the last heathen European state, in 1386. In 1444 they tried in vain to topple Constantinople, in the course of which the young king Władysław IV lost his life in a battle near Warna (now in Bulgaria). In 1683 the Polish king Jan III Sobieski commanded a multinational army which saved Vienna from the Turks.

Above: Pope John Paul II (Karol Wojtyła) on a visit to his homeland. Right: These stone figures are relics of the natural religion of the Prussians who lived in the northeastern part of the country (Museum in Olsztyn).

During the partition period of 1795-1918, the Protestant (Prussian) and Russian Orthodox (Russian) occupiers gave the Catholic Church no opportunity to negotiate with them. This strengthened the Church's popularity as the protector of the people.

The Nazi and communist regimes, which both openly fought the Church, could do nothing to lessen its popularity – and in fact achieved precisely the opposite. The Polish Pope John Paul II, whose election helped undermine communist power in Poland, is the country's great national hero.

It is, paradoxically, democracy and the market economy that have begun to empty the churches. While their political influence was still very strong during the military rule of 1981-1983, it is now on the wane. The old assumption that all Poles are Catholic is no longer quite as applicable. Newspapers even run historical articles which present a much more complex view of the Church than they might have only a short while ago.

The idea that people of other faiths can also be patriotic Poles, such as the current president Jerzy Buzek, who comes from the strong Protestant minority centered around Cieszyn on the Czech border, is something the population is now having to come to terms with.

Piast Dynasty (966-1370)

The name and origins of the Polish state go back to the Polians, one of the West Slavic tribes that populated the country along the Vistula and Odra starting around the fifth century A.D. After the state they established near Poznań had been in existence for several decades, the Polians' ruler Duke Mieszko I (reigned 960-992), one of the successors of the legendary tribal chief Piast, was converted to Christianity. This event, which took place in 966, is considered to mark the formal birth of the state of Poland.

When his successor Bolesław I Chrobry ("Boleslaus the Brave" 992-1025) founded the archbishopric of Gniezno in the year 1000, this already included the bishoprics of Poznań, Cracow, Wrocław and Kołobrzeg. The coronation of Bolesław as the first Polish king in 1025 established the country as part of Christendom, thus putting an end to the repeated attempts of the Holy Roman Empire to force the Polish dukes into a position of feudal dependency.

The reign of Bolesław III Krzywousty ("Boleslaus the Wry-Mouthed"; 1102 to 1138) who came to power after a period of unrest, restored stability to the country. He divided Poland into four sections in order to provide for each of his sons. The principle of seniority, designating the oldest son as ruler in Cracow, with power over the other provinces, was implemented to guarantee the existence of the central state. Though meaning well, this proved a disaster: it resulted in the division of Poland for almost two centuries into individual principalities, and ushering in a period of highly complex internal conflicts. In Silesia alone, there were for a time 14 separate territories. It was at this time that Poland lost Pomerania, and the Silesian duchies gradually began to transfer their allegaince to the kingdom of Bohemia. When Kazimierz III Wielki (Casimir the Great) agreed to the separation of Silesia from Poland in the Treaty of Trentschin in 1335, he was simply acknowledging a *fait accompli*.

At the northern border, the Polish principalities were confronted with an increasingly powerful neighbor who was later to become their arch enemy. Duke Konrad I of Mazovia, a ruler who was overwhelmed by his country's constant internal conflicts, was unable to control the pagan Prussians, a Baltic tribe in the present northeastern part of Poland. In 1230 he offered the Teutonic Knights – a German order previously active in Palestine and Hungary – a stretch of land north of Toruń in exchange for help with repelling the invaders. The Knights subjugated

HISTORY AND CULTURE

the Prussians and established the theocratic, centrally administered Teutonic state of Prussia. However, when in 1308 they seized Gdańsk – capital of a Slavic duchy, which Poland had acquired a few years earlier – the initial peace with Poland came to an end.

The country was eventually reunified under Władysław II Łokietek, although at his coronation as King of Poland in 1320 his territory consisted only of Great Poland and Little Poland. The foundations for an efficient state were laid by his successor Kazimierz III Wielki (1333-1370), who was the only ruler in Polish history to receive the sobriquet of "Great."

He consolidated the state, organized the legal and tax systems and regulated the revenue of the royal family. These measures made him a popular king, who also acquired a reputation as a great architect said to have found Poland built of wood and left it built of stone. He extended Poland's boundary east to Lvov (Ukrainian name: Lviv) by means of skilled negotiation rather than armed conflict and opened the country to the Jewish refugees from the Empire, giving them many privileges because of their contribution to the country's development. In 1364 the modernized country established a university in Cracow, the second in Central Europe after Prague. None of the king's wives gave him a son (although he had a large number of illegitimate ones), so that with his death the main Polish line of the Piast dynasty came to an end.

Anjou and Jagiellonian Dynasty (1370-1572)

To regulate the succession after his death, Kazimierz III Wielki had made a testamentary contract with the Hungarian royal house of Anjou. In accordance with this agreement, Ludwik Węgierski (Louis of Hungary) succeeded to the Polish throne in 1370. This rather unpopular ruler was followed by his daughter Jadwiga (reigned 1384 to 1386), who stood high in the affections of the people. She is the only queen in Poland's history and was canonized in 1997.

In 1386 she was forced for reasons of state to marry a much older "savage" – the Lithuanian prince Jagiello, who became Władysław II Jagiełło, King of Poland. He committed himself to christianizing Lithuania, uniting it with Poland and tackling their common enemy, the Teutonic state of Prussia. The subsequent conflict was not merely due to German-Polish antagonism, but a struggle for supremacy in Eastern Europe. Subsequent to its crushing defeat of the Teutonic Knights at Tannenberg (Grunwald) in 1410, the Polish-Lithuanian state became the dominant power of the next 250 years.

Wars against the Teutonic Knights were waged throughout the 15th century, until Poland finally took Eastern Pomerania, Gdańsk, Warmia (part of Prussia) and even Malbork (1466). What was left of the Prussian state became the Protestant Duchy of Prussia, under Polish suzerainty (1525).

The era (1506-1572) of the last two Jagiellonian kings, Zygmunt I Stary (Sigismund I the Old) and Zygmunt II August (Sigismund II Augustus), was a "golden age" for Poland. The Union of Lublin (1569) finally made the multinational Polish-Lithuanian double state a single indivisible entity, and geographically the largest country in Europe. The kingdom extended to Smolensk in the East, and, after the oath of allegiance in Livland of the last of the land-owning Teutonic Knights (1561), its northern boundary lay well beyond Riga.

A sophisticated humanist culture flourished in the country, with Renaissance art, Polish poetry (Jan Kochanowski) and social utopias such as that of Frycz

Right: The tomb of Kazimierz the Great is a masterpiece of High Gothic art (Coronation Cathedral in Cracow, Wawel).

Modrzewski, the friend of Erasmus of Rotterdam. The kingdom also achieved economic prosperity through the export of grain, construction timber, domestic animals and hemp – via the port of Gdańsk to Western Europe.

King Zygmunt II, who was personally indifferent to religion, guaranteed complete religious freedom, on the premise that "I am not king of your consciences." Although Catholicism predominated, over half of the aristocratic members of Parliament were Protestant. The burning of heretics at the stake and "St. Bartholomew's Day-type Massacres" were unknown, and Jews, Moslems and Armenians could openly practice their respective religions. The various Protestant sects, such as the anti-Trinitarians (Arians), which were cruelly persecuted even in Lutheran and Calvinist countries, had their universities and printing presses in Poland. However, even during this golden age, the first signs of trouble were beginning to appear, as the aristocracy acquired increasing influence, weakening the power of the throne, and it became much more difficult to introduce political reforms.

The Era of the Elected Kings (1573-1795)

Poland-Lithuania became a "Rzeczpospolita" (respublica), a republic under the rule of the nobility, who comprised only 10 percent of the population and enjoyed all the rights.

This aristocratic class, whose members all had the same privileges, whether they were powerful rulers with their own territories (such as the Radziwiłłs or Potockis), or landless officials at the courts of more wealthy individuals, decreed that all kings should be elected by a general assembly of noblemen. The elected king was obliged to guarantee the rights of the nobility, or risk being deposed.

The rapid spread of Reformation ideas into Poland was halted in Poland at the beginning of the 17th century. The religious tolerance still fostered during the

HISTORY AND CULTURE

1576-1586 reign of Stephen Bathory (Polish: Stefan Batory), gave way to an increasingly militant Catholicism under the three Waza kings.

The reigning monarch was the arch-Catholic Zygmunt III Waza (Sigismund III Vasa) when the Union of Brest, 1595, made the provision that under a "Uniate Church" the Orthodox population of eastern Poland could continue to worship according to the Orthodox rite but was obliged to acknowledge the supremacy of the Pope. Since this agreement was not universally accepted, religious and social conflict continued to escalate in this area, where the peasants were Ukrainians and the land-owners Poles.

The 1648 Cossack uprising in the Ukraine, lead by Bohdan Chmielnicki, undermined Poland's position of power abroad. The Ukraine east of the Dnieper river resisted Polish influence and in 1667, after many years of conflict, finally sided with Moscow. Preceeding this, the situation in Poland had already gotten completely out of hand in the First Nordic War against Sweden in 1655-1660 (subject of a novel by Henryk Sienkiewicz). Sweden controlled the entire country with the exception of Gdańsk, Zamość, Lviv and the Pauline monastery in Częstochowa. In Poland's hour of need, King Jan II Kazimierz Waza (John II Casimir Vasa) proclaimed the Black Madonna of Częstochowa, Queen of Poland, who became the inspiration for the Polish troops. The war began to turn in the country's favor and the Madonna became the enduring symbol of the unity and freedom of Catholic Poland (cf page 114).

The Swedes were forced to withdraw, leaving behind them devastation on an unprecedented scale. Even the splendid victory of King Jan III Sobieski (reigned 1674-1696) over the Turks (Chocim 1673, Vienna 1683), in the war waged against them by Poland, Bavaria and Austria, could not hide the fact that Poland was no longer the supreme power in Eastern Europe.

The country's foreign policy problems were compounded by decline on the domestic front. The enduring economic crisis following the wars with Sweden, and the unrestricted power of various sections of the nobility that had replaced central governance by the king, gave rise to the saying "Polonia confusione regitur" (Poland is ruled by disorder).

The first disruption of a parliamentary session occurred in 1652, when one member walked out before a resolution was formally passed. This set a precedent and the *liberum veto* became part of the constitution, meaning that a resolution could not be passed if even only one member of the nobility expressed disapproval. The parliament became largely incapable of achieving anything, since any member of the nobility, and even foreign powers (by bribing a national representative), could undermine any reform attempted by the state. What was intended to be a legal principle of the highest order ended by destroying the entire state.

The Partition of Poland

The disintegration of power continued during the reigns of the Saxon August II Mocny (the Strong) and August III (1697-1733 and 1733-1763). Under Russian dominance Poland also fell into the hands of other foreign powers. In 1764 Catherine the Great's lover Stanisław August Poniatowski was elected king.

With the Russian-Turkish wars in the Balkans, Catherine the Great realized that Russia could not continue to control the whole of Poland by itself and decided to exploit this powerless country to appease Prussia and Austria. This is what lead to the First Partition of Poland in 1772. The Russians annexed a section of East Po-

Right: From 1697 to 1733 the Saxon, August II (the Strong) was King of Poland.

HISTORY AND CULTURE

land and handed over Galicia to the Austrians, to avoid conflict with this ally of Turkey, while Prussia took over the Baltic regions.

The partition served as an indication to the Great Powers that borders in East-Central Europe could apparently be shifted at will – setting a dangerous precedent for the region.

The shock of the First Partition of the country made the king all the more determined to reform the state. The May Constitution – the first basic national law in Europe – came into force on 3 May 1791 at which time Poland was declared a parliamentary, hereditary monarchy. War was the result.

Russia and Prussia were panic-stricken by the prospect of the ideas of the French Revolution making their appearance on the Vistula. The two armies took military action against the reformers, resulting in the Second Partition of Poland in 1793 and further areas of the country being annexed. This resulted in an armed uprising, led by Tadeusz Kościuszko (1794 - 1795), a former adjutant of George Washington in the American War of Independence.

The suppression of this rebellion was followed by the Third Partition of Poland (1795). What was left of the country was divided between Russia, Prussia and Austria and, for the next 123 years, Poland disappeared from the map as an independent state.

Poland Divided (1795-1918)

In the 19th century Poland vacillated between uprisings and hopes of independence, resignation and waves of emigration. Great hopes were also placed in Napoleon; the Polish legions fought in all his wars (a hymn that was written later – "Poland is not lost, as long as we still live" – originated from their ranks). After his victory over Prussia, Napoleon founded the Grand Duchy of Warsaw, which existed from 1807 to 1813 – however this was but a poor substitute for a Polish state.

HISTORY AND CULTURE

At the Congress of Vienna in 1815 the borders were redrawn yet again, in what is is sometimes referred to as the "Fourth Partition of Poland." A kingdom of Poland was created, though annexed to Russia and known as "Congress Poland," as well as a second entity known as the "Free State" of Cracow.

The November Insurrection of 1830-1831 against the Russian overlords was at first successful, but was soon violently suppressed.

The storming of Warsaw in September of 1831 marked the end of Russia's relatively liberal stance toward Poland and the beginning of outright Russianization. The defeat resulted in a mass emigration, particularly to Paris – which was becoming the new home of the country's cultural elite – and including the poets Adam Mickiewicz and Juliusz Słowacki and composer Frédéric Chopin.

Another uprising in Cracow in 1846 was followed by the annexation of this last autonomous part of Poland by Austria. The Poznań uprising against the Prussians in 1848 was equally unsuccessful. The uprising with the most serious consequences took place in 1863 in the Russian sector (January Insurrection). It was avenged mercilessly by the Russians, with executions, exile to Siberia and dispossession.

The aristocracy was decimated and powerless, with a corresponding improvement in the position of the middle classes and city intellectuals. The so-called positivists rejected armed resistance with its romantic connotations and called for "organic work," by means of which the education and the prosperity of the nation was to be improved, without which greater political independence was not possible. Parallel to this, both the Russians and the Prussians stepped up their efforts to eradicate Polish culture in their sectors.

It was only in Galicia, the Austrian sector which included the towns of Cracow and Lviv, that the situation was bearable. In 1867, with the founding of the imperial and royal monarchy, Galicia became largely autonomous, with Polish reinstated as the official language, and its own universities and a provincial parliament. When Poland was recreated in 1918, it was the experienced Galicians that were sent to Warsaw and Poznań as the initial officials and employees of the new state.

The Second Republic (1918-1939)

It was a miracle of history which enabled Poland to regain its independence: the defeat of two of the powers that dominated it in the First World War, and the elimination of the third great power's influence in the turmoil following the October Revolution. Before this, however, the Great Powers tried to outdo each other with concessions to the "Polish issue," as a means of persuading hundreds of thousands of Polish soldiers to fight on their side.

The most serious proposition was made by the American President Woodrow Wilson, who advocated (as part of the "14-point declaration" of January 8th, 1918) an independent state of Poland, with access to the Baltic.

It was some time before the borders of the new state were properly defined. In the east there were battles against the Ukrainians, who wanted their own state, and there was ultimately a major war with Soviet Russia. Although the Poles were initially successful (they occupied Kiev in May 1920), the Russians launched a counterattack that was halted just short of Warsaw – the "miracle on the Vistula."

As a result of this victory, however, Polish territory was extended a long way to the East. Under the Treaty of Ver-

Right: "The capture of the arsenal in Warsaw" by the rebels in the revolution of 1830-31 (Painting by Marcin Zaleski, 1831).

sailles, Poland was awarded most of former Prussian provinces of West Prussia and Great Poland, but the plebiscites in Warmia and Masuria were less successful. Gdańsk, with its predominantly German population, became a free city, albeit within the Polish customs area and represented abroad by Poland.

In Upper Silesia the plebiscite and subsequent armed conflict led to a division of the region – a third of the territory, with most of the industry, went to Poland.

Throughout the period between the world wars, the Germans continued to demand a redrawing of the border, a demand that was supported by all the political parties of the Weimar Republic.

Polish politics between the wars were dominated by Józef Piłsudski, who assumed the leadership of the Republic in November 1918, a dominating figure, who still today has both passionate defenders and sworn enemies. After an electoral defeat in 1922 he initially withdrew from politics, but then returned in May 1926.

Disappointed by Polish parliamentarianism, which had resulted in an unstable situation and a rapid succession of governments, despite the economic successes that had been achieved (stabilization of the currency, building of Gdynia etc.), Piłsudski staged a coup and installed a new government. Until his death in 1935 he exerted a major influence on politics as the country's *eminence grise*. His rule was authoritarian, and he occasionally even imprisoned members of his parliament or made the opposition the object of a show trial. His "moral dictatorship" was nevertheless not motivated by nationalism.

Piłsudski openly expressed his abhorrence of Hitler, and in 1933 suggested to France that a preemptive strike should be waged against Germany. France did not agree, leading Piłsudski to sign a nonaggression pact with Hitler in 1934.

When this political realist died in 1935 and was buried alongside the kings in the Wawel Royal Cathedral in Cracow, he was mourned by millions, many sus-

HISTORY AND CULTURE

pecting that another leader of his caliber would be a long time in coming. We know now that his successors would not only be unable to halt the developing national catastrophe, they would even play a role in intensifying it.

The Second World War (1939-1945)

On August 23, 1939 the Hitler-Stalin pact was signed, which contained a secret protocol concerning the renewed partition of Poland. The Second World War was provoked by an attack by the German army on the Polish munitions depot on the Westerplatte in Gdańsk, at dawn on September 1, 1939. The Polish units, fighting alone, were attacked from the rear by the Red Army on September 17, which went on to take control of more than half of Poland. On September 27, after a siege lasting almost three weeks, Warsaw surrendered to the Germans, and by October 5 all resistance by the Polish army had ceased.

The Polish state was divided into Soviet-occupied East Poland, the areas annexed outright by the German Reich (the former provinces of Poznań, West Prussia and the eastern part of Upper Silesia), and the so-called General Government, under German administration.

The Nazi terror unleashed here from 1939 to 1945, based on a primitive scientific theory of race, was unprecedented in the history of Poland and, indeed, in the history of the world. The people under the General Government were essentially in a state of slavery. Between five and six million Polish citizens fell victim to the Nazis, half of them Jews (cf page 226)

The "Eastern Plan" included a scheme to deport Poles to Siberia or Brazil, to make room for the arrival of Germans, and this was partially accomplished, especially in the area around Zamość.

The first stage was to try to eliminate the intelligentsia of Poland, so that the "simple people" could be exploited more easily as slave labor. A chilling description of the school system that was introduced in Poland is contained in a set of Heinrich Himmler's notes, referring to a four-year primary school: "The aims of this primary school are limited to simple arithmetic up to 500 at the most, teaching pupils to write their names and instructing them that it is a divine commandment to obey the Germans, and to be honest, industrious and good. I do not consider reading to be necessary."

As a result of the "Extraordinary Pacification Actions" – referring to the imprisonment of the intelligentsia in concentration camps – and similar initiatives, 10,000 doctors, 6,300 professors and university lecturers, 5,600 lawyers, 2,600 priests, and 800 artists and writers were among those who lost their lives.

Everyday life in Poland under the Nazis was appalling: numerous street raids, with the victims hauled off to the Reich

Above: Jósef Piłsudski dominated Polish politics between the two World Wars.

HISTORY AND CULTURE

POLAND 1939

Map showing Poland's borders with dates of territorial acquisitions: West Prussia (1919), Posen, Upper Silesia (1921), Olsa (1938), West Galicia (1918), East Galicia (1918), Vilnius State (1922), Polesia (1921), Wolhynia, Kingdom of Poland (before 1914). Neighboring regions: German Empire, Czechoslovakia, Austria, Hungary, Romania, Soviet Union, Lithuania. Cities marked: Danzig (Free City), Posen, Breslau, Warsaw, Brest, Lublin, Teschen, Minsk, Kiev, Shitomir. Rivers: Neiße, Elbe, Odra, Warta, Vistula, Bug, Nemunas, Duna, Dniepr, Pripet, Dnester.

into forced labor, punishment for the activities of the many partisan associations, whereby whole villages were burned to the ground and their inhabitants shot, the death throes of the Warsaw Ghetto in 1943, and finally the massacre of those who took part in the Warsaw Uprising of 1944.

The Soviets, who occupied the eastern part of the country until 1941, were of the same mind as the Germans with respect to the elimination of the intelligentsia of Poland. An estimated half million Polish citizens, many of which were Jews, Belorussians and Ukrainians, were deported from their traditional homes in eastern Poland after the invasion of the Red Army, most of them to Siberian or Kazak camps, where large numbers of them were executed or died of cold or hunger. Katyń, a small locality near Smolensk, where over 4,000 reserve officers were shot, including the elite of the nation, is symbolic of the atrocities of the Soviets.

Sometimes, however, more pain is caused by failure to act than by criminal actions. To this day the Poles have not forgiven the Russians for their behavior during the Warsaw Uprising which started on August 1, 1944. This counter-attack was organized by the Home Army (AK), an underground organization with 300,000 members, under the direction of the legitimate Polish government from its exile in London.

At the time the Red Army was positioned in Praga, on the eastern bank of the Vistula outside Warsaw, and looked on passively while Himmler's SS units crushed the insurgence. There were even Russian leaflets in circulation, which outlined Stalin's strategic position of allowing others to destroy a future civil opposition.

In the two months of the uprising – the largest Polish battle of the Second World War – over 200,000 people died a death that could have been avoided.

There is no national holiday in Poland to celebrate the unconditional surrender of the Germans. At the conferences in Teheran and Yalta, the decision was made

HISTORY AND CULTURE

over the heads of the Poles to shift the borders West, leaving the whole of eastern Poland in Stalin's hands. Stalin got his way: instead of running east of Lviv and Vilnius, the Polish border runs along the Odra-Nysa line and west of Szczecin.

As a consequence, nine million Germans fled from these areas or became the victims of enforced displacement, in the ensuing period. Thousands of people were killed by plundering bands of Poles in the "Wild West," by the People's Police or in camps, such as Łambinowice – a fact that was never mentioned in Polish history books and has only been openly discussed since 1989.

At the same time, the Soviet secret service was busy making preparations for the establishment of a communist regime in Poland. Many of the heroes of the Home Army and the Polish exile armies were arrested and executed. This was the beginning of the new and supposedly better world.

The People's Republic of Poland (1945 - 1989)

Joseph Stalin once remarked that imposing communism on Poland was "like trying to saddle a cow." Since there had never been a communist movement to speak of in Poland (in contrast to, for instance, Czechoslovakia), the establishment of the communist system after 1945 was only possible with the aid of force and by falsifying the electoral results. Poland became a satellite of the Soviet Union, which constantly interfered in the country's internal affairs, even resorting to military intervention in 1956, 1970, 1980 and 1981.

The beginning of the communist era was marked by violent actions against the middle-class opposition and civil war with the Ukrainian minority in the southeastern part of the country. With the founding of the Polish United Workers' Party (Polska Zjednoczona Partia Robotnicza, or PZPR) in 1948, a Stalinist regime was finally established in Poland. It introduced agricultural collectivization, an open campaign against the Catholic Church (which included the imprisonment of Cardinal Stefan Wyszyński, from 1953-1956) and isolation of the country from western influence.

After the death of party leader Bierut and the uprising of the Poznań workers in 1956, which was put down by force, the so-called thaw began. The party leadership was assumed by Władysław Gomułka, a communist of the prewar era, who's past dissenting views had provided him with first-hand experience of Soviet prisons. Promising to introduce a more humane form of socialism, he managed to avert a general uprising similar to the one in Hungarian in October 1956 and, at the last moment, prevented the Soviets from directly intervening.

Although Gomułka put an end to agricultural collectivization, the general liberalization of the system that the population was anticipating did not materialize.

The worst atrocities of this era were committed in March 1968, when student unrest was used by the secret service as an excuse to persecute intellectuals and Jews, who were accused of not supporting the communist regime. About 20,000 people were forced to emigrate.

A third new beginning was promised by Gomułka's successor, Edward Gierek (party leader from 1970-1980), a technocrat who set out to modernize Poland with the help of western credit. An initial boom was followed by another period of crisis – the loans were not properly administered, or were directed into projects that were of no economic benefit. The party leadership was revealed to be corrupt and thoroughly inept. Both the intellectual elite and the working class, which

Right: On Hitler's orders, Warsaw was completely destroyed in 1944; 850,000 of its citizens were victims of the war.

was of course supposed to be the system's main pillar of support, lost all remaining faith in the leadership. Subsequently, only blatant opportunism remained as a motivator for being an active member of the Communist Party.

Workers' strikes were called for in June of 1976, and were promptly supported by the KOR, the Workers' Defense Committee , an organization run by the intellectual elite. The further erosion of the system, coupled with a severe economic crisis, led to the dock-workers' strikes in Gdańsk, the "Gdańsk Agreement" of August 31, 1980 and – in accordance with this agreement – the founding of the independent labor union *Solidarność* (Solidarity).

In the months that followed, almost 10 million workers joined Solidarność. The struggle between the union and the government, which from October 1981 on was under the leadership of First Party Secretary General Wojciech Jaruzelski, ended with the proclamation of military rule on December 13, 1981. Thousands of people were arrested and Solidarność was banned.

The following years saw the country in the grip of a severe economic depression that affected public life in general. Under-cover experiments were made with alternative power structures based on Solidarność, there was a thriving counter-culture and serious investigations into the possibility of transforming the state-run economy into a free market economy were made. After Mikhail Gorbachev came to power in Moscow, the communists embarked on half-hearted reforms, which only served to increase the social pressure that brought on strikes and other forms of civil disobedience.

The change of the system began in the spring of 1989, with discussions between representatives of the Party, the church and the underground Solidarność. The debate about the division of power lasted almost three months, resulting in a set of roundtable agreements, which became a model for the peaceful rejection of the Communist dictatorship in other coun-

HISTORY AND CULTURE

tries. Semi-free elections followed, and in the late summer of the same year, Tadeusz Mazowiecki was installed as the first non-Communist prime minister in the Soviet bloc.

Poland after the Change of Power (since 1989)

The legacy of 40 years of communist rule included an inflation rate of approximately 1,000 percent and foreign debts of 40 billion dollars. This was compounded by other fundamental shortcomings of the socialist planned economy: scarcities of currency and goods, endless line-ups at near-empty shops, and food rationing.

This set the stage for Leszek Balcerowicz, an economist and finance minster under the presidency of former union

Above: "High noon" in the 1989 election campaign. Right: Lech Wałęsa, leader of Solidarność, and a practising Catholic; in 1990 the Poles elected him as their first president after the change of power.

leader Lech Wałęsa (1990-1995). Balcerowicz had already decided that any attempt to find a third way between a planned and a market economy would be a sheer waste of time. His name was to become synonymous with what was probably the most daring and ambitious economic experiment in post-communist Eastern Central Europe. East Germany needed astronomical financial support from former West Germany to achieve what Poland's new finance minister did in his country with no cushioning at all: on January 1, 1990, after only three months' preparation, the country took the plunge into the icy waters of the market economy.

Balcerowicz stopped all tax relief and supplements overnight, allowed almost all prices to be regulated by the free market, and put a damper on pay increases by means of a hefty wage increase tax. He introduced positive real interest, made the złoty a freely convertible currency within the country and opened the borders to allow imports, so that Polish industry would be forced to rationalize and modernize to meet the competition from abroad. Hyperinflation was stopped and in the shops the shelves filled up with goods.

The resounding success of these measures was overshadowed by an unavoidable decline in production and growing unemployment, an opportunity which was seized by the enemies of radical transformation. Post-communists, Christian Nationalists, Radical Nationalists and the Agricultural Party promised the people the earth, proclaimed the good news of a painless transition to the market economy and even wanted to summon the "Father of the Polish reforms" before a state tribunal for selling out the nation's wealth. Just as the country was over the worst, Balcerowicz was obliged to leave his position.

In 1993, the post Solidarność parties joined him in opposition, thus not only reaping the harvest of their own shock therapy, but also falling victim to their own internal divisions, numerous scandals and an unfortunate (since amended) election regulation with no five percent limit.

Their successors, from 1993 to 1997 – postcommunists from the left-wing Democratic Alliance (SLD) and the Agricultural Party (PSL) – had an easier time of it. They were the major beneficiaries of the Balcerowicz reforms. Although he was now the bogeyman of Poland, his policies had to be continued, if the economy was to be put back on its feet.

For all their angry words, all the left-wing parties were able to achieve was to continue with the monetary reform. Success was not slow in coming: unemployment dropped from 16 percent to nine percent, inflation to nine percent (1998), and from 1994-1997 the gross national product increased by about six percent a year – setting a European record.

In 1995 the legendary electrician who had become the first president of the Third Republic of Poland, Lech Wałęsa, lost the election to the clever post-communist candidate Aleksander Kwaśniewski. It seemed as if the population had a very short memory, thinking they could easily switch their allegiance to the vociferous ex-apparatchiks, who were now claiming to be West-European-oriented.

Fortunately their success was soon tarnished by their failure to implement the necessary reforms, their greed for power, and scandals such as the Oleksy spy affair, which exposed the leader of the post-communists as a Soviet secret agent. The negative consequence of this choice of government was that the *lustracja,* the law that was intended to investigate the activities of all public servants from the days of the communist dictatorship, was never passed, the endless debates having degenerated into a farce.

The next dubious step came in 1997 with the victory of the united right-wing parties, Solidarity Electoral Alliance (AWS). This extremely heterogeneous alliance of right-wing parties, which pre-

HISTORY AND CULTURE

viously wanted nothing to do with one another, included the unionists and the nationalist parties. With their Polish-Catholic orientation, they often take a "socialist" line in economic affairs, promising the electorate social security, even when this runs counter to the laws of the market economy.

In 1997 the liberal Freedom Union (UW) became the third largest political coalition, after the AWS and the post-communists. Its members include former dissidents as well as respected prime ministers in office between 1989 and 1993 (Tadeusz Mazowiecki, Jan Krzysztof Bielecki, Hanna Suchocka). Under the leadership of Leszek Balcerowicz, the Freedom Union achieved its best-ever result (15 percent) which, given that it is a typical intelligentsia party, drawing its support almost entirely from students, university graduates and business people, is not likely to be bettered.

At the end of a decade of democracy, the political scene is dominated by five or six large parties ranging from right to left, and this is not likely to change noticeably in the immediate future.

A new constitution (adopted in 1997) limits the power of the president, who is elected every five years, but who still has the power of veto over the decisions of the Sejm.

With the Sejm, the lower chamber of Parliament that makes the laws, and the Senate, the upper chamber with its more advisory role, Poland is now a well-functioning parliamentary democracy. Eight prime ministers in ten years and two early parliamentary elections are an indication not of political chaos, but rather of a trial-and-error method which will in the end, it is hoped, produce an efficient system and a new political class. The rift between the former opponents of the system and the "communists" is, however, still very deep and is unlikely to be resolved soon.

Above: in the 1990s, modernisation of the country's economy and infrastructure proceeded apace. Right: Poland gears up for its leap into the EU.

HISTORY AND CULTURE

The two present ruling parties, the right-wing AWS and the Freedom Union, are continuing – though not without a certain amount of conflict with one another – with the projects which were abandoned for four years after the shift to the left in 1993 – the reform of the administration, education, health and state social security systems.

In 1999, Poland's forty nine small jurisdictions (województwa), heavily dependent on Warsaw, were replaced by sixteen large ones, which are to have their own budget and, to some extent, their own economic policies.

The infrastructure is urgently in need of improvement, particularly the roads. The construction of freeways is essential if the country is not to grind to a halt in one enormous traffic jam. This is all vital for the continuation of economic growth and the decentralization of the country, without which Poland will scarcely be in a position to reach its long-term objectives.

There is a surprisingly widespread consensus among all the main political parties as to what these goals are, which certainly helped in facilitating the country in joining NATO in March 1999.

There is also little doubt that Poland will play a leading role when the European Union expands eastward. In view of its past, often tragic history, the country does not want to be caught between the existing power structures, but to be anchored in the West and at the same time open and cooperative towards the East, especially Russia.

ART IN POLAND

Ask anyone who knows something about art, and is perhaps familiar with the Dresden Art Gallery, the Louvre or the Uffizi Gallery in Florence, what he or she associates with Polish architecture and painting, and the answer will likely be a long silence. At best Malbork (Marienburg) might be mentioned – which can hardly be called Polish – and perhaps even Cracow. Gericault is well-known, but not Michałowski, Mucha, but not Wyspiański, Corinth, but not Malczewski, Prague, but not Cracow – although Polish artists can hold their own in every way when compared to their better-known counterparts in other countries.

Poland has a vast number of fascinating and valuable art treasures, and above all a great variety of styles. For centuries Poland was the country where East met West, with artists often visiting from Germany, the Orthodox East, Italy or Holland.

The pure form of the Florentine Renaissance was, for instance, supported at the court of the Jagiellonian kings, by the same dynasty that a hundred years previously had favored the Byzantine style (as in the castle chapel in Lublin; cf page 86).

All the patrons of the arts tried to bring the great artists of their time to Poland. Sometimes they were highly successful, as when the Cracow aristocracy commis-

HISTORY AND CULTURE

sioned the work of the great Nuremberg wood-carver Veit Stoss – sometimes less so, as with Hans Dürer, who painted the frescoes on the walls of the Wawel castle in Cracow. His brother Albrecht would have brought the royal residence greater fame.

There was also, however, a flow of artists in the other direction. In 1694 the future king of Prussia, Friedrich I, commissioned Andreas Schlüter the Younger (1660-1714). Schlüter was the greatest North German sculptor and architect of the Baroque era (Berlin Palace). He decided to make the move from the city of Gdańsk, after he had made a name for himself in Warsaw (cf page 51).

There are distinct problems associated with a summary of Polish art. The dilema is epitomized by asking oneself if this study should include the Teutonic Knights' castle in Malbork (Marienburg) or perhaps a Hapsburg structure such as the Krezszów Abbey in Silesia? What people are visiting now is a country whose borders have been shifted west hundreds of kilometers after the end of the war in 1945. If we decide that we should limit ourselves to present-day Polish territory, much of what is really Polish art in Ukrainian Lviv and Lithuanian Vilnius would have to be omitted.

On the other hand, the Silesian or Pomeranian art that is to be found in Poland often has little to do with Poland. That is why it is possibly more appropriate to speak of "Art in Poland" rather than "Polish Art."

Romanesque Art

The first stone buildings were constructed at about the same time that the Polish state was founded. Prior to this time, there had been only earth fortresses and mud houses, which were the relics of older cultures. An example of such a relic might be the extremely well preserved settlement from the Lusatian Culture at Biskupin (cf page 76). The first monuments of any substance are the round churches dating from the 10th century. An example of this type of round church is the one in a later building of the Wawel castle in Cracow (exhibition "The Lost Wawel"). A similar rotunda, or rather only the remains of its walls, is to be found on the island of Lednica. This island lies between Poznań and Gniezno.

Large numbers of Romanesque churches were built at a later date. For example, Tum which is near Łęczyca, St. Andrew's Church in Cracow, Opatów in central Poland, Czerwińsk in Mazovia, and Wysocice which is near Cracow. These are ll attractive buildings. They are, however, much smaller and less decorative than the German or French churches built at the same time. They do, though, have some individual artistic features. These include the sculptured pillars of Strzelno as well as the doors of the St. Mary Magdalene Church in Wrocław. Along with the bronze doors in Gniezno, these rank as some of the finest examples of Romanesque art in Europe.

The Cistercians were already in Poland by the 12th century, some had come directly from Burgund (Morimond), whereas some had arrived via their German or Danish filiations.

The Cistercians brought new features – ribbed vaults and pointed arches – and their churches are hence typical of the transitional style between Romanesque and Gothic architecture. The most interesting of these buildings are the Cistercian monasteries in southern Poland which includes Wąchock, Sulejów, and Mogiła, as well as the Danish Oliwa monastery near Gdańsk. Also of note are the monastery built by the monks of Bad Doberan in Mecklenburg and Pelplin Abbey (west of Malbork), which latter was already pure Gothic.

Right: The sculptured pillars of Strzelno, a highlight of Romanesque art in Poland.

HISTORY AND CULTURE

There are other buildings typical of the transitional period. These include the Dominican church in Sandomierz, which displays a certain Italian influence, and the church of the Cistercian nuns in Trzebnica (in Silesia).

Gothic Art

The Gothic era began in Poland with four great cathedrals. Each of these required the major reconstruction of an older sacred building: the Polish coronation cathedrals of Poznań, Gniezno and Cracow as well as the Cathedral of Wrocław.

A number of castles were built by Kazimierz III Wielki (1333-1370). Among these castles were the so-called "eagle's nests" which have remained as picturesque ruins located between Cracow and Częstochowa, (Olsztyn, Mirów and part of Ogrodzieniec). The same king also built a number of churches with two naves. This unusual architectural construction was probably influenced by French architecture (e.g. Wiślica) and contributed to the transformation of his capital, Cracow, with a number of fine buildings. These include St. Mary's Church, St. Catherine's Church, the town hall tower and the Collegium Maius of the university which are brick buildings. These buildings, however, differ from the architecture of the Teutonic state in that ashlar has been used for the structural and main decorative elements, such as supports, borders, portals and window frames.

Silesia, which also went its own way politically, developed its own style of Gothic architecture. Silesia's Gothic architecture included elaborate forms such as the ribbed vault of St. Mary on the Sand in Wrocław. The town hall, the Holy Cross Church and the cathedral in Wrocław are all masterpieces of Silesian Gothic.

The Teutonic state of Prussia favored the Gothic brick architecture typical of northern Germany. Monumental castle complexes and forts – often square in

HISTORY AND CULTURE

shape – still dominate the surrounding countryside (Toruń, Radzyń Chełmiński). The large Hansa towns – Gdańsk, Toruń and Elbląg – put up impressive buildings as symbols of their importance. The monumental medieval brick church in Gdańsk, St. Mary's, and the huge town hall in Toruń are both examples of architectural displays of power.

Other important historical monuments include the cathedral in Frombork and the Bishop's Castle in Lidzbark Warmiński. The crowning architectural achievement in the Teutonic state of Prussia, however, was the castle built by the Teutonic Order of Knights in Malbork (Marienburg). This was designed as the main seat of their Grand Master, and is the largest and most magnificent of all the brick buildings in the Gothic era.

Above: St Mary's Church in Toruń – a splendid example of brick Gothic architecture. Right: the arcaded courtyard of the Wawel castle in Cracow was built during the Renaissance.

The most important medieval sculptor by far was a guest from Nuremberg: Veit Stoss (1447-1533; Polish name: Wit Stosz or Stwosz). None of his pupils or successors was ever able to approach his genius. This will become immediately obvious when one seees the magnificent figures on the high altar of St. Mary's Church in Cracow.

Painting in the 15th century was briefly, but nonetheless quite significantly influenced by the Byzantine style of Ruthenia (i.e. the Orthodox countries east of Poland). This style was favored by King Władysław Jagiełło and his successor Kazimierz IV. The churches of Wiślica and Sandomierz, a chapel in the Wawel Cathedral in Cracow and the exquisite castle chapel in Lublin are painted in this style.

Renaissance

Poland's most glorious artistic era was without a doubt the Renaissance. In 1502, when the architecture of Germany and Bohemia was still exclusively Gothic, the rulers of Poland embarked on the ambitious project of the rebuilding of the royal castle on the Wawel Hill in Cracow. The architectural style of this royal complex originates in Florence. It is particularly evident in the arcaded courtyard of the palace, and the Jagiellonian chapel next to the Wawel Cathedral (1517-1533, from a design by Bartolommeo Berrecci). This direct adoption of the Italian style was initiated by Queen Bona Sforza from Bari. She was the wife of Zygmunt I Stary (Sigismund the Old), who brought not only artists to Poland, but also such practical commodities as herbs and vegetables for making soup and salad.

The new style in architecture and sculpture was limited, at first, to members of the royal court. The local artists at first had no interest in domes, the golden section or the world of ancient symbols. Outside the court, architects continued to

HISTORY AND CULTURE

build in the Gothic style for a considerable period: the beautiful log churches that are to be found throughout Little Poland (Dębno, Haczów, Grywałd etc.), for example, also have their origins in the same period.

From around 1550 the nobility began to favour the Italian fashion and started building large palaces in this style, most of them surrounded by massive bastion fortifications (*palazzo in fortezza*). The Renaissance ideals then gradually gave way to Mannerism. The new thinking or style, Mannerism, abandoned the classic rules of proportion to indulge in a unbridled display of pomp, which is evident at Krasiczyn, Baranów and Sandomierski. The Residence of Krzyżtopór in Ujazd which is near Sandomierz ignored all the previous dictates of good taste. There you could find marble and mirrors in the stables and an aquarium as the ceiling of the ballroom. It was a crass example of the incredible extravagance and delusions of grandeur exhibited by the Polish nobility in the 16th century.

The architects of these palaces were Italians and included such well known practitioners of architecture as Santi Gucci, Galleazo Appiano and Lorenzo Senes. At the same time there was a new artistic influence from the north, known as Dutch Mannerism. This was represented by a number of outstanding artists such as Anthonis van Opbergen, Abraham van den Blocke and Hans Vredemann de Vries. Dutch Mannerism was particularly popular in Gdańsk.

Characteristic examples of the sculpture of this period are found on gravestones, for example on those of the last Jagiellonian kings, who were Johann Olbracht 1501, Zygmunt I Stary and Zygmunt August in the Wawel Cathedral in Cracow. As well, this type of sculpture could be found on the innumerable graves of the nobility (Poznań, Gniezno, Tarnów). Two of the leading names among the many sculptors who were active at this time were Gian Maria Padovano and Jan Michałowicz from Urzędów.

HISTORY AND CULTURE

A very popular decorative feature in the palaces during the Polish Renaissance, in addition to paintings, was the *arrasy*, or tapestries. The largest collection of these tapestries, named for the town of Arras, was amassed by King Zygmunt August for his Wawel castle. Of the original 350 tapestries hanging in the castles, as as many as 137 are still hanging in the castle rooms. They depict scenes from both the Old and New Testaments, animals and plants as well as the coats-of-arms and emblems of the king.

Baroque Art

The Baroque style came to Poland with the Jesuits. In 1597 they started building the Church of St. Peter and St. Paul in Cracow, which is actually a smaller version of the Il Gesù Church in Rome. In the first half of the 17th century, Polish architecture was dominated by the Wasa style. With its particularly elegant forms and restrained ornamentation it reflected the serious religious nature of the dynasty from which the style took its name (e.g. the Royal Castle in Warsaw and the palace in Kielce).

The Wasa style was then followed in the 17th and 18th centuries by the Italian Baroque style. There are numerous, representative churches, and these include the Jesuit Church in Poznań, the Church of the Nuns of the Visitation in Warsaw as well as the Parish Church in Chełm. The Italian Baroque style is also represented by magnificent residences such as the large building with three wings and a cour d'honneur: Warsaw-Wilanów, Białystok. The main representative of the northern European Baroque style in the second half of the 17th century, which with its more restrained forms was closer to the classical style, was the Dutch architect Tilman van Gameren (e.g. Krasiński Palace in Warsaw, Nieborów Palace, St. Anne's Church in Cracow).

The Baroque buildings of Silesia are in an area that, at the time of their building, was outside the borders of Poland. These buildings were modeled along the lines of Bohemian and Viennese architecture. They include splendid abbeys, among them Krzeszów, Lubiąż and Legnickie Pole. These were were designed and decorated by such famous artists as Kilian Ignaz Dientzenhofer and Cosmas Damian Asam, and stand out as masterpieces of the European Baroque architecture.

From Neoclassicism to the Period between the Wars

Polish neoclassicism is closely linked with the last Polish king, Stanisław August Poniatowski. During his politically unsuccessful reign (1764-1795) Warsaw acquired a number of important new

Above: Valuable tapestries (arrasy) from the 16 th and 17th centuries still hang on the walls of the Wawel castle. Right: Polish Baroque – the Church of SS Peter and Paul in Kraków.

HISTORY AND CULTURE

buildings, including the Łazienki Palace built by Domenico Merlini and the Protestant Church built by Simon Bogumil Zug. Famous painters such as Bernardo Bellotto (known as Canaletto; 1720-80) and M. Bacciarelli also worked for the court.

After the Congress of Vienna in 1815, neoclassicism acquired a more severe and monumental form. This more sober style can be considered to be represented, for example, by the Grand Theatre and the building complex on Plac Bankowy (Bank Square) in Warsaw (architect: Antonio Corazzi). The famous Dane, Bertel Thorvaldsen, who was one of the two leading sculptors of this epoch – the other being Antonio Cannova – created two monuments for Warsaw. One was created in memory of Prince Józef Poniatowski and one for Nicholas Copernicus.

Architecture in partitioned Poland up to the First World War progressed through all the bizarre forms of the epoch, from romantic parks and ruins (Arkadia, Puławy) via a wide range of "neo" styles to an eclectic mixture which is now being taken seriously. The buildings that stand out from this period are the creations of Karl Friedrich Schinkel: in Silesia (Kamieniec Ząbkowicki) and for the nobility of Great Poland (Antonin). Art Nouveau was featured in Łódź and Warsaw (Chopin Monument) at the beginning of the 20th century. The Art Nouveau style was followed by a search for a form of national architecture, which materialized in the Zakopane style (cf page 125). This 200-year period, however, produced not only remarkable achievements in architecture but also outstanding works of art. These would not perhaps normally include the paintings of Jan Matejko (1838-1893), even though for every Pole with a basic knowledge of art history he is the greatest painter of all. The significance of Jan Matejko, creator of large historical paintings à la Makart and Piloty, lay in the social standing he enjoyed during the partition period. Whether it was the "Prussian Oath of Allegiance" (Cracow Cloth Hall) or "King Bathory at Pskov"

HISTORY AND CULTURE

(Warsaw National Museum) – his works gave the humiliated nation hope. The paintings tell of a past age when the subsequent occupiers of Poland bowed down before the powerful realm. As so often in art history, the truly innovative artists went almost unnoticed. One of these innovative artists is Piotr Michałowski (1800-1855). His Somosierra Battle Scenes (in memory of the Polish troops who helped Napoleon fight his way to Madrid over the pass of the same name) are reminiscent of J. M. William Turner. Another of these innovative artists is Stanisław Wyspiański (1869-1907). His works contain a wonderful symbiosis between Japanese woodcuts, Art Nouveau elements and the influence of Gauguin. Further outstanding artists are Władysław Ślewiński (1854-1918; a member of the Pont Aven school), Witold Wojtkiewicz (1878-1909) whose paintings are characterized by a morbid symbolism and Jacek Malczewski (1854-1929), whose works are full of color with a very wide range of motifs. The West has unjustifiably neglected the avant-garde artists who were active in the period between the wars. Some of these artists were influenced by Soviet art, such as Malewicz, while others developed their own theories of art (Władysław Strzemiński, 1893-1952; Katarzyna Kobro, 1898-1951).

The Postwar Period

The wasteland of rubble left in 1945 gave rise to a dispute as to whether the socialist world should use a new art form or whether the old should first be rebuilt. The conviction that only the reconstruction of the most important towns in their old form could hold the nation together carried the day; the reconstruction of Warsaw gave the Poles the feeling that

Above: "The creative moment—sleeping harpy" (painting by Jacek Malczewski, 1907). Right: Socialist realism – the Mickiewicz Monument in front of the Palace of Culture and Science in Warsaw.

HISTORY AND CULTURE

their state at least had some historical continuity. Given the trauma of the war, the new political system as welll as the shifting of the country's borders, this was by no means irrelevant. By 1952 the Warsaw Old Town was back in place, almost more beautiful than it had been before the war. Whole streets were reconstructed to appear, as nearly as possible, as they had around the year 1780, based on the paintings of Canaletto (Bernardo Bellotto). Only the Royal Castle had to wait until 1970 for its reconstruction, because Party Secretary Gomułka found it "ideologically undesirable." The Warsaw Old Town was followed by Lublin, Gdansk and Poznań. This was followed by the less extensive reconstruction of Wrocław. While the restoration of the Old Towns is a glorious chapter in Polish history, nevertheless the new world created was also an architectural disaster. The total conformity to socialist realism set the tone in the 1950's and produced such monstrosities as the Warsaw Palace of Culture. This still dominates the city panorama despite the new skyscrapers that have sprung up since then. With the passing decades, however, the wedding-cake style has come to be judged less harshly, and some of its products – such as the MDM settlement in Warsaw – have even been added to the list of designated landmarks. The reason is probably that the panel construction of the sixties and seventies was even worse. Looking at the endless, soulless concrete blocks, it is harder to decide which is more catastrophic, the defective materials or the architects' lack of imagination. Even the numerous modern churches that were built in the eighties do nothing to relieve the dreariness of the housing developments.

In the art world, however, developments in recent decades have been much more positive. The broad spectrum of work ranges from the surrealists such as Władysław Hasior (cf Zakopane, page 124) to woven art (Magdalena Abakanowicz), and the endless columns of figures of Roman Opałka, who now lives in the West. The best institutions where one can get to really know Polish modern art are the *Muzeum Sztuki,* which is in Łódź, Ujazdowski Palace and the Zachęta Gallery in Warsaw.

The Polish speciality of the postwar period was poster art. Starting in the fifties on, a number of young artists rejected the commercial poster of the prewar period and elevated this medium to an independent art form. Among them were Jan Lenica, Henryk Tomaszewski, Jan Młodożeniec, Franciszek Starowieyski and Waldemar Świeży. In 1968 the Poster Museum was founded in Wilanów (near Warsaw), where their works are collected, evaluated in terms of the history of art and documented. Although in the eighties Polish poster art lost some of its important representatives through death and emigration, the museum should on no account be omitted from your itinerary.

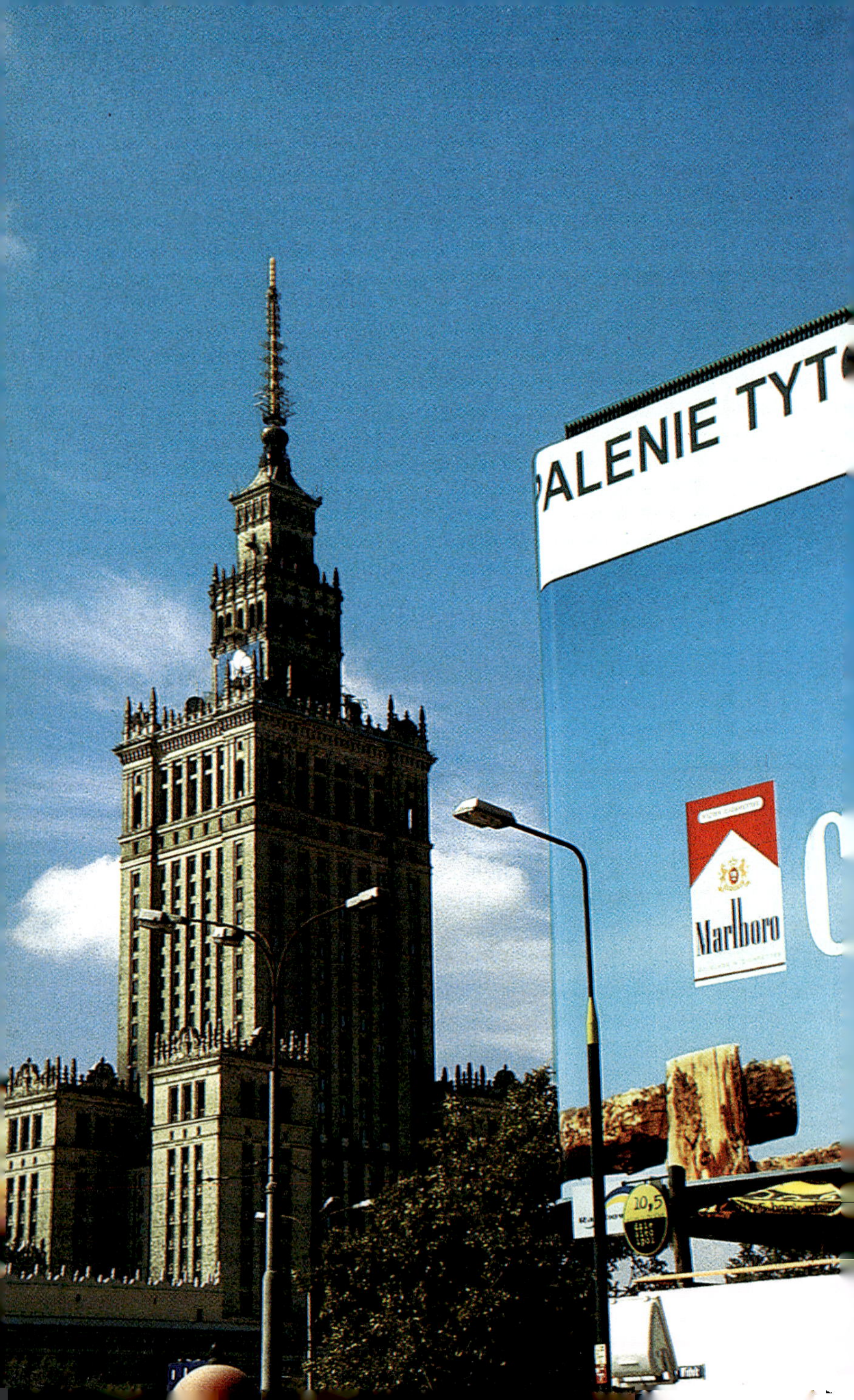

PALENIE TYT
Marlboro
10,5

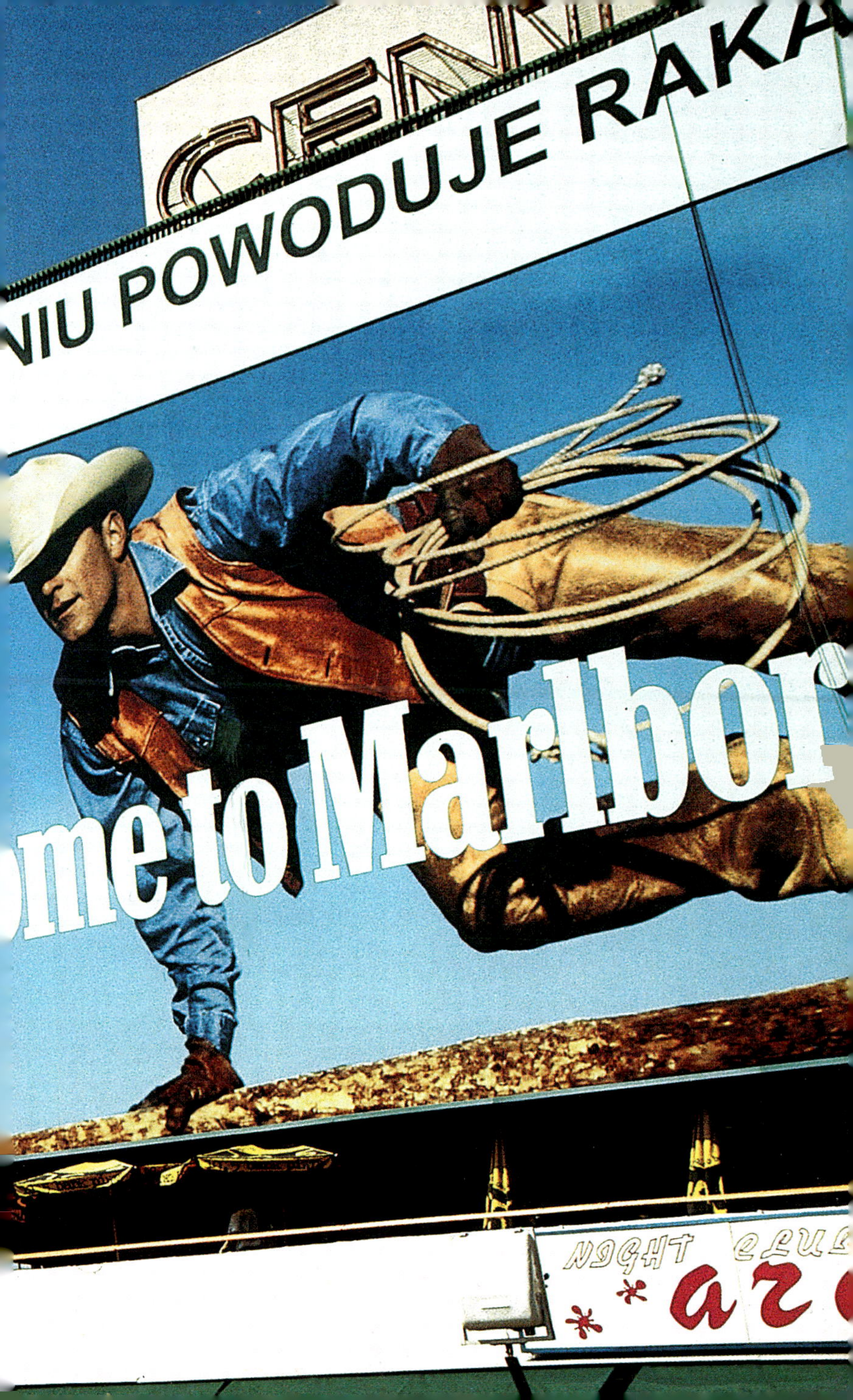
NIU POWODUJE RAKA
ome to Marlbor
NIGHT

WARSAW

WARSAW
A Phoenix from the Ashes

THE MODERN CENTER
JEWISH WARSAW
OLD TOWN / NEW TOWN
THE ROYAL WAY
ŁAZIENKI PARK
WILANÓW PALACE

WARSAW (WARSZAWA)

Acres of concrete blocks, a center without a plan and an Old Town in which nothing is actually old. The people who live in this mixed environment have a hectic life style and are considered by the rest of Poland to be unfriendly and arrogant. The hotels are crowded, the taxi drivers are not always honest and in the Old Town a cup of coffee costs almost as much as it does in front of the cathedral of Notre Dame in Paris.

It would nevertheless be wrong to be influenced by first impressions: on closer inspection the attractions of the city will soon become apparent and you will suddenly feel quite at home. Warsaw is a city that 50 years ago had neither much of a population nor many buildings. From the expanse of ruins, which provided only a few hundred people with provisional shelter in 1945, the present Old and New Towns with the Royal Way were recreated and Warsaw became the largest historic city in the world to have been reconstructed exactly according to its original form.

Previous pages: Warsaw in transition from socialism (Palace of Culture and Science in the socialist realism style) to competitive capitalism. Left: Western elegance.

This tremendous achievement was acknowledged by UNESCO, which placed the Warsaw Old Town, rebuilt in minute detail, on the World Cultural Heritage list. You will not, however, look in vain for something genuinely old, even though it means venturing a little way out of the city: in this category are the two royal residences, Łazienki and Wilanów, which also have charming parks in which to recover from the hectic pace of life in Warsaw.

History

The poor fisherman Wars and and his wife Sawa are said to have founded the first settlement on the Vistula, which acquired a city charter around the year 1300. Warsaw, which by comparison with other medieval towns in Poland was of only medium size, became the capital of the Duchy of Mazovia in 1413 (and was incorporated into the kingdom of Poland in 1526). Its last dukes, Stanisław and Janusz, were only 24 and 26 when they died, leaving no heirs. Two innocent women were burned at the stake for their deaths, allegedly laying a curse on the city as they departed this life and condemning it to suffer repeated destruction by fire, something which did in fact happen all too often.

WARSAW

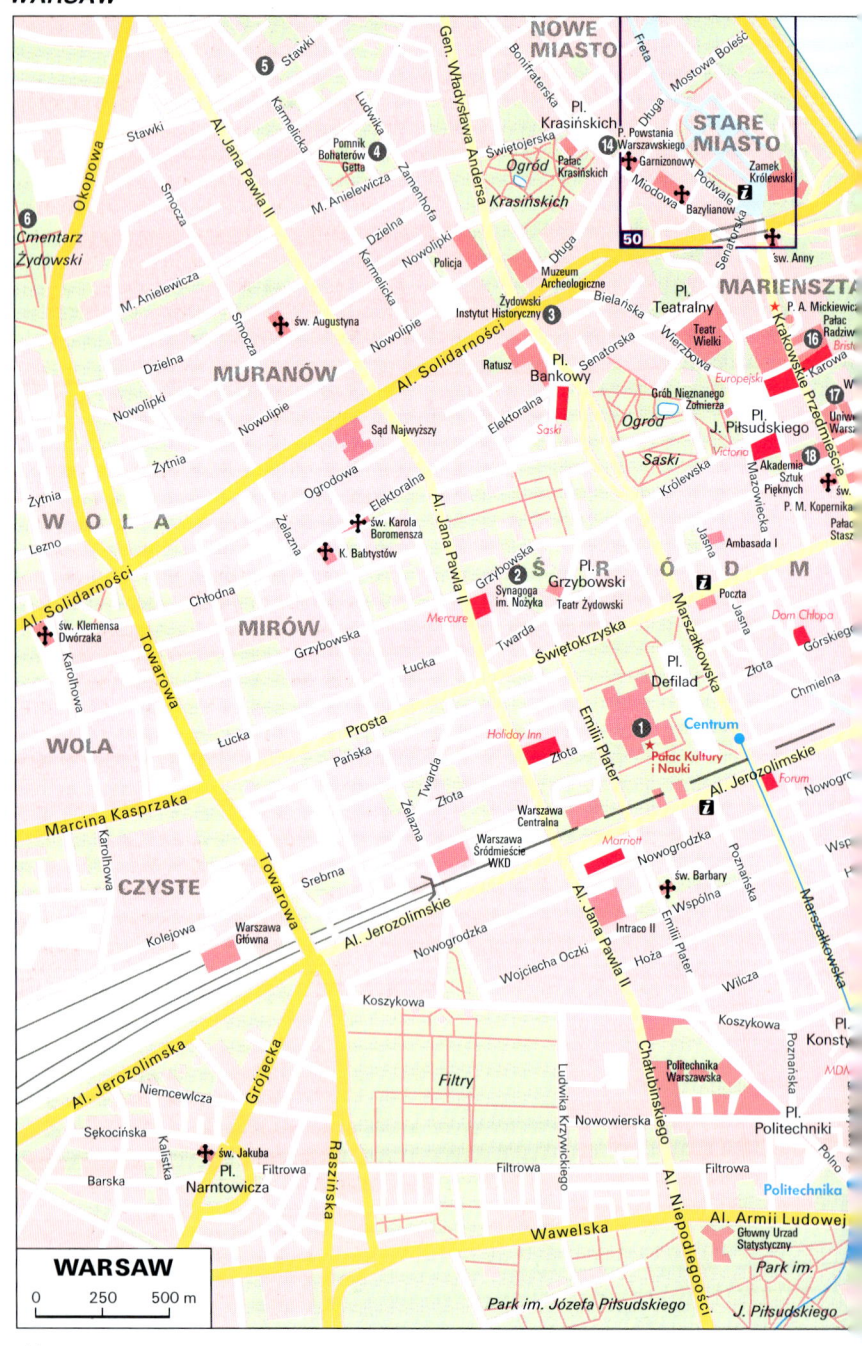

WARSAW

Warsaw burned down for the first time in 1655/56, when it was destroyed by the Swedish army. By then it had already been the kingdom's capital for half a century – an honor it owed to King Zygmunt III Waza (Sigismund III Vasa), who would really have preferred to live in Stockholm. In order to come a little closer to this unattainable goal he transferred the royal residence from Cracow to Warsaw. Unfortunately he also foolishly involved Poland in wars with the Swedish army.

From the partitioning of Poland at the end of the 18th century (cf page 23) onwards, periods of destruction alternated with periods of rebuilding. Because of its strategic, central position, Warsaw became the most frequently besieged and fought over capital of modern Europe. The constantly changing claims on its territory led to repeated attacks that were still continuing in the 20th century. There was a short breathing space with the independence of Poland after the First World War and within a very short period of time the city had new municipal districts, administrative buildings, museums and theaters.

During the Second World War the city was ravaged by the worst fires in its history. In 1939, during the three-week siege by the German army, some ten percent of Warsaw was destroyed. The ghetto uprising, which cost the Jewish population 60,000 lives and the Warsaw uprising, which claimed around 200,000 civilian victims, reduced half the city to a sea of rubble.

Anything that was left was systematically destroyed by special units of the SS, which were instructed by Hitler to raze Warsaw to the ground. When the districts on the left bank of the Vistula were taken on January 17, 1945 by the Red Army, the Russian soldiers found a situation that not even the vengeful women at the stake could have envisaged. Eight hundred and fifty thousand citizens of Warsaw had

Information pages 56-57   47

THE OLD TOWN OF WARSAW

died – more than all the English and American victims of the war put together.

Of Warsaw's 957 historic buildings, 782 had been completely and 141 partially destroyed; only 34 buildings had remained unharmed. The city had to be completely reconstructed.

THE MODERN CENTER

The Palace of Culture and Science ❶ (*Pałac Kultury i Nauki*), which marks the center of the city, was built from 1952-1955. It was a present from the Soviet Union, a present of massive proportions that many Warsaw residents would gladly have returned. The building, 274 meters high and with approximately 3000 rooms, includes four theaters, three cinemas, two restaurants, two museums, a swimming pool and a conference hall. It was built by the Soviet architect Lev Rudniev in the socialist realism style (disrespectfully known as the "wedding-cake style"), which was intended to emphasise the power of the new ideology by incorporating elements of classical architecture. When compared with similar buildings in Moscow, such as Lomonosov University, the Palace of Culture and Science has distinct Polish traits: the "attics," decorative parapets at the top of the walls, are also familiar from the Renaissance buildings of Cracow.

The Palace of Culture is extremely useful for travelers to Warsaw: since it can be seen from almost everywhere in the city, you always know exactly where you are. A further aid to orientation in the chaotic layout of the streets is the view from the 30th floor; from here there is an excellent panorama of the old town and the course of the Vistula.

The area in front of the palace is taken up by department stores and the new subway station "Centrum," but there is no overall planning concept. The *Marriott* luxury hotel and the huge block that is the main train station are also close by.

The **ul. Marszałkowska**, Warsaw's main shopping street, is lined with shops and is always full of people, but it has irrevocably lost its prewar elegance.

At its southern end it opens out into the spacious **Plac Konstytucji**, which is the center of the MDM district and a textbook example of Stalinist architecture (MDM stands for *Marszałkowska Dzielnica Mieszkaniowa*, a housing development on the Marszałkowska).

The entire square, with giant candelabras in the center and monumental buildings on all four sides, which are decorated with reliefs depicting heroic pioneers of socialism, has already been placed under a preservation order.

JEWISH WARSAW

Behind the façade of modern Warsaw there are still a few remnants of the Jewish town. The dreary postwar architecture north of the Palace of Culture and Science has replaced the ghetto created in 1939. It was here, cut off from the rest of the world, behind a wall topped with barbed wire, that 600,000 people lived in unspeakable misery, many of them dying of hunger and epidemics; it was here that they attempted in an uprising to defend their right to a dignified death, and from here that they were transported to the death camp Treblinka.

Today the mounds which are now the site of houses built in the sixties mark the ruins of the ghetto. All that was left was the neo-Romanesque **Nożyk Synagogue** ❷ behind the state Jewish Theatre on the Plac Grzybowski, built from 1898 to 1902, and the main synagogue of Warsaw on the Plac Bankowy, now the site of a glass skyscraper.

Behind this is the **Jewish Historical Institute** ❸ (*Żydowski Instytut Historyczny*), with its valuable archive of grim

Right: The Old Town Market Square – completely rebuilt after total destruction in the war.

THE OLD TOWN

documents from the ghettos and extermination camps. The Jews' hopeless struggle for survival is commemorated by the emotionally charged **Monument to the Heroes of the Ghetto** ❹ dating from 1948, and depicted in newspapers round the world when Willy Brandt went down on his knees in front of it on his visit in 1970 (ul. Zamenhofa, corner ul. Anielewicza). Thousands of names are engraved on the **Umschlagplatz (Assembly Point) Monument** ❺, (ul. Stawki), the walls of which are as high as the walls of the ghetto once were. From this square over 300,000 people were sent to the gas chambers.

Among those buried in the **Jewish Cemetery** ❻ (*Cmentarz Żydowski*; ul. Okopowa 49/51) is the inventor of Esperanto, Ludwik Zamenhof.

THE **OLD TOWN (STARE MIASTO)

The "old" town of Warsaw that was reconstructed in the fifties begins on the **Castle Square** ❼ (*Plac Zamkowy*), with the **Column of Zygmunt III Waza** dating from 1633 in a dominant central position. High above the square with sword and cross is the arch-Catholic king who chose Warsaw as his residence over the old town of Cracow (Sigismund III Vasa, reigned 1587-1632).

The east side of the square is dominated by the ***Royal Castle** ❽ (*Zamek Królewski*), blown up by the Germans in the late autumn of 1944; its reconstruction, in its original 17th century form, was not begun until 1970. Since substantial parts of the interior were removed and rescued when the bombing began in 1939 (e.g. 300 paintings, 70 sculptures, six fireplaces and thousands of architectural fragments), the decoration inside is largely original.

The guided tour includes the Knights' Hall, where the first constitution in Europe, the May Constitution, became law in 1791; the magnificent ballroom from the time of the Saxon kings; and the Canaletto Hall with 23 vedutas of the city

THE OLD TOWN

roof surfaces provided lighting for the stairwell.

The **Historical Museum of Warsaw** (*Muzeum Historyczne miasta Warszawy*), is housed in three of the restored houses on the northwest side of the square and traces the development of the metropolis. The film about the destruction of the city, based on German newsreels from 1939-1945, is shown several times a day in several languages and should on no account be missed. It is only then that it is possible to fully appreciate what was achieved with the reconstruction. The original function of the square as a market has been exploited not only by the craft and souvenir stalls but also by a wide range of amateur painters selling their pictures. Like Łazienki Park, the Old Town is one of Warsaw's most popular spots, and with its ice-cream stands, cafés and restaurants is a pleasant place for a stroll. Street musicians provide entertainment, and the crowds of people on Sundays add to the attractions of this atmospheric quarter.

by Bernardo Bellotto, known as Canaletto (1720 to 1780), on the basis of which it was possible to reconstruct whole streets when Warsaw was rebuilt after 1945.

The **Old Town Market** ❾ (*Rynek Starego Miasta*), which is surrounded by elegant residences, forms the center of the Old Town. Originally built in the Gothic period, in the 16th to 18th centuries the houses acquired Renaissance, Baroque or neoclassical façades.

Some of them are crowned with fine Renaissance parapets (a decorative wall above the main façade) e.g. No. 32, others have unusual decorative elements, such as the head of a black African (No. 36), probably intended to represent the extensive trade contacts of the 16th century house owner. The terraced roofs are also a special feature of the Warsaw residences; the windows between the two

The most important Old Town church is the Gothic brick **St. John's Cathedral** ❿ (*Katedra św. Jana*), which was also completely reconstructed after 1945. Some of the tombstones were preserved beneath the ruins, such as that of Henryk Sienkiewicz, the author of "Quo Vadis," (in the crypt) and that of the last Mazovian dukes Stanisław and Janusz (in the right-hand side aisle). It shows two figures embracing, with their helmets lat their feet to show that with them the dynasty came to an end. The baptismal font is also original and dates from 1632.

Around the Old Town runs a double **fortified city wall**. The best known section is the **Barbican** ⓫, built in 1550 by Giovanni Battista da Venezia and marking the boundary between the Old Town and the New. It is authentically crowned with an attic, as depicted in old engravings. The elliptical projection from the medieval city gate is however only a poor

Right: The Barbican – 16th-century fortifications reconstructed on the basis of old engravings.

50   *Information pages 56-57*

THE NEW TOWN

relation of the building it was modelled on in Cracow.

THE NEW TOWN (NOWE MIASTO)

Despite the name, the New Town also has its share of important historical monuments. The **New Town Square** ⓬ with its Baroque domed **Church of the Nuns of the Holy Sacrament** (*Kościół Sakramentek*) is particularly worth a visit. The church was built in 1689-1692 by Tilman van Gameren, one of the most important Baroque architects in Poland, and lends a dignified air to this square – a peaceful place after the bustle of the Old Town Square.

On the way here you pass the **Birthplace of Marie Curie** ⓭ (ul. Freta 16; small museum). The scientist who twice won the Nobel prize was born here in 1867 as Maria Skłodowska; Curie was her married name. She was the discoverer of radium and polonium, which she named after her home country.

From the New Town a small detour can be taken to Krasiński Square, with its **Monument to the Warsaw Uprising** ⓮ of 1944, which was built as recently as 1989. This late successor of socialist realism with its larger-than-life soldier figures aroused vehement protest while it was being built and is often described as the communists' last revenge.

The west side of the square is taken up by the **Krasiński Palace** (*Pałac Krasińskich*), built in 1677-1683 by Tilman van Gameren and bordered by an attractive park. The reliefs on the tympanum of both façades, depicting the alleged ancient Roman ancestors of the Krasiński family, are by the Gdańsk sculptor and architect Andreas Schlüter, and are his first authenticated works.

THE ROYAL WAY

*Krakowskie Przedmieście

Krakowskie Przedmieście ("Cracow Suburb"), Warsaw's grand avenue, is part

Information pages 56-57

THE ROYAL WAY

of the Royal Way that leads from the Castle Square to the residences in Łazienki Park and in Wilanów. It is the location of the magnificent palaces built by the aristocracy, the large churches, the university and the monuments to the country's famous, still guarded by soldiers.

At the beginning of the Royal Way, near Castle Square, is **St. Anne's Church** ⑮ (*Kościół św. Anny*), with its mixture of Gothic, Renaissance, Baroque and neoclassical styles. The late Baroque façade, which was completed in 1786-1788 from a design by Chrystian Piotr Aigner, is based on Palladio's Il-Redentore Church in Venice. In the postwar period the church was in imminent danger of sliding down the high bank of the Vistula and was saved only when the slope was reinforced with concrete.

The Royal Way continues past the 1898 **Monument to Adam Mickiewicz**, which was dismantled during the war and rebuilt in its original place in 1950, to a former aristocratic residence. **Radziwiłł Palace** ⑯, the neoclassical backdrop for the **Equestrian Statue of Prince Poniatowski,** is the official residence of the Polish state president. It was here, in 1989, that the round-table discussions took place to arrange the peaceful transition from dictatorship to democracy – a solution that set an example for other Eastern Bloc states.

Warsaw's boulevard is not however just a succession of churches, monuments and palaces. Here the best hotels were built; the most prestigious is the **Hotel Bristol** (built in 1901 in neo-Renaissance style). It was renovated and upgraded after the change of power to reclaim its former reputation as the best hotel in the country. Opposite is the oldest existing hotel in Warsaw, the **Europejski** (mid-19th century), which has been unable to shed the influence of the socialist era.

Right: The Akwarium Jazz Club, recommended for an evening of good jazz!

The **Church of the Nuns of the Visitation** ⑰ (*Kościół Wizytek*) is considered by connoisseurs to be the finest sacred building in Warsaw. Its imaginative Rococo façade was created by the Toruń architect Efraim Schroeger in 1754-1766; the pulpit is shaped like a boat.

At the southern end of the Krakowskie Przedmieście is Warsaw **University,** housed in a number of Baroque palaces, which was founded in the 19th century. Opposite it is the Baroque Czapski Palace which houses the **Academy of Fine Arts** ⑱. A few steps further on is the **Holy Cross Church** (*Kościół Św. Krzyża*) with its dominant double towers. In accordance with the last will of Frédéric Chopin, who is buried in Paris, the urn containing his heart was brought to this church; it is walled into the first pillar on the left. The neoclassical **Staszic Palace** ⑲ and the **Monument to Copernicus** (1830) – like the Poniatowski Monument the work of the Dane Bertel Thorvaldsen – form a fitting conclusion to the most beautiful street in Warsaw.

Detour to the Saxon Gardens

Situated behind the hotel *Europejski* is Piłsudski Square with the **Tomb of the Unknown Soldier** (*Grób Nieznanego Żołnierza*), where a ceremonious changing of the guard takes place at noon every day. Before the Second World War the tomb was surrounded by the gigantic pillars of the Saxon Palace, the rebuilding of which is a current source of controversy. It is behind this monument that the **Saxon Gardens** (*Ogród Saski*) are located; the large central axis was designed by Matthäus Daniel Pöppelmann, who built the Dresden Zwinger.

On the nearby Theater Square (*Plac Teatralny*) is the largest neoclassical building in Poland, the **Opera House**, built in 1825-1833 by Antonio Corazzi and extended after 1945 to hold an audience of 1900. Opposite it is the most re-

THE ROYAL WAY

cently reconstructed architectural monument in Warsaw, the **Old Town Hall**, of which the facade alone was rebuilt in 1997, on the basis of old documents.

Nowy Świat

In the south Krakowskie Przedmieście continues as the **Nowy Świat** ("New World"), a boulevard lined with beautifully restored 19th century residences of the bourgeiosie.

At the crossing with the Aleje Jerozolimskie is the so-called **White House** 20, the former seat of the Polish United Workers' Party (PZPR).

It is one of the ironies of history that after the change of power this was the building that was taken over by the new and expanding Polish stock exchange.

A few steps down the road in the direction of the Vistula is the massive **National Museum** 21 (*Muzeum Narodowe*). Among the highlights are the collection of medieval art, the gallery of 19th and 20th century Polish painting and, not to be missed, the Christian frescoes from Pharos (Sudan; 8th-12th century), rescued by a Polish excavation mission before the region was flooded by the Aswan reservoir.

Aleje Ujazdowskie

The third section of the Royal Way, the leafy Aleje Ujazdowskie which follows Krakowskie Przedmieście and Nowy Świat, is lined with old villas now housing embassies.

This avenue starts at the **Plac Trzech Krzyży** 22 (*Three Crosses Square*) and continues along a way of the cross built in the time of King August II to Łazienki-Park.

The ruins of **Ujazdowski Castle** 23 were torn down in 1954, and it was not until the 1970's that the 17th century fort with its four corner towers was rebuilt.

Today it houses the **Center of Modern Art**, one of the best places in Warsaw to see exhibitions of contemporary Polish and international art.

ŁAZIENKI PARK

After the walk along the Royal Way, you can also enjoy a pleasant meal at the gallery's terrace restaurant.

*ŁAZIENKI-PARK

Łazienki Park is the largest of all the gardens along the Aleje Ujazdowskie. On Sunday mornings, regardless of the weather, the people of Warsaw head for this splendid 18th century country park.

In the summer they gather at the Art Nouveau **Chopin Monument** 24 (1904, erected here in 1926; like almost everything else in Warsaw a postwar copy), where piano music is played every Sunday from 12 noon. Or they stop to eat ice cream in the cafés or feed the squirrels, the fat carp and the peacocks.

The first buildings on this site were baths (called *łazienki* in Polish) which were built here in the 17th century to take advantage of the healing springs.

At a much later date the last Polish king, Stanisław August Poniatowski (reigned 1764-1795), chose the spot for his summer residence. While he was not necessarily renowned for his statesmanship, his good taste certainly left nothing to be desired.

From 1775-1793, he built the **Palace upon the Water** 25 (*Pałac na Wyspie*) on an island in the middle of the park.

Originally a bathhouse by Tilman van Gameren (1690), the building was gradually extended and transformed into a palace under the direction of the Italian Domenico Merlini. Today it houses a section of the National Museum.

The Petit Trianon in Versailles was the model for the **White Cottage** 26, a garden residence used by the king and located between the Chopin Monument and the Palace upon the Water, while the **Open Air Theater** 27, was inspired by Herculaneum and the Temple of Baalbek (today in Lebanon).

Above: Łazienki Park, a good place to unwind, popular with both locals and tourists. Right: A classical concert in a late-Baroque setting (theatre in the Old Orangery).

WILANÓW PALACE

In this theater the stage is separated from the audience by a canal, so that real boats can be introduced into the productions. An enthusiastic theater-goer, the king had a second theater built in the **Old Orangery** ㉘ (*Stara Oranżeria*), decorated with illusionistic paintings of boxes occupied by very lively looking spectators. This exquisite late Baroque creation provides an atmospheric setting for classical concerts.

*WILANÓW PALACE

Ten kilometers south of Łazienki in **Wilanów** ㉙ is the summer residence *Villa Nova* built by Jan III Sobieski. Its present appearance – its magnificent façade is crowned with sculptures – dates from 1684 to 1696, when Agostino Locci transformed the villa into a large palace. The two monumental side wings were added in the 18th and 19th centuries. The artistic taste of the king and the successive owners of the palace is displayed by the interior: the Chinese Room, the Dutch Cabinet and the Bedroom in which the hero of the ceiling fresco, Apollo on his sun chariot, represents the king. The exterior of the palace is decorated with sculptures glorifying the king's military successes and comparing him with ancient heroes such as Alexander the Great and Hercules.

The palace is surrounded by a French style Baroque **Garden** of ordered proportions, which is in turn bordered on all three sides by an English landscape park with romantic buildings including a Chinese pagoda, a Japanese bridge, and a water tower, built to look like a medieval castle. It is the perfect place in which to escape for a little while from the hectic pace of Warsaw.

Hidden behind the façade of an old riding arena is the attraction of a modern building containing the **Poster Museum** (to the right of the palace gate), which merits at the very least a brief visit, on account of the international reputation of Polish posters from the 1960's and 1970's.(cf. page 41).

City map pages 46-47, Information pages 56-57

WARSAW

WARSAW (WARSZAWA) ☎ 022

WCIT, Pl. Zamkowy 1/3, Tel. 6351881, Fax 8310464, on the Castle Square. There are also tourist information desks at the main train station, at the airport and at Pl. Powstańców Warszawy 2. **Orbis Tourist Offices:** ul. Bracka 16 (Tel. 8260271), Marszałkowska 142 (Tel. 8278031). They offer city tours, tickets, etc.

ARRIVAL: The easiest ways to travel from the **airport** into the city center are the bus line 175 (from the airport to the main railway station and Old Town, but watch out for pickpockets!) and with the expensive airport bus (every 30 minutes), which makes stops at the major hotels. You are better off not taking a taxi. Visitors traveling by rail arrive at the centrally located main **train station**, the Warszawa Centralna. The trains also make stops at the east station, Wschodnia, and the west station, Zachodnia. Most of the trains depart from Warszawa Centralna. (Informacja PKP, Tel. 6200361; for international trains 6204512). The long-distance **bus station** for most routes, Centralny Dworzec PKS, is inconveniently located in the western part of the city, next to the west railway station. (Bus 130 to the city center; Information PKS, Tel. 8224811).

LOCAL TRANSPORTATION: **Bus** and **trolley** tickets valid for a single ride without transfer cost 2.40 Zł (*bilet*) and must be canceled (stamped) immediately when you enter the vehicle. It is getting easier to find kiosks which sell the money-saving day ticket (*bilet jednodniowy*, 7.20 Zł, cancel only at the beginning of the first ride). It is not recommended to take a **taxi** from the airport, main railway station, Castle Square, ul. Kilińskiego, Nowy Świat and Marszałkowska; you will be charged an exorbitant fare. Company/radio taxis are more reasonable in cost than the private taxis; there is no danger of being fleeced. (Tel. 919, 9623, 9661, 9624, among others).

◉◉◉ **Bristol**, ul. Krakowskie Przedmieście 42/44, Tel. 6252525, Fax 6252577, www.bristol.polhotels.com. Historical hotel in the most elegant quarter of the capital; Poland's most expensive accommodation. **Marriott**, Al. Jerozolimskie 65/79, Tel. 6306306, 6307141, Fax 6305239, 8300311. In a skyscraper next to the main railroad station; offers all amenities, including a bar on the fortieth floor. **Sheraton**, ul. B. Prusa 2, Tel. 6576100, Fax 6576200. At the Pl. Trzech Krzyży in the southern part of the Royal Way. **Europejski**, ul. Krakowskie Przedmieście 13, Tel. 8265061, 8263104, Fax 8261111, www.orbis.pl/hot_eur.html. Good location, somewhat run down, rooms in several price categories. **Victoria**, ul. Królewska 11, Tel. 6578011, 6578012, 6579051, Fax 6578057, www.orbis.pl/hot_vic.html. Near the Old Town, recommendable. The following hotels are located in the modern but not very interesting city center: **Holiday Inn**, ul. Złota 48/54, Tel. 6200341, 6206534, Fax 8300569. Near the main train station; handicapped access. **Mercure**, Al. Jana Pawła II. 22, Tel. 6200201, Fax 6208779. **Jan III. Sobieski**, Pl. Zawiszy 1, Tel. 6584444, 6595501, Fax 6598828. **Forum**, ul. Nowogrodzka 24/26, Tel. 6210271, 230364, Fax 6250476. Very large and noisy; showing its age. ◉◉ Since most of the hotels in Warsaw are in the better categories, advance reservations for the following are usually necessary: **Harenda**, Krakowskie Przedmieście 4/6, Tel. 8260701, 8262625. In one of the best areas along the Royal Way near the Copernicus Monument. **Dom Chłopa**, Pl. Powstańców Warszawy 2, Tel. 8279251, 8274943. Near Harenda. **MDM**, Pl. Konstytucji 1, Tel. 6229432, Fax 6214173, www.syrena.com.pl/mdm.htm. Named after the housing compound in pure Stalinist style; recently renovated; Syrian cuisine featuring sesame specialties in *Ugarit*, the best Syrian restaurant in the city. ◉ **Belfer**, ul. Wybrzeże Kościuszkowskie 31/33, Tel. 6252600, 6250571. An old teachers' hotel near the bank of the Vistula River, not far from the National Museum; a 20 minute walk to the Old Town (also reachable by bus); reserve ahead!

Youth Hostels: ul. Smolna 30, Tel. 8278952. located in the same area as the Belfer; central but spartan. A second hostel at ul. Karolkowa 53 a, Tel. 6328829. In the western part of the city; open year round.

Campgrounds: The most popular one lies on the route to the airport and also offers cabins (ul. Żwirki i Wigury 32, Tel. 2543391). Among the remaining five, the one at the address ul. Grochowska 1 (Tel. 6106366) deserves recommendation. **Private rooms**: can be found through the information center on the Castle Square and at the Syrena office, ul. Krucza 17, Tel. 6287540.

✖ Warsaw is not for the budget-minded travelers seeking a layover on the way home from trekking in Annapurna. *GOOD AND EXPENSIVE:* **Belvedere**, Nowa Oranżeria, Tel. 8414806. Elegant restaurant in the Łazienki Park (look at the prices on the menu before your order); Polish and international cuisine. **La Bohème**, Pl. Teatralny 1, Tel. 6920681. Inside the National Theater; Specialties include mushroom soup and tagliatelle with mussels. **La Gioconda**, Plac Piłsudskiego 9, Tel. 8279442. This restaurant has hosted a wide spectrum of guests, from Umberto Ecco to the Gipsy Kings. **Nowe Miasto**, Rynek Nowego Miasta 13/15, Tel. 8314379. Elegant vegetarian restaurant on the New Town Market Square. All the **luxury hotels** have good restaurants. *IN THE OLD TOWN:* **Fukier**, Rynek Starego Miasta 27, Tel. 8311013. Rich in tradition, high level of Polish cuisine, good selection of wine. **Świętoszek**, ul. Jezuicka 6/8, Tel. 8315634. **Rycerska**, ul. Szeroki Dunaj 9/11, Tel. 8313668. **Kamienne Schodki**, Rynek Starego

WARSAW

Miasta 26, Tel. 8310822. Relatively inexpensive. **Bazyliszek**, Rynek Starego Miasta 3/9, Tel. 8311841. The showcase restaurant of the People's Republic has seen better days, but still serves good duck. *ETHNIC RESTAURANTS:* **Tsubames**, ul. Foksal 16, Tel. 8265127. Sushis. **Kahlenberg**, ul. Koszykowa 54, Tel. 6308850, 6308851. Viennese cuisine with, among other specialties, "tafelspitz." **Pod Samsonem**, ul. Freta 3/5, Tel. 8311788. Almost directly across from the birthplace of Marie Curie; Jewish cooking, specialty: *karp po żydowsku* in aspic and sweet as an appetizer; a touch of the atmosphere of old Warsaw; worth the price. *WILANÓW:* Try to tie in this visit with lunch. **Wilanów**, ul. St. Kostki Potockiego 27, Tel. 8421852. Polish and international cuisine. **Kuźnia**, ul. St. Kostki Potockiego 24, Tel. 8423171. The "forge" – a secret tip in communist Poland – seems in the meantime to be resting a bit on its laurels. *SIMPLE:* **Dom Chłopa**, Pl. Powstańców Warszawy 2, Tel. 6251545. **Mazowsze**, ul. Marszałkowska 55/73, Tel. 6216776. When money is tight there are the milk bars (**Bary Mleczne**); the best ones are the ones at the Barbican (Mostowa 27/29) and the ones between the Copernicus Monument and the main gate of the University (Krakowskie Przedmieście 20; English menu on request at the cashier's desk). *CAFÉS:* Good ice cream is served at the outdoor cafés on the Old Town Market Square. **Nowy Świat**, ul. Nowy Świat 63. Quiet; with current newspapers from Western Europe. One of the customs of Warsaw residents is the Sunday visit to the **Hortex** (ul. Świętokrzyska 35 and Pl. Konstytucji 7) or the **Blikle Bakery** (Nowy Świat 35), where the best jelly doughnuts, *pączki*, can be had. Another custom is to sip a cup of hot chocolate in the **Wedel** (corner of ul. Szpitalna and Górskiego).

The best jazz clubs with live music are **Akwarium**, ul. Emilii Plater, Tel. 6205072, and **Remont**, ul. Waryńskiego 12, Tel. 6256031.

Palace of Culture and Science (Pałac Kultury i Nauki). Panorama view from the 30th floor. Mon-Fri 9:00 a.m. – 6:00 p.m.; Sat, Sun 10:00 a.m. – 6:00 p.m. **Museum of the Jewish Historical Institute** (Żydowski Instytut Historyczny), ul. Tłomacka 3/5. Mon-Fri 9:00 a.m. – 3:00 p.m.; tours in English, French, and German: Tel. 8271843, 8279221, Fax 8278372. **Jewish Cemetery** (Cmentarz Żydowski), ul. Okopowa. Sun-Thurs 10:00 a.m. – 3:00 p.m. **Royal Castle** (Zamek Królewski): Tues-Sun 10:00 a.m. – 4:00 p.m. On Thursdays and Sundays you can visit on your own; on other days, guided tour (several languages). Expect long line-ups in summer, so arrive early. **Historical Museum of Warsaw** (Muzeum Historyczne miasta Warszawy), Rynek Starego Miasta 42. Ticket reservations Tel. 6351625. Tues, Thurs 11:00 a.m. – 6:00 p.m.; Wed, Fri 10:00 a.m. – 3:30 p.m.; Sat, Sun 10:30 a.m. –2:30 p.m. **National Museum** (Muzeum Narodowe), Al. Jerozolimskie 3, Tel. 6211031, www.ddg.com.pl/nm/index.html. Tues, Sun 10:00 a.m. – 5:00 p.m.; Wed, Fri, Sat 10:00 a.m. – 4:00 p.m., Thurs 12:00 – 7:00 p.m. **Łazienki**, Castle, Theater (teatr w Starej Oranżerii), White House (Biały Domek), Tel. 6218212. Tues-Sun 9:30 a.m. – 3:00 p.m. **Center of Contemporary Art** (Zentrum Sztuki Współczesnej), ul. Armii Ludowej, in the Ujazdów Castle (Zamek Ujazdowski), various temporary exhibitions. Tel. 6281271-73. Tues-Thurs, Sat, Sun 11:00 a.m. – 5:00 p.m.; Fri 11:00 a.m. – 9:00 p.m. **Wilanów**, Interior of the Castle: Wed-Mon 9:30 a.m. – 2:30 p.m.; park open daily from 9:00 a.m. to sunset. **Poster Museum** (Muzeum Plakatu w Wilanowie): Tues –Sun 10:00 a.m. – 5:00 p.m. (in winter to 4:00 p.m) www.poster.com.pl.

A performance of the **Jewish Theater** is worthwhile even if not "high art" (Teatr Żydowski, Pl. Grzybowski 12/16, Tel. 6207025). Performances are in Yiddish; Polish translation with earphones. If you understand German, you will be able to understand a lot of the Yiddish as well. *CINEMA:* The ever more cosmopolitan cinema scene offers movies from all over the world in the original language (with Polish subtitles).

FESTIVALS: **July**: Mozart Festival in various churches and music houses of Warsaw. **September**: Warsaw Fall (Warszawska Jesień; Tel. 8310607) of modern electronic music; **End of October**: Jazz Jamboree – one of the most important jazz festivals worldwide (Tel. 8262824). The **International Chopin Competition**, a prestigious event, takes place every five years and was most recently held in the year 2000. The current **program of cultural events** is published in the monthly *Warsaw What, Where, When* (English, German, Polish; www.inter.com.pl), available gratis at the tourist office on the Castle Square, among other places. You can also purchase the more comprehensive English language magazine *Warsaw Insider*. *CONCERTS:* **Filharmonia**, ul. Sienkiewicza 10, Tel. 8267281 (concerts: ul. Moniuszki 5), and **Operetka Warszawska**, ul. Nowogrodzka 49, Tel. 6920754, for operetta. The **Opera** (Teatr Narodowy, Pl. Teatralny 1, Tel. 8265019) is located in an interesting building and provides the opportunity to get to know the national operas. ("Halka" or "Straszny Dwór," by Stanisław Moniuszko are recommended). English subtitles (more accurately "supertitles") appear above the stage. *FOLK MUSIC:* The ensembles *Mazowsze* (Mazovian) and *Śląsk* (Silesia) perform folk music for discriminating audiences whenever they are home in Warsaw and not on a their foreign tour. The *Europejski* Hotel offers folk music events during the summer at 8:00 p.m.

MASOVIA AND ŁÓDŹ

MAZOVIA AND ŁÓDŹ
Chopin's Birthplace and the City of Poland's Industrial Revolution

KAMPINOS NATIONAL PARK
PŁOCK
ŁOWICZ AND ITS ENVIRONS
ŁÓDŹ

Mazovia (Polish: Mazowsze), the wide, flat region within a 100 kilometer radius of Warsaw, was once characterized by sandy soil and straw-thatched huts. While ugly concrete dormitory towns are now to be found on the outskirts of Warsaw, the farther away from Warsaw you go, the more natural the scenery becomes, with the occasional characteristic white willows. These are a typical feature of Mazovia and are often featured on the covers of Polish music recordings by the greatest Mazovian, the composer Frédéric Chopin. Although by no means as exciting for visitors as the Carpathian Mountains or Masuria, Mazovia nevertheless has its own special charm. Large medieval castles, Baroque palaces, a thriving folk art tradition and unspoiled nature in the Kampinowski National Park are all waiting to be discovered on day trips from Warsaw.

Diversions of a rather different kind are provided by the town of Łódź, often called the Manchester of the East. Here the world of factories and palaces created by the barons of the textile industry has been preserved intact, and coming here is almost like walking onto a film set. It is

Left: In Łowicz the Corpus Christi processions are particularly colorful occasions with the participants in traditional costumes.

an open-air museum of the days when capitalism was still young, aggressive, and greedy.

KAMPINOWSKI NATIONAL PARK

There is probably no other capital in the world that has a national park right outside its gates. Until 1992, when the Biebrza marshes in the northeast were turned into a national park, the 670-square-kilometer **Kampinos National Park** (Kampinowski Park Narodowy) ❶ near Warsaw was even the largest nature reserve in Poland. It extends along the former course of the River Vistula, with marshes in the East and sand dunes in the West.

Since the forest in this area of dunes and marshes was for centuries the hunting ground of the Polish kings, it remained largely unspoiled. In the last two centuries, however, villages were built within its boundaries and it can no longer be described as isolated. After 1974 the state bought up several of the villages, pulled them down and reforested these areas. The park thus has a mixture of strictly protected reserves and settlements in an attractive natural setting and can be explored on any of the various hiking trails.

Map page 61, Information page 65

PŁOCK

The essential guide to the 300 kilometers of marked trails is the "Kampinowski Park Narodowy" hiking map. A good starting point is the trail marked in red leading from the Warsaw suburb of Dziekanów to Brochów which, although over 50 kilometers in length, can be tackled in shorter stretches due to its numerous access points.

Other starting points for the exploration of the park are the villages of Truskaw, Palmiry and Kampinos, which are easy to reach. It is not advisable to go walking on a Sunday or public holiday, when the paths are overcrowded. On any other day there is a better chance of seeing one of the 100 elks that live in the National Park. They are, however, extremely shy and usually stay hidden in the impenetrable undergrowth.

Apart from foxes, wild boar, cranes and storks, the park has the largest colony in Europe of the rare black stork.

Above: Frédéric Chopin (sculpture by J. Borrell-Nicolau) – Mazovia's most famous son.

On the western edge of the park, 50 kilometers from Warsaw, is the **Birthplace of Frédéric Chopin** ❷ in Żelazowa Wola near Sochaczew. Chopin spent the first few months of his life in 1810 in a building adjacent to a manor house until his family moved to Warsaw. Today this house is a museum: the exhibits include portraits and facsimiles of manuscripts.

Chopin's father, Mikołaj Chopin, a French music and language teacher who had taken Polish citizenship earned his living as a tutor in the manor household; his mother came from an impoverished branch of the Mazovian aristocracy. Sunday morning is the best time to come to Żleazowa Wola; the attractive manor house garden provides the setting for beautifully played piano music – naturally works by Chopin.

PŁOCK

A pleasant excursion can be made along the Vistula from Warsaw to **Płock** ❸ (around 100 kilometers). On the banks of the Vistula, it is a blend of small provincial town with an charming market square and endless suburbs of concrete blocks, which house the employees of Poland's largest petrochemical factory *Petrochemia Płocka S.A.* Płock is proud of its history: from the early 11th century to 1495 it was the capital of the Duchy of Mazovia. For a short time, from 1079 to 1138, it was actually the capital of the whole of Poland.

The most interesting part of the city is the **Cathedral and Castle Hill**, on the cliff above the Vistula. This is the location of the **Mazovian Museum** (*Muzeum Mazowieckie*) which is a must-see, even if museums are not normally your first priority. In 1967 a collection of Art Nouveau objects of every category was begun. The result is a fully reconstructed dining room, a drawing room in the Viennese style, and a bedroom, all furnished with works by the great artists of the era

ŁOWICZ

such as van de Velde, Mucha and Lalique, and firms such as Tiffany.

The adjacent **Cathedral** incorporates a range of styles from Romanesque to Art Nouveau, which are reflected in the frescoes inside. In 1825 the remains of the Polish rulers who had resided here, Władysław Hermann and Bolesław III Krzywousty ("the Wry-Mouthed"), were transferred to the royal chapel.

Particularly outstanding among the numerous works of art in this church is the copy of the **Plotzker Bronze Door**. It was made in Magdeburg in the 12th century for the cathedral of Płock, and consists of twenty four panels with reliefs depicting subjects from the Old Testament and the Gospels, as well as allegories. The original was stolen and carried off to Novgorod (Russia) in the Middle Ages.

ŁOWICZ AND ITS ENVIRONS

Five Baroque churches dominate the town center of **Łowicz** ❹ (80 kilometers west of Warsaw). For over 600 years the town was under the control of the Gneizno archbishops, the highest religious authority in the country. Next to the **Cathedral** and the **Town Hall** on the market square (*Rynek Kościuszki*) is a large building that was once the missionary seminary, with two small farms eking out an existence in its courtyard.

These are part of the **Regional Museum** accommodated in the monastery complex that was rebuilt for this purpose. The collection also includes sculptures, painting, pottery, embroidery, national costumes and household implements.

The folk tradition in Łowicz is not, however, confined to the museum. On the Feast of Corpus Christi the townspeople, beautifully dressed in their colorful traditional costumes, file through the streets in a long procession behind a splendidly decorated portrait of the Mother of God.

Outside Łowicz are two villages with extensive parks for pleasant walks. In **Nieborów** is the imposing palace of Cardinal Radziejowski, built in 1690-1696.

Information page 65

ARKADIA

The creator of this magnificent building with its two corner towers was the Dutch architect Tilman van Gameren. Now a branch of the Warsaw National Museum, the palace has a rich collection of paintings and antique sculptures (e.g. a José Ribera and the famous head of Niobe). Behind the palace is a French-style park, decorated with the mysterious, prehistoric female figures originating from the Scythians of the Black Sea coast.

If the Nieborów Park is too ordered and geometric for your taste, three kilometers further on is *Arkadia, created in 1778 for Princess Helena Radziwiłł. Laid out quite in the romantic style, this park has a number of buildings in artistically designed "natural" settings: the Temple of Diana, the "High Priest's House" with original "spoils," this is Renaissance details removed from a Łowicz tombstone and added here – and the burgrave's house where the walls are covered with numerous tufa stones, imported specially from Italy. And the romantic scene would not be complete, of course, without its Sybilline grotto, a "Gothic" house and a "Roman" aqueduct.

Above: Nieborów Palace near Łowicz. Right: Girl Guides on a visit to Łódź.

ŁÓDŹ

The second largest town in Poland is widely thought to be the ugliest, and on top of this, full of swindlers from the shadow economy. Even so, an increasing number of people are beginning to discover the town's morbid charm, its once derided architecture from the turn of the twentieth century and its fascinating history.

In 1820 **Łódź** ❺ had a population of 800. It was in this year that the plans of the philosopher of the Enlightenment, Stanisław Staszic, who wanted to make this small place the center of the Eastern European textile industry, began to take shape: Łódź was transformed into a city with straight roads laid out like a chess board. It grew dramatically and in only

Map page 61, Information page 65

two generations the population grew to over 300,000.

After 1850, when the customs barriers between Russian-dominated Poland and Russia were abolished, more industrial plants were built. The textile magnates cultivated a pseudo-aristocratic lifestyle, their power based neither on aristocratic titles nor particular services to the state, but on their property alone. This, as is very evident from their palaces, was of vast proportions.

One anecdote will serve to illustrate the wealth of Łódź society: Moritz Poznański decided he wanted to cover the walls of his palace with gold rubles. He asked the czar for permission, since the likeness of the czar was displayed the coins. Back came the inspired answer from St. Petersburg that the czar had nothing against this project in principle, on condition that the coins were to be mounted at right-angles to the wall. However it is not known whether Poznański actually followed these instructions or not.

Given the fact that the population was made up of only two classes, it is no surprise that in Łódź the Marxist slogans fell on open ears. In 1861 there was an uprising by the weavers, and in 1905 hundreds of workers died in violent clashes with the Russian military.

The face of the town, which they renamed "Litzmannstadt" was changed indelibly by the Nazis: over 360,000 people died in the Kulmhof extermination camp (Chełmno nad Nerem). Not yet having refined their extermination techniques, the captors crammed their victims into trucks disguised as X-ray vans and, with the exhaust fumes directed inside, drove around until they suffocated. Of the population of Łódź, 30 percent had been Jews. After the war, all that was left of their world was the **Jewish Cemetery**, the largest in Europe (ul. Chrysantem, northeast of the town center), and memories of those who had fled in time, including the Łódź musician Arthur Rubinstein (1887-1982).

After the war, Łódź became famous for its Film School with Polański, Wajda and

Map page 61, Information page 65

ŁÓDŹ

cent neo-Renaissance buildings. The **Poznański Palace**, northwest of Plac Wolności, looks primarily neo-Baroque although it is in fact more of a hybrid that includes the neo-Gothic and other architectural styles. It now houses the Historical Museum of Łódź. Adjoining the palace is the **Poznański Factory**, with weaving and spinning mills and warehouses concealed behind its huge brick façade.

Opposite is the **Factory Workers' Housing**. This is the setting of the novel by the Nobel prize winner Władysław Reymont, "The Promised Land" (1899), which portrays the inhuman face of early capitalism. Reymont described Łódź as "a polyp, which ground up people and goods, heaven and earth in its massive jaws and for this gave a handful of people unnecessary millions but vast armies of people nothing but hunger and trouble." The novel was brilliantly filmed by Andrzej Wajda (1974).

The title of the novel has been borrowed by the city map, *Pałace Ziemi Obiecanej*, ("Palaces of the Promised Land," obtainable in the Historical Museum), which is a guide to further historic buildings. Among them are beautiful examples of Art Nouveau design such as the **Villa of the Kindermann Family** (west of Piotrkowska) and the **Palace of the Herbst Family** (in the eastern part of the town) with rooms typical of the palace of an industrial tycoon around 1900, some of which are original and some reconstructed.

Kieślowski among its students. Its more recent history has been dominated by recession, since many of the textile factories were unable to survive in the market economy and went bankrupt after the loss of the eastern markets.

A stay in Łódź is an exciting voyage of discovery into the age of early capitalism. The tour begins where the special atmosphere of the town is at its most evident, on *****ul. Piotrkowska**, the central north-south axis. At the southern end of the elegant pedestrian precinct is the **White Factory** (*Biała Fabryka*; 1835-37) of the Geyer family which has a large mechanical spinning mill, and is now the location of the **Textile Museum**.

Łódź created for itself that past that it did not have with the façades of the palaces and residences. Meyer Street, once a private road and today called **ul. Moniuszki** (a small street perpendicular to Piotrkowska), is lined with magnificent

Finally, Łódź also has the best **Museum of Modern Art** (*Muzeum Sztuki*) in Poland, accommodated in another Pozański Palace. It includes works by the great artists of classical modernism, such as Chagall, Picasso, Léger, Nolde, and Ernst, as well as the unjustifiably neglected Polish artist, Władysław Strzeminski, and the Polish-born Jankiel Adler, the greatest painter of the Jewish world, apart from Chagall.

Above: Splendid Art Nouveau window in the Villa of the Kindermann (Łódź).

MASOVIA AND ŁÓDŹ

KAMPINOWSKI NATIONAL PARK, ŁOWICZ ☎ 046

Zacisze, ul. Kaliska 5, Łowicz, Tel. 8376244, Fax 8373326.
Hotel **Zacisze** in Łowicz has a pleasant restaurant. **Kuźnia Napoleońska**, ul. Sochaczewska 5, Paprotnia in Żelazowa Wola (on the main road between Warsaw and Poznań), Tel. 8615213, 8615214. Pub in an old forge, in which Napoleon is said to have dined; Polish specialties such as borscht, pea soup and pickled pork knuckle in jelly.
Chopin's Birthplace, Żelazowa Wola. Tues-Sat 10:00 a.m. – 5:00 pm (in winter to 4:00 p.m.), Sunday to 2:30 p.m.). **Regional Museum**, Rynek Kościuszki 4, Łowicz. Tues-Sun 10:00 a.m. – 4:00 p.m. **Castle Museum**, Nieborów, Tues-Sun 10:00 a.m. – 3:30 p.m. **Park**, Arkadia, daily, 10:00 a.m. to sunset.
Hiking in the Kampinowski National Park: Bus line 701 goes from Warsaw's Pl. Wilsona to Dziekanów; Line 708 from the PKS station Marymont to Truskaw. PKS buses depart the PKS station Warsaw Zachodnia for Płock by way of Palmiry, Nowy Kazuń, and for Sochaczew by way of Leszno, Kampinos and Żelazowa Wola. The map "Kampinowski Park Narodowy" can be purchased in bookshops in Warsaw.
Żelazowa Wola, Piano recitals: Sundays at 11:00 a.m. and 3:00 p.m., May to October.

PŁOCK ☎ 024

ul. Tumska 4, Tel. 2629497.
Petropol, ul. Jachowicza 49, Tel. 2624451, Fax 2624450, www.orbis.pl/hot_pet.html. The exterior of the city's best hotel looks like a cement block building.
Apart from an unremarkable restaurant in the Hotel **Petropol** you have the choice between a Hawaii steak at the **Literacka** on the Market Square (Stary Rynek 8, Tel. 2641111) and the chicken Masala in Polish-Indian style at the **Hollywood** (ul. Tumska 8, Tel. 2622545).
Mazovian Museum (Muzeum Mazowieckie), ul. Tumska 2. Tues-Sat 9:00 a.m. – 3:00 p.m., Sunday and holidays 10:00 a.m. – 3:00 p.m.

ŁÓDŹ ☎ 042

WCIT, ul. Traugutta 18, Tel. 6337169. **Orbis Tourist Office**, ul. Piotrkowska 68, Tel. 6366126. **PTTK Office**, ul. Wigury 12, Tel. 6361946.
Grand, ul. Piotrkowska 72, Tel. 6339920, Fax 6337876. The best hotel in the city; like much else here, it has seen better times. Nevertheless, worth a recommendation. **Centrum**, ul. Kilińskiego 59/63, Tel. 6328640, Fax 6369650. Good hotel; offers the ambience of modern banality. **Déjà Vu**, ul. Wigury 4, Tel. 6362060, 6367081, Fax 6367083. New, in a former factory in the city center; furnished in the style of the twenties. **Savoy**, ul. Traugutta 6, Tel. 6329360, Fax 6329368. Seven-story "skyscraper" of the turn of the (19th-20th) century; today it offers only the reflected splendor of the epoch in which Joseph Roth wrote his novel of the same name. **Garnizonowy**, ul. Obrońców Stalingradu 81, Tel. 6338023. Former army lodgings. **Youth Hostels**, ul. Zamenhofa 13, Tel. 6366599, in the city center; open all year round; also one at ul. Legionów 27, Tel. 6306680. **Campground**, ul. Rzgowska 247.
In contrast to the culinary tedium characteristic until the recent past, the city does offer a few possibilities today: **Maharaja**, ul. Traugutta 4, Tel. 6334045. Specialties from India. **Malinowa** in the *Grand* Hotel, ul. Piotrkowska 72, Tel. 6330111. Exquisite Polish cuisine. **Złota Kaczka**, ul. Piotrkowska 79, Tel. 6332261. Chinese. **Frutti di Mare**, ul. Piotrkowska 92, Tel. 6302008. Good pizzeria. **Dracena**, Al. Kościuszki 68, Tel. 6364806. International cuisine; the wild boar with cranberries is delicious. **Halka**, Moniuszki 1. Modest; reasonably priced Polish meals
Textile Industry Museum (Centralne Muzeum Włókiennictwa), ul. Piotrkowska 282, Tel. 6832684, www.muzeumwlokiennictwa.muz.pl. Tues, Sat 10:00 a.m. – 4:00 p.m.; Wed, Fri 9:00 a.m. –5:00 p.m. (free entrance); Thurs 10:00 a.m. – 5:00 p.m.; Sun 10:00 a.m. – 3:00 p.m. **City Historical Museum,** Poznański-Palais, ul. Ogrodowa 15, Tel. 6540323. Tues, Sat 10:00 a.m. – 2:00 p.m.; Wed 2:00 p.m. – 6:00 p.m.. The adjacent **Poznański Factory** (Ogrodowa 17) is still in operation and is not open to tourists. **Chimera Gallery**, the Villa of the Kindermann Family, ul. Wólczańska 31/33, Tel. 6322416. Opening times vary. **Museum of Modern Art** (Muzeum Sztuki), ul. Więckowskiego 36 (reached by way of ul. Piotrkowska and Więckowskiego), Tel. 6339790, www.ddg.com.pl/msl.html. Tues 10:00 a.m. – 5:00 p.m.; Wed, Fri 11:00 a.m. – 5:00 p.m.; Thurs 12:00 – 7:00 p.m. (entrance free); Sat, Sun 10:00 a.m. – 4:00 p.m. **Herbst Family Mansion** (Rezydencja Księży Młyn), ul. Przędzalniana 72, Tel. 6749698. Tues 10:00 a.m. – 5:00 p.m.; Wed, Fri 12:00 – 5:00 p.m., Thurs 12:00 – 7:00 p.m.; Sat, Sun 11:00 a.m. – 4:00 p.m.
Opera (Teatr Wielki), Pl. Dąbrowskiego 1, Tel. 6339960. **Philharmonic**, ul. Piotrkowska 243, Tel. 6371506. **Music Theater** (Teatr Muzyczny), ul. Północna 47/51, Tel. 6783511. Program listings for these theaters are printed in the Łódź newspaper *Welcome to Łódź*, available from tourist information offices.

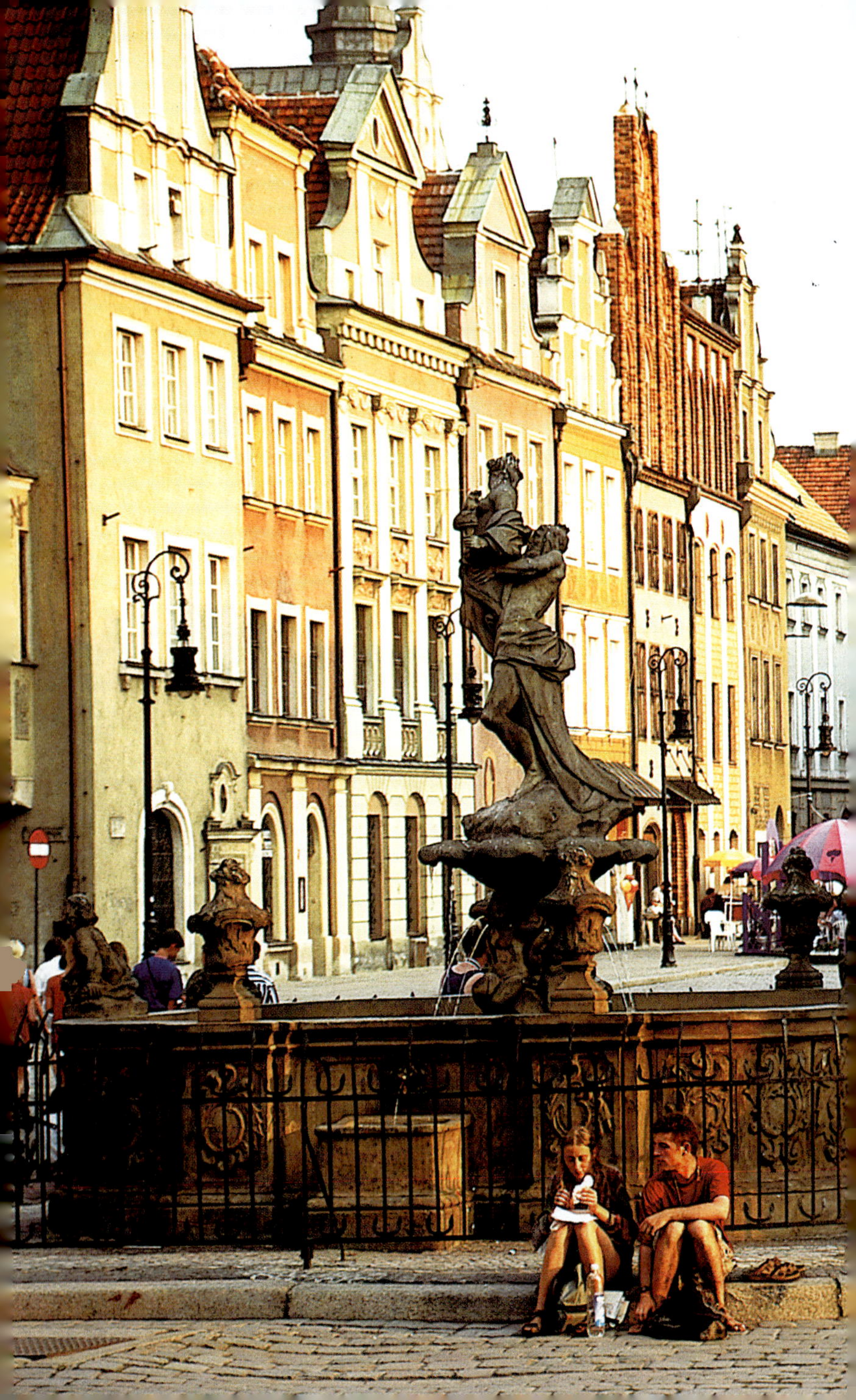

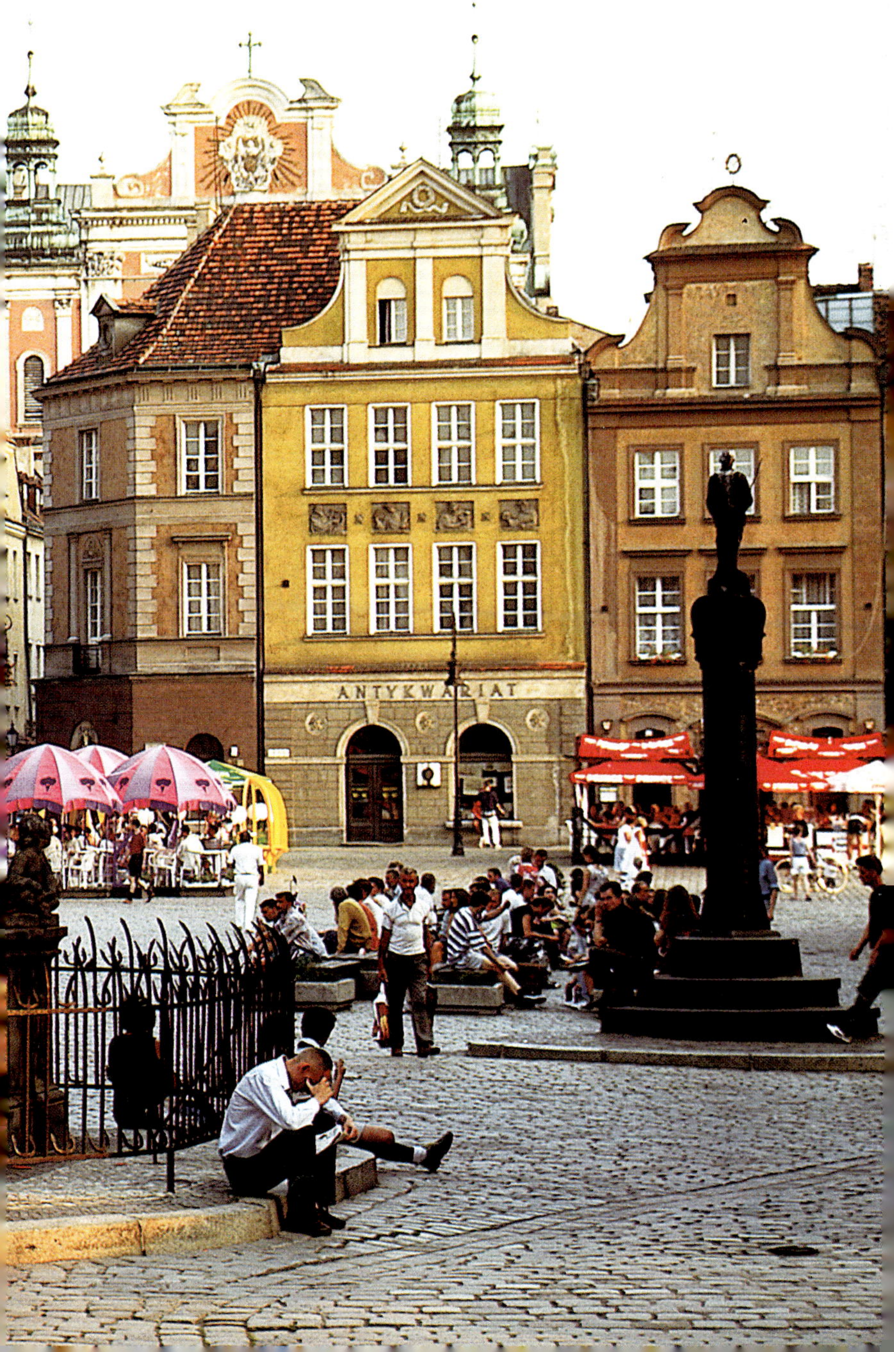
ANTYKWARIAT

POZNAŃ AND GREAT POLAND

POZNAŃ AND GREAT POLAND
The Cradle of the Polish State

POZNAŃ
THE PALACES OF
GREAT POLAND
GNIEZNO
KUJAWY

The area which surrounds Poznań is known as *Wielkopolska*, or Great Poland. It was the home in the 10th century of the Polians, the Slavic tribe who played a decisive role in the emergence of the state of Poland in 966. By then Prince Mieszko I (reigned approximately 960-992) was already ruling over a relatively stable state. It was not until later that the area around Cracow, which then became known as *Małopolska*, or Little Poland, was incorporated into the new state.

Poznań, the most important town in Great Poland, and with a population of 600,000 the fifth largest town in the country, is worth more than a short stop on a journey from Berlin to Warsaw.

The Old Town Square has a charming southern Mediterranean atmosphere and there are many other interesting features waiting to be discovered in the place that is now a dynamic trade centre.

An initial impression of the region can be obtained on day trips from Poznań. The cathedral of Gniezno, in which numerous Polish kings were crowned, is a must, and no itinerary should omit the countryside; the lakes of the Great Poland

Previous pages: On the Old Town Square of Poznań. Left: The Cathedral of Gniezno, for centuries the Polish kingdom's coronation church.

National Park are much more than a weekend refuge for nearby city dwellers.

POZNAŃ

It is impossible to overemphasise the historical importance of **Poznań** ❶. Like Ostrów Lednicki and Gniezno, it was one of the residences of Prince Mieszko I, who, as was the custom in the early Middle Ages moved with his court from one palatinate to another.

In 1253 a commercial center was founded on the opposite, left bank of the Warta, which had a Magdeburg town charter. Its wealth was based on a trade law established 1394 which offered traveling merchants, as they passed through, the right to offer their wares for sale in the city for a limited time.

In 1793, in the course of the Second Partition of Poland, the town became part of Prussia. The peaceful coexistence of Germans (30-40 percent of the total population of the region) and Poles came to an abrupt end in the second half of the 19th century with the unsuccessful Polish uprising of 1848 and the cultural campaign of Bismarck (1871-1887). Bismarck campaigned against the Catholic Church and the Polish aristocracy in the hope that it would then be easier to germanicize the people in the villages. At

POZNAŃ

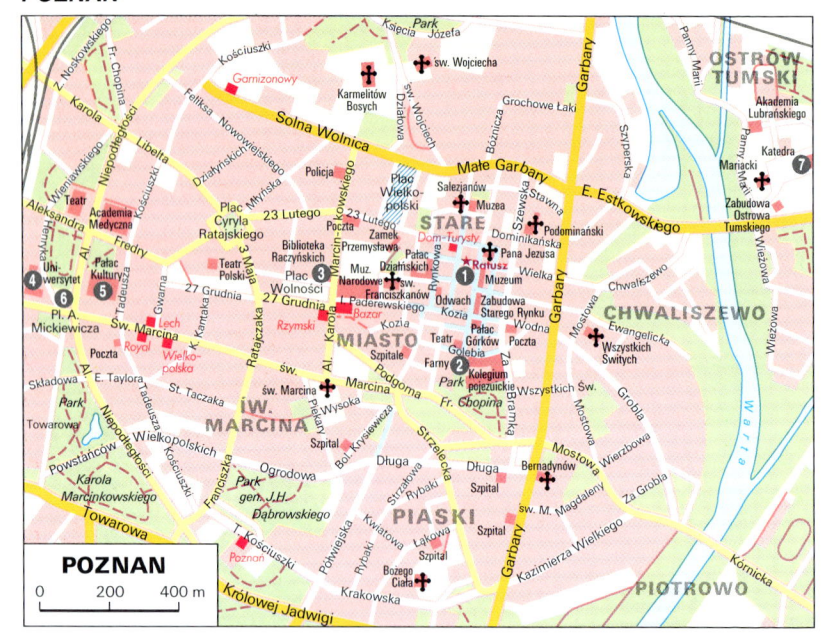

the same time he passed restrictive laws which included the prohibition of the Polish language in the schools, with the aim of suppressing the Poles.

The conflicts between the nationalities, once inflamed, were impossible to extinguish. After 1918, when Poznań had once again become a commercial center, expulsion of the Germans was the declared aim of the Polish government. In 1939 one million Poles were driven out of Warthegau, the area around Poznań, into the so-called General Government (cf page 26). At the end of Nazi rule, all the Germans were again expelled from the Poznań region, but at the same time the Old Town also suffered heavy damage.

It is presumably because of the close connections of the two nations that the people of Poznań are said by their fellow-countrymen to have "typical German" characteristics. They are considered to be

Right: The Town Hall of Poznań, a beautiful Renaissance building and a popular meeting point in the town centre.

industrious to the point of being greedy, sober to the point of being unimaginative, reliable but not very hospitable.

They seem to make good use of their positive characteristics: every year the largest industrial trade fair in the former Soviet block, apart from the one in Leipzig, is held in Poznań. The town can show strong economic growth in its statistics, with the result that numerous foreign firms are now established here.

Old Town Square

The main sights can all be reached on foot but are nevertheless located in three separate districts: in the Old Town, in the newer district west of this, and on the Cathedral Island.

Begin your tour of the town with the Old Town Square, dominated by what is undeniably Poznań's finest building, the **★Town Hall** ❶. Between 1550 and 1560 the original Gothic structure was completely rebuilt in the Renaissance style by the Italian architect with the fine-

70 *Information pages 76-77*

POZNAŃ

sounding name of Giovanni Battista Quadro di Lugano. The main façade consists of a three-story arcaded loggia, crowned with a high attic.

At noon every day two metal goats spring out of the town hall clock, in memory of the saviors of the town. The story is that two goats once escaped onto the roofs of Poznań. While they were being pursued, a fire was discovered, in time for it to be extinguished; this happy coincidence saved the town from being reduced to ashes.

The Historical Museum of Poznań in the Town Hall is well worth a visit; one of its outstanding features is the large hall on the first floor with its coffered ceiling beautifully decorated with stucco work. As in all medieval towns, the **Market Place** was the location not only of the town hall but also of small shops. These little houses have since been rebuilt; they originally sold such commodities as salt, herrings and candles. The square is closed off by the Weigh House, the neoclassical main police station and two ugly 20th century buildings that are used for exhibitions.

Of all the many churches in Poznań, the **Parish Church** ❷, which originally belonged to the Jesuits, is the most unusual (Koś ciół farny; ul. Gołębia). The building, begun in 1650 by the Italian Tommaso Poncino, is an excellent example of Baroque illusionism: the 16 massive marble columns are only there for decoration and have no structural function.

On the elongated square, Plac Wolności, is the town's finest neoclassical building, the **Raczyński Library** ❸, dating from 1829 and modeled on the Louvre. The large colonnade was built of cast iron, which was then one of the latest forms of technology. The east side of the square is taken up by the **National Museum**. The exhibition of western artists is one of the best in the country and includes Ribera, Zurbarán, Bellini, Bronzino, and one of the few women painters of the 16th century, Sofonisba Anguisciola. In the Polish section there is a large collection of so-called coffin portraits – Poland's most unusual art form. It was the custom of the aristocracy in the 16th to 18th centuries to paint a portrait of the deceased, which was then attached to the end of the coffin and left there until burial. The Polish dignitaries thus depicted stare down glassily from the strange trapezoid metal plates.

Ulica św. Marcina

The main axis of present-day Poznań is the **Ulica św. Marcina**, which is dominated by modern department stores. At its western end there are also historic buildings, such as the present-day **Adam Mickiewicz University** ❹. The neo-Baroque Collegium Maius and neo-Renaissance Collegium Minus were once Prussian school and government buildings. Nearby is the **Palace of Culture** ❺, the former residence of Emperor Wil-

Information pages 76-77

POZNAŃ

Above: The Cathedral Island with Poznań Cathedral is the oldest part of the town.

helm II. It was built in 1910 by Franz Schwechten, the architect of the Berlin Memorial Church, in a somber, neo-Romanesque style, modeled on the imperial palaces of the dynasty of Hohenstaufen

The **Monument to the Victims of June 1956** ❻ commemorates the workers who protested against the communist regime in June 1956 and whose rebellion was literally crushed by tanks, leaving 76 dead and 600 injured.

Cathedral Island

The oldest part of Poznań lies east of the Warta in the present *Ostrów Tumski* district (Cathedral Island). This is also the location of **Poznań Cathedral** ❼, a massive Gothic basilica fronted by two towers that are finished in the Baroque style. It was preceded by two buildings dating from the 10th and 12th centuries, the remains of which can be seen in the basement. The church, which is supported on oak piles in marshy soil, repeatedly had to be renovated, and each time its outer shell was altered to match the architectural style of the day. After 1945 the exterior was renovated primarily in the Gothic style.

Inside the church you will see a number of valuable **Tombstones**, including that of the Górka family (1574) by Canavesi and that of Bishop Izbieński (after 1533) by Jan Michałowicz, the most famous Polish sculptor of the epoch. The **Golden Chapel** (*Złota Kaplica*), the walls of which are paneled with real gold, is not something you can walk past without noticing. This room, which is certainly not one of the wonders of western architecture, contains the symbolic tombstones of the first Polish rulers – Mieszko I and Bolesław the Brave – and was built in 1835-1841 by the Italian, Maria Lanci, in a style which might somewhat generously be described as neo-Byzantine.

AROUND POZNAŃ

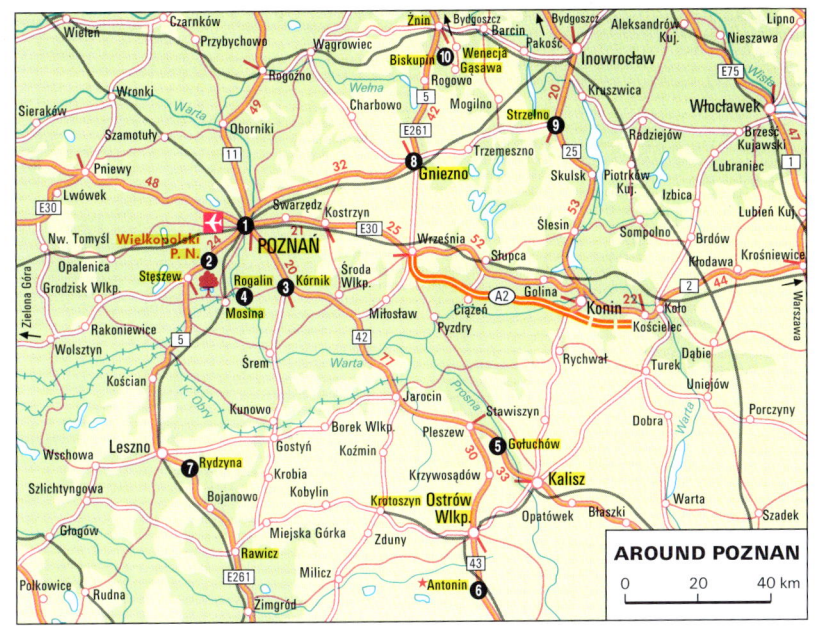

Excursion to the National Park

Practically bordering the southern edge of the town of Poznań, is the perfect place in which to unwind after the many cultural challenges of the city: the **Wielkopolska National Park** ❷ (*Wielkopolski Park Narodowy* or Great Poland National Park). Set in an ancient glacial landscape, the park has a total of 16 lakes among the mixed forest.

Good places to set out from are the parking lot near Mosina or the little station of Osowa Góra, which can be reach by train arriving several times a day from Poznań.

The path with red markings passes the small Lake Kociołek and continues to Lake Górecki – a long lake surrounded by forest, and the most beautiful spot in the park. The trail then continues to Puszczykowo, which also has a rail link with Poznań. Also attractive is the path with blue markings, which initially follows the same route and ends in Stęszew on the Poznań – Zielona Góra road.

THE CASTLES OF GREAT POLAND

In the 18th and 19th centuries the self-assured local aristocracy constructed magnificent residences for themselves, which today are showpieces of the southern part of Great Poland.

Families such as the Leszczyńskis, Raczyńskis and Radziwiłłs produced kings and governors, and were also related by marriage to the elite of western European nobility.

Many of these palaces have been turned into museums and – even more importantly for travelers – some have been converted into accommodation with special flair.

Twenty kilometers along the expressway running southeast from Poznań is **Kórnik** ❸, location of the fairy-tale castle of the Działyński family.

It was rebuilt in its present, primarily neo-Gothic form by the then owner Tytus Działyński in 1845-1860, on the basis of a design by Karl Friedrich Schinkel. In

Information pages 76-77

ROGALIN

the well-preserved interior you are back in the world of the 19th century aristocracy. The members of this upper class liked a touch of the exotic in their Polish homes, as is demonstrated by the Moorish Hall on the first floor, distinctly influenced by the Alhambra in Granada. Beside a lake behind the castle is the **Arboretum**, botanical gardens containing around 3,000 plant species, many of them exotic and most planted by the same Działyński.

Baroque ornamentation is the dominant feature of the palace 13 kilometers to the west in **Rogalin** ❹. Built for the Raczyński family in 1768-1784, it consists of a main building with semicircular galleries. It is part of the Poznań National Museum, with works primarily from the 19th century exhibited in an adjacent building. Outside the complex is the family **Mausoleum**, built in 1817-1820 – a miniature copy of the Maison Carrée located in Nîmes.

There are three oak trees in the large romantic park, said to be a thousand years old and named Lech, Czech and Rus after the legendary brothers who founded the Polish, Czech and Russian states. Rus is by far the most massive of the three trees.

Gołuchów ❺, on the main road to Kalisz (80 kilometers) will appeal particularly to admirers of Loire Valley castles. The steep roofs, high chimneys, octagonal towers and a courtyard with arbors, make it look decidedly French.

Here, in the 16th century, not far from Kalisia (or Kalisz) – the oldest settlement in Poland, dating to Roman times – the prosperous Leszczyńskis built themselves a manor befitting their station in society.

When the wife of subsequent owner Działyński – Izabella Czartoryska – had it completely rebuilt in 1872-1885, with the help of the famous Viollet le Duc, the older parts were integrated into an elegant neo-Renaissance Palace.

Above: Rogalin Palace, built by the Raczyński family in the 18th century. Right: the shrine of St Adalbert in Gniezno Cathedral.

ANTONON / GNIEZNO

*Antonin ❻, is one of Karl Friedrich Schinkel's most unusual creations. The wooden hunting lodge was built in 1822-1824 for Prince Antoni Radziwiłł, governor of the Grand Duchy of Poznań, which was subject to Prussian supremacy. The four-story cruciform building is supported by the central pillar, which has the chimney inside it. This is a good place to spend an evening by the fire and the night in one of the hotel rooms. To get there from Gołuchów, take the road running south from Ostrów Wielkopolski (46 kilometers).

The final palace on the itinerary is **Rydzyna**, ❼ in the western part of Great Poland near Leszno (110 kilometers). A little more luxurious than Antonin, it also offers accommodation. Rydzyna was built in 1696-1704 by Pompeo Ferrari for Stanisław Leszczyński, who later became king of Poland.

GNIEZNO

Gniezno ❽ is now a sleepy provincial town that seems oblivious of its great past. There is little evidence to show that, in the 10th century, this was the center of the new Polish state. Kings were crowned here until the 14th century, and it was visited by Emperor Otto III who came in the year 1000 on a pilgrimage to the tomb of St. Adalbert, which was said to have miraculous properties.

Other than the *Cathedral, dominating the town's skyline, and an archaeological museum, there is not much to see in Gniezno. The massive brick building, the façade of which has two towers, and which dates from the 14th century, replaced a pre-Romanesque and a Romanesque cathedral. As in Poznań, the successive phases of reconstruction put the exterior in disaccord with the interior. However, the famous 12th century **Gniezno Bronze Door** has fortunately been preserved. The door is decorated with scenes from the life of St. Adalbert (Św. Wojciech in Polish), probably Poland's most important saint. A total of 18 pictures (clockwise starting from the bottom left) show Adalbert leaving Gdańsk to go as a missionary to christianize the Prussians, celebrating mass, preaching, and being martyred. This is the first – and also one of the last – representations of the Prussians in European art.

The unusual ribs in the interior vaulting are made of ashlar and stucco and are richly decorated with sculptured or cast motifs of plants and figures. An interesting feature in the interior, however, is the silver **Shrine of St. Adalbert** (1662) which was partially destroyed in 1986 in a spectacular art robbery (but has since been reconstructed). Furthermore you can admire a **Tombstone** which is the work of Veit Stoss.

KUJAWY

The Kujawy region begins east of Gniezno and runs north to Bydgoszcz. The separation of this region from Great

KUJAWY

Poland is due primarily to the fact that, in the late Middle Ages, Kujawy was a separate duchy. **Strzelno** ❾, located in the middle of Kujawy, has two famous Romanesque churches.

The interior of the Baroque *****Premonstratensian Church of the Holy Trinity** (*Kościół Św. Trójcy*)contains a most unusual treasure: by pure chance four sculptured Romanesque columns were discovered here some time after the Second World War. Two of these nave colums, set in blind arcades, are carved with female figures representing the various virtues and sins.

The origin of this most rare form of column is just as puzzling as the function of Strzelno's second Romanesque church, the adjacent **St. Procopius' Church**. It is built in the form of a castle chapel with a circular ground plan, a highly unusual construction for an abbey church.

Biskupin ❿, 36 kilometers north of Gniezno near Żnin, also became famous by chance. In 1933 a teacher noticed pieces of wood on a marshy peninsula near the village. These were excavated to reveal a *****Settlement of the Lusatian Culture**, considered to be the best preserved in Europe.

Inhabited between around 700 and 400 BC, the village had a population of approximately 1000, that lived in 106 identical houses – an indication that there were no marked social differences among the inhabitants. The settlement was protected by diagonal wooden stakes rammed into the earth and a six-meter earth rampart fortified with oak logs. To preserve it from decay, much of the complex has been re-buried. Replicas of the entrance gate and a road have been constructed and are open to the public, together with a small excavated area.

An additional attraction of this area is the **Narrow-gauge Railway** between Gąsawa and Żnin, which stops at the excavation site.

WIELKOPOLSKA / GREAT POLAND

POZNAŃ ☎ 061

WCIT, Stary Rynek 59, Tel. 8526156, Fax 8553378; Plac Wolności, Tel. 8519645, **Orbis Tourist Office**, ul. Roosvelta 20, Tel. 8471792, and ul. Marcinkowskiego 21, Tel. 8532052.

Poznań, Pl. W. Andersa 1, Tel. 8332081, Fax 8332961. The best known hotel in the city is a monstrous block that dominates the silhouette of the city. Restaurant, bars, sauna, shops, travel office, car rental, etc. available; lovely view of the city from the higher floors, looking direction northeast. In spite of the large number of rooms, you should reserve early – as with all the hotels in Poznań – during, for example, trade fairs. During busy times (See last section of Info on Poznań.) the prices almost double.

Merkury, ul. Roosvelta 20, Tel. 8558000, Fax 8558955. Frequented mostly by business travelers because of its proximity to the exhibition center. **Novotel**, ul. Warszawska 64/66, Tel. 8770011, Fax 8773654. Typical representative of the well known hotel chain; inconveniently located on the periphery of the city. All beds American size (disliked by Europeans, who are used to wider ones and consider these appropriate only for honeymooners). **Polonez**, Al. Niepodległości 36, Tel. 8699141, Fax 8523762. long-established; convenient location not too far from the Old Town Market. **Meridian**, ul. Litewska 22, Tel. 8471564, Fax 8473441. Modern and comfortable. **Park**, ul. Majakowskiego 77, Tel. 8794081, Fax 8773830. New structure with all comforts. **Dorrian**, ul. Wyspiańskiego 29, Tel. 8674522, Fax 8674559. Relatively new; for discriminating guests. The following hotels offer similar standards of comfort and are located directly west of the Old Town, so they are within walking distance: **Wielkopolski**, ul. św. Marcina 67, Tel. 8527631, Fax 8515492. **Lech**, ul. św. Marcina 74, Tel. 8530151, Fax 8530880. **Rzymski**, Al. K. Marcinkowskiego 22, Tel. 8528121, Fax 8528983, www.rzymskihotel.com. Pricey, but the best in the area. **Dom Turysty PTTK**, Stary Rynek 91, Tel. 8528891 to 5, Fax 8528893. This is the only PTTK hostel in Poland that falls into the middle price category, because of the unique location on the Market Square. Although the visitors here are not primarily business travelers, inexpensive accommodation is nonetheless continually booked up, making early reservations advisable. **Zacisze**, ul. św. Marcina 71, Tel. 8525530. **Dom Studenta Hanka**, Al. Niepodległości 26, Tel. 8529083. The five **Youth Hostels** are open year round but, from the standpoint of lo-

POZNAŃ AND GREAT POLAND

cation, only two can be recommended: ul. Dzymały 3, Tel. 8485836, and ul. Berwińskiego 2/3, Tel. 8663680, 8664040. **Campgrounds**, ul. Krańcowa 98, Tel. 8766155. Also cabins; an acceptable distance from the city center, a good place to unwind on the banks of Lake Malta. Ul. Koszalińska 15. In the section of the city called Strzeszynek. Baranowo, Tel. 8482812. West of the city. **Private rooms**: Biuro Zakwaterowania, ul. Głogowska 16, Tel. 8666313.

Poznań offers the strongest proof that competition enlivens business. Not only do several restaurants advertise through Internet addresses; they also try to outdo each other in the most exotic dishes they can come up with. **Cztery Pory Roku**, ul. Winogrady 9, Tel. 8532177, www.vivaldi.pl. Exclusive. Specialty: quail in juniper sauce. **Orfeusz**, ul. Świętosławska 12, Tel. 8519844. Eccentric, unusual dishes such as chicken with grapes in lily blossoms. **Rzymska**, Al. Marcinkowskiego 22, Tel. 8528121, www.rzymskihotel.com. In the hotel of the same name. Outstanding chanterelle sauce accompanies meat dishes. **Ratuszowa**, Stary Rynek 55, Tel. 8515318. Conveniently located, succulent duck stuffed with apple. **Club Elite**, Stary Rynek 2, Tel. 8529917. In a cellar on the Market Square, specialty: beef steak with porcinos.
ASIAN CUISINE: **Azalia**, ul. św. Marcina 34/36, Tel. 8532442. Sea cucumbers. **Bambus**, Stary Rynek 64/65, Tel. 8530658. Peking duck. **Pekin**, ul. 23 Lutego 33, Tel. 8526370. Seafood. **Taj India**, ul. Wiankowa 3, Tel. 8766249. Chicken in yogurt-safran sauce. There is no lack of Italian restaurants: **Colosseo**, Pl. Wolności 5, Tel. 8521128. **Casa Mia**, ul. Szpitalna 27b, Tel. 8477194. **Figaro**, ul. Ogrodowa 10, Tel. 8522812. **Tivoli**, ul. św. Czesława 3, Tel. 8336252.

Town Hall, **Historical Museum of Poznań** (Muzeum Historii Miasta Poznania), Tel. 8525613. Mon, Tues, Fri 10:00 a.m. – 4:00 p.m., Wed 12:00 – 6:00 p.m., Sun 10:00 a.m. – 3:00 p.m. Friday entrance free. **National Museum**, (Muzeum Narodowe), Al. Marcinkowskiego 9, Tel. 8528011, http://mpn.info.poznan.pl. Tues 10:00 a.m. – 6:00 p.m., Wed-Sat 10:00 a.m. – 4:00 p.m., Sun 10:00 a.m. – 3:00 p.m. Friday free entrance.

The pamphlet *Poznań What, Where, When* is available in the tourist office. Here you can inquire about the schedule for the **Opera** (Teatr Wielki, ul. Fredry 9, Tel. 828291), **Philharmonic** (ul. św. Marcina 81. Tel. 8522266), the renowned **Ballet** (Polski Teatr Tańca, ul. Kozia 4, Tel. 8524241) and for the most famous boys' choir in Poland, the **Poznań Nightingales** (Słowiki Poznańskie).

HIKING: in the Great Poland National Park. The map "Wielkopolski Park Narodowy" is available in local bookshops. Park administration: Jeziory, PL-62-050 Mosina, Tel./Fax 8136299.

East of the Cathedral, surrounding **Lake Malta**, is an extensive park with such attractions as a small railway that brings you to the zoo, and a ski slope open year round – a good place to unwind from the bustle of the big city. Every year in July the grounds west of the main railway station become the scene of a large industrial trade fair. Unless you are here to take part in it, it is rather a disincentive to be in town: crowds everywhere, booked out hotels and sky-high prices (Information: Tel. 8692592).

THE PALACES OF GREAT POLAND

Kalisz: **CIT**, ul. Garbarska 2, Tel. 062/7642184
Prosna, ul. Górnośląska 53/55, Kalisz (22 km from Gołuchów), Tel. 062/7644974, Fax 7644994. **Pałac Myśliwski**, Antonin (in Palace), Tel. 062/7348114, Tel./Fax 7361651 (Reservations also in Kalisz, Tel. 7645893, Fax 7672318). **Zamkowy**, Pl. Zamkowy 1, Rydzyna, (in Palace), Tel. 065/205847. **Europa**, Al. Wolności 5, Tel. 062/7672031 bis 33. Gołuchów: **Youth Hostel**, ul. Borkowskiego 2, Tel. 062/7617087.

Kórnik, Castle Museum: Mar-Nov. Tues-Fri, Sun 9:00 a.m. – 3:00 p.m., Sat 9:00 a.m. – 2:00 p.m.
Rogalin, Castle Museum, Tel. 061/8138030. Wed-Sun 10:00 a.m. – 4:00 p.m. (in summer Saturdays to 6:00 p.m.).**Gołuchów**, Castle Museum, Tel. 062/7617030. Tues-Sat 10:00 a.m. – 3:30 p.m., Sun 10:00 a.m. – 4:30 p.m. (with guided tour)

GNIEZNO / KUJAWY ☎ 061

Gniezno: ul. Warszawska 5, Tel. 4263701.
Lech, ul. Bł. Jolanty 5, Gniezno, Tel. 4261294, Fax 4262385. In a sports center somewhat outside of the city; swimming pool, sauna, bar, etc. **Pietrak**, ul. Bolesława Chrobrego 3, Gniezno, Tel. 4261497, Fax 4263715. In the city center. **Youth Hostel**, ul. Pocztowa 11, Tel. 4262780.

Królewska, ul. Bolesława Chrobrego 18, Gniezno, Tel. 4263715. All under one roof, Polish, Italian and Chinese dishes.

Cathedral, Gniezno: Mon-Sat 10:00 a.m.–5:00 p.m., Sun 1:30–5:30 p.m. **Archeological Museum** (Muzeum Początków Państwa Polskiego), ul. Prof. Jerzego Kostrzewskiego 1, Gniezno: Tues-Sun 10:00 a.m.–5:00 p.m. **Settlement of the Lusatian Culture,** Excavations at Biskupin: May-Sept daily 8:00 a.m –7:00 p.m.

A historic narrow-gauge railway runs during the season May 1 to September 30, often on the stretch Żnin Wąskotorowy – Wenecja (medieval castle ruin) – Wenecja Muzeum (Museum of the Narrow-Gauge Railway) – Biskupin Wykopaliska – Gąsawa; station in Żnin: ul. Potockiego 5, Tel. 052/3020492.

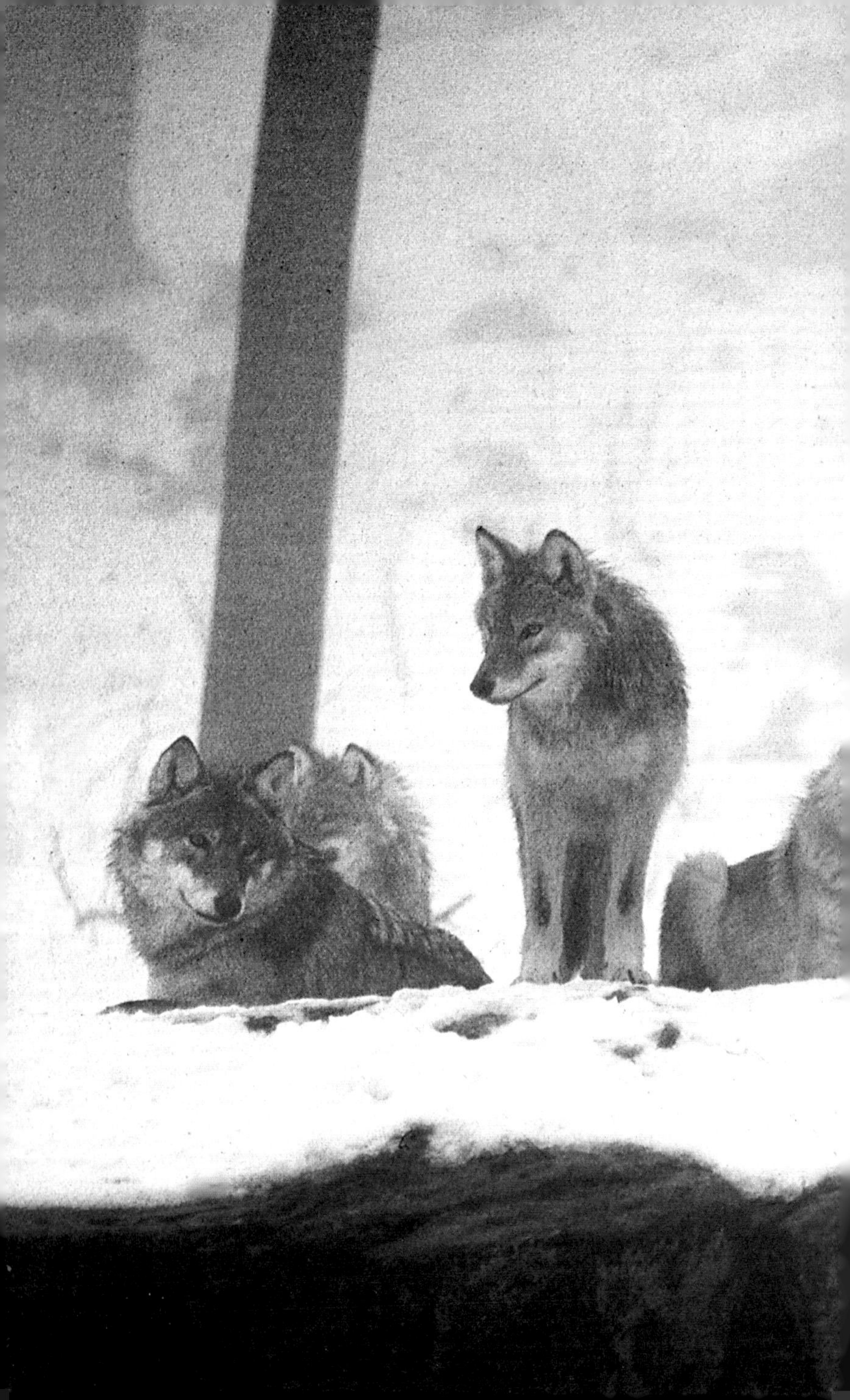

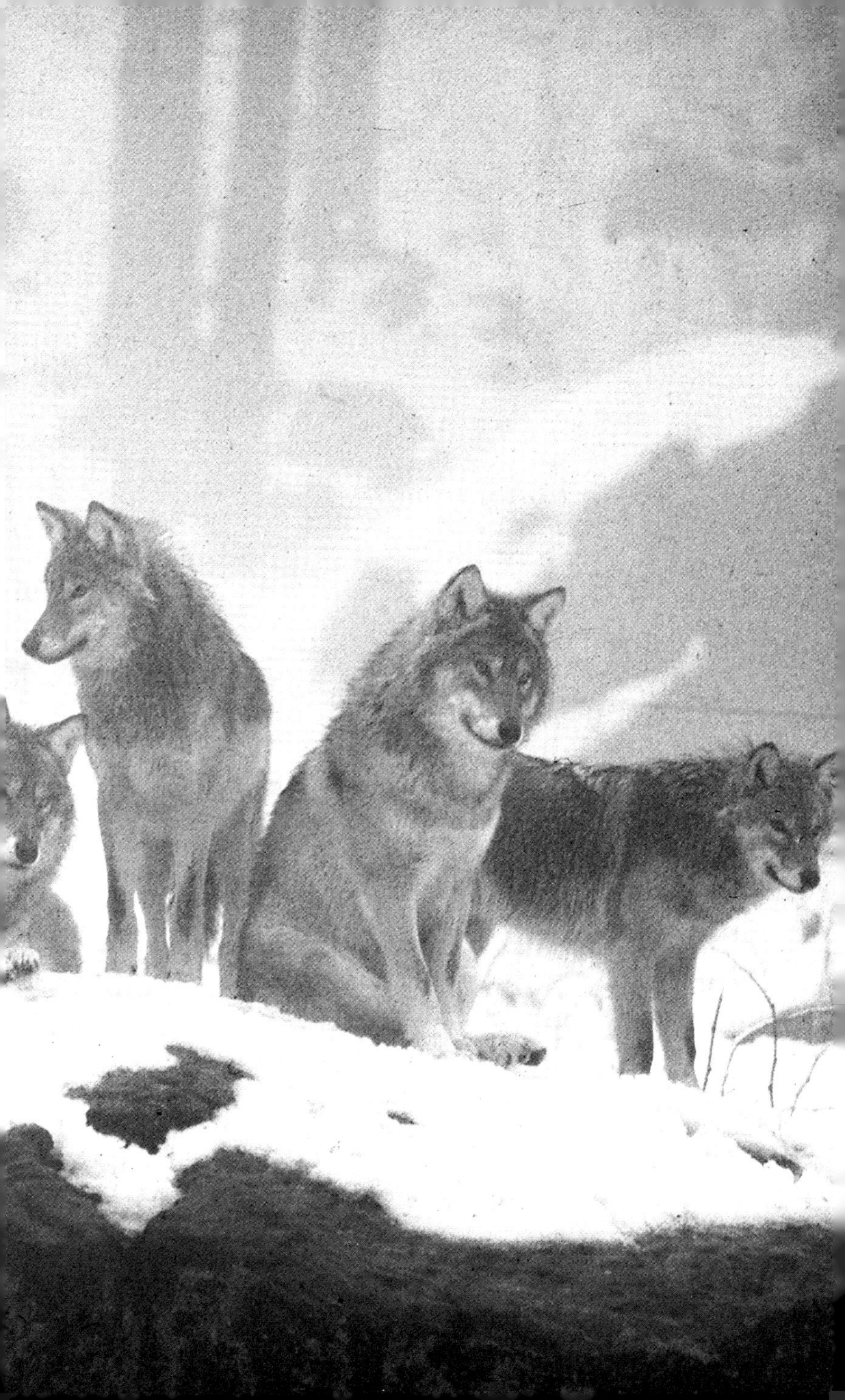

KIELCE AND LUBLIN

KIELCE AND LUBLIN
Witches, Renaissance Highlights and Partisans

KIELCE
GÓRY ŚWIĘTOKRZYSKIE
SANDOMIERZ, BARANÓW
KAZIMIERZ DOLNY
LUBLIN
ZAMOŚĆ

The center of Poland, although equally accessible from Cracow and Warsaw, is relatively unknown.

Unjustifiably so, since it is well worth a journey both for its scenery – Góry Świętokrzyskie (the Holy Cross Mountains), which are perfect for hiking, and the wild countryside of the Roztocze mountains – and for its art, with gems from the Romanesque and Renaissance eras.

Well away from the areas frequented by most western tourists in Poland, visitors will discover genuine miracles of architecture and town planning, as well as walks along the Vistula and interesting cafés on attractive market squares.

KIELCE

The largest town between Warsaw and Cracow, the industrial town of **Kielce** ❶ (population 200,000), while not the most beautiful town in the world, is a good starting point for excursions to the Góry Świętokrzyskie.

The town's most interesting building is the **Cracow Bishops' Palace**, 1637-1641, in a restrained, transitional style between Renaissance and Baroque known as the Waza style.

The main section of this building, rectangular in shape and with four octagonal towers, resembles an Italian mansion.

It is the best example of the Waza style and even more beautiful than another, more famous building in the same category, the Warsaw Royal Castle.

The **National Museum** in the castle has valuable interiors and a magnificent collection of Polish painting.

In the **Portrait Hall** (former dining hall) the walls are decorated with a frieze of Cracow bishops.

One of the most remarkable episodes in Polish history is depicted in a painting from the school of the Venetian Tommasso Dolabella, on the ceiling of the adjacent hall: *The Judgment of the Arians*.

This Protestant sect, also known as the anti-Trinitarians or Polish Brothers, denied the existence of the Holy Trinity, was against capital punishment and called on the aristocrats to redistribute their wealth to the poor. Their adherents – cruelly persecuted in 16th-century Europe – found refuge in the Kielce region and were even allowed to practice their religion in peace. All that changed in 1658. Accused of collaboration with the Swedes, who had just been chased out of

---

Previous pages: Wolf pack in winter in Roztoczański National Park. Left: Keeping the wooden houses warm in the winter is hard work.

AROUND KIELCE AND LUBLIN

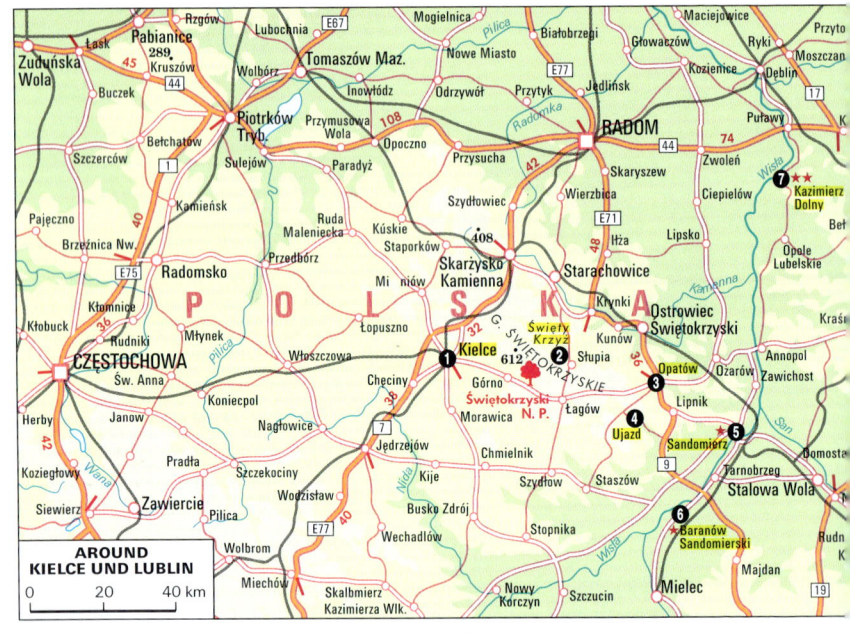

Poland, they were forced to convert to Catholicism or leave the country.

GÓRY ŚWIĘTOKRZYSKIE

East of Kielce are the **Góry Świętokrzyskie** (Holy Cross Mountains) an old geological formation encompassing more gently rolling wooded hills than mountains. Although it has only a few summits higher than 600 meters, this is nevertheless an impressive range. In the national park that surrounds it are unusual heaps of broken quartzite rock from the ice age and dense pine and larch forests (with the Polish larch, *larix polonica*, a species which is only found here). These forests were not always as deserted as they sometimes may appear to be today: they concealed heathen places of worship, were the gathering place of medieval witches said to fly here on their broomsticks on the Witches' Sabbath, and echoed with shots from the numerous partisan units during the Second World War.

The best way of getting to know this area is to explore the quiet, 13 kilometer hiking trail (marked in black and red) along the ridge of Święta Katarzyna.

The highest point on this tour, which ends at the former Benedictine monastery of **Święty Krzyż** ❷ is Łysica, (612 meters).

The crypt of the monastery church of Święty Krzyż has a somewhat macabre exhibit – the embalmed body of Jeremi Wiśniowiecki (1612-1651). He acquired a reputation as an excellent but ruthless general in the battles against the Ukrainians in the 17th century and his fame was such that the nobility chose his son Michał Korbut to be king in 1678. He proved, however, in contrast to his father, to be completey incompetent, and died as a result of gluttony three years after the election.

*Krzyżtopór Castle

In **Opatów** ❸ (60 kilometers east of Kielce), with **St. Martin's Parish**

Information pages 90-91

SANDOMIERZ

gers in the stables were made of Carrara marble, and built into the ceiling of the octagonal dining room was an aquarium with goldfish swimming in it for the entertainment of bored guests.

*SANDOMIERZ

*Sandomierz ❺, today an inconspicuous provincial town perched on a hill above the Vistula, has an illustrious past. Like Cracow, it was a center of the second duchy of Little Poland, although here periods of prosperity and catastrophe alternated with regularity. Much of what was built up by the town at the crossroads of the trade routes along the Vistula and from Kiev was destroyed by rampaging hordes of Mongols, Tartars and Swedes.

The central point of the town is the spacious main square, which slopes slightly towards the east, and the fine **Town Hall** (mid-16th century). This Renaissance building – as might be expected in Poland – is embellished with a high parapet with an arcade frieze, which is capped with stone masks and volutes.

Northwest of the square is the former **Benedictine convent** with a rare external pulpit, designed to enable a larger audience to hear the sermons. From the top of the neighboring **Opatów Gate** you can look out over the town and along the Vistula valley.

Southeast of the square and only a short distance away is the **Cathedral** (interesting Orthodox frescoes in the choir; cf Lublin, page 86) and a little further on **St James' Church** (*Kościół św. Jakuba*), the first brick building in Poland. Built in 1226 by the Dominicans, it was clearly influenced by Lombardian architecture, most noticeably in the elegant portal on the long side.

Many of the houses in the picturesque narrow streets of Sandomierz are in poor condition and constantly have to be renovated, due largely to the fact that the foundations are constantly sliding down

---

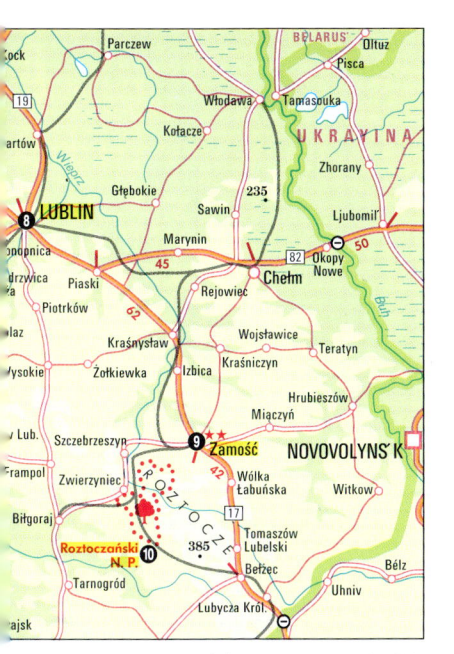

Church, a beautiful Romanesque building worth a stop, there is a turn-off in the road which leads south to the village of **Ujazd** ❹ (16 kilometers).

The object of this highly recommended detour is ***Krzyżtopór Castle**, built in 1627-1644 by Lorenzo Senes, Its owners, the Ossoliński family, lived here for only 13 years: in 1655 the castle was burned down by the Swedes. Even if the occasional claim that it is the largest castle to have been built in Europe before Versailles is an exaggeration, it was certainly a huge complex, with as many towers as seasons, and as many halls as months of the year; it had 52 rooms corresponding to the number of weeks in the year, and 365 windows.

The relatively well-preserved ruin is surrounded by a five-point star of bastions and has a portal flanked by gigantic bas-reliefs of a cross – Krzyż – and an axe – Topór – (the elements of the family coat-of-arms and together the origin of the name Krzyżtopór). The interior was of unparalleled magnificence. The man-

Information pages 90-91

BARANÓW SANDOMIERSKI

the high bank of the Vistula. This is primarily because of the labyrinth of interconnected **medieval wine and grain cellars**, which spreads out underneath the entire municipal area. From 1964 to 1977 the cellars were filled in as part of an attempt to save the town, with the exception of a 400 meter section which was opened to the public. The entrance is at the back of the Oleśnicki residence on a corner of the main square; the exit is in the town hall.

*BARANÓW

Approximately 25 kilometers southwest of Sandomierz is the castle of *Baranów Sandomierski ❻, where it is worth planning an overnight stay: within the castle walls a stylish hotel has been opened. Built between 1569 and 1609,

the **residence of the Leszczyński family** still retains something of its former elegance. The rectangular building has three wings, joined by a wall on the fourth, front side. In addition to the entrance tower on this side there are also four cylindrical corner towers.

The outer façades were kept deliberately plain, with the exception of the Renaissance parapets, as a contrast to the richly arcaded courtyard with its oval stairwell inside. The restoration of the castle, which also contains a museum showing the achievements of the sulphur industry, was financed by the sulphur concern Tarnobrzeg located not far from the castle – as if, given its poor environmental record, it were anxious to do something positive.

**KAZIMIERZ DOLNY

Shortly before Lublin is **Kazimierz Dolny ❼**, a town on the Vistula with its own very special charm. This small place, consisting of only a few streets, a

Above: The Vistula, the dominant feature of the countryside. Right: The former prosperity of Kazimierz Dolny is reflected by the façade of the St. Christopher House.

KAZIMIERZ DOLNY

large main square and a few hills; all of this clinging to the bank of the fast-flowing river, radiates an atmosphere of peace and tranquillity.

The Vistula, here a powerful, unregulated current, flows through a wide fluvial landscape, with thickly wooded shores, sandbanks and tributaries; this romantic setting, not surprisingly, is source of inspiration for numerous artists. For tourists, the chief attractions are a stroll through the town ending with a stop in a café on the square to sit and admire the richly decorated façades. The picturesque surroundings of the Vistula valley with its deep loess gorges add to the pleasures of a stay here.

The town was founded in the 12th century by Duke Kasimierz the Just, who gave it his name. Its prosperity, which is clearly reflected in its architecture, was based on trade along the Vistula. Grain was stored here in huge **granaries**, (some of which are still extant), before being shipped to Gdańsk.

The most attractive aspect of Kazimierz is probably the provincial architecture of its houses. During the period of prosperity there was an endless supply of money, but little sense of what was good art and stylish architecture – a situation that was to repeat itself two hundred years later in Łódź.

When the Baroque style had long taken over everywhere else, the grain merchants in Kazimierz were still building their houses in a rather naive Renaissance style.

Examples of this are the **Houses of the Przybyło Brothers** (1616) on the main square, known as the St Christopher House and the St Nicholas House after their respective owners' patron saints, whose bas-relief figures are on the façades. Another example is the 1635 **House of Bartłomiej Celej** (*Kamienica Celej-owska*; ul. Senatorska 11), which has a decorative parapet that is almost higher than the house itself.

All the houses are completely covered with bas-reliefs of figures, as if the artists had a "horror vacui," a horror of empty spaces. Other interesting houses in the ul. Senatorska are the **Górski House** (No. 2; built in 1607) and the **White House** (No. 17; 1635).

LUBLIN
The Center of East Poland

After the borders of Poland were shifted west in 1945 and (Ukrainian Lviv) and Vilna (Lithuanian Vilnius) were lost, **Lublin** ❽ became the largest town in East Poland.

On the ancient trade route between Warsaw and Lviv, it is still a trade center, as is evident from the numerous traveling hawkers from the neighboring eastern countries.

Mentioned in documents as early as the 10th century, Lublin became prosperous in the 15th and 16th centuries. The town was the scene of important historical events: it was here, in 1569, that the Par-

LUBLIN

liament met to decide on the final unification of Poland with Lithuania, and in 1944-1945 it was the seat of the first communist government of Poland, installed by Stalin.

The existence of the Catholic university of Lublin (KUL), founded in 1919, was probably a thorn in the side of the government in this people's republic as the only non-communist institution of higher learning in the Eastern bloc.

The Marie Curie-Skłodowska University (founded in 1944), its state-run rival was always a poor relation.

On a short visit to Lublin it is best to concentrate on the castle and the old town. The neo-Gothic **Castle**, which does not look particularly interesting from the outside, has one exquisite feature inside: the *Holy Trinity Chapel (*Kościół Św. Trójcy*).

Above: The Byzantine frescoes in the Holy Trinity Chapel of Lublin Castle. Right: the 16th-century Cracow Gate is the symbol of the town of Lublin.

The interior of the 14th-century church is covered with colorful Byzantine frescoes, which contrast vividly with the standard Gothic architecture of the church.

The work is signed by a Master Andrej and dated 1418. In addition to scenes from the Old Testament and episodes from the life of Jesus, secular figures are also depicted, such as King Władysław Jagiełło who is portrayed as a knight bringing Christianity to the Lithuanians, and as the chapel's founder kneeling before the Virgin.

Where, then, does this astonishing symbiosis of Eastern and Western art originate? It came about because, although in Lithuania the official creed, until 1386 was the natural religion, the Orthodox religion was evidently also quite widespread.

After Jagiełło had converted to Christianity, he brought traditional Byzantine artists to Poland. Of all the frescoes that have remained from this short period (e.g. in the Holy Cross Chapel of the Cracow Cathedral, in Sandomierz and in Wiślica), the frescoes of the Lublin castle chapel are without a doubt the finest. They had been whitewashed over and were only rediscovered a hundred years ago. They were not opened to the public until 1997, after 21 years of painstaking restoration.

The other castle rooms, which now house the **Regional Museum**, include a table with an unusual mark on it.

There is of course an accompanying legend: in the 16th century, the Polish Crown Tribunal, the highest court in the country, sat here in Lublin.

A widow who had been cheated by the court asked the devil for help. He duly appeared, and left his claw-print on the judge's table as a mark of his successful intervention in this worldly affair.

On a hill opposite the castle is the **Old Town** (*Stare Miasto*). The magnificent façades of the houses on the Market Square are an indication of Lublin's former importance as a trade metropolis. However, all that glitters is not gold. After the destruction of the war the communist rulers set a limit of ten years for rebuilding and repairing the damage that had been done. Under this kind of time pressure the quality of the restoration measures naturally suffered.

Looked at in a more positive light, it could also be said that the Old Town was restored so shoddily that today the crumbling plaster makes it look really old.

There are, however, several buildings of importance such as the **Burghers' Residences** of the Lubomelski and Konopnica families on the main square (Rynek 8 and 12), which are clearly of Renaissance origin, even though the Lubomelski House was subsequently rebuilt in the neoclassical style.

The nearby **Cracow Gate**, originating from the 16th century with subsequent Baroque additions, is the dominant feature of the town.

Of the many churches in the Old Town, one particularly worth a visit, in addition to the the **Cathedral**, is the **Dominican Church** (east of the town hall). As with

LUBLIN

the churches of Kazimierz and Zamość, it is built in the blend of architectural traditions from northern Italy and the Lublin region referred to as the Lublin Renaissance style.

The churches typically have late Gothic vaulting richly decorated with stucco work. Thus in the Dominican Church the simple barrel vaulting has been uniquely decorated with varied bands of ornamentation featuring hearts and circles.

After visiting the churches, stop off at the Old Town's **Café Pod Czarcią Łapą** ("The Devil's Claw").

Majdanek Concentration Camp

Lublin also has its grim reminders of the Nazi era. Before the war, the Jewish quarter of town was located at the foot of the castle. One of the largest centers of Chassidism, it also had one of the most famous Talmud schools in the world. This fascinating world, brought to life in Isaac Bashevis Singer's "The Magician of Lublin," was completely wiped out.

Among the approximately 240,000 victims of the **Lublin-Majdanek Concentration and Extermination Camp** were practically all the Jews of Lublin.

It has remained as a memorial with a museum – its proximity to the town center still comes as a shock to all who visit it (on the road to Zamość).

*ZAMOŚĆ
Pearl of the Renaissance

Less than 90 kilometers from Lublin is a very special town totally out of character with this region: sitting on a mild summer day in one of the street cafés of **Zamość's** ❾ market square sipping a glass of red wine, you could be forgiven for thinking you were in Italy.

Zamość, the "Padua of the North," is one of the few towns in Europe that did

Above: The Armenian merchants' houses in Zamość were painstakingly restored. Right: A wild cat in Roztoczański National Park.

not develop naturally but was planned on the drawing board. The idea of a town in which social and aesthetic aspects are unified goes back to Plato and Aristotle and was taken up again in the Renaissance age by Leonardo da Vinci and Dürer. However, these ideas only actually resulted in the building of very small towns (e.g. Palmanova near Udina and Sabbionetta near Mantua).

The chancellor Jan Zamoyski and his architect Bernardo Morando from Padua, who completed the plans for Zamość in 1579, envisaged a combination of magnate residence, trading and cultural center.

In 1594 the Akademia Zamoyska was founded, and the town with its population of Poles, Sephardic Jews, Armenians, Germans, Greeks and Scots became famous as a center of learning.

Completed in the first quarter of the 17th century, the town was surrounded by massive bastions, which soon had to prove their worth when Zamość was attacked by the Swedes in 1655.

Zamość was designed with a pentagonal bourgeois town district adjoining a smaller, four-sided section which contained the residence of the town's owners. Until 1821 it was the property of the Zamoyski family.

A tour of the town is best begun on the **Market Square**, with its Renaissance houses built nearly all in the same style.

The **Town Hall**, with its high tower at the front and huge flight of steps, added in the 18th century, was built on the north side of the square rather than in the middle, so that it did not compete with the residence of the nobility.

The houses on the square have arcades and once also had beautiful Renaissance parapets, most of which were however removed in the 19th century.

They were only reconstructed on the side occupied by the **Armenian merchants' houses**, (*domy kupców ormiańskich*; today it is a museum (which also includes a model of the town), the façades of which are decorated with oriental motifs.

ZAMOŚĆ

From the Market Square the two main axes run through the town: the north-south axis, which connected all three markets in the town, and the east-west axis, which ran between the residence, now substantially rebuilt, and the town's most important bastion. Other architectural gems in the town center are the **Collegiate Church** (*Kolegiata*), located southwest of the Market Square, built by Morandi in 1587-1600, and the former **Orthodox Uniate Church** (*Kościół św. Stanisława*), located southeast of the square and the **Synagogue**.

Two events link Zamość with German history. Its most famous daughter is Rosa Luxemburg, the famous activist of the Polish and later the German labor movement, who was born here in 1871 (in No. 37 on the Market Square).

The Nazi ideologists pursued ideas of a different kind, testing a new concept of racial politics in the town they called "Himmlerstadt" and also "Pflugstadt."

Between November 1942 and August 1943 the populations of almost 300 villages in the surrounding area were completely or partially resettled and replaced by Germans from Eastern Europe.

Zamość is located in Roztocze, a region consisting of a low range of chalk and limestone hills (up to 390 meters). In 1974, the **Roztoczański National Park** ❿ was established around the nearby town of Zwierzyniec, with a variety of wild animals including lynxes, wolves, wild cats and Aesculapian snakes.

The intact natural environment is explained by the fact that from the 16th century on the Zamoyskis had their own private zoo here with tarpans, bison and elk, in which hunting was prohibited (hence the name Zwierzyniec, which is Polish for "zoo"). Ornithologists have counted over 200 species of bird in the park.

Into this attractive terrain, the rivers have cut deep gorges, and there are a number of waterfalls. There are relatively few tourist facilities.

KIELCE AND LUBLIN

KIELCE ☎ 041

WCIT, Pl. Moniuszki 2 b, Tel./Fax 3446240, www.complex.com.pl/~itkielce. **PTTK-Office**, ul. Sienkiewicza 34, Tel. 3445914.

Exbud, ul. Manifestu Lipcowego 34, Tel. 3326393, Fax 3326440, www.exbud.com.pl/cb/eindex.html. This business hotel meets all expectations. **Bristol**, ul. Sienkiewicza 21, Tel. 3682460, Fax 3663065. Centrally located. **Świętokrzyski**, Cedzyna, Tel. 3680051, Fax 3680052. In a quiet location in the woods (roughly 5 km east of the city on the road to Lublin); good restaurant. **Centralny**, ul. Sienkiewicza 78, Tel. 3662511. Located next to the train station; you will not fail to hear it. **Youth Hostel**, ul. Szymanowskiego 5, Tel. 3423735. **PTTK-Hostel**, Święta Katarzyna, Tel. 3110111. **Jodłowy Dwór**, Huta Szklana (2 km west of the Święty Krzyż monastery), Tel. 3025028. On the connecting road to Kielce.

Winnica, ul. Kryniczna 4, Tel. 3444576. Ukrainian cuisine. **Promont**, ul. Sienkiewicza 59. Pizza.

National Museum (Muzeum Narodowe), Pl. Zamkowy 1, Kielce (inside Castle): Tues-Sun 9:00 a.m. – 3:15 p.m. **Former Benedictine Abbey** (today Museum of the Świętokrzyski National Park), Święty Krzyż: Tues-Sun 10:00 a.m. – 4:00 p.m.

SANDOMIERZ, BARANÓW ☎ 015

PTTK-Office, Rynek 26, Tel. 8322305.

Siarkopol, ul. Zamkowa 20, Baranów Sandomierski, Tel. 8555900. In the Renaissance Palace (more modest, unpretentious rooms in the adjacent building). **Zajazd pod Żółtą Ciżemką**, Rynek 27, Tel. 8320550. Located at the Market. **Zacisze**, ul. Portowa 3, Tel. 8321905.

Ludowa, ul. Mariacka 5, Sandomierz, Tel. 8322724. Good borscht with meat ravioli. **Ciżemka**, Rynek 27, Sandomierz, Tel. 8323668. **Oskar**, ul. Mickiewicza 17a, Sandomierz, Tel. 8321144.

Opatów Gate, Sandomierz. Can be climbed daily in summer 10:00 a.m. – 5:30 p.m., as part of the visit to the adjacent former **Merchants' Cellar**. (Podziemna Trasa Turystyczna): Tues-Sun 10:00 a.m. – 5:00 p.m.

KAZIMIERZ DOLNY ☎ 081

PTTK-Office, Rynek 27, Tel./Fax 8810046.

Dom Architekta, Rynek 20, Tel./Fax 8810544. View of the Market; meeting place of Warsaw's architects. The following have similarly high standards: **Łaźnia**, ul. Senatorska 21, Tel. 8810298, 8810249. In the old Jewish bath house. **Zajazd Piastowski**, ul. Słoneczna 3, Tel. 8810346, Fax

KIELCE AND LUBLIN

8810351. Located 2 km east of the city. 🟢 **PTTK Hostel Murka**, Krakowska 59, Tel. 8810036. Housed in an old warehouse. **Youth Hostel**, ul. Puławska 64, Tel. 8810327. **Campgrounds**, ul. Krakowska 59/61, Tel. 8810036. Next to the warehouse. **Private rooms** can be found through the PTTK office or the Biuro Zakwaterowania, ul. Lubelska 7, Tel. 8810101.

❌ **Staropolska**, ul. Nadrzeczna 14, Tel. 8810236. Succulent duck with apple and buckwheat grits. **Zajazd Piastowski**, see under "Hotels". Recommendable Polish cuisine. **Zielona Tawerna**, ul. Nadwiślańska 4, Tel. 8810038. Good pierogis (*pierogi ruskie*). **Cezary Sarzyński**, ul. Nadrzeczna 6 (near the crossing ul. Klasztorna). Glitters with imaginative yeast pastries that have sometimes been ordered for delivery to Paris. You should plan in some time for the many cafés in the center of town (for example Galeria, U Dziwisza).

LUBLIN ☎ 081

ℹ️ **WCIT-Office**, ul. Krakowskie Przedmieście 78, Tel. 5324412. **PTTK-Office**, ul. Grodzka 3.

🏨 😀😀😀 **Unia**, Al. Racławickie 12, Tel. 5332061, Fax 5333021, www.orbis.pl/hot_uni.html. West of the Old Town next to the KUL University. 😀😀 **Victoria**, ul. Narutowicza 58, Tel. 5327011, Fax 5329026, e-mail vicoria@lublin.top.pl. **Lublinianka**, ul. Krakowskie Przedmieście 56, Tel. 5324261. Within walking distance of the Old Town. 🟢 **PTTK-Hostel**, ul. Krakowskie Przedmieście 29, Tel. 5323941. **Youth Hostel**, ul. Długosza 6b, Tel. 5330628. Open year round, 2 km west of the city center. **Campgrounds**, ul. Krężnicka 6, Tel. 7441070.

❌ The restaurants in the **Victoria Hotel** (specialty: Caribbean turkey) and the **Hotel Unia** (tender Chateaubriand) are counted among the gourmet temples of the city.

Hades, ul. Peowiaków 12, Tel. 5328761, 5325641. As the name infers, situated in a deep cellar; everything revolves around tatar here (even salmon tatar); evenings often with live music (www.uhc.lublin.pl/hades). **Karczma Słupska**, Al. Racławickie 22, Tel. 5338813. Inexpensive but appetizing dishes. There are some nice cafés in the Old Town, including: **U Rajcy** (Rynek 2) and **Pod Czarcią Łapą** (ul. Bramowa 6).

🏛️ A visit to the **Castle Chapel** (kaplica zamkowa) is part of a visit to the **Regional Museum** (Muzeum Lubelskie): Wed-Sat 9:00 a.m. – 4:00 p.m., Sun 9:00 a.m. – 5:00 p.m. **Concentration and Extermination Camp Majdanek**, ul. Droga Męczenników Majdanka 67, Tel. 5341955. Tues-Sun 8:00 a.m. – 4:00 p.m. (Oct-April to 3:00 p.m.); no admission under 14 years of age; trolley bus lines 153 and 156 from the Cathedral. (www.majdanek.pl/en/oboz.htm)

🎭 **Philharmonic Hall** (Filharmonia Lubelska), ul. Kapucyńska 7, Tel. 5321536. **Classical Theater** (Teatr im. Osterwy), ul. Narutowicza 17. **KUL University Theater** (Scena Plastyczna KUL-u), Al. Racławickie 14, Tel. 5330392. Leszek Mądzik stages half-hour "visions," in which shapes, figures, masks and cloth move to celestial sounds. **Gardzienice Theater**, Büro ul. Grodzka 5 a, Tel. 5329840, 5329637 (Advance ticket orders also call Tel. 7446251). A small theater named after a village near Lublin. Under the direction of Włodzimierz Staniewski, its performing troupe, now known throughout Europe, presents "ethno-oratoria," which resemble medieval mystery plays. Both avant-garde theater groups are often abroad, so it is best to ask in advance about their schedules. (www.galeria.pl)

ZAMOŚĆ ☎ 084

ℹ️ **Informacja Turystyczna**: Rynek Wielki 13, Tel./Fax 6270813, 6392292. **WPT Roztocze**, ul. Łukasińskiego 5a, Tel. 6271006. **PTTK Office**, Staszica 31, Tel. 6385687.

🏨 😀😀 **Renesans**, ul. Grecka 6, Tel. 6392001 bis 3, Tel./Fax 6385174 (advance reservations recommended). An ugly concrete dissonance in the center of the Old Town, but still the best address in town. **Jubilat**, Al. Prymasa Wyszyńskiego 52, Tel. 6386400 –5, Tel./Fax 6386215. Close to the bus station, relatively far from the Old Town. 🟢 **Sportowy**, ul. Królowej Jadwigi 8, Tel. 6386011, Fax 386202. **PTTK-Hostel Marta**, ul. Zamenhofa 11, Tel. 6392639. In the center of the Old Town. **Youth Hostel**, ul. Zamoyskiego 4, Tel. 6279125 (July-Aug). **Campgrounds**, ul. Królowej Jadwigi 14, Tel. 6392499.

❌ **Jubilat** and **Renesans** in the hotels of the same names serve the local specialty *kotlet po zamojsku* (stuffed pork cutlet). **Royal Night Club**, ul. Żeromskiego 22. One of the most beautiful cellar restaurants in the city; good cuisine, but in the late evenings the music is deafening. The restaurants on the Market Square turn into outdoor cafés during the summer: **Ratuszowa**, Rynek Wielki 13, Tel. 6271557. Meatballs Spanish style (*zraz po hiszpańsku*). **Arkadia**, Rynek Wielki 9, Tel. 6386507. Hungarian-style saddle of pork. **Padwa**, ul. Staszica 23, Tel. 6386256. Rounds out its exotic offerings with beef Mexican style.

🏛️ **County Museum** (Muzeum Okręgowe), ul. Ormiańska 30, Tel. 6386494. Tues-Sun 10:00 a.m. – 5:00 p.m. **Synagogue**, ul. Zamenhofa. Used as a library today; visits are possible.

🎭 *FESTIVALS*: **June-July**: Zamość Theater Summer with theatrical performances on the Market Square. **September**: International Gathering of Jazz Vocalists (Międzynarodowe Spotkania Wokalistów Jazzowych).

91

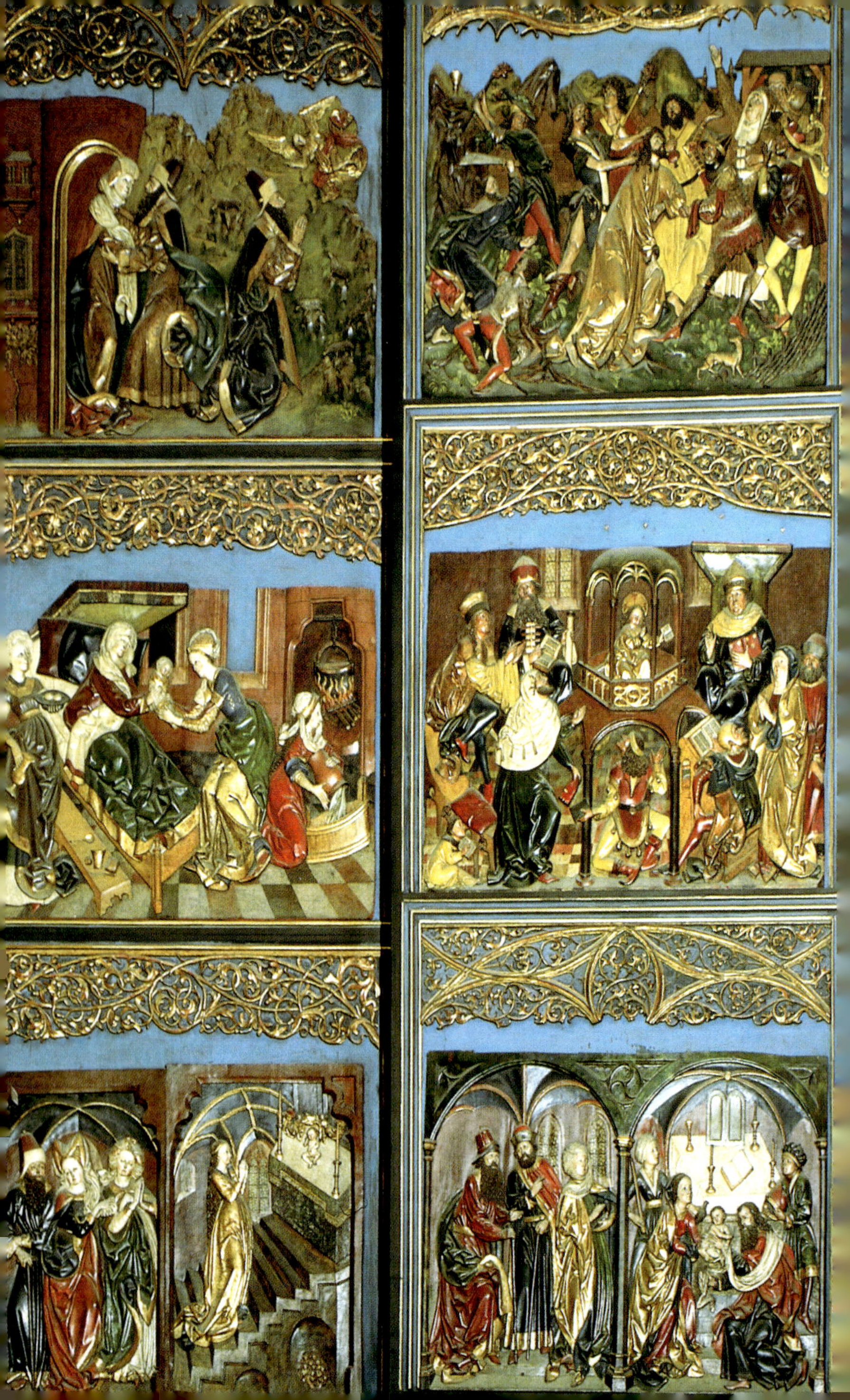

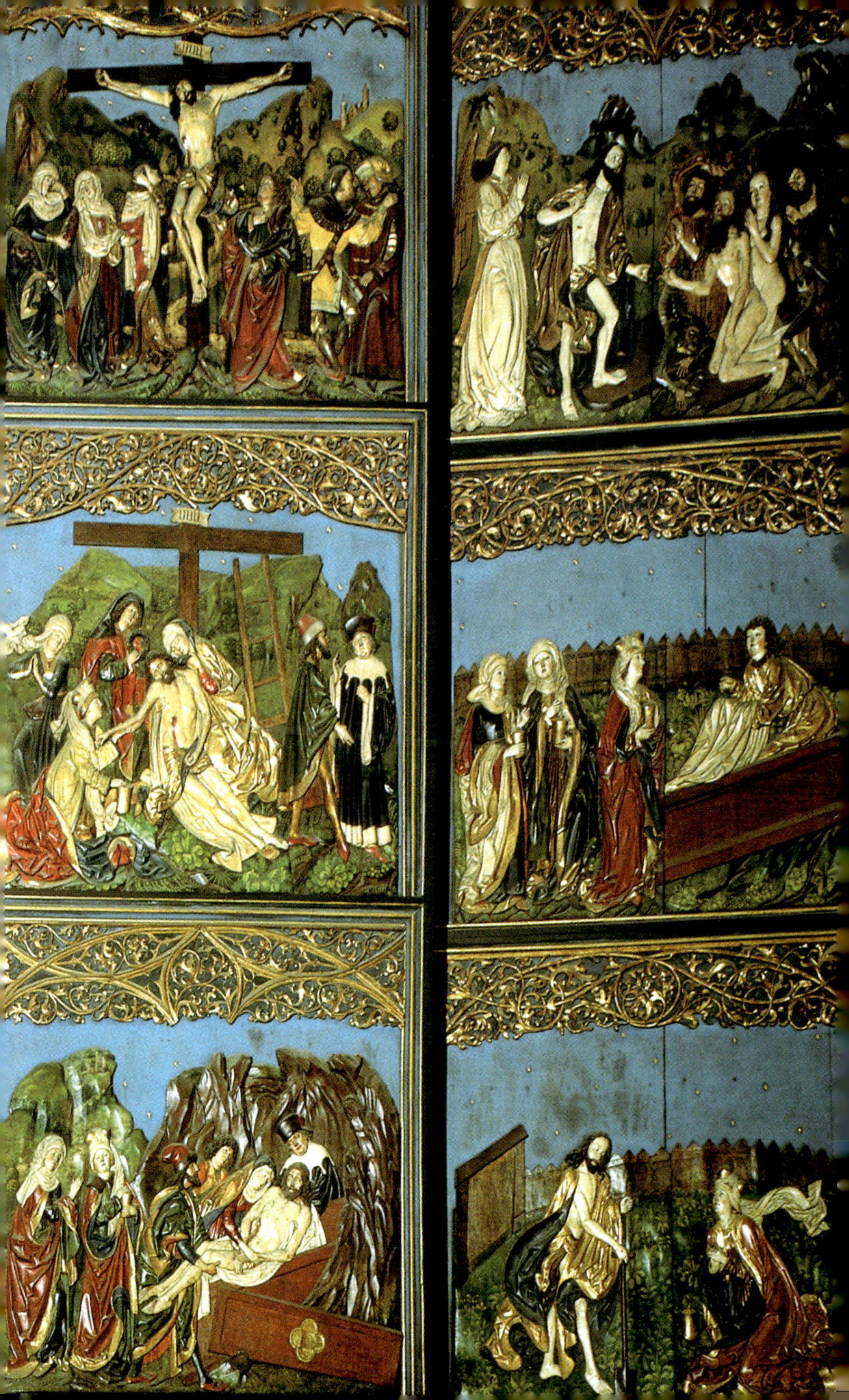

CRACOW

CRACOW
City of Royal Splendour

MAIN MARKET SQUARE
UL. FLORIAŃSKA
WAWEL
KAZIMIERZ / WIELICZKA
AUSCHWITZ (OŚWIĘCIM)
CZĘSTOCHOWA

**CRACOW

If you have time to go to only one place in Poland, then you should choose Cracow. As a center of the arts it was known as the "Florence of the North," with its 140 churches it was a "Second Rome" and because of its university (the second oldest in Central Europe) it was the "New Athens." Cracow is on UNESCO's World Cultural Heritage list and is proud of its 5,500 listed historic houses and around 2.5 million works of art.

Apart from Prague it is the only large town in Central Europe which survived the inferno of the Second World War almost unscathed. The purest form of Italian Renaissance architecure north of the Alps, the largest and probably the most beautiful carved altar of the Gothic period, the many stone monuments of Jewish history – there are more than enough reasons to go to Cracow.

And though it might sound a little sentimental: in Cracow, time really does seem to slow down and life is lived at a less frenetic pace, possibly because its inhabitants are in daily contact with the town's rich past. Here everyone knows everyone else at least by sight, and people meet all their acquaintances by chance on the Market Square once a week at the very minimum. Then they address each other with all kinds of honorary titles and it becomes clear to visitors that if they are not at the focal point of Europe, then they are certainly in the most important town in Poland. Here the traditions of the "imperial and royal" Austro-Hungarian Empire are alive and well, but coexist with the characteristics of a provincial town. The atmosphere here is at all events one of great charm.

With its theaters and cabarets, Cracow is without question the country's cultural capital. It is also the home of the winner of the Nobel prize for literature, the authoress Wisława Szymborska, of the dramatist and satirist Sławomir Mrożek and of the master of science fiction Stanisław Lem. Allow a few days not only to see the musts on the tourist itinerary, but also just to wander around the streets of this fascinating town.

History

Cracow was first mentioned in a document written in 965 by Ibrahim ibYaqub, a Jewish traveler, sent by the Caliph of Córdoba. Even at this time there was al-

Previous pages: The altar in St Mary's, a medieval masterpiece by Veit Stoss. Left: Trusting to the point of impertinence: the pigeons on Cracow's Main Market Square.

CRACOW

Above: The procession at the Lajkonik Festival is led by a Tartar horseman (cf. p 117).

ready a settlement, as indicated by the two mysterious mounds of earth to the east and south of the present town, which date from the eighth century.

It was not until 992, however, that the trade center on the Amber Route was absorbed into the new Polish state founded in the area around Poznań.

After destruction by the Mongols in 1241, Cracow was reestablished with a Magdeburg town charter in 1257. It became a powerful town and strove for greater autonomy, which led in 1311 to the first uprising against the throne.

With the coronation of Władysław Łokietek in 1320, Cracow finally became the country's capital. From then on, with the exception of only two rulers in the 18th century, all the kings of Poland were crowned here. Cracow's golden age, which was marked by the creativity of the Nuremberg sculptor and painter Veit Stoss and the patronage of Queen Bona Sforza, began with the founding of the university in 1364.

The hospitality and religious tolerance of the Jagiellonian kings attracted many foreigners to Cracow. The tone of the town was set not only by Poles but also by the German patriciate, Italian artists and bankers, many of whom came from Genoa, and Jewish merchants.

Many of them attained high office and acquired houses and palaces. Even their names gradually became Polish: *Wierzynek*, the name of the excellent restaurant on the main Market Square, is an adaptation of Wirsing, the name of a German patrician who settled here in the 14th century.

King Zygmunt III Waza (Sigismund III Vasa) transferred his royal court to Warsaw at the beginning of the 17th century: from then on Cracow was only the coronation city and the final resting place of the kings.

By the end of the 18th century, when Cracow became part of Austria with the Third Partition of Poland, its population had gone down from 30,000 in the 16th century to a mere 9,000.

After a short period as a "Free City" it was annexed by Austria again in 1846, and it was not until 1867 that things once more began to improve.

It is, however, due to this happier period that Austrian rule is still thought of positively in Cracow. Galicia, including Cracow, became an autonomous province with Lvov as the capital, and Polish became the official language; cultural institutions of all kinds were able to develop freely.

A Polish civil service also developed here, some of which was "exported" after 1918 to Warsaw and Poznań, where all Polish activities had been prohibited until then.

In the 20th century there were two attempts to destroy Cracow. It escaped almost certain destruction towards the end of the Second World War through a sur-

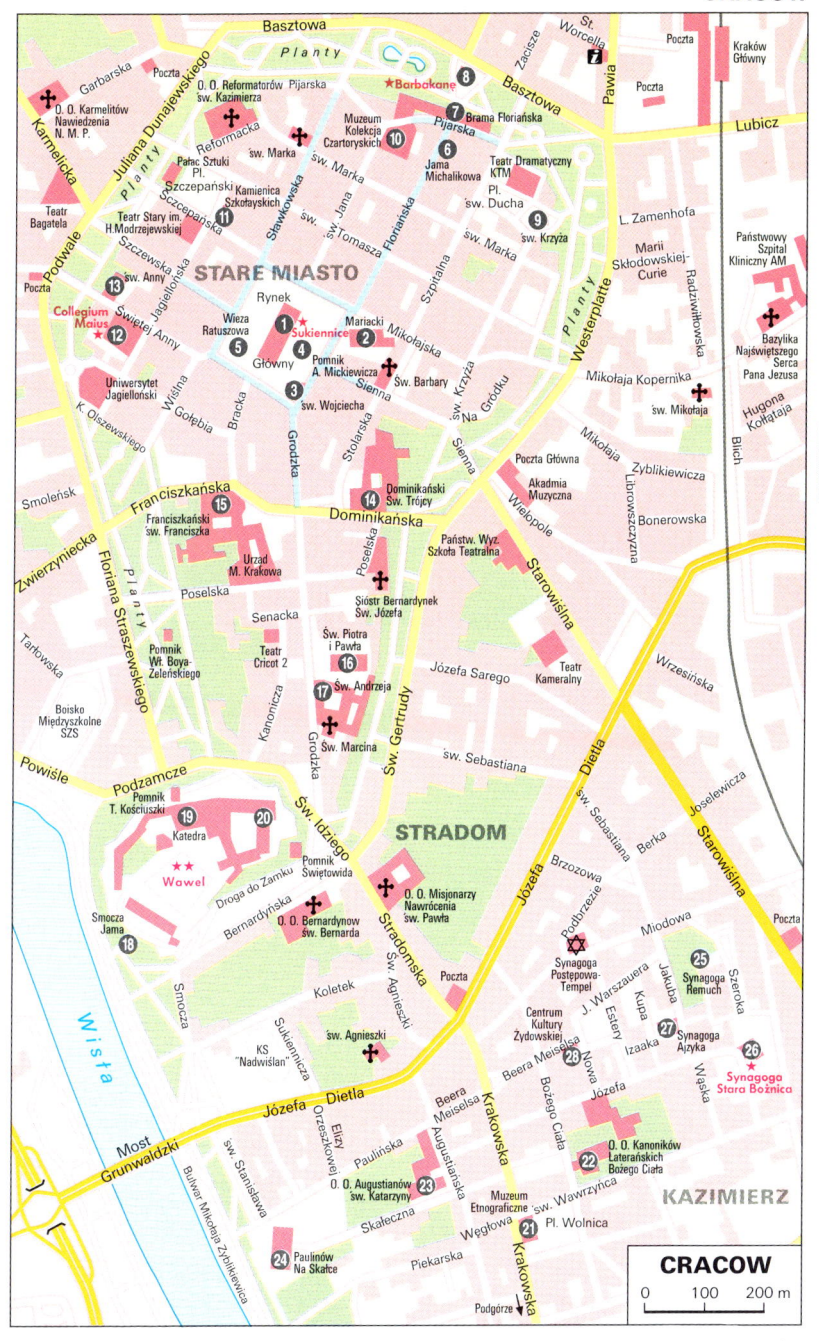

CRACOW

MAIN MARKET

prising maneuver by the Red Army: the encircled German Army, in a state of panic, was given the opportunity to flee, so that this time it withdrew without razing everything to the ground.

The new rulers, however, dismissed the town as a clerical, provincial backwater and refused to allow it any resources for renovation.

Now, presumably by order of Stalin himself, a second attempt was made to destroy the town, which differed only in that it was more subtle. The iron foundry Nowa Huta was built just outside Cracow with the idea of diluting the Cracow bourgeoisie with a strong labor force.

The severe air pollution from the iron foundry attacked the building substance and for decades the effect of the noxious fumes was visible on every street corner in the form of mutilated sculptures and dull gray walls. Strangely enough, it has been the effects of the recent economic crisis which has been the saving of the town.

Since the drastic reduction of foundry production and the restructuring of the Upper Silesian industrial area, the inhabitants can now breathe more freely. House walls can once more be painted white and the air is cleaner.

THE MAIN MARKET SQUARE (RYNEK GŁÓWNY)

Cracow's **Old Town** (*Stare Miasto*) is surrounded by the **Planty**, a ring-shaped park which follows the original course of the town walls. The streets are laid out in a regular, chess-board pattern, originating from the rebuilding of the town in 1257. The only features that do not fit in with this scheme are the small St. Adalbert's Church and St. Mary's Church on the Market Square, which both stand at an angle to the surrounding streets, and ul. Grodzka, which runs diagonally, all originating from an earlier period of the history of the town.

Above: Flea market in front of the Cloth Hall. Right: St Mary's Church lit up at night.

CLOTH HALL

The center of the Old Town is the **Main Market Square**, with its numerous summertime street cafés. With a length of 200 meters, the *Rynek Główny* is one of the largest medieval squares in Europe.

The burghers' residences surrounding it all date from the Middle Ages, and only the façades were changed in subsequent architectural epochs up to and including Art Nouveau.

Many houses still retain their Gothic timber ceilings, portals and, as in house No. 17, beautiful vaulting.

In the center of the Market Square is the impressive *****Cloth Hall** ❶ (*Sukiennice*). This Gothic building, designed as a center for the textile trade, was remodeled during the Renaissance and extended in 1875-1879 with external, neo-Gothic arcades.

Almost all European towns in Central Europe had cloth halls, and most were pulled down in the 19th century as a result of the widespread town improvement activities. The Cracow building is thus a great rarity.

The richly decorated wall supporting the roof, the so-called "attic" or Renaissance parapet is the Polish contribution to the Renaissance style and was added in 1556-1560.

Attics were used to hide the high gable roofs, which were necessary in this climate, because of the winter snowfalls, but which did not match the rest of the Italianate architecture.

This parapet wall of the Cloth Hall, with its grotesque faces (*mascarons*) served as the model for numerous other buildings throughout the country – including the monstrous Warsaw Palace of Culture. The original function of the building is echoed by the small shops inside selling wooden figures, woolen sweaters from the High Tatra, jewelry and other souvenirs.

On the top floor is the **Gallery** of Polish painting, which has mainly works from the 19th and 20th centuries – the most interesting gallery in Poland apart from the Warsaw National Museum. Look out for the paintings of Piotr

City map page 97, Information pages 115-117

ST. MARY'S CHURCH

Michałowski, which are comparable with works by Delacroix and Gericault. Jan Matejko's "Prussian Oath of Allegiance" (*Hołd Pruski*), is of historic interest, showing the last Grand Master of the Teutonic Knights, Albrecht von Hohenzollern-Ansbach, swearing the oath of allegiance on the Cracow Market Square in 1525. The picture by Władysław Podkowiński entitled "Frenzy" and depicting a naked woman on a horse, on the other hand, says something about the social attitudes at the turn of the 20th century: at the time it caused a major scandal.

*St. Mary's Church

The next architectural masterpiece on the Market Square is **St. Mary's Church** ❷ (*Kościół Mariacki*) with its two towers. As the third church on this site, it was built in its present form in 1355-1408

Above: The Town Hall Tower, all that remains of the original 14th-century town hall. Right: In the Radio Zet Club.

and, with the exception of a few later additions, has never been substantially altered.

The two towers of the basilica are of unequal heights. According to a legend, two brothers competed to build the highest tower and eventually one was killed by the other. The instrument of murder, a rusty knife, is still hanging in one of the arcades of the Cloth Hall.

An unmistakable Cracow custom has its origins in an event which took place in the Middle Ages. From a small window in the higher tower of St. Mary's church, which is topped with a spire, the legendary alarm call (*Hejnał Mariacki*) is sounded over the town every hour by a trumpet.

This ritual goes back to a Mongol invasion in the year 1287, which the watchman on the tower was the first to spot. His fanfare, which warned the town's inhabitants just in time, was broken off abruptly when a Mongolian arrow pierced his throat, and today the melody still stops at the same point.

ST. MARY'S CHURCH

The best place from which to see the trumpeter is the small square south of the church, next to the little St. Barbara's Church.

In the dark interior of St. Mary's Church the focal point is the huge **high altar**. Fourteen meters high and eleven meters wide, it is the work of the Nuremberg sculptor, Veit Stoss, and is the largest medieval altar in the world.

Even more important than its size, however, is the artistic quality of the work. The large central panel features the Death of the Virgin (bottom scene), her Assumption (center) and her Coronation (above the altar).

The bas-reliefs of the opened triptych show the six joys of the Virgin (Annunciation, Birth of Christ, Adoration of the Magi, Resurrection of Christ, Ascension of Christ, Outpouring of the Holy Spirit).

The scenes are realistic down to the last detail, and even include emotional expressions: sorrow, anger and doubt are clearly reflected in the faces of the larger-than-life size apostle figures.

Stoss, who worked on the altar from 1477 to 1485, lived in the royal city for 20 years, where he was known as Wit Stwosz. The altar is ceremoniously opened at noon every day and remains open until 6:00 p.m., which is scarcely enough time to appreciate this masterpiece to the full.

The second work in the church by Veit Stoss is a late Gothic **stone crucifix** (in the right hand side aisle). Its distressingly naturalistic portrayal of a man in agony is unparalleled.

Around the Cloth Hall

The small **St. Adalbert's Church** ❸ (*Kościół św. Wojciecha*), looks rather lost in the huge Market Square.

It dates from the 10th century and its history is documented in the permanent exhibition inside. Not far from the church stands the greatest romantic poet of Poland, Adam Mickiewicz, surrounded by figures personifying the fatherland, knowledge, poetry and heroism.

City map page 97, Information pages 115-117

ULICA FLORIAŃSKA

Cast in 1898, the **Mickiewicz Monument** ❹ was melted down after 1939 by the Nazis, who spared only one Cracow monument: the one commemorating a mayor with the sufficiently German name of Dietel.

The present monument is thus a reconstruction, which makes it no less popular as a meeting point for the residents of Cracow.

On the other side of the square is the **Town Hall Tower** ❺ dating from the 14th century, all that has remained of the medieval town hall that was pulled down in 1820. There is an excellent view from the top.

ULICA FLORIAŃSKA

Running north from the Market Square is the **ul. Floriańska**, a lively pedestrian precinct with lavishly decorated burghers' residences.

In the top section a sign with the inscription **Jama Michalikowa** ❻ points visitors to the most beautiful café in town. Numerous fin-de-siècle artists and Bohemians paid their bills here with drawings and caricatures on the walls.

With its two very individual back rooms in Viennese Secession style, you will not find another café like this in any other European town; in addition to admiring the walls, however, you should also take the time to sit down here and have a cup of coffee and a slice of cake.

At the end of the Floriańska is the **Florian Gate** ❼ (*Brama Floriańska*), the only remaining gate in what was once a massive, double row of fortifications.

It was built before 1307; today its walls are always covered with works by Cracow's amateur painters. There are also three towers named after the occupational groups which were supposed to defend it in time of war, the **Carpenters'** and the **Joiners' Tower** (west of the city gate) and the **Trimmings Manufacturers' Tower** (east of the gate).

The most massive part of the fortifications is the ★**Barbican** ❽ (*Barbakan*) a round defensive structure – the word is of Arabic origin. It was not added until 1489-1499, when the town feared an invasion by the Turks. Of all the European barbicans (Carcassone, Görlitz, Naumburg, Warsaw) this is by far the largest.

With the exception of the short section by the Florian Gate, the town walls were pulled down during the alterations in the 19th century and were replaced with a park.

East of Planty Park is another architectural gem, the **Church of the Holy Cross** ❾ (*Kościół Św. Krzyża*). Built in 1300, it was redesigned in 1528-1533 with highly original vaulting supported on a single central column. The frescoes are a tasteful potpourri of Gothic, Renaissance and Art Nouveau styles.

The various sections of the **Cracow National Museum** (*Muzeum Narodowe*) are housed all over the city. Its most important collections are those amassed by Princess Izabella Czartoryska in the 19th century and displayed in the **Kolekcja Czartoryskich** ❿ near the Florian Gate. Among the works exhibited here are "The Lady with the Ermine" by Leonardo da Vinci – Poland's most valuable painting, with the exception of the "Last Judgement" by Memling in Gdańsk. It is a portrait of Cecilia Gallerani, mistress of the patron Prince Lodovico il Moro. His nickname was *ermelino*, hence the animal the lady is holding.

If museums are your priority, the **Szołayski House** ⓫ on Plac Szczepański offers religious painting and sculptures. The showpieces of the collection are the sandstone relief "Christ on the Mount of Olives" by Veit Stoß and the famous, beautiful "Madonna of Krużowa."

Right: The arcaded courtyard of the Collegium Maius, the old main building of the Jagiellonian university.

UNIVERSITY QUARTER

University Quarter

Ul. Świętej Anny leads from the Market Square to the **Jagiellonian University** complex.

The second university in Central and Eastern Europe after Prague, it was founded in 1364, but only rose to importance in 1400, when Queen Jadwiga (the wife of Władysław II Jagiełło) presented it with her entire collection of jewelry, so that she was buried with only wooden insignia of power.

In the 15th century, the university had one of the most important departments of astronomy, where the young man who was probably the university's greatest student, Nicholas Copernicus, studied.

His statue stands in the *Planty* by the Collegium Novum. Other famous students have included Jan III Sobieski, the father of British social anthropology, Bronisław Malinowski, and Pope John Paul II.

The 15th-century ***Collegium Maius** ⑫, the old main building, is one of the very few university buildings in Europe from this period.

Built like a monastery, it consists of four residential wings forming a four-sided arcaded courtyard. The magnificent interior houses the university museum, with exhibits including the rectors' scepter portraits and antique globes.

The Baroque **St. Anne's Church** ⑬ (*Kościół św. Anny*), the university church, was built in 1689-1703 from a design by the Dutchman Tilman van Gameren. It has a particularly interesting façade, designed to be seen from the narrow perspective of the street, in such a way that its graphic form, and the light and shade this creates, can be seen to the best effect.

On the Way to the Wawel

Ul. Grodzka is the so-called Royal Way leading from the Market Square to the royal castle on the Wawel. Facing one another across the first street crossing are two fine churches, the Gothic **Dominican**

WAWEL

Church ⑭ (*Kościół dominikański*), the interior of which was rebuilt after a fire in the 19th century, and the **Franciscan Church** ⑮ (*Kościół franciszkański*).

The latter dates from the second half of the 13th century and was clearly influenced by Lombardian architecture. As is appropriate for a mendicant order, it has no tower and its façade and the interior are only sparsely decorated.

Its historical importance, by contrast, cannot be overestimated. It was here that Władysław II Jagiełło, the ruler of the last non-Christian state in Europe, Lithuania, was baptized in 1386.

This marked the beginning of the Jagiellonian dynasty and the powerful Polish-Lithuanian double kingdom. The main attractions of the church are the Art Nouveau windows by Stanisław Wyspiański (in 1900). The Franciscans were on the point of firing the artist when the Madonna was portrayed in one of the windows with bare feet and the face of a Cracow peasant-woman.

In the end the Madonna was banished to a place behind the main altar, where she can hardly be seen. By contrast the glass window on the west wall depicting God creating the world is easy to see, and is particularly beautiful in the afternoon sun when the church is flooded with color.

An interesting contrast is provided by two further churches on the Royal Way. The **Church of St. Peter & St. Paul** ⑯ (*Kościół śś. Piotra i Pawła*) with its magnificent Baroque façade and the 12 apostles depicted on columns in front of the church was the first Baroque building in Poland-Lithuania apart from the Vilnius Church and was built after 1596. Immediately adjacent to it is the austere Romanesque **St. Andrew's Church** ⑰ (*Kościół św. Andrzeja*), in which the town's inhabitants took refuge from the plundering Mongolians in 1241. It has a Baroque interior.

Above: Thunderstorm brewing over the Wawel.
Right: The golden dome of the Sigismund Chapel, a focal point for visitors.

CATHEDRAL

The last part of the Royal Way continues on the parallel **ul. Kanonicza**, the most picturesque of all Cracow's streets. Its 16th-century houses have stone portals and the coats-of-arms which once functioned as house numbers.

**Wawel

The Wawel, a limestone hill by the Vistula, which is actually the final hill in the Cracow-Częstochowa Jura terrain, bears witness to the country's former greatness.

The residence of the town's rulers from a very early stage of its history, it later became a royal seat. Its remote past – like much else in Cracow – is interwoven with numerous legends.

A cave in the hill was said to shelter a fearsome dragon, which was constantly on the lookout for human nourishment, preferably attractive virgins.

It was finally dealt with by a poor shoemaker, who presented it with a sheep filled with sulphur. The monster had such a thirst after devouring the sheep that it drank until it burst.

The legend seems to be a reference to the invasions of the Vikings, whose ships were decorated with dragon heads. The little **Dragon's Cave** can be seen at the foot of the Wawel hill. At its entrance is a bronze dragon, which breathes real fire every few minutes.

Cathedral

A wide, paved approach lined with postcard vendors and street musicians leads up the hill, first to the **Coronation Cathedral**, with an ancient mammoth bone hanging by the door – a curiosity that has been here since the Middle Ages.

The church in its present form is the third building on this site, dating from the Gothic era but in reality is an amalgam of all the artistic styles of the last thousand years, and can scarcely be appreciated in all its aspects without a detailed guide.

The first thing to catch the eye is the Baroque **Shrine of St. Stanislaus**. The gleaming silver sarcophagus of the saint, borne by four angels, rests under a domed canopy of black marble and gilded bronze (made in 1669-1671 by the Gdańsk artist Pit van der Renen).

Also among the highlights of the cathedral are the **tombs** of Władysław Jagiełło (after 1434) and Kazimierz III Wielki (sandstone and red marble; after 1370). They are both to be found under the arcades that separate the main nave from the southern side aisle.

The most important of the 18 side chapels is on the south side: the **Holy Cross Chapel** with its Byzantine frescoes by a Russian painter from Pskov (end of the 15th century) includes a masterpiece by Veit Stoss, the tombstone of King Kazimierz IV Jagiellończyk. In the neo-classical **Potocki Chapel** is a figure of Christ by Bertel Thorvaldsen. This is followed by the Baroque **Waza Chapel** and

ROYAL CASTLE

the famous **Sigismund Chapel** *(Kaplica Zymnutowska)*. This architectural gem was designed in 1517 by Bartolommeo Berrecci, a master from Florence, and also contains the tombstones of the last two Jagiellonian kings. With its classical proportions and gilded dome, the Sigismund Chapel has the purest Renaissance style north of the Alps, originating at a time when the architecture of Poland, Bohemia and Germany was still Gothic.

From the northern side aisle there are flights of stairs leading up to the largest bell in Poland in the **Sigismund Tower**, and down into the **Royal Crypts**. The spacious Romanesque crypt and the surrounding rooms are the final resting place of almost all the Polish kings since the 16th century. National heroes were also buried here, such as Tadeusz Kościuszko, Marshall Józef Piłsudski and General Władysław Sikorski, who died in Gibralter in 1943.

Above and right: Impressions of the Jewish cemetery of Kazimierz.

A further **crypt** under the north aisle contains the remains of Adam Mickiewicz and Juliusz Słowacki, the great romantic poets of Poland, who were thus equated with the kings.

Royal Castle

Wawel Castle [20] had modest beginnings. The first building on the site was the round **St. Mary's Church** *(Rotunda Feliksa i Adaukta)* in the south wing, which dates from the 10th century, and there was continuous development from this time on.

The royal castle, built in the 14th century, was rebuilt in the Renaissance style which dominates its appearance today; the large **arcaded courtyard** was begun in 1502 by the Florentine architects Bartolommeo Berrecci and Francesco Fiorentino.

Their creation however differs significantly from the arcaded courtyards of Italy: its proportions are not regular, the steep roof is a concession to the northern European rain and snow, and the high slender columns of the upper floors are not in conformity with the Renaissance style at all.

The columns were originally painted in purple and gold and the walls decorated with frescoes by Hans Dürer (brother of the famous Albrecht Dürer) so that the whole bore more resemblance to a manneristic stage set than to a tranquil Renaissance palazzo.

The comprehensively restored rooms of the castle, which was used by the Austrians as a barracks in the second half of the 19th century, still have original 16th-century portals and coffered ceilings, the most famous of which is to be found in the **Ambassadors' Hall**.

The carved wooden heads of men and women decorating the ceiling were presumably intended to represent the various classes (early 16th-century, probably by Hans Schnitzer of Silesia).

Of the original 194 heads, only 30 remain. There is a guided tour of the other ceremonial halls on the second floor, including the **Senators' Hall**, in which the kings held audience; this is without a doubt the most magnificent of all the rooms.

The **Royal Chambers** contain a number of old Gobelin tapestries. They were ordered in the 16th century by the last Jagiellonian king, Zygmunt August, for the decoration of his residence.

Named after the French town of Arras where many of them come from (as well as from Brussels), all Gobelin tapestries are called *arrasy* in Polish.

Although only 136 of the original 350 have remained, it is still the largest collection of its kind in the world. The tapestries have primarily biblical themes, such as the outstanding cycle depicting the Flood.

They were taken for safe keeping to Canada in 1939 when war seemed likely and were not returned until 1961. The tour of the castle includes a visit to the **Crown Treasury** (on the ground floor) with the famous *Szczerbiec*, the sword of the Polish kings. The exhibition **Orient of the Wawel** in the west wing consists largely of Turkish booty acquired by Jan III Sobieski after the Battle of Vienna in 1683. The most valuable exhibits are the magnificent tents of the Turkish commanders-in-chief, only some of which can be exhibited, for reasons of preservation.

KAZIMIERZ

The section of the city called **Kazimierz** is located southeast of the Wawel Hill.

Two hundred years ago, at the end of only a 20-minute walk you would have been in another town. It was founded in 1335 by Kazimierz III Wielki, who wanted a new Polish town to counterbalance the unpopular Cracow with its German aristocracy.

The **Renaissance Town Hall** ㉑, which today houses a very interesting

KAZIMIERZ

Ethnographic Museum towers over the Plac Wolnica, the old marketplace of Kazimierz.

North of this is the Gothic **Corpus Christi Church** ㉒, (*Kościół Bożego Ciała*) which somewhat resembles St. Mary's Church on the Cracow Market Square. It is also built of brick, which was used however only as filling material; the portals and window and building frames are of sandstone.

St. Catherine's Church ㉓ (*Kościół św. Katarzyny*) a little further to the west is of similar design and is considered a masterpiece of Gothic architecture. Only a few steps away is the Baroque **Pauline Church** ㉔ (*Kościół Paulinów na Skałce* i.e. on the rock) which was built as a consequence of a cruel murder.

It is here that the Cracow Bishop Stanisław (Stanislaus) – today the town's most important saint – was said to have been condemned to death by the vengeful King Bolesław II Śmiały (the Bold) in 1079; according to legend the king carried out the sentence himself.

After 1495, when Jews were forbidden to settle in Cracow, Kazimierz became the most famous Jewish town in Poland. It reached a peak of prosperity in the 16th century, but then went into decline. Even when, at the end of the 18th century, Jews were given freedom to settle, the east of Kazimierz remained very poor. The terrible end of this community came after 1939 when the country was occupied by the Germans. The Jews were transferred to the ghetto in the city district of Podgórze and to the concentration camp of Cracow-Płaszów. Eventually they were transported to the gas chambers of Bełżec and Auschwitz.

Of the 68,000 Jews in Kazimierz less than 1,200 survived, and these did so because they were taken to Bohemia by the German industrialist Oskar Schindler under the pretext that he needed them to work in his factory. This story is now widely known thanks to the film "Schindler's List" made by Steven Spielberg in 1994. **Schindler's Enamel Factory** still exists (in Cracow-Podgórze on the right-hand shore of the Vistula, ul. Lipowa 4) even though it closed after the change of power. Some of the film was shot there.

In Kazimierz there are still many traces of Jewish history and tradition. The seven synagogues were classified by the Nazis as "museums of the extinct race" and were thus spared destruction. On **ul. Szeroka** ("Broad Street"), the center of the Jewish quarter, you can find one of the two prayer houses still in use as such, the small Renaissance **Remuh Synagogue** ㉕.

Behind the synagogue is a **cemetery**, dating to 1533. The gravestones were probably buried in 1704 to save them from desecration by invading Swedes. The cemetery that was later laid out on top of them was destroyed by the Nazis, who had no idea that there were more gravestones hidden under the earth. Discovered by chance after the war, it is the most important 16th-century Jewish cemetery in Europe. The most important grave, the destination of pilgrims from all over the world, is that of Orthodox Rabbi Moses Isserles, also known as Remuh.

At the end of ul. Szeroka is the ★**Old Synagogue** ㉖ (*Stara Bożnica*), built around 1500 and rebuilt in 1557-1570. It is one of the few Jewish prayer houses from the Middle Ages and the early modern age that still exists (the others are in Prague, Worms and Toledo) and it today houses the Museum of History & Culture of the Cracow Jews. The synagogues on the side streets have also been restored: one of these is the beautiful Baroque **Isaac Synagogue** ㉗ (ul. Izaaka) only a few steps away from the Old Synagogue. The **Center of Jewish Culture** ㉘ (*Centrum Kultury Żydowskiej*) at ul. Meiselsa 17 has films and exhibitions – and incidentally serves a good cup of coffee.

108　　　　　*City map page 97, Information pages 115-117*

WEST OF CRACOW

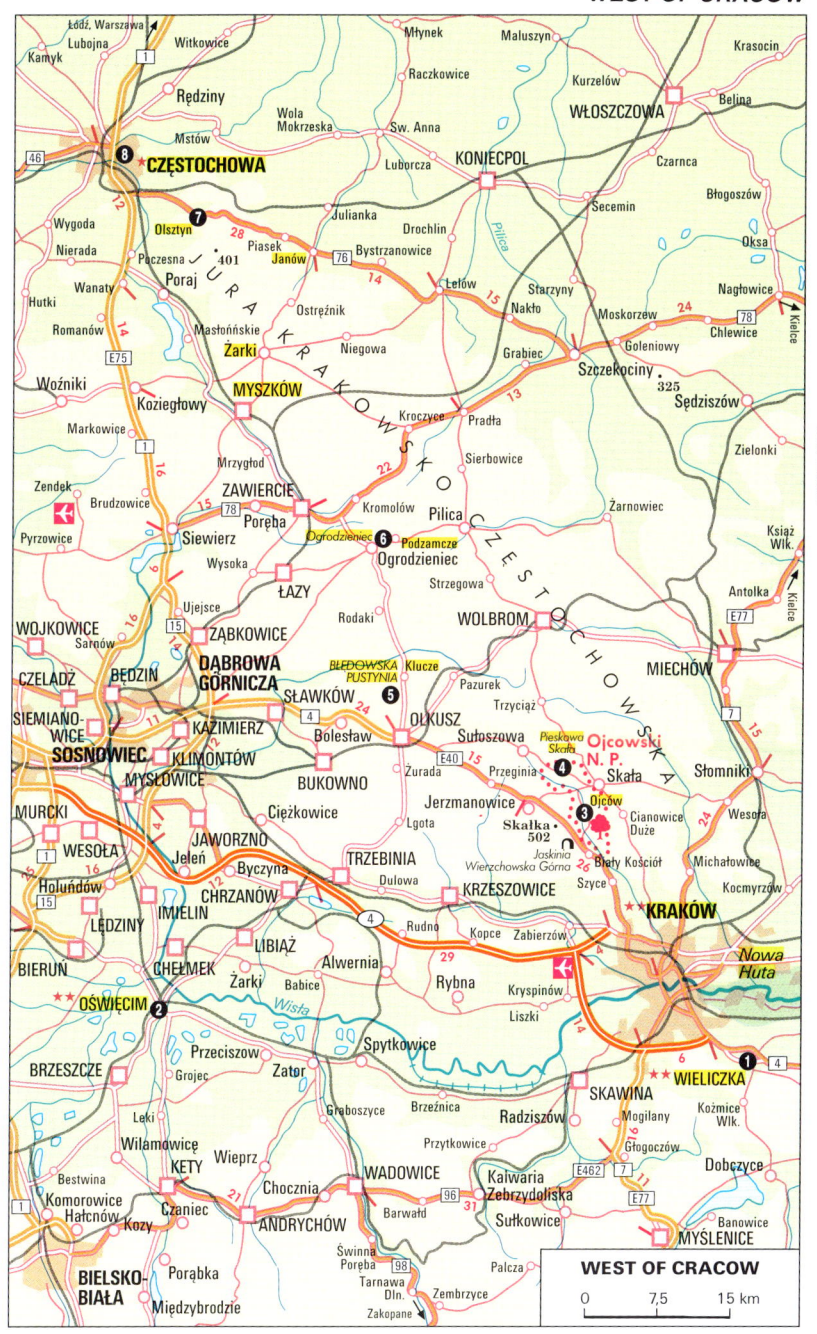

WIELICZKA

Until recently it seemed as though Kazimierz had lost its former inhabitants but not its poverty: run-down houses, tired and rather inhospitable residents, and in the opinion of many Cracow people, not a place to go walking at night. Slowly this is changing: the houses on ul. Szeroka are being restored, some have good Jewish restaurants in them, and thousands come here for the annual festival of Jewish music.

**WIELICZKA

While Nowa Huta is not exactly a tourist attraction, the nearby historic **Wieliczka mine** ❶, which is on the UNESCO World Cultural Heritage list, is a highlight of any trip to Poland. Recently, however, there were doubts as to whether it would ever be accessible again: in 1992

Above: A magnificent chandelier made of salt crystals in the Wieliczka mine. Right: Auschwitz, Main Camp I, where the Nazis imprisoned Polish intellectuals.

an underground river flooded the tunnels, putting the most valuable sections of the mine as well as the town itself in acute danger. A successful rescue operation has now been completed, and the safety of the two- to three-hour guided tours of the salt mine is once again assured.

On the tour you see only a three-kilometer stretch of the total 300 kilometers of galleries, which reach a depth of 327 meters. A fascinating world is revealed with salt lakes and natural grottoes, mining equipment from the last 400 years with gigantic scaffolding, and sculptures and bas-reliefs chiselled in salt by anonymous miners. One hundred and one meters under the earth is the **Chapel of the Blessed Kinga** – actually more cathedral than chapel with a length of 54 meters and a height of 12 meters – with its altars and figures made of salt, which celebrated its centenary in 1996. The huge underground cave with its artistic decoration takes your breath away.

Salt has been mined in Wieliczka since prehistoric times; in the 11th century it was already known as "Magnum Sal." In the 14th century Kazimierz III Wielki issued the statutes for the miners and modernized the mining of the salt, which from then on took place underground. The importance of the royal salt monopoly is demonstrated by the fact that for centuries it was the source of a third of Poland's entire state income.

**AUSCHWITZ (OŚWIĘCIM)

While this town should not be omitted from any itinerary of Poland, only those who have no soul could think of comparing a visit to **Auschwitz (Oświęcim)** ❷ with a visit to places like Malbork or Częstochowa. Auschwitz, where a million people were the victims of dehumanised killing machinery, is unique in history, even given the existence of the other Nazi camps, the Stalinist Gulag archipelago, and the killing fields of the Khmer Rouge. A visit here has a deeper meaning, which is expressed in the words over the entrance to the fourth German block: "Whoever forgets the past is doomed to repeat it."

There were two, in fact even three camps in Auschwitz: the **Main Camp I** was created in April 1940 as a concentration camp for the Polish intellectual elite who were to be "eliminated." Later, prisoners from almost all European countries were detained here, of whom 100,000 died – victims of the heavy work or epidemics and hunger, or gassing or shooting. Nevertheless here there was still a chance, albeit a small one, of survival.

By contrast Auschwitz II, **Birkenau** (Brzezinka) was not primarily a concentration camp but an extermination camp. In this death factory, from 1941 on, over a million Jews and over 20,000 Roma and Sinti were killed. The figure of four million deaths, which was formerly quoted in all the publications of the Eastern bloc, was an erroneous calculation on the part of the Soviets in 1945, based on the capacity of the crematoria.

In Auschwitz-Birkenau, which apart from Kulmhof was the only extermina-

CRACOW-CZĘSTOCHOWA JURA

tion camp within the borders of the Third Reich, the same procedure was followed as in the extermination camps in the General Government, i.e. on Polish territory (Treblinka, Bełżec, Sobibór, Majdanek). On arrival, the people were herded out of the trains onto the ramp; those fit for work were picked out, and the rest were sent directly to the gas chambers, which were disguised as showers. "Between two goals of the football game between the camp teams, a whole trainload of Jews was burned," wrote Tadeusz Borowski, a former concentration camp inmate, in his memoirs. But no matter how much one reads, it will never be possible to understand Auschwitz.

Oświęcim is 60 kilometers west of Cracow and easily accessible by train and car. Up until the 15th century the town belonged to Silesia, and it was only then that it was transferred to the ownership of the Polish monarchy.

What visitors see is the main camp with the notorious gate bearing the inscription "Arbeit macht frei" – "Work shall Make you Free." Thirty barracks, a gas chamber and a crematorium are all still standing. It was here that the first experiments with cyanide B were carried out, the victims of which were Soviet prisoners-of-war. A shattering documentary (available in several languages) about the liberation of the camp in 1945, is shown at regular intervals. It is possible to visit the camp on your own, as exhibits are informatively labeled, but guided tours are available.

Birkenau, to which you can either walk or take the free shuttle bus, is less like a museum. Here you stand in the middle of a seemingly endless space, with a few barracks, mostly ruined and the remains of the four gas chambers. At the end of the railway lines, which form the main axis of the camp, there is a memorial to those who died, put up in 1967.

Right: West Galician countryside near Cracow.

CRACOW-CZĘSTOCHOWA JURA

Northwest of Cracow is the **Cracow Częstochowa Jura** (Wyżyna Krakowsko-Częstochowska), an upland region, with its deep valleys and limestone bedrock formed into bizarre shapes by the processes of erosion. The porous limestone also resulted in the development of typical karst features, including deep dripstone caves.

The picturesque hilly countryside, with summits of up to 500 meters, is also dotted with numerous castle ruins, the so-called eagles' nests, most of which were built by Kazimierz III Wielki (Casimir the Great), to protect the trade route to Silesia.

The most beautiful part of this region is the ***Ojców Valley** (dolina Ojcowska*, also known as the *dolina Prądinika*), with a stream named *Prądnik* flowing through it. It has been turned into a national park, primarily to protect the many plants that are found only here, such as *betulia oycoviensis*, a type of birch. Short walks can be taken from the road which winds through the bottom of the valley. A map is a necessity.

The National Park is Cracow's local getaway spot, as it is only 25 kilometers from the city, and it is equally popular with tourists, day-trippers and school groups. With its many trees it is at its peak of beauty in the fall, when the colors are magnificent.

The old spa of **Ojców** ❸ is the closest to Cracow. It has the ruins of a medieval fort, the National Park Museum, and a Regional Museum – both at the foot of the castle hill. The trail marked in black leads from the castle in Ojców to Cracow Gorge (*Wąwóz Kraków*) and the Łokietek Cave (*Jaskinia Łokietka*) in which, according to the legend, the later King Władysław Łokietek took refuge from the troops of the Bohemian King Wenceslas II. Today the only inhabitants of the cave are bats – of which there are nevertheless twelve different species. The trail marked in yellow leads to a longer cave, the *Jaskinia Wierzchowska Górna* (a walk taking one and a half hours).

At the northern end of the nature reserve is **Hercules' Club** (Maczuga Herkulesa), a particularly interesting example of cliff erosion.

On the "Dog Cliff" (Polish: *Pieskowa Skała*), a few hundred meters further west, is **Pieskowa Skała Castle** ❹. Originally a medieval fortress, it was rebuilt as a Renaissance palace in the 16th century, in the same style as the Cracow royal residence. The attractive arcaded courtyard is clearly modeled on the Wawel, with a series of caricatures carved in stone. The state rooms and living rooms are open to the public, and have been furnished with exhibits typical of the styles of various epochs from the Wawel Museum.

En route to Częstochowa are more bizarre rock formations, and a string of castles. Near the village of Klucze (around five kilometers north of Olkusz) are 30 square kilometers of quicksand, rather facetiously referred to as "the only desert in Europe." The **Błędowska Pustynia** ❺, which has been reported to have sand dunes, an oasis and even fata morganas, is gradually being overgrown by grass. It was nevertheless sufficiently desert-like for German General Rommel's Africa corps to have used it as a training area.

The castles are distinctly more photogenic, in particular **Ogrodzieniec** ❻, a huge 16th-century ruin in a rocky setting near the village of Podzamcze. It has been placed under a preservation order, and is open to visitors. Continuing on toward Częstochowa, via Myszków, Żarki and Janów, the country road passes more eagles' nests at **Mirów** and **Bobolice**. Though already visible from a long way off, the most well known feature of Częstochowa, the ruin of the medieval **Olsztyn Castle** ❼, is finally reached, just outside the town. It was one of the most important strongholds, not only in the Cracow region, but in all of Poland.

Map page 109, Information pages 115-117

*CZĘSTOCHOWA

Above: The Black Madonna of Częstochowa (here a copy in the monastery courtyard) – destination of pilgrims and the symbol of national consciousness.

The industrial town of ***Częstochowa** ❽ (population 260,000) owes its fame to an incident in its history. In 1382 the Silesian duke Władysław Opolczyk had a monastery built for the Paulite order which had emigrated here from Hungary, and presented them with a miraculous painting of Our Lady.

The dark color of the **Black Madonna of Częstochowa** (*Matka Boska Częstochowska*) was intentional and has nothing to do with the smoke from the candles.

The origin of the painting is unknown. Some believe it was painted by St. Luke, others think it is a sienna painting or a Russian icon acquired by the duke as booty from some military exploit. The question will probably never be answered definitively, since the picture was badly damaged in an attack by the Hussites and was later completely restored by Russian artists. The two sword marks on the Madonna's cheek are also said to have been made by the Hussites. There was, however, a Byzantine tradition of "wounded" pictures, where violence was simulated to promote reverence for a work of art. It was then that the Black Madonna began her career as a miracle worker: the horses that were supposed to carry the picture back to Bohemia refused to participate in this scandalous deed and would not move.

The picture is said to have saved the monastery from the Swedes in 1655: during the siege there were daily processions with it along the wall to give the defenders courage.

Military success against the Russians in 1770 and the saving of the monastery in 1945, when attempts by the Germans to blow it up on retreat were defeated by a damp fuse, were also attributed by many people to the power of the Black Madonna.

CRACOW

Częstochowa plays a central part in the religious culture of Poland. The popular belief in the Black Madonna has also become closely associated with national consciousness. Hundreds of thousands of pilgrims come here every year for the town's most important holiday, the Assumption of Mary on August 15th. Anyone who visits the town at this time and sees the vast crowds of people will need no convincing of the power of the Polish Catholic Church.

The monastery was built on a hill, *Jasna Góra* (Bright Mountain), three kilometers west of the present center, at the end of the wide *Aleja Najświętszej Marii Panny* (Mother of God Avenue), a stretch of road which some pilgrims cover on their knees. The monastery is surrounded by bastions. Clustered around the four consecutive **gates** of the fortifications, is a pilgrims' fair – complete with inflatable rubber animals, cotton candy, devotional articles, and balloons with the Pope's image on them.

Inside the monastery, however, the atmosphere is more serious. The first building you come to is the **Monastery Church** with its high, slender tower and a magnificent Baroque interior.

Also well worth a visit are the **Knight's Hall** (*Sala Rycerska*), with paintings from the 17th century illustrating the exciting history of the monastery, and the **Treasury** with precious votive gifts from various kings and national heroes.

At the heart of the complex is the **Chapel of the Birth of Mary** (entrance through the Monastery Church or the Treasury), where the picture is kept on the main altar. It is protected by a silver cover dating from 1673, which at intervals is ceremoniously opened, to the accompaniment of a fanfare. Together with hundreds of pilgrims, and from an respectful distance, you can gaze on the patron saint of Poland. Here you are never alone.

CRACOW ☎ 012

Center for Tourist Information, ul. Pawia 8, Tel. 4226091, Fax 4220471.

ARRIVAL: There are several **flights** daily from Warsaw; you can also fly directly from Frankfurt/Main and Vienna (Info: LOT, ul. Basztowa 15, Tel. 4224215, 4777451). **Trains** from Warsaw leave several times daily; the ride requires 2 hours and 40 minutes. Daily trains also connect Cracow with Frankfurt/Main and Prague. Until construction of the freeway through Silesia is finished, coming by **car** is relatively trying. Drivers from Warsaw are advised to use the longer but better maintained stretch of road through Częstochowa and Katowice. *LOCAL TRANSPORTATION:* All the tourist sights in the Old Town and Kazimierz can be reached easily on foot. Tickets for the bus and trolley can be purchased at the MPK kiosks (one-hour tickets 2 Zł (bus), 2.50 Zł (trolley); full-day tickets 8 Zł. Some possibly useful routes: Bus No. 100 runs from Plac Matejki (near the Barbican) to Kościuszko Hill, No. 109 from Zwierzyniec (west of the Old Town) to Bielany. Taxis can be called under the numbers Tel. 919 and 936. Driving inside the city can be very complicated due to the many one-way streets; a better idea is to park at one of the large, attended parking lots (Plac Szczepański, Plac Św. Ducha) and continue on foot.

Hotel rates in Cracow are climbing rapidly from one year to the next, and alas do not always correspond to levels of quality and service. ☻☻☻ **Forum**, ul. M. Konopnickiej 28, Tel. 2619212, Fax 2690080. e-mail: cracow@interconti.com. Giant concrete building on the bank of the Vistula; offers swimming pool, sauna, nightclub, casino; some rooms have a lovely view of the Wawel. **Holiday Inn**, ul. Armii Krajowej 7, Tel. 6375044, Fax 6375938. Inconveniently far from the city center. **Cracovia**, Al. Focha 1, Tel. 4228666, Fax 4219586, www.orbis.pl/hot_cra.html. A relic from the communist years; however the standard of comfort has improved. Ten-minute walk to the Old Town. **Francuski**, ul. Pijarska 13, Tel. 4225122, Fax 4225270, www.orbis.pl/hot_fra.html. The best choice in the Old Town; built in 1912; the furnishings and decor provide a touch of the atmosphere of the past. **Grand**, ul. Sławkowska 5/7, Tel. 4217255, Fax 4218360. Relatively expensive. **Pod Różą**, ul. Floriańska 14, Tel. 4229399, Fax 4217026. Least reccommended because of its noisy casino. ☻☻ **Royal**, ul. Św. Getrudy 26/29, Tel. 4213500, Fax 4214979. Best possible location, directly at the foot of the Wawel Hill; some of its rooms reasonably priced and not necessarily inferior. **Pollera**, ul. Szpitalna 30,

CRACOW

Tel. 4221044, 4221128, Fax 4221389. Located in the Old Town, as is the **Polski**, ul. Pijarska 17, Tel. 4221144, Fax 4221426. Both offer rooms with and without private bath. **Logos**, ul. Szujskiego 5, Tel. 6323333, Fax 6324210, www.interkom.pl/logos. New and recommendable; in a modern building, between the older structures; not far from the Old Town. Near the train station: **Polonia**, ul. Basztowa 25, Tel. 4221233, Fax 4221621, e-mail: polonia@bci.krakow.pl. **Europejski**, ul. Lubicz 5, Tel. 4220911. **Warszawski**, ul. Pawia 6, Tel. 4220622. The first of these is the best and quietest. **Hotel D** (Dom Turysty), ul. Westerplatte 15, Tel. 4229566. Has 800 beds in 2-, 3-, 4- and 8-bed rooms. Has become rather expensive considering the standard of comfort offered. **Youth Hostel**, ul. Oleandry 4, Tel. 6338822. In the west of Cracow; within walking distance of the city center. Alternatively a second youth hostel is located at ul. Grochowa 21 (Tel. 6532432). **Campgrounds**: Krak, ul. Radzikowskiego 99, Tel. 6372122. In the western part of the city, next to the Motel *Krak*. Cracowianka, ul. Żywiecka 4, Tel. 2664191. Other Campgrounds in the south along the road to Zakopane.

Wierzynek, Rynek Główny 15, Tel. 4221035. During the communist years, this was the most renowned restaurant in Cracow, if not in Poland. As early as 1364 it hosted an emperor, four kings, and several dukes, who gathered to discuss marriage politics and defense against the Turks. A visit is worthwhile, even if cynics say you are paying for the period rooms, the view, and the lute music rather than for the food. **Hawełka**, Rynek Główny 34, Tel. 4224753. Unpretentious ground floor and elegant main floor (*Hawełka Tetmajerowska*). This restaurant is second to none, not even the *Wierzynek*, even if it has "only" existed since 1876. Both restaurants serve classical Polish noble cuisine with a lot of game and poultry; the duck with apple and the porcino soup are first-rate. **Staropolska**, ul. Sienna 4, Tel. 4225821. A few steps from the Market Square; tasty Polish dishes. **Balaton**, ul. Grodzka 37, Tel. 4220469. Hungarian specialties. **Cyrano de Bergerac**, ul. Sławkowska 26, Tel. 4117288. High-class French cuisine. **Chiński Pałac**, ul. Sławkowska 3, Tel. 4213542. Chinese restaurant in the *Saski* Hotel. **Da Pietro**, Rynek Główny 17, Tel. 4223279. Pizzeria on the Market Square. **U Szkota**, ul. Mikołajska 4, Tel. 4221570. Palate-pleasing dishes from Scotland. **Paese**, ul. Poselska 24, Tel. 4216273. Corsican cuisine. **Vega**, ul. Św. Getrudy 7, Tel. 4223494. Inexpensive vegetarian cuisine, which for Polish people is still exotic. Kosher restaurants in Kazimierz: **Ariel**, ul. Szeroka 17, Tel. 4213870, www.ariel.krakow.pl. **Koszerna**, ul. Szeroka 39, Tel. 4226790. *Cafés:* **Jama Michalikowa**, ul. Floriańska 45, Tel. 4221561. A leading café; also as a tourist attraction; often offers cabaret in the evenings.

The best place for great jazz is **Piwnica pod Jaszczurami**, Rynek Główny 7/8. On weekends mostly a disco. **U Muniaka**, ul. Floriańska 3, Tel. 231205. Club of the famous Polish jazz musician.

NATIONAL MUSEUM: **Czartoryski Collection** (Muzeum Narodowe, Kolekcja Czartoryskich), Pijarska 15, Tel. 4225566, www.gwc.net/czartor. Tues-Thurs, Sat, Sun 10:00 a.m. – 3:00 p.m., Fri 10:00 a.m. – 5:00 p.m.; July and Aug Tues-Sun 10:00 a.m. – 6:00 p.m. **Gallery of Paintings** in the Cloth Hall (Galeria Sukiennice), Rynek Główny 1/3, Tel. 4221166. Tues-Sun 10:00 a.m. – 3:30 p.m. (Thurs to 6:00 p.m.). **Szołayski House** (Kamienica Szkołayskich), pl. Szczepański 9, Tel. 4227021. **Tower of the Town Hall**: can be climbed Wed-Sun 9:00 a.m. – 3:00 p.m. (only in summer). **Collegium Maius**, University Museum, ul. Jagiellońska 15, Tel. 4220549, www.uj.edu.pl/Muzeum. Mon-Fri 11:00 a.m. – 2:30 p.m., Sat 11:00 a.m. – 1:30 p.m. Guided tours in Polish 3x daily and English once daily; advance recommendations are advisable. The court is open until sunset. **Wawel**, Castle Hill, Tel. 4225155, www.cyf-kr.edu.pl/wawel. Accessible daily from 6:00 a.m. – 6:00 p.m. (Oct-March to 5:00 p.m.). Cathedral and royal tombs: May-Sept Mon-Sat 9:00 a.m. – 5:00 p.m., Sundays and holidays 12:15 – 5:00 p.m.; April-Oct daily 9:00 a.m. – 4:00 p.m.; Nov-March daily 9:00 a.m. – 3:00 p.m. Royal Apartments, Treasury, Exhibition of Oriental Art: May-Sept Tues 9:30 a.m. – 4:30 p.m., Wed-Fri 9:30 a.m. – 3:30 p.m., Sat 9:30 a.m. – 3:00 p.m., Sun 10:00 a.m. – 3.00 p.m.; Oct-April Tues-Thurs, Sat 9:30 a.m. – 3.00 p.m., Fri 9:30 a.m. – 4:00 p.m., Sun 10:00 a.m. – 3:00 p.m. "Lost Wawel" exhibit (Wawel zaginiony): Wed, Thurs, Sat 9:30 a.m. – 3:00 p.m., Fri 9:30 a.m. – 4:00 p.m., Sun 10:00 a.m. ndash 3:00 p.m., Mon 9:30 a.m. – 3:30 p.m. Dragons' Cave (Smocza Jama): May-Sept daily 10:00 a.m. – 5:00 p.m. Expect large crowds in summer, especially waiting for entrance to the Royal Apartments; it pays to arrive before the ticket booth opens. **Synagogue and Remuh Cemetery**, ul. Szeroka 40: Mon-Fri 9:00 a.m. – 4:00 p.m. **Old Synagogue**, Museum of Culture and History of the Jews of Cracow (Stara Bożnica), ul. Szeroka 24, Tel. 4220962: Wed-Thurs, Sat-Sun 9:00 a.m. – 3:00 p.m., Fri 11:00 a.m. – 6:00 p.m. (closed the first Saturday and Sunday of each month). **Isaak Synagogue** (Synagoga Ajzyka), ul. Kupa 18: Sun-Fri 9:00 a.m. – 7:00 p.m. (closed on Jewish holidays). **Jewish Cultural Center** (Centrum Kultury Żydowskiej), ul. Meiselsa 17, Tel. 4235595, 4235587. **Ethnographic Museum** (Muzeum Etnograficzne), Plac Wolnica, Kazimierz: Mon 10:00 a.m. – 6:00 p.m., Wed-Sun 10:00 a.m. – 3:00 p.m.

Cricot 2. The best known avant-garde theater in Cracow still occasionally stages the last works by its

CRACOW

founder, Tadeusz Kantor (died 1990). It is worth enquiring. Tel. 4228332). The two best-known traditional theaters in Cracow: **Teatr Stary**, ul. Jagiellońska 1, Tel. 4228566; **Teatr im. Słowackiego**, pl. Św. Ducha 1, Tel. 4224364. The later is worth a visit if only for its impressive interior. Frequent opera and ballet performances.

FESTIVALS: **February**: Shanty Festival. **May**: Juwenalia (Student Festival). **May-June**: Festival of Short Films. **June-July**: Festival of Jewish Culture in Kazimierz. **July-August**: Festival of Early Music (Letni Festiwal Muzyki Dawnej), court of the Collegium Maius, in the Villa Decius and in some churches; Info: Tel. 4220064; Festival of Street Theater. The months of **September to November** are big months for jazz music (Solo-Duo-Trio Jazz Festival and Zaduszki Jazzowe). The Triennial of Graphic Arts is held every three years (next in 2003; Info Tel. 4217787). Folk Festival *Lajkonik*: The parade, from the Church of the Premonstratensian Order in Zwierzyniec to the Market Square, takes place eight days after the Feast of Corpus Christi. A dancing horse (*lajkonik*) leads the parade, its rider in traditional Tatar dress, commemorating the raftsman, who in 1287 killed a Mongolian emperor and donned the emperor's clothing for his triumphal entry into the city. In **December** Cracow's nativity scenes (*szopki*), exhibiting papier-maché models of Cracow's churches.The weekly magazine *Miesiąc w Cracowie* (Polish / English) prints information about exhibitions, cultural events, and the film schedules.

WIELICZKA ☎ 012

ARRIVAL: Local trains from Cracow central train station; from the station in Wieliczka the walk to the Salt Mines is about 15 minutes.

Museum in the Salt Mines of Wieliczka (kopalnia soli w Wieliczce), ul. Daniłowicza 10, Tel. 2782653, www.muzeum.wieliczka.pl. Daily 8:00 a.m. to 6:00 p.m. (Off-season to 4:00 p.m. Three-hour guided tour with break; reserve for tours in other languages than Polish.

AUSCHWITZ (OŚWIĘCIM) ☎ 033

ARRIVAL: Trains from Cracow central train station by way of Trzebinia 6:38 a.m. and 8:05 a.m. or from the Cracow Płaszów station by way of Skawina. Buses from Cracow often, (8:30, 9:30, 10:30 a.m.).

Memorial Museum in both sections of the camp: daily July-Aug 8:00 a.m. – 7:00 p.m.; May, Sept 8:00 a.m. – 6:00 p.m.; April, Oct 8:00 a.m. – 5:00 p.m., March, Nov 8:00 a.m. – 4:00 p.m.; Dec-Feb 8:00 a.m. – 3:00 p.m. No children under the age of 14 are permitted to visit the museum. Tel. 8432022.

CRACOW-CZĘSTOCHOWA JURA ☎ 012

In Ojców there are plenty of **private rooms** (arranged by the Ojcowianin office, Tel. 3892089). Acceptable overnight accommodation are also offered by the guesthouse **Zosia** (Ojców 4, Tel. 3892008) and the **PTTK Hostel** (Dom noclegowy PTTK, Ojców 15, Tel. 3892010). There is also a **camp site** in the town. Nearby is a **Youth Hostel** (Skała, ul. Szkolna 4, Tel. 3891065; July-Aug). The **Motel Krystyna** (Będło, Tel. 6372298) is on the main road near the National Park. Modest accommodation in the Jura area can be found in Olkusz (Olkusz, ul. Kazimierza Wielkiego 61, Tel. 035/6433613) and also in the **Youth Hostels** housed in the village schools of Ogrodzieniec (Podzamcze) Bobolice and Olsztyn.

Zamkowa, in the Castle in Pieskowa Skała, Tel. 3891103. Terrace with beautiful view.

The **Caves** Łokietka and Górna Wierzchowska can be visited daily from 9:00 a.m. – 4:00 p.m. (May-Oct).
Museums in Ojców (Muzeum Regionalne, Muzeum Przyrodnicze for Flora and Fauna): Tues-Sun 9:00 a.m. – 4:00 p.m. **Castle Museum**, Pieskowa Skała, Tel. 3896004. Tues-Sun 10:00 a.m. – 3:00 p.m., (in summer Sat, Sun 10:00 a.m. – 5:00 p.m.).

CZĘSTOCHOWA ☎ 034

Al. Najświętszej Marii Panny 65, Tel. 3241360.

Patria, ul. Ks. J. Popiełuszki 2, Tel. 3247001, Fax 3246332, www.orbis.pl/hot_pat.html. Best hotel in the city; c. 10 minute walk to the monastery grounds. **Motel Orbis**, Al. Wojska Polskiego 281/287, tel. 3610233, fax 3655607, www.orbis.pl/hot_motcz.html. City periphery; attractive rooms. There are many **church-run guest houses** (Dom Pielgrzyma next to the monastery, ul. Ks. Wyszyńskiego 1/31, Tel. 324701, or Diecezjalny Dom Rekolekcyjny, ul. Św. Barbary 43, Tel. 3241177), often full, as are the hotels in Częstochowa, especially around August 15. **Youth Hostel**, ul. Wacławy Marek 12, Tel. 467995. Far from city center. **Camping**, ul. Oleńki 20/30, Tel. 3146285.

The best restaurants in the city are in the *Patria* Hotel and the *Motel Orbis* listed above. Chinese and Vietnamese restaurants: **A-Dong**, ul. Niepodległości 48, Tel.3 630351. **Chińska**, ul. Racławicka 3, Tel. 3246235. **Wietnamska**, ul. Warszawska 9, Tel. 3246735.

The painting of the **Black Madonna** is usually accessible for viewing at these hours: 6:00 a.m. – 12:00 noon, 3:30 – 4:40 p.m., and 7:00 – 7:45 p.m. **Treasury:** Mon-Sat 9:00 – 11.30 a.m. and 3:30 – 5:30 p.m, Sun 9:00 a.m. – 1:00 p.m.

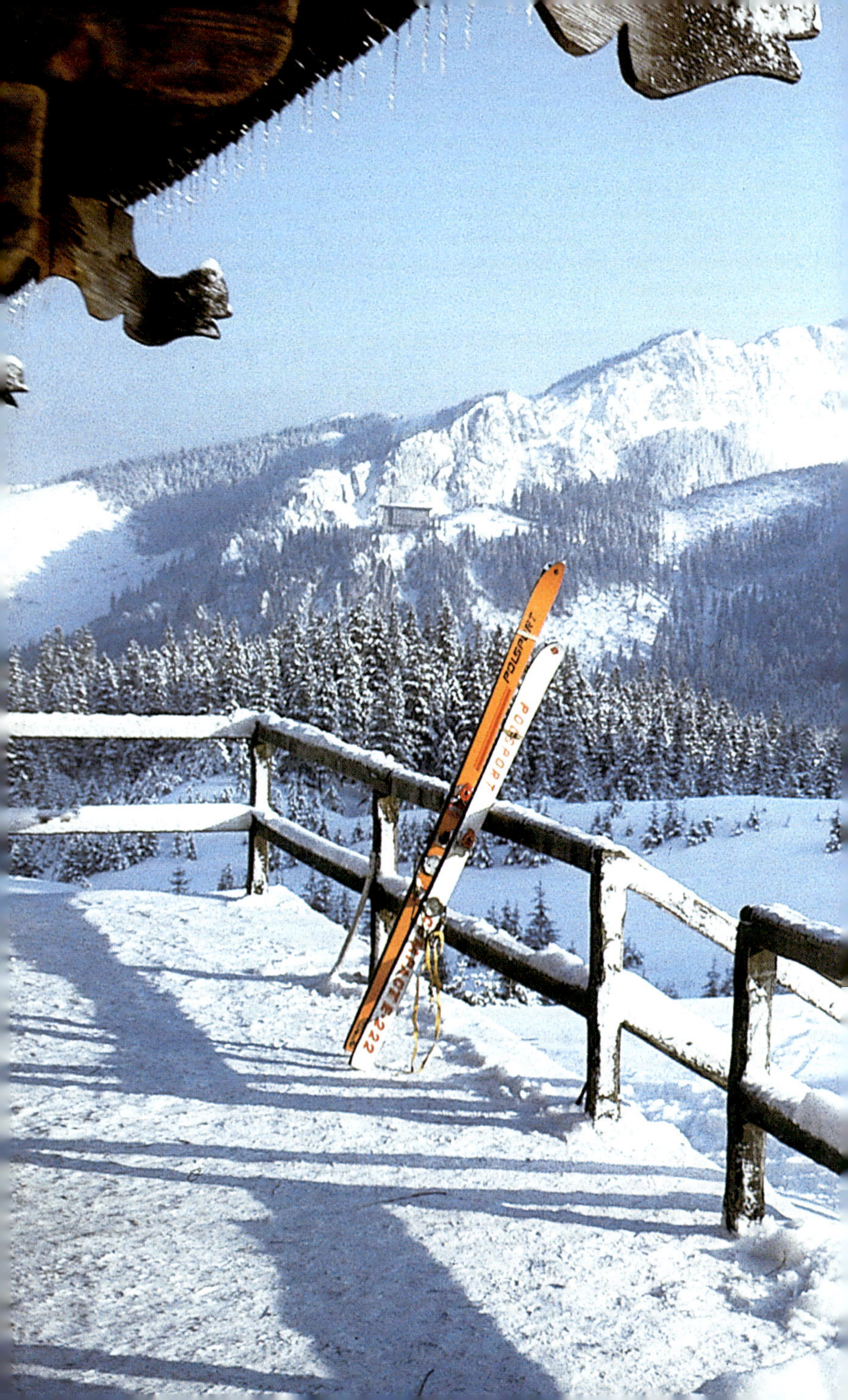
E-222

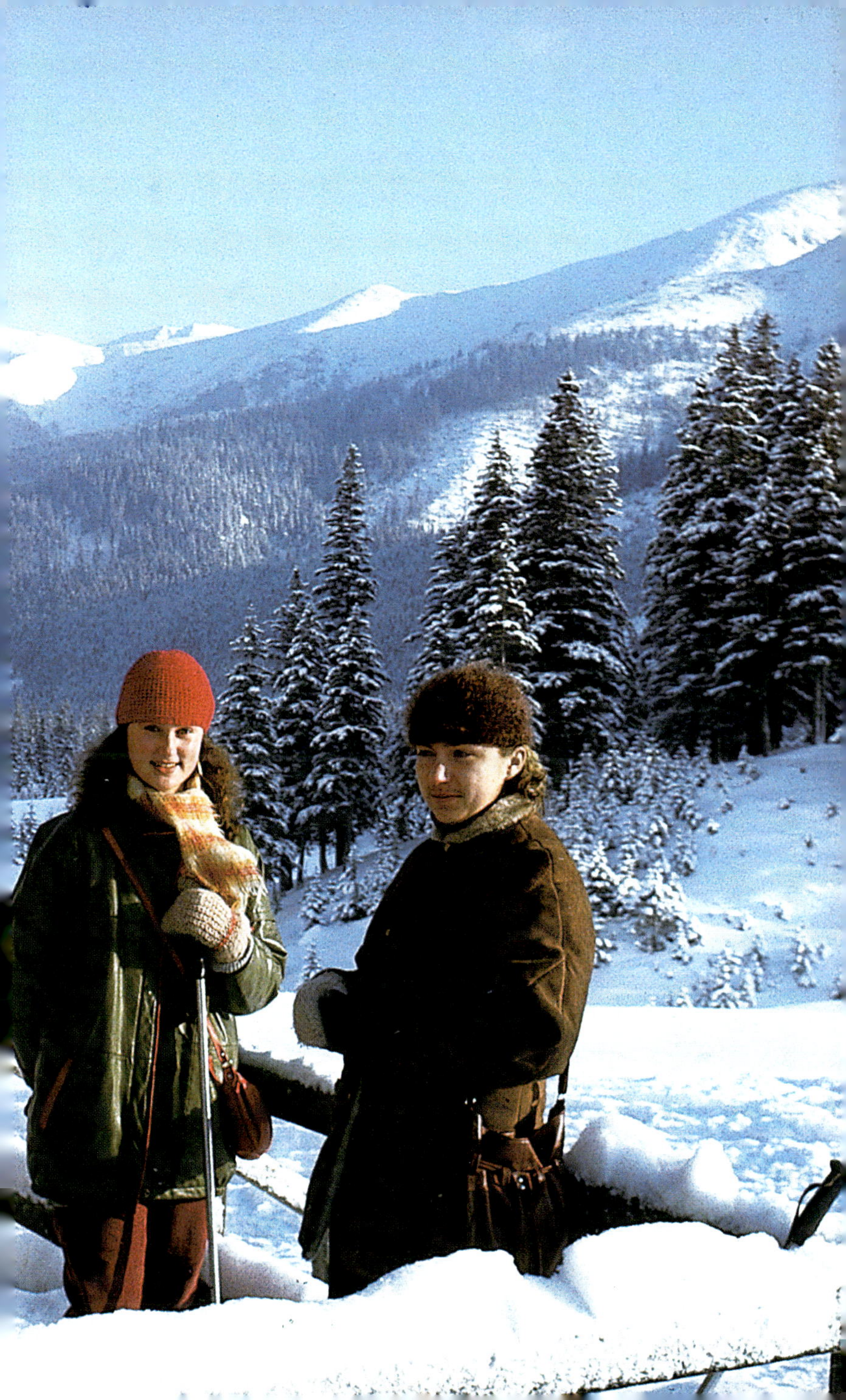

LITTLE POLAND

LITTLE POLAND
Galicia – The Lost World

**PODHALE AND
THE HIGH TATRA
PIENINY MOUNTAINS AND
THE DUNAJEC GORGE
BETWEEN CRACOW
AND PRZEMYSL
BIESZCZADY**

Dominated by the Carpathian mountains and their foothills, Southeast Poland offers travel destinations ranging from the rugged peaks of the High Tatra mountains with their alpine landscapes to the soft, wooded ridges of the Beskin mountains. Nature is at its best here. Within a 100 kilometer radius of Cracow, there are no less than five national parks. Another two are located just a little farther to the east. A hike to the lakes in the High Tatra as well as river rafting through the Pieniny Mountains are adventures not to be missed when visiting this beautiful region.

The farther you travel to the East, the more untamed the scenery. There are few human settlements; instead, wolves, lynx and brown bears roam the countryside. You will come across the remains of Ukrainian villages, with wooden Orthodox churches, characteristic of the region. Farther north, the splendid residences of the Polish nobility await your visit as well. The travel destinations described here are not recommended as day excursions from Cracow. It would be better to arrange overnight accommodation, avail-

Previous page: The High Tatra Mountains offer great hiking and skiing areas. Left: The climb from Czamy Staw up to Mt. Rysy (2499 meters), Poland's highest mountain peak.

able at Zakopane, Nowy, Sącz, Przemyśl and Sanok. When exploring the eastern part of the Bieszczady, you will have to bear with very modest hotels; or better yet, pack a tent.

Little Poland or Galicia?

The names given this region are rather confusing. Whereas the Poles speak of "Little Poland" (Małopolska), this region is better known outside of the country as "Galicia." The different names owe their origins to the region's history.

The area around Cracow, Lviv, Kielce and Lublin had been known as Little Poland since the Middle Ages, and the region around Poznań had been known as Great Poland. In 1772 during the First Partition of Poland, when Austria annexed parts of the country south and east of Cracow, Empress Maria Theresa gave historical justification to the name Galicia, basing it on a fictitious detail: she claimed to be heiress to the throne of the medieval duchies of Halicz and Volhynia, of which the Latin names are Galicia and Lodomeria.

In 1867 Galicia became an autonomous province in the Austro-Hungarian Empire, which had its capital at Lviv (today in the Ukraine). The present-day border between Poland and the Ukraine is

Map pages 122-123, Information pages 132-133

LITTLE POLAND

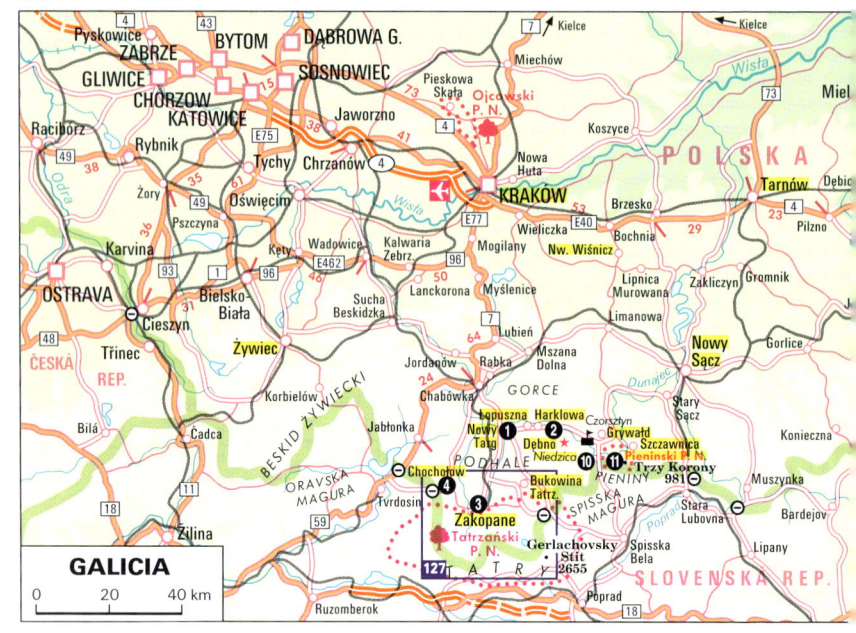

the result of the Hitler-Stalin pact of 1939. The eastern portion of Galicia was annexed to the Soviet Union, from which the independent Ukrainian state has since evolved (1991). The border is not the ethnic boundary between the Poles and the Ukrainians, as many people believe. The ethnic boundary ran West of the present border; however, even to the East, up until 1939 the cities were still primarily populated by Poles and Jews.

Today's relationship between Poland and the Ukraine as seen by Warsaw and Kiev is exemplary. However, from Lviv or Przemyśl it is seen as more complicated, sometimes irritating, and burdened by the past. Don't let this prevent you from considering an excursion by bus from Przemyśl to Lviv, two hours away, the former capital of Galicia and a very beautiful city. (Don't forget the visa requirement!)

Galicia was synonymous for poverty and backwardness in the 19th century. Life was lived against a background of overpopulation, waves of emigration from Galicia to America, and bloody peasant revolts and Ukrainian uprisings. The world of the Galician Jewry and the cultural autonomy of this land during the partition, however, were unique. Joseph Conrad and Pope John Paul II, among other prominent figures, were born in Little Poland / Galicia. It is also the spiritual home of Joseph Roth and the great visionary Bruno Schultz, often regarded as an equal of Franz Kafka.

An essence of the exotic still lingers in the present day image of this region. There are mountainsides with countless small, irregularly shaped grain fields, villages in which the houses sometimes still have straw-covered roofs and blue walls, pathways lined with wayside devotionals and shrines; and wooden churches packed on Sundays with people in traditional costumes.

But take heed: asphalt jungles are encroaching on the wooden houses, tractors are driving out the horses, and the typical embroidered felt pants of the Tatra people are being swapped for jeans.

Information pages 132-133

PODHALE

ities that can be partly traced back to the influence of Balkan shepherds. Górales call all non-Górales "*ceper*" and amusingly look a bit down on them even though the non-Górales who come as tourists from the flatlands provide a considerable share of the Górales' yearly income. The Górales are known for their sense of humor and for their pronounced sense of honor. Despite attempts by the German National Socialists during the Second World War to make an Arian people out of them, they remained loyal and patriotic Poles throughout the ordeal.

Local folk culture is very much alive. But you don't need to visit the annual highlanders folklore festival in Zakopane in September to be aware that this cultural heritage is still thriving. You can admire the traditional costumes commonly worn to the Sunday church services. The women dress in flowered skirts and scarves, white blouses and red coral necklaces. The men are clad in white embroidered cloth pants and artistically decorated fur waistcoats. Their costumes are completed with braided leather shoes, a round felt hat, and the so-called "cucha," a cloth jacket thrown over the shoulder.

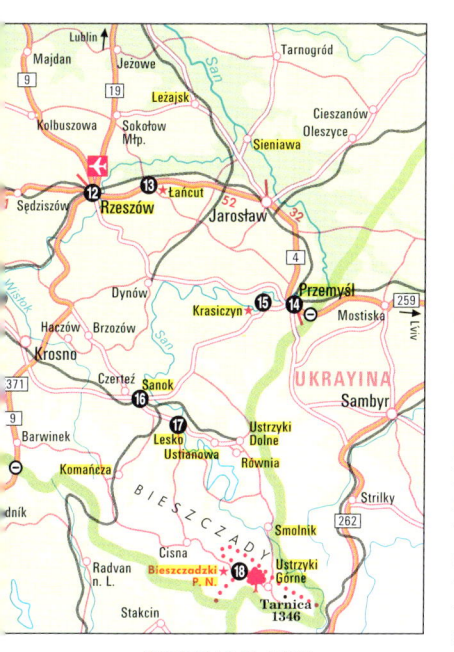

PODHALE AND ⋆THE HIGH TATRA

Podhale is a flat basin surrounded on all sides by mountains. The High and Western Tatra are located to the south; the Beskid Zywiecki and Gorce to the west and north; and the Pieniny are to the east. This highland, (the name means "alpine meadows") borders to the southeast and southwest the regions of Spisz and Orawa without a mountainous barrier.

The 100 kilometer trip from Cracow to Podhale leads over two mountain passes. to Nowy Targ (New Market), the old capital of the Górale. "Górale" simply means "mountain dweller" and the residents of the towns Nowy Sącz and Zywiec can be correctly depicted as such. Of course, if it is to be taken at all seriously, only those from the Podhale region can be designated the "true Górales." Their language (actually a Polish dialect featuring its own word intonation), their music, architectural construction and their folk traditions display characteristics and peculiar-

Podhale

Nowy Targ ❶ (New Market) is not particularly interesting from a tourist's point of view. The best time to visit the city, though, is on a Thursday when a sizeable market takes place on the banks of the Biały Dunajec. Here you can literally buy everything under the sun – from horses, sheep and pigs to wooden toys and cowbells. You can also see tiny lively wooly balls that grow steadily into the famous Tatra sheep dogs (*owczarek podhalański*) that command great respect. It is said that these dogs come to a dismal end and die if taken out of the Tatra region. To a certain extent, this applies to the Górales, also. Nevertheless, they have been emigrating to "Hámerika," as they

Information pages 132-133

ZAKOPANE

call it, on a massive scale for the past 100 years. Supposedly every second Górale has a relative in Chicago who sends him money for a new home. Perhaps this is the reason why so many new homes are going up everywhere in Podhale – and probably nowhere in Europe will you see as much construction underway as here. The truth of the matter is that construction takes a number of years to complete because with each new money gift, an additional wall of a home can be financed.

Several of the most beautiful wooden churches are situated east of Nowy Targ on the way to the Pieniny Mountains in **Łopuszna**, **Harklowa** and **Grywałd**. The most magnificent of all is located in *Dębno ❷. It features a shingled roof and is dedicated to the Archangel Michael. This church dates from the 15th century. (Ask for the key at the parish house across the street.) It is built out of

Above: Traditional wooden cabins in Chochołów. Right: View from Zakopane looking out to the High Tatra.

larchwood using wooden dowels (no metal nails). The ceiling and walls are covered with unique late Gothic stencil paintings. Behind the altar is a copy of Poland's oldest panel painting, dating from the 13th century (the original can be seen in Cracow's Wawel Royal Castle). To prevent danger from fire, the church has no electrical wiring, and each individual section of the church interior is illuminated with a lamp, enhancing the magical setting and atmosphere. It is not all that surprising to hear that Americans (or so the story goes) wanted to buy the church for one million dollars, so that they could rebuild it on their side of the Atlantic.

Zakopane

The center of Podhale is **Zakopane ❸**, the heart of tourism, ski capital of Poland, and home base for excursions into the High Tatra mountains. However, many vacationers prefer the surrounding villages (Bukowina, Murzasichle, and Kościelisko) to the smog-covered valley basin of Zakopane.

The snobs from Warsaw and Cracow flaunt their brand new ski suits on **Krupówki Boulevard**, the main street in Zakopane. During the summer months, on days when bad weather discourages hiking, you can observe coffeehouse guests on Krupówki Boulevard looking determinedly relaxed as they do some "people-watching".

Zakopane's busy city center is architecturally unimpressive. Many restaurants, shops, cafés and the **Tatra Museum** (*Muzeum Tatrzańskie*) are located downtown. The museum displays the past culture and folklore of the shepherds and villages of Podhale in an impressive manner. The private **Władysław Hasior Art Gallery** (east of the center, via ul. Kościuszki) offers a contrasting program. The world-famous doyen of modern art, who died in 1999, displayed collages,

HIGH TATRA

which he assembled using everyday articles.

The characteristic architecture of the city deserves your attention. Zakopane was originally a Górale village dotted with typical peasant cabins similar to those still standing in the **ul. Kościeliska** (a side street off ul. Krupówki, running down the valley). In the second half of the 19th century, Cracow artists discovered Zakopane. One of these artists – the painter Stanislaw Witkiewicz – conceived a new architectural style. High, pointed roofs, special ornamental forms derived from Górale cabins, and wood as the main building material characterize the "Zakopane style." This design has evolved into a building style synonymous with Polish national architecture. However, the Zakopane style seldom appears anywhere outside of Podhale.

The oldest and finest examples of this architecture are displayed in two **villas** and a picturesque **chapel**. The villas are located in Koziniec in the southeast part of Zakopane and are called *Koliba*, ul. Kościeliska, and *Pod Jedlami*, ul. Droga na Antałówkę. The chapel was built in **Jaszczurówka**, an eastern suburb of Zakopane. If you are truly looking for authentic village architecture, a trip to **Chochołów** ❹, 15 kilometers northwest of Zakopane, is highly recommended. Old wooden houses line the streets with their gabled walls facing front.

*The High Tatra

The Tatra Mountain Range encompasses an area of 715 square kilometers of which 215 square kilometers lie in Poland. The highest point of the range is called Gerlachovský štít (Gerlach Peak) (2655 meters), and it is located on the Slovakian side. The higher eastern region is called the **High Tatra**. The West Tatra is slightly lower in elevation. Both Poland and Slovakia have designated their respective shares of the mountain range as national parks, for the distinctive flora and fauna were being increasingly endangered by reckless tourism. The vegetation

HIGH TATRA

of the Tatra range grows according to the characteristic climatic zones of a high elevation (deciduous and coniferous woods, mountain pine and above the elevation of 1800 meters the alpine growth). Swiss pine grows at the upper edge of the woodlands. You may spot some unusual animals, such as brown bears, wildcats, and lynx in the wooded areas, or marmots, chamois, and golden eagles around the alpine meadows.

Hikers and mountain lovers alike are drawn to this splendid, pristine scenery. During the summer, however, the lower mountain region is literally trampled on, and more often than not, you will have to stand in line for your turn to climb the famous Giewont Peak. The National Park Service has therefore reduced the number of overnight stays and prohibits hikers from leaving the marked hiking trails.

September is not only the best month weather-wise to explore the Tatra, but also the least crowded, for the hordes of tourists typical of the summer months slow to a trickle. Trail hikes leading to the peaks of Mt. Rysy (2499 meters), Mt. Giewont and Mt. Zawrat (2159 meters) are not recommended in the months of July and August. The West Tatra Mountains are much less crowded (with the exception of a few valleys). Beware that the climate conditions in the Tatra are unpredictable. Each year many unfortunate deaths are attributed to sudden weather changes or to imprudent tourists taking shortcuts off the marked trails. Often, the rescue actions carried out by the volunteer Tatra Rescue Unit (GOPR) are, unfortunately, too late.

Mountain climbers and hikers who have purchased the *Tatrzański Park Narodowy* map can choose from hundreds of trails and hikes. The shortest excursion starts in Zakopane and leads through the beautiful valleys of **Białego** and **Strążyska**. Both are easy to reach. From Zakopanes's city center, take ul. Do Białego or ul. Kasprusie. The road

Above: Gentiana asclepiadea – this colorful flower is at home in the High Tatra.

Information pages 132-133

TATRZAŃSKI NATIONAL PARK

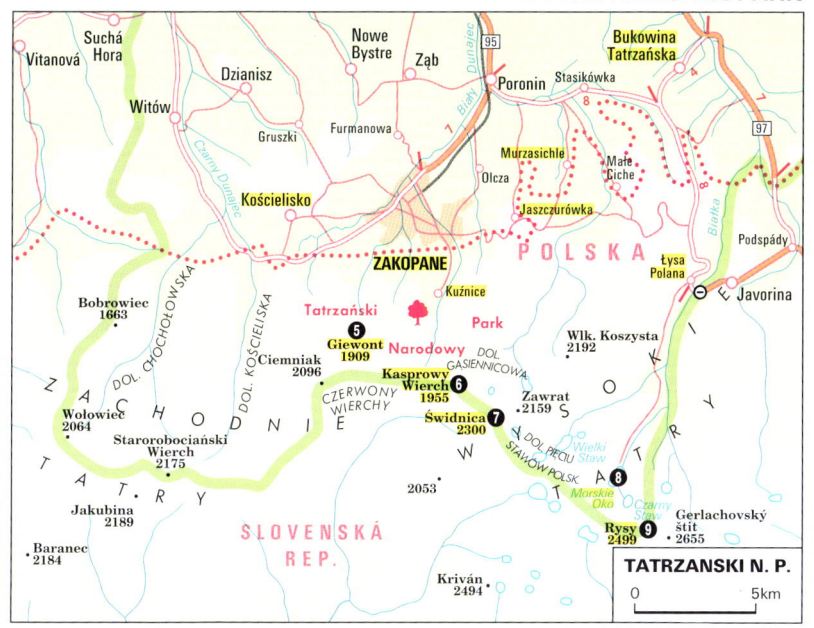

through Strążyska Valley converts into the congested trail leading to **Mt. Giewont ❺** (1909 meters) (trail marked red). Mt. Giewont towers directly above Zakopane, resembling a sleeping knight. The peak can also be reached from Kuźnice (parking lot) via Kalatówki and Polana Kondratowa (mountain lodging; trail marked blue).

The **West Tatra** mountain range lies west of Zakopane. These mountains are less steep than those in the High Tatra, and the mountain floor usually consists of limestone instead of granite. The two most beautiful valleys are the popular Kościeliska and Chochołowska valleys. Their mountain lodgings have been built in the typical Zakopane architectural style. At the south end of **Kościeliska Valley**, hikers approach the Onark mountain hut. From here, a trail marked yellow leads over a pass, Iwaniacka Przełęcz (1459 meters); to **Chochołowska Valley**. On a short side trip to the idyllic pond, Smreczyński, you may stir up a few black grouse (return trip on the same trail). The small wooden cabins dotting the countryside are reminders of the earlier presence of the shepherds, banished from the park in the 1950's because of the damage caused by the sheep. Nowadays, environmental considerations have changed, and a limited amount of grazing is being reconsidered.

The peak of **Kasprowy Wierch ❻** (1955 meters) rises into the sky on the border between the West and High Tatra. It can be comfortably reached via a suspended cable car from Kuźnice, a section of Zakopane. Reserve tickets for the ride in advance (cf page 133). From the cable car station on the mountain, a trail leads to the west across the mountain ridge of **Czerwony Wierchy.** Its rounded, rolling terrain, however, has frequently been a fatal trap for many a hiker (do not leave the trail marked red!) The soft slopes toward the North suddenly turn into abrupt precipices. To the east along the state borderline, the trails become increasingly steep. After three hours of hiking, the third peak, **Mt. Świdnica ❼** (2300 me-

Little Poland (Galicia)

Information pages 132-133

PIENINY

ters), can be climbed with the help of chains and footholds secured in the mountain walls. From this point, only experienced hikers and mountaineers should attempt the challenging climb. **Orla Perć** (*Eagle's Trail*) is marked red and leads in about six hours over several peaks eastward to Krzyżne Pass. From here, the trail marked yellow takes you down in another one or two hours, to either the east or the west. The view is breathtaking, but so are the precipices that dangerously open up beneath your feet. This impressive adventure is nothing for the fainthearted and lightheaded. The trail also has iron hand and footholds.

There are many paths leading from the Orla Perć trail, such as the two trails down into two of the most important valleys of the Tatra from Zawrat Pass (2159 meters) or Kozia Przełęcz to **Dolina Gąsiennicowa** and **Dolina Pięciu Stawów Polskich** (Valley of the Five Lakes). Mountain lodgings await the weary hiker. Don't expect much more than a space on the floor for your sleeping bag; however, no one may be turned away, even if they arrive late in the afternoon.

The Valley of the Five Lakes is named after the five lakes with deep blue water located here (actually there are six lakes, two of them being very small). Two trails proceed from this point (the yellow trail via Szpiglasowa is more difficult but less crowded and more scenic) to the last Polish valley to the east, where there is a large lake.

The **Morskie Oko** ❽ (meaning "eye of the ocean") is the largest and most beautiful of all the high-lying lakes in the Tatra. It is 51 meters deep and according to legend, connected to the Adriatic Sea.

Life is in full swing again at this spot because it can be easily reached by car from Zakopane. Park two kilometers south of the border crossing at Łysa

Right: Don't miss river rafting through the Dunajec Gorge.

Polana and walk the remaining nine kilometers to the lake, or take a horse-drawn carriage there.

Above Morskie Oko lies the 70-meter-deep **Czarny Staw** (Black Lake), and from here, you can follow the red signs taking you on a three-hour steep and precarious climb to the highest mountain in Poland, **Mt. Rysy** ❾ (2499 meters).

PIENINY MOUNTAINS AND *DUNAJEC GORGE

About 50 kilometers northeast of the High Tatra lies the **Pieniny** mountain range. On the way to Nowy Targ, you first come across a dam completed in 1994. The protest actions of environmental groups could not stop this controversial and (for many) absurd project. Villages with beautiful folk architecture were flooded as a result of the dam. The charm of the landscape was forever lost. The only thing that gained from the flooding is the **Niedzica Castle** ❿, which now has a beautiful reflection in the nearby reservoir. The Hungarian family Horvath built this castle at the beginning of the 14th century. At the beginning of the 17th century, the lower castle was added.

The border between Poland and Hungary ran along here. Later on, the border between Galicia and the Hungarian region of the Austro-Hungarian Empire was drawn at this place. This made Niedzica Polish as late as 1918. On the other side of the reservoir, on the historical Polish side, you can see the ruins of a royal border castle, **Czorsztyn**.

There is a retreat center for members of the art history association in Niedzica. Sometimes even the average weary traveler can stay overnight there. There is also the small **Museum of Spisz**. Spisz is the surrounding area of Niedzica, which for the most part belongs to Slovakia. The museum tells of a mysterious fortress secret. In the 16th century, the daughter of

Map page 127, Information pages 132-133

DUNAJEC GORGE

Tupac Amaru, the last of the legendary Inca rulers of Peru, sought protection here from Spanish assassins. In 1946, a quipu document (made of Inca knots) was discovered in the castle. It was supposed to give directions to the site of the Incas' lost treasures in Lake Titicaca. However, the rest of the story about the document remains in the dark.

Pieniny ⓫ is also a national park. It is a small, low limestone mountain range of great scenic charm. The main attraction is *****Dunajec Gorge**. The gorge can be crossed on a raft ride. This type of ride, offered from 9:00 a.m. to about 4:00 p.m., May through September, looks more dangerous than it really is. Even small children can participate in the ride over the rapids between the jagged mountains. Ten people are crowded together on a raft captained by a guaranteed humorous Pieniny Górale. The ride lasts approximately two hours from the villages of Kąty to Szczawnica.

The river twists and turns to such an extent that it is sometimes impossible to anticipate which on side of the mountain the raft will pass. The steep cliffs jutting out of the water and the dense forests that are home to the black storks create a romantic, adventurous atmosphere.

The **hiking trails** in the Pieniny mountains are worth your while. You can climb **Mt. Sokolica** (747 meters) by following the trail marked blue from Szczawnica, which includes a short ferry ride at first. At the top, you will have a fantastic, breathtaking picture postcard view upon the river.

The hike continues on **Mt. Trzy Korony** (Three Crowns, 981 meters) for another four hours. This peak is the highest in the Pieniny. The alert and knowledgeable hiker will recognize a type of juniper (*Juniperus Sabina*) growing that is native only to this area.

There is also a green lizard living here that is very rare in other areas of Poland. You should be sure to purchase a trail map of the *Pieniński Park Narodowy* (at one of the kiosks in Szczawinca or Krościenko).

Little Poland (Galicia)

ŁAŃCUT, PRZEMYŚL

BETWEEN CRACOW AND PRZEMYŚL

On the main road from Cracow to Lviv lies the city of **Rzeszów** ⑫. It has a population of 159,000 and is the largest city in southeastern Poland today, but has little to interest tourists. From Cracow, you reach the city of ***Łańcut** ⑬ where a castle of considerable importance is located. The castle was built by the Lubomirskis from 1629 to 1641 and remodeled several times over. In the 19th century, it was turned over to the Potocki familiy (after the Radziwiłłs the second most influential aristocratic family in Poland. Massive towers with fantastic roofs in front of the impressive castle dominate its exterior.

The castle is home of the **Museum of Interior Design**. Decorated according to the fashion of the 18th century, you can see Chinese rooms, a private theater, and

Above: Hay harvest in Krosno, west of Przemysl. Right: The castle of Przemysl serves as a theater today.

Turkish chambers – a Polish specialty. At the classical **riding arena,** you will discover the largest coach museum in Europe. Among the 50 exhibits dating back to the 18th and 19th century, there are state carriages, hunting wagons, and stagecoaches in every size and style imaginable. A side wing of the castle serves as a hotel. The **Synagogue** of Łańcut, recently restored as a museum, testifies to the active Jewish life in the cities of Galicia before the Holocaust. The synagogue was erected in 1760 and is located west of the castle near the entrance to the park. It represents the culture of the Jewish people, who once made up half of the urban population in many parts of this region. The synagogues of Lesko and Rzeszów, and above all the cemeteries of Lesko, Tarnów, Wiśnicz Nowy, Sieniawa and Leżajsk, are practically all that is left. Łańcut is just 70 kilometers from **Przemyśl** ⑭. Przemyśl is a picturesque city on the San River. Next to the castle, archaeologists have discovered relics from a church dating back to the 10th century, the oldest church in southern Poland. Przemyśl itself finally became Polish in 1340, but retains a significant Ukrainian minority. The city was built into a fortress in the 19th century. In the First World War, it was twice besieged, but played a key role in the defense against the attacks, comparable to that of Verdun. Today, the **forts** scattered within a 10-kilometer radius of the city are a popular tourist attraction. In the city the many churches, especially the cathedral, the castle and an intact Old Town, encourage the visitor to stroll around.

The most enchanting Renaissance castle in all of Poland is located not far from Przemyśl, in **Krasiczyn** ⓯ (1592-1614). Italian builder Galeazzo Appiani erected it for the Krasicki family. The castle presents a striking silhouette featuring four different towers and an arcaded courtyard. The façade appears yielding and softer by the use of antique designs and sgraffito motifs of the Polish kings. As in Łańcut, you should certainly consider staying overnight in the castle, which since 1998 has been operating as a comfortable hotel.

BIESZCZADY

For Poles, there is an almost magical quality to the sound of this name. In the 1960's, hippies and adventure seekers came to this sparsely inhabited region. They were lured by the unspoiled, natural countryside. It had no cultural monuments, no industry. You could wander for days without seeing another person. Of course, the situation has changed today.

The few villages, which have not increased in number, attract more tourists from year to year, who prefer comfortable hotels to tents and modest boarding houses. The designation of this region as a national park in the 1980's came just in time. The unique fauna and flora of the mountains were becoming increasingly endangered.

The Bieszczady is the only part of the East Carpathian mountain range to lie in Poland, and is composed of many ridges

BIESZCZADY

running from northwest to southeast with low valleys in between. Its typical feature are the open meadows on the mountain summits, the *połoniny*, with panoramic views. On hikes through the region, you may encounter the tree-dwelling snake Asclepius and maybe even brown bears, wild cats, lynx or wolves.

The mountains were home to a Ukrainian people called the Boyks not too long ago. Long after the Second World War, this group fought for Ukrainian independence, along with another Ukrainian group, the Lemks, under the leadership of the Ukrainian Insurgent Army. As collective punishment for this resistance, the village inhabitants were forcibly resettled in the new West Polish area in an action called "Operation Vistula." Only the beautiful Orthodox churches in **Smolnik**, **Równia**, **Ustianowa** and **Komańcza** bear witness to the lost culture.

Begin your exploration of the region in Sanok or in Lesko. **Sanok's** ⑯ pride is an ***Open Air Museum** featuring more than 100 buildings on an area of 38 hectares. Two beautiful, wooden Orthodox churches containing an outstanding icon collection are of special interest.

The captivating scenic countryside in **Lesko** ⑰ begins with a tour along the Bieszczady Loop, a 78-kilometer-long road, through Ustrzyki Dolne and Ustrzyki Górne. Use a good trail map and hike from Ustrzyki Górne into the ***Bieszczadzki National Park** ⑱. The most beautiful of the marked trails runs from the northwest over the peaks of Mt. Połonina Caryńska and Mt. Wetlińska to Mt. Wielka Rawka (in the border triangle of Poland, the Ukraine and Slovakia); and up to the peak of Mt. Tarnica, the highest mountain in the region (1346 meters). The red trail leads across Szeroki Wierch, Tarnica and Halicz to Rozsypaniec peak on the Ukrainian border. From here, a comfortable 10 kilometer-long road into the valley takes you back to Ustrzyki Górne (approximately seven hours).

LITTLE POLAND (GALICIA)

ZAKOPANE
☎ **(Zakopane and Podhale) 018**

IT Office, ul. Chramcówki 35, Tel. 2014000. **CIT Tatry**, ul. Kościuszki 17, Tel. 2012211, Fax 2066051. **Orbis Tourist Office**, ul. Krupówki 22, Tel. 2012238. Organizes excursions, raft ride down the Dunajec.

Kasprowy, Polana Szymoszkowa, Tel. 2014011 bis 20, Fax 2015272, www.orbis.pl/hot_kas.html. Above the city, view of the Tatra Mountains. Large, comfortable, with pool, nightclubs, etc. **Giewont**, ul. Kościuszki 1, Tel. 2012011 to -15, Fax 2012015, www.orbis.pl/hot_gie.html. **Gazda**, ul. Zaruskiego 2, Tel. 2015011, Fax 2015330; city center. Suitable for excursions into the National Park: **Biały Potok**, ul. Droga do Białego 7, Tel. 2014380. **Pan Tadeusz**, Droga do Białego 20, Tel. 2012228. **Telimena**, Droga do Białego 7 b, Tel. 2012228. Tip: Former **Recreation Complex of the Party**, c. 15 km west of the city, in the National Park, Polana Zgorzelisko 1, Tel. 2012051, Fax 2012052. Late communist charm, located in unsurpassed tranquility; restaurant, small ski lift. **DOM Turysty PTTK**, ul. Zaruskiego 5, Tel. 2063207, 2063281, Fax 2012358. **Youth Hostel**, ul. Nowotarska 45, Tel. 2066203. Open all year, very large. **Private rooms** through Orbis (Tel. 2012238), CIT Tatry (Tel. 2012211) and Gromada (ul. Zaruskiego 2). **Campgrounds**: Zakopane, ul. Żeromskiego, Tel. 2012256, Droga do Olczy 12, Tel. 2066250. **Mountain huts** in the **High Tatra**: Dolina Pięciu Stawów Polskich, Tel. 2077607; Dolina Roztoki, Tel. 2077442; Hala Gąsiennicowa, Tel. 2012633; Morskie Oko, Tel. 2077609. In the **West Tatra**: Hala Kondratowa, Tel. 2015214; Kalatówki, Tel. 2063644; Ornak (end of Kościeliskiej valley), Tel. 2070520; Polana Chochołowska, Tel. 2070510.

Snack bars and stands on ul. Krupówki, where highlanders (Górale) sell *Oscypki* (goat cheese). Stylish restaurants with "Górale" interior: **U Wnuka**, ul. Kościelska 8, Tel. 2066147. In an authentic peasants' hut. **Karczma Redykołka**, Kościelska 9, Tel. 2066332. Mutton. **Karczma Obrochtówka**, ul. Kraszewskiego 8, Tel. 2063987. Delicious potato pancakes (*placki ziemniaczane*).

Tatra Museum (Muzeum Tatrzańskie), ul. Krupówki 10, Tel. 2015205. Wed-Sun 9:00 a.m. – 3:00 p.m. (July-Aug until 4:30 p.m., also Tuesdays). **Galerie Władysław Hasior**, ul. Jagiellońska 18 b, Tel. 2066871. Wed, Thurs 1:00 p.m. – 7:00 p.m., Fri-Sun 9:00 a.m. – 3:00 p.m. **Muzeum Stylu Zakopańskiego** (Villa Koliba), ul. Kościelska 18, Tel. 2013602. Wed-Sun 10:00 a.m. – 2:30 p.m.

Map pages 122-123

LITTLE POLAND (GALICIA)

An unforgettable experience, even if you don't speak Polish: **Avant-garde Theater in Witkacy**. Teatr Witkacego, ul. Chramcówki 15, Tel. 2068297, www.witkacy.zakopane.pl.

Zakopane is the ideal starting point for hikes into the Tatra. The higher you stay (i.e. farther south, in Kuźnice, Rondo, Jaszczurówka) the better. Don't forget hiking boots, rain gear and the map "Tatrzański Park Narodowy"!

MOUNTAIN TRAINS AND CABLE CARS: Rack railroad on **Gubałówka**: Open all year, except end of April and October, in summer daily 7:30 a.m. – 9:00 p.m. Lift to **Kasprowy** in Kuźnice: December 15 – May 10 (7:30 a.m. – 4:00 p.m.), June 20 – October 20 (7:30 a.m. – 8:00 p.m.), due to the crowds and lines (winter and summer), you should book tickets 4 days ahead at an Orbis office.

GOPR (Volunteer Mountain Rescue Unit), Tel. 018/2063444.

FESTIVALS: **July**: Karol Szymanowski Festival with musical compositions of unjustifiably neglected composers of the turn of the 20th century (Villa Atma, ul. Kasprusie 19; also Museum: Tues-Sun 10:00 a.m. – 4:00 p.m). **September**: International song and dance festival "Autumn in the Tatra" (*Jesień w Tatrach*).

PIENINY ☎ 018

Szczawnica: **PTTK Office**, ul. Główna 1, Tel. 2622295, **Podhale Office**, ul. Główna 20, Tel. 2622370. **House of Art Historians** (Stowarzyszenie Historyków Sztuki, Dom Pracy Twórczej), Niedzica, in the castle, Tel. 2629489. **PTTK Hostel Orlica**, Szczawnica, ul. Pienińska 12, Tel. 2622248. Tourist information offices also arrange room reservations. Many **workers' hostels**, such as Nawigator, ul. Zdrojowa 28, Tel. 2622346, Fax 2622271).

River rafting on the Dunjec, from Kąty (at Sromowce) to Szczawnica, approx. 2 hours. May – September from 8:00 a.m. – 4:00 p.m. Continuous departures when a raft is full. Reservations: Tel. 2629793.

Museum in **Castle Niedzica**: May-Sept. 9:00 a.m. – 5:00 p.m; off-season Tues-Sun 10:00 a.m. – 4:00 p.m.

HIKING: In Pieniński National Park. Starting point: Szczawnica, Krościenko, Sromowce, Czorsztyn. The hikers' map "Pieniński Park Narodowy" can be purchased everywhere.

ŁAŃCUT, PRZEMYŚL ☎ Rzeszów (Łańcut) 017, Przemyśl 016

Rzeszów: ul. Asnyka 6, Tel. 8524612. Przemyśl: ul. Władycze 3, Tel. 6751664.

Budimex, Rzeszów, ul. Podwisłocze 42, Tel. 626835, Fax 627741, **Hotel Rzeszów**, al. Cieplińskiego 2, Tel. 8523441, Fax 8533389.

Zamkowy, Łańcut (in the castle), ul. Zamkowa 1, Tel. 2252672. **Marko**, Przemyśl, ul. Lwowska 36 a, Tel./Fax 6789272. **Zamkowy**, Krasiczyn (in the castle), Tel. 016/6718321, Fax 6718316. **Krokus**, Przemyśl, ul. Michiewicza 47, Tel. 6785127. **Youth Hostel**, ul. Lelewela 6, Tel. 6706145. **Camping ground**, Wybrzeże Piłsudskiego 8 a, Tel. 6785642.

Zamkowa, Łańcut, ul. Zamkowa 1, Tel. 2252805, **Pizzeria Veneziana**, Łańcut, ul. Piłsudskiego 8, Tel. 2253414. **Eger**, Przemyśl, ul. Grunwaldzka 72, Tel. 6709283.

ŁAŃCUT: **Castle Museum** and Carriage Exhibit: April-Oct Tues-Sat 9:00 a.m. – 2:30 p.m., Sun 9:00 a.m. – 4.00 p.m., Nov-March from 10:00 a.m. Former **Synagogue**, Pl. Sobieskiego: June 15 to September 30, Tues-Sun 10:30 a.m. – 4:30 p.m. Closed Oct 1 - June 14.

Bus Tour to Lviv, in the Ukraine: hourly from 6:00 a.m. (2 hours). Ticket sales at the bus station. Dworzec PKS, ul. Czanieckiego, Tel. 6785435. A visa is required.

FESTIVALS: **Łańcut**, May: Chamber Music Festival. **Przemyśl**, May: Polish festival of street bands.

BIESZCZADY ☎ 013

PTTK Office, Sanok, ul. 3 Maja 2, Tel. 4632171. **Sanok**, Autosan, Sanok, ul. Lipińskiego 113, Tel. 46350221. **Turysta**, Sanok, ul. Jagiellońska 13, Tel. 46330922. **Dom Turysty PTTK**, Sanok, ul. Mickiewicza 29, Tel. 46331439, 46331013. **Campgrounds**, Sanok, ul. Wojska Polskiego, Tel. 46330257. **Pension Zamek**, Lesko (in the castle), ul. Piłsudskiego 7, Tel. 4696268. **Campgrounds**: Nad Sanem, Tel. 4696689. **Dom Wycieczkowy Laworta**, Ustrzyki Dolne, ul. Zielona 12, Tel. 4611177 to -8. In the mountains: **Leśny Dwór**, Wetlina, Tel./Fax 4696454. Quiet pension in the Bieszczady heartland. **Mountain lodging**: **Pod Małą Rawką** and **Połonina Wetlińska**; beautiful location. With the exception of Jabłonki, Lesko and Wetlina, all **Youth Hostels** (Sanok, Czarna, Cisna, Komańcza, Rzepedź, Solina) are open only in the summer. **PTTK Hostel** in Ustrzyki Górne (Tel. 4611036, extension 104). **Campgrounds** in Solina (Tel. 4691833) and Ustrzyki Górne (Tel. 4611036, ask for extension 50).

Jagiellońska, Sanok, ul. Jagiellońska 49, Tel. 4631208. French, Italian and Asian cuisine. **Koliba**, Lesko, Rynek 8, Tel. 4696303, 4698088. **Zajazd u Kmity**, Podstołów bei Lesko, Tel. 4698176. Among the sparse offerings in Ustrzyki Dolne, **Bieszczadzka**, Rynek 19, Tel. 4611072, is the best choice.

Open Air Museum ("skansen"), Sanok, ul. Traugutta 3: daily in the summer from 8:00 a.m. – 6:00 p.m., in the winter 9:00 a.m. – 3:00 p.m.

GOPR (Volunteer Mountain Rescue Unit, Tel. 4632204, 4634611.

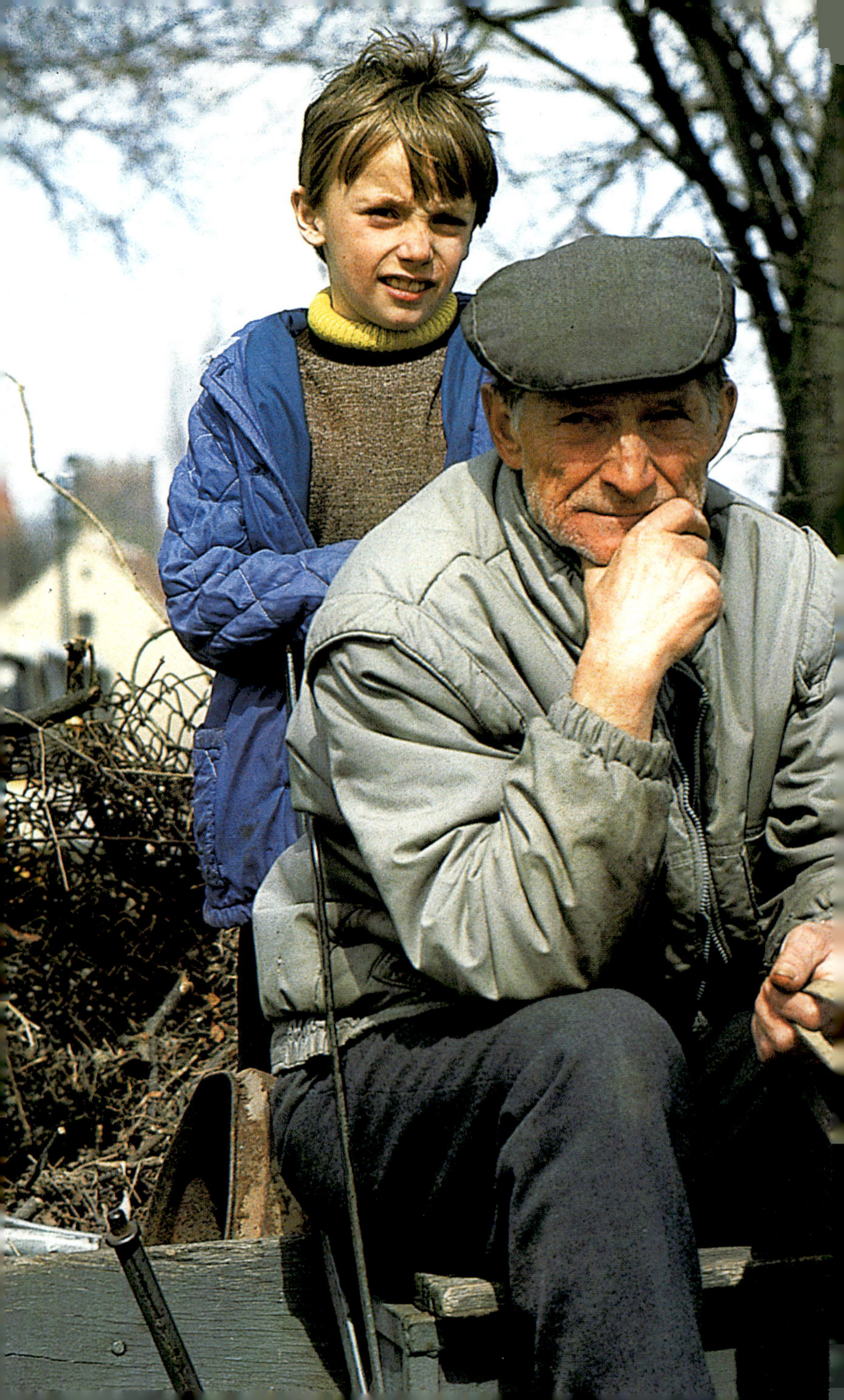

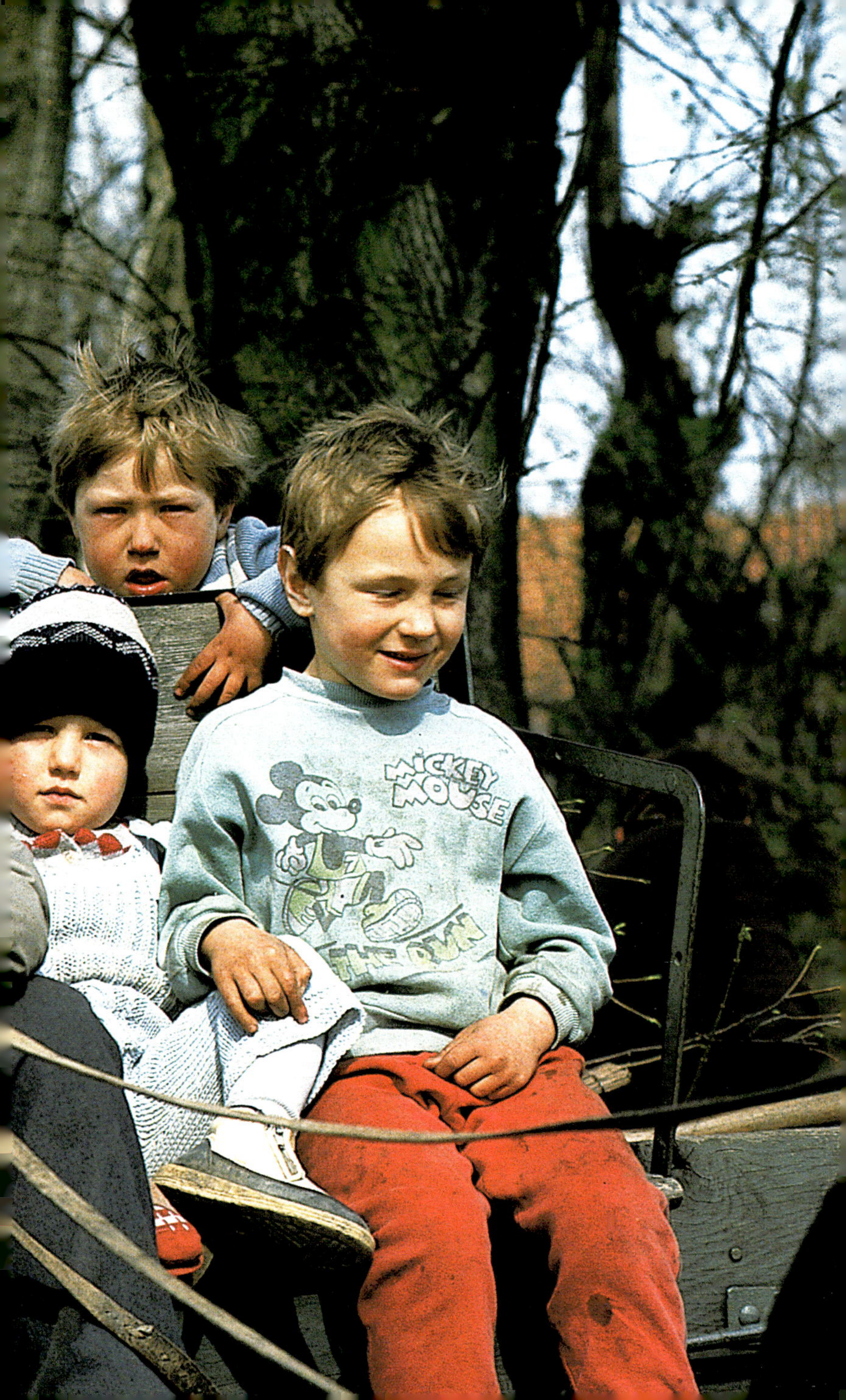
MICKEY MOUSE

SILESIA

SILESIA
From the Karkonosze to the Coal Barons

WROCŁAW
KŁODZKO
SWIDNICA
THE KARKONOSZE MOUNTAINS
OPOLE COUNTRY
UPPER SILESIA

Contrary to popular belief, Silesia (Śląsk) is not typified by factory smokestacks and gray skies, but by numerous national parks in the Sudeten mountains. Nor is it a region of of overcrowded concrete housing, but rather of idyllic villages with cultural monuments of European significance. Nationalistic tensions are not dominant, but there are richly diverse cultural backgrounds. The 400 kilometer-long Odra River (English: Oder) is the backbone of this region.

Silesia offers the visitor metropolitan flair in Wrocław, where the market square is doubtless one of the most beautiful in all of Europe. To the south is the 300 kilometers long Sudeten mountain range, the highest section of which is the Karkonosze (or Giant) Mountains that form the border to the Czech Republic. The bare, rounded summits are as unforgettable as the sweeping views from the highest peak, Mt. Śnieżka (1602 meters).

History of the Region

There is hardly a region in Europe which has changed its national identity

Previous pages: A day outing with Grandfather in Myslakowice. Left: Left undamaged by the war: the east gable of Wrocław's city hall, with its impressive, ornate Gothic openwork.

more often than Silesia. In the first centuries A.D., a Germanic people lived in this region, but they started moving westward by the 6th century. Soon after, Slavic peoples settled in their place. Since the 10th century, Silesia has been part of Poland, maintaining a bishopric in Wrocław (formerly Breslau). Around 1138, when Poland began to be divided into individual principalities, the Silesian princes gradually drifted away from their close ties to Cracow. The Silesians incorporated the chivalrous customs of the Germans, who were part of the Holy Roman Empire, and by the 13th century, more courts spoke German than Polish. The spread of the German language encouraged German-speaking settlers to immigrate to the east by the thousands.

Silesia, whose principalities had been increasingly paying homage to the Bohemian Crown, became part of the Habsburg Monarchy in 1526. Silesia was not just another of the many Austrian provinces but rather one of the most prosperous, particularly due to the flourishing trade of its cities and its booming weaving industries. In 1741, when Austria had to surrender Silesia to Prussia, it suffered a severe political and economical defeat.

At that time the region was divided into Upper and Lower Silesia. While Lower Silesia (including Wrocław) was primar-

WROCŁAW

ily Protestant and, since the 17th century, for the most part German-speaking, Upper Silesia has remained Catholic and multilingual, even to this day. Most Upper Silesians spoke Polish (with the exception of the upper classes and many city residents) or Slonzak, a Polish dialect interspersed with German, which was disparagingly known as "watery Polish."

In 1921, a vote was held on where to draw the boundary of Upper Silesia. Approximately forty percent of the population voted to annex Silesia to Poland. As a result of this plebiscite, and the ensuing military conflicts (the Third Silesian Uprising), Silesia was again divided. Poland annexed one third and Germany took over two thirds of the region. After this redrawing of the border, which was considered by many to be arbitrary and unjust, many German-speaking citizens remained on the Polish side, especially in the towns of Katowice and Chorzów. On the other side, much of the rural ethnic Polish population around Opole was now on the German side of the border. At the end of the Second World War, almost all of Silesia was surrendered to Poland, and the majority of the German-speaking Silesians were expelled from the country.

Today the exact boundary between Upper and Lower Silesia is even harder to discern. Upper Silesia (Górny Śląsk) is comprised chiefly of the industrial center around Katowice. Further to the west lie Opolszcsyzna (Opole Country) and Dolny Śląsk (Lower Silesia), around Wrocław. Silesia has a homogenous Polish population with the exception of the residents of the villages and towns around Opole, where the Upper Silesians were allowed to stay after 1945. The German minority in this region is numbered at approximately 300,000.

WROCŁAW

Wrocław ❶, located on the Odra River, is the capital of Silesia. With a population of 640,000, it is the fourth largest city in Poland. Today it has more or less the same population as before the Second World War, yet the makeup of this population has a complete renewal. In 1945, Poles, who had been driven out of this region during the war, were returning and replacing the expelled Germans. These Poles still had a love and longing in their hearts for the Polish city of Lviv, which they had had to leave because of the Soviet takeover. This is presumably the reason why Wrocław still exudes an exotic flair, though the lilting eastern accent has gradually vanished with successive generations.

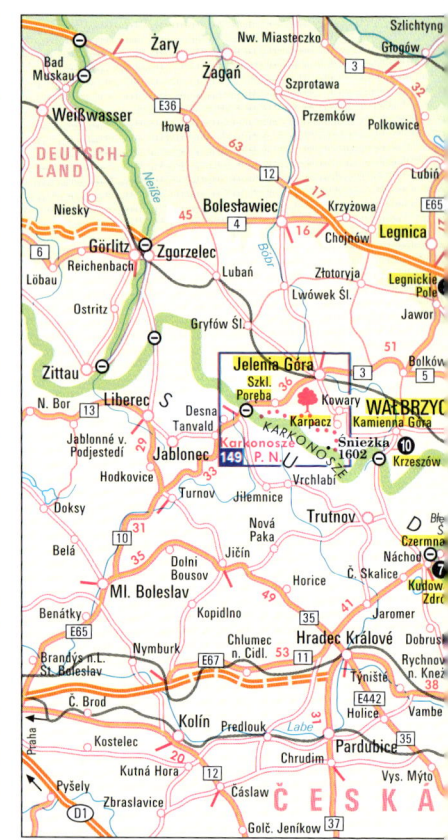

Priding itself on its university and many other institutions of higher educa-

SILESIA

tion (a total of 40,000 students), its museums, numerous modern theaters, the largest Polish library (the Ossoliński Library, brought over from Lviv), as well as world-renowned classic and jazz festivals, Wrocław is ranked third directly behind Cracow and Warsaw in the quality of its cultural life. The City Hall, the Racławice Panorama, the cathedral, and Centenary Hall draw visitors by the thousands. On sunny summer days, tourists and locals enjoy in the many garden cafés at the newly renovated market square. Wrocław is known as the "green city" due to it extensive parks and gardens.

Despite this pleasant and amiable side of the city, you cannot help but notice the randomness with which Stalinist architecture and socialistic housing have been constructed right next to old architectural monuments. Many areas (Plac Dominikański, Plac Powstańców Warszawy) resemble bomb craters, which will slowly but surely be filled with shopping centers, hotel complexes and similar buildings.

History

It is not exactly clear when the first settlement occurred at the present location of Wrocław. There is evidence that a Slavic tribe, the Ślężanie, settled on the Cathedral Island (Ostrów Tumski) as early as the ninth century. In 1000 AD, a bishopric was established here, under the auspices of the Archbishopric Gniezno

WROCŁAW

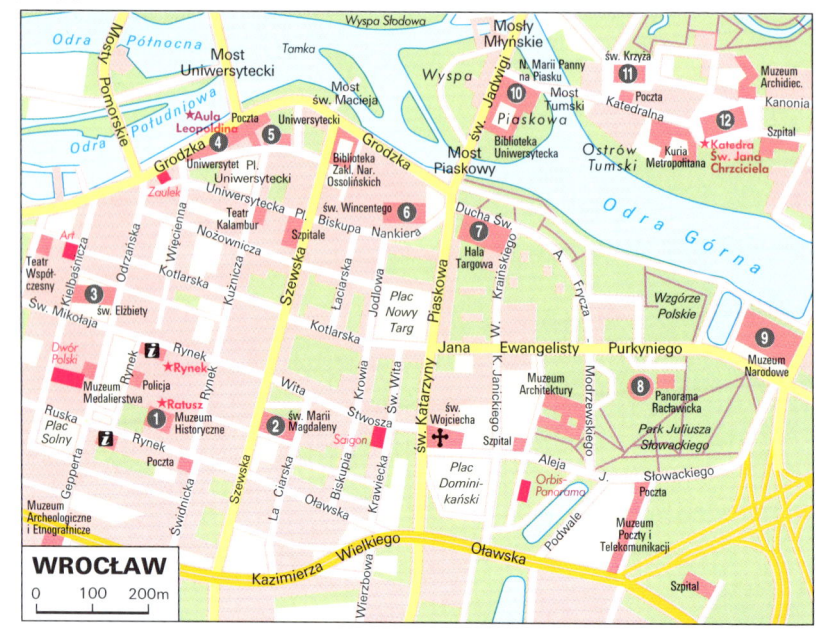

near Poznań. With this the Polish state secured its claim to Silesia and maintained its stance against Bohemia. In 1226 when *Wratislavia* (Wrocław's Latin name) was endowed with a city charter, Germans settled on the southern banks of the Odra River. The Slavic residence of the Polish Piasts was to the north. In the following centuries, this flourishing economic center, located along the Nuremberg – Cracow – Kiev trade route, experienced its prime. In the 19th century Wrocław, the capital of the Prussian province Silesia, developed into an elegant metropolis possessing economic zest and enjoying a vibrant cultural life.

This prosperity ended abruptly with the atrocities of 1945. In a three-month attempt to defend the city against attack, seventy percent of the historical buildings and architecture was reduced to rubble. Entire streets were destroyed in order to enlarge the field of defensive fire. At the

Right: A look at the fantastic interior vaulted ceiling of the Gothic city hall in Wrocław.

present site of Plac Grunwaldzki where the area had been leveled off, an airstrip was constructed. The irony of the story is that from this airstrip only a single plane ever took off. The German commanding officer, *Gauleiter Hanke,* escaped with a plane after having given orders to defend the city to the very last man.

Wrocław (then Breslau) surrendered on May 6, 1945 after 170,000 civilians had lost their lives. After the remaining German residents were expelled between 1945 and 1947, Breslau's name was changed to Wrocław. In December 1948, at the World Congress of Intellectuals, Pablo Picasso painted his famous dove of peace, which has become the international peace symbol. It seemed to him that the ruins of the city had admonished him to do so.

Wrocław's latest misforune was the was the 1997 flood, the worst of the century. Many newly constructed areas and streets were covered in water up to seven meters deep. The authorities had failed to save the city, but the commitment and un-

MARKET SQUARE

tiring efforts of the city residents alone saved the Old Town, Cathedral and Sand Islands, as well as the residential areas northeast of the city from the flooding.

*Market Square (Rynek)

Despite the many disasters that Wrocław has suffered through the years, it offers the visitor a number of interesting sights, which rank among the best of Europe. The starting point for a tour of the city is the **Market Square**, whose large size (207 x 172 meters) gives you an inkling of the status the city once had. Its old-world name "ring" from the Polish word *rynek* (from which the word for market squares originated) more describes its character. At one time, a ring road encircled a block of Cloth Halls, public buildings and small stores.

These buildings later made way for residences, to which the *City Hall ❶ is now adjoined. Maintaining its original appearance, the City Hall dates back to the years between 1343 and 1528. The east gable of the building was remarkably spared from damage during the war and is truly a prime example of medieval architecture. The artistically elegant, decorative openwork may remind you of the French flamboyant style (named after its resemblance to the design of leaping flames). The small gnomes or demons on the windowsills are fascinating and have an apothropaic function – evil should be frightened away at the sight of itself. The only element that was later added to the gable is the remarkable astronomical clock dated 1580.

You should not miss a visit to the city hall's extraordinary dining room, council chambers and Knights' Hall with their fantastic vaulted ceilings. You should have a look at the Museum of City History exhibits, which will also give you an idea of the beauty of the city before its destruction 1945.

To the south of city hall is the entrance to the *Piwnica Świdnicka* (Świdnica cellar), where you can indulge yourself in the pleasures of a beer as they did hun-

Information pages 153-155

CHURCH OF ST MARY MAGDALENE

dreds of years ago. While the tasty beer originally came from the city of Świdnica (formerly Schweidnitz), you will now find a *Piast* from Wrocław or an *EB* from Elbląg smoothly flowing down the throats of happy revelers.

A statue of the comedy writer Graf Aleksander Fredro, who was expelled from the city of Lviv, sits in solitary splendor above the market. His **memorial** dating from the 19th century took over the memorial site of Frederick the Great after the war. Here, on the west side of the market, are the most beautiful of the city's restored town houses. One of them, the ***Dwór Wazów*** (Vasa Court) has been turned into an elegant restaurant and luxurious hotel (Hotel *Dwór Polski*).

Among a row of Renaissance and Baroque houses, one modern ten-story building stands out. This is not a Polish addition built after 1945 as many tourists complain, but is a **bank** built from 1929 to 1930 when skyscraper fever had hit the country. The plan was to cover the Old Town with skyscrapers, but luckily this never happened. In the meantime, the tall art-decobank has been put on the preservation list of historical monuments.

It is just a short walk from the ring street to the **St. Mary Magdalene Church** ❷ (*Kościół św. Marii Magdaleny*) whose south façade exhibits an especially precious architectural piece, the most beautiful **Romanesque Portal** in Poland (12th century). It came from the old Benedictine monastery Ołbin, at the edge of town which was torn down in the 16th century. The archivolt figures, whose origins are said to lie in southern France, represent the life of Jesus Christ.

The Bank of the Odra River in the Old Town

Proceeding towards the Odra River, you will pass the Gothic **Church of St.**

Above: The Baroque and Renaissance façades of Wrocław houses testify to the city's former importance. Right: The magnificent entrance to the Aula Leopoldina.

142   *City map page 140, Information pages 153-155*

AULA LEOPOLDINA

Elizabeth ❸ (*Kościół św. Elżbiety*) with the highest steeple in the city. From here, continue to the awesome main building of the **University** ❹. The university was established and endowed in 1702 by the Emperor Leopold I and was formerly a Jesuit place of higher education. By 1810, it had expanded into the University of Silesia, incorporating the faculties of the University of *Viadrina* in Frankfurt on the Oder because this institute had been closed. After the fall of the Berlin wall in 1989, the Viadrina University was reestablished at its original location as a German-Polish university.

The most important part of the Wrocław campus is the **Collegium Maximum** (1728-1740). If you enter through the monumental south portal (figuratively depicting the cardinal virtues of justice, courage, wisdom and moderation), you will be led into the *Aula Leopoldina (assembly hall). Unfortunately, the assembly hall featuring a Baroque composition of architecture, fresco paintings and sculptures (1731 – 1732) has lost some of its cultural wealth. The round portraits of those who had well served this place of learning fell victim to a brazen robbery but have, however, been replaced with copies.

This assembly hall, elaborately decorated with gold, still radiates an atmosphere of stateliness and splendor, which is emphasized by the muted lighting. Besides the rich stucco work, you will be impressed by the ceiling fresco of the apotheosis or deification of heavenly wisdom. All this makes a perfect setting for special occasions and ceremonies, such as the awarding of honorary doctorates or the conferring of professorships.

Walking along the Odra River, you will first pass the Baroque **Jesuit Church** ❺ (*Kościół Uniwersytecki*), which serves as the church of the University. Further along, you will come across the Gothic **St. Vincent's Church** ❻ (*Kościól św. Wincentego*), where the Greek-Catholic Ukrainians, who settled here in 1947, hold their services. The icons and the Orthodox music build an atmospheric contrast to the Gothic interior of the building. Finally you reach the Neogothic **Market Hall** ❼. The hall's interior is certainly worth viewing because of its bold, daring construction (1908), and the wide range of food offered for sale.

Finally, you will reach a round modern building, which is the highlight of every Wrocław school field trip. Displayed inside this building is the famous **Panorama Painting of the Battle of Racławice** ❽ (1893-1894). The giant painting portrays the victory of the Polish rebells over the Russians in 1794 under the leadership of the Polish hero, Tadeusz Kościuszko, who had been an adjutant of George Washington during the American Revolution. Impressively depicted are the fighting peasants who, with scythes in their hands, won the battle for Poland.

The panorama type of painting was especially popular in the second half of the 19th century. It could be spread out in a

CATHEDRAL ISLAND

round room or rotunda and gave the impression of being three-dimensional. The painting of the Battle of Racławice was originally from Lviv and was brought to Wrocław after 1944. It was first exhibited in its new home no earlier than 1985 because of the concern that the picture could provoke resentment against the Russians. The viewing (with a recorded commentary in three foreign languages) takes about thirty minutes.

Reserve an afternoon tour early in the morning to avoid a long wait to get in. You can visit the neighboring **National Museum** ❾ *(Muzeum Narodowe)* while waiting. The exceptional collection of medieval Silesian stone and wood sculptures (for example, the tombstone of Duke Henry III Probus) is one of the best parts of the exhibit.

Cathedral Island

Ostrów Tumski, formerly **Cathedral Island** (but no longer an island since one of the arms of the Odra River has since been filled in), and **Sand Island** (*Wyspa Piaskowa*) were the cradle of the city. The ducal residence was located at this spot, and today there are seven Gothic churches still standing here.

Of special interest is the church of **St. Mary on the Sand** ❿ (*Kościół św. Marii Panny na Piasku*) with an unconventional spring vault in the side aisles. The contrast between the old interior furnishings with numerous Gothic winged altars and the modern glass windows is striking. This does not detract whatsoever from the beauty of the church.

A few steps away is the elegant **Holy Cross Church** ⓫ (*Kościół Św. Krzyża*; 1288-1400). This church has two floors, which is unusual in the Gothic style. The upper floor housed the tombs of the dukes; religious services open to the public were regularly held on the ground floor.

The city's most important religious building is the **★Cathedral of John the Baptist** ⓬ (*Katedra św. Jana Chrzciciela*). It is an impressive Gothic basilica with a twin tower façade. Construction began in the 10th century. Even if time is short and you feel you have reached the saturation point with the many Wrocław churches, do take a look at the three chapels of the chancel gallery. While the **St. Elisabeth's Chapel** (1680-1700; to the south) represents a fine example of Italian high Baroque, the **St. Mary's Chapel** (center) with the tombstone of a bishop from Wrocław, made by the Nuremberg metal caster Peter Vischer, is completely Gothic. The oval **Elector's Chapel** (1716-1724) is the most prominent work of the Viennese royal architect Johann Bernard Fischer von Erlach. The marble bust of Cardinal Friedrich of Hesse-Darmstadt located above the portal of the St. Elisabeth Chapel is among the most prominent and valuable of the art works. It came from the workshop of Gian Lorenzo Bernini around the year 1668.

Outside the City Center

South of the city center is the **Jewish Cemetery** (*Cmentarz Żydowski*; ul. Ślężna), which was established in the year 1856. It covers an area of approximately four hectares. A number of famous people were buried here, among them Ferdinand Lassalle, who was born in Wrocław in 1825. He was a forerunner of the first Social Democrats and founder of the German labor movement, the General German Workers' Association. This cemetery is considered one the of most beautiful in Europe. It has tall trees and artistically impressive gravestones originating from the turn of the 20th century. The cemetery brings to mind how

Right: The most important sacral building in Wrocław is the Cathedral of St. John the Baptist.

AROUND WROCŁAW

properous and influential the residents, including the Jewish minority, had been before the unfathomable horrors of the Holocaust began.

Another witness to the former importance of the city lies east of the city center at **Szczytnicki Park**. The Centenary Hall ***Hala Ludowa**, was built by Max Berg on the occasion of the centennial anniversary (1913) of the wars of independence against Napoleon. This mammoth building's architecture was ahead of its time. It's dome measures 65 meters in diameter and is constructed of reinforced concrete. The dome was at that time the second largest in the world after the Roman Pantheon. As you look at it, you can well imagine that the Breslau Academy of Arts, with such members as Hans Scharoun and Hans Poelzig, was one of the most important centers of modern architecture in the 1920's. Ask at the tourist information center at the market place if some cultural event or performance is scheduled in the Centenary Hall, for example "Carmen." This could be the crowning finale of your visit to the city of Wrocław.

Around Wrocław

Trzebnica ❷, 25 kilometers north of Wrocław, is famous for its pilgrimages to the burial site of the patron saint of Silesia, Hedwig (canonized in 1267). The wife of the Silesian Duke Henry I the Bearded (Henryk Brodaty), she founded the first **Cistercian convent** in Silesia in 1202. After having given birth to the Duke's seven children and after the Duke's death, she decided to enter a convent to live a life of asceticism, and here she died in 1243.

The convent church, built in the first half of the 13th century, was remodeled during the Baroque period. The late Romanesque **west portal**, portraying King David playing an instrument and Bathsheba posing left next to the entrance, belongs to one of the more interesting parts of the church. In front of the main altar, you will find the **double tomb**

KŁODZKO

(1680) of Henry I and Conrad von Feuchtwangen, Grand Master of the Teutonic Order, who died here during a journey. To the right, **St. Hedwig's Chapel** (1680) adjoins the chancel and holds the tomb of the saint. Erected in the year 1268, it is considered the first building constructed in pure Gothic style in Poland.

West of Wrocław, you can take a day trip to **Legnickie Pole** ❸ located near Legnica (62 kilometers). In 1241, the famous Battle of Legnica (Liegnitz) took place between the Mongolians and the Polish-German troops under the Silesian Prince Henry II the Pious (Henryk Pobożny). A son of Hedwig, he died on the battlefield at Legnica. After the defeat of the Europeans, a pure coincidence saved the Western World from a devastating end. The news of the death of the Mongolian emperor in far-off Karakorum made the Mongolian leader Batu withdraw his troops from the area to return and play a part in the selection of the emperor's successor.

Visitors are fascinated by a huge *****Benedictine Abbey** located across from a small Gothic church holding a **Battle Museum.** The convent church was built by Kilian Ignaz Dientzenhofer from 1727 to 1731 and was dedicated to Saint Hedwig. A masterpiece, the architectural style, in which a straight line is hard to find, is called "ultra Baroque." The Dientzenhofers were masters in this field. The façade with its two towers has alternating concave and convex curves, and the interior consists of diagonal girders and trusses gracefully flowing together.

The frescoes of Cosmas Damian Asam complete the Baroque interior. For example, one scene shows Hedwig who recognizes her dead son on the battlefield by his six toes. As well, you can see Mongolian soldiers swinging dragonheads from

Right: Harvest time in Silesia. Work by hand is still necessary.

which "a stinking smell came," as the medieval chronologist Długosz reported.

The third excursion leads you to the southeast where, between Wrocław and Opole, the city of **Brzeg** ❹ is located. The city's monumental *****castle** (1541-1560) has an elaborate gate, considered to be the principle work in the Renaissance style in Silesia. Two rows of busts, one above the other, portray the Polish kings and dukes of the Piast Dynasty (top) and the related princes of Silesian (bottom). Sculptures of Duke George II and his wife Barbara are located beneath the ancestral line. The museum-like interior is also worth seeing.

The castle has a three-story courtyard arcade that is the work of Italians Giacomo and Francesco Parr. Only the courtyard was destroyed (with the exception of a single arcade) in the Seven Years War (1757 – 1764). The castle resembles the Polish castle Wawel in Cracow. These Polish features may be why the authorities decided to have the courtyard arcade restored in 1970.

EN ROUTE IN LOWER SILESIA

Kłodzko

Kłodzko ❺ is located about 90 kilometers south of Wrocław in the center of the Kłodzko Vaslley, *Kotlina Kłodzka*. The ridges of the Sudeten Mountains surround it on all sides. During the course of history, this region, called the Duchy of Glatz (Kłodzko), belonged at times to Bohemia before it fell to Prussia along with Silesia in 1742. On the map, the region is easy to spot as an area shaped like a rhombus reaching into the Czech Republic.

The **Stone Bridge** in Kłodzko from the 14th century brings Bohemia to mind. With its Baroque sculptures, the bridge looks very slike the little sister of the Charles Bridge in Prague. Next to the **City Hall**, the **Fortress of Frederick II**

ŚWIDNICA

is the biggest attraction in the town. The fortress features bastions and underground tunnels and facilities. It is also home to a small fire brigade museum.

The many spas made the region around Kłodzko well known even before the Second World War. Today, nothing much has changed, except that the German word "Bad" (spa) has been replaced by the Polish word "Zdrój." Among the traditional spas are **Duszniki Zdrój** ❻, where the Chopin Festival is held every August; and **Kudowa Zdrój** ❼, located directly on the border to the Czech Republic. A macabre curio awaits you in a northern suburb of Kłodzko called **Czermna**. A chapel here, built in 1776, has walls and ceilings completely covered with human skulls – those of soldiers killed in the Thirty Years and the Silesian Wars.

Kłodzko is a good place to start trips into the **Góry Stołowe** mountains. The Polish name means "table mountains" and accurately describes this unusual geological formation. The mountains rise up incredibly steeply and their summits are quite flat. Marvelous hiking destinations are the Szczeliniec (919 meters) or the natural reserve Błędne Skały, where you have a wonderful view to the west. Here you can hike through a labyrinth of stone, which has taken on fantastic shapes over time due to erosion (trail marked red).

Świdnica, Książ, Krzeszów

The majestic town houses and the **St. Stanislaus and St.Wenzel's Church** (*Kościół śś. Stanisława i Wacława*), with the highest tower in all of Silesia (104 meters), testify to the former importance of **Świdnica** ❽. The city was a flourishing center of beer brewing, textile weaving and merchandise exchange with commercial interests stretching all the way to Russia.

Near the city center there is a unique monument, the Protestant ***Trinity Peace Church** (*Kościół protestancki Trójcy Świętej*). This church will even in-

KSIĄŻ CASTLE

Above: Hiking in the Karkonosze Mountains – a short rest before the next climb.

terest those who are tired of art. According to regulations of that time, the church was supposed to have been Built outside the city limits, made of wood, clay, sand and straw and should have had no steeples. It was also supposed to have been erected within a year's time. Those were the strict conditions under which Catholic Vienna, in 1648, granted the Silesian Protestants of Silesia permission to build three so called "peace churches" (two are still standing – next to Świdnica Jawor). The contrast between the modest half-timbered construction style and the magnificence of the interior is impressive. Yet, the elaborate interior is hardly to be expected in a Protestant church. The gold from the altar, pulpit and organ frankly seems to smother the nave, which was constructed to hold 7500 persons.

There is not much to draw you to the big city of **Wałbrzych** ❾ with its coal-mines and coke plants, except for the huge **Książ castle**. The castle is in a scenic park setting at the south edge of the city. The huge complex featuring 415 halls is a conglomeration of all architectural styles starting with the Gothic period when Prince Bolko I had begun building the high fortress.

From 1507 until 1944 the castle belonged to the Hochberg family (the owners of Pszczyna, cf page 152), who in the 17th and 18th centuries remodeled it into a castle. In 1944, while it was being remodeled to seve as a residence for Hitler, parts of the interior were destroyed. During the years immediately after the Second World War, the castle stood vacant and soon almost every house in the region owned a small piece of furniture from its chambers. The castle has since been renovated and is now a museum, hotel and convention center.

On your way from Wałbrzych to the Karkonosze Mountains, you will soon come across the town of **Krzeszów** ❿ located south of Kamienna Góra and a rewarding destination. In the complex of

KARKONOSZE NATIONAL PARK

the *Benedictine Monastery (1242-1292; later a Cistercian monastery), a twin-towered church built in early in the 18th century dominates the scene. The church has an immense interior, and east of its apse, is the Dukes' Chapel where the Dukes of Świdnica, the Bolkos, are buried.

The monastery's demonstration of might, chiseled in stone, is probably not as inspiring as the quaint St. Joseph's Church (*Kościół św. Józefa*) located in the immediate vicinity of the abbey. Michael Willmann, a Protestant from Königsberg (now Kaliningrad), who converted to Catholicism and spent 35 years as a monk in the monastery Lubiąż, created a fantastic fresco sequence here (1692-1695). The scenes from the life of the young and attractive spouse of the Virgin Mary come alive through the use of brilliant colors and daring, almost impressionistic, brush strokes. In recognition of this talent, Willmann has rightly been given the name, "the Rembrandt of Silesia."

*THE KARKONOSZE MOUNTAINS

The highest section of the Sudeten, the **Karkonosze Mountains**, also known as the Giant Mountains, is an outstanding vacation destination. The mountains are characterized by unsual flat, rounded summits that rise to an impressive 1602 meters. They are also the home of the legendary mountain gnome, Liczyrzepa or Rubezahl. Overnight accommodation can be found, for example, at **Jelenia Góra** ⓫, in the Kotlina Jeleniogórska Valley. This basin is surrounded on four sides by mountain ridges. Jelenia Góra is the largest town in the region. You are closer to the mountains if you stay in Karpacz or Szklarska Poręba. **Karpacz** ⓬ is so conveniently located that you can step right out of your hotel onto a hiking trail leading to the highest peak **Mt. Śnieżka** ⓭ (1602 meters). Of course, it may be more comfortable to take a shortcut by the chair lift to the *Mała Kopa* and walk the rest (about one and a half hours).

Information pages 153-155

KARKONOSZE MOUNTAINS

As you enter the city of Karpacz, you will see a surprising building, the **Stave Church** from Vang (known in Polish as Wang) in Southern Norway. It was in danger of being torn down; and in 1844, with the help of Prussian King Friedrich Wilhelm IV, it was rebuilt here. The church, with its projecting roofs and dragonheads resembles a Viking ship. Some researchers see this as evidence of the spiritual return to a pre-Christian, Germanic religion and its concept of a sacral or holy ship. The most noteworthy parts are the masts and portals, whose interlacing ornamentation are full of symbolic scenes, such as winged dragons, faces with two tongues, and the Snake of Midgard, which by biting its own tail forms a ring as long as the world exists.

From the vantage point of the granite summits, you will come across unparalleled scenery in these mountains. Their ridges stretch out over a length of 50 kilometers and mark the border to the Czech Republic. At 1200 meters, where pine trees are the only large plants, the flat ridges are used for pasture. The high plateau suddenly breaks off to the north into five steep, basin-like glacier valleys.

The giant, eroded, solitary rocks are another strange sight. Their curious shapes have led to them receiving such names as Pilgrim (*Pielgrzymy)*, and Sunflower S*ł*onecznik). Both these rocks are located near Wielki Staw (Great Lake).

In 1959, a national park was established on both the Polish and Czech sides of the Karkonosze Mountains. This conservation measure has not been extensive enough to properly preserve the area, as can be seen in the thin crowns of the trees. That mysterious legendary mountain spirit Liczyrzepa, also known as Rubezahl, is certainly not responsible for the poor condition of the forest, but rather the acid rain from Upper Silesia, from the Bohemian coal mining area, and the

Above: Transferred from Norway to the Giant Mountains – the stave church from Vang has been erected in Karpacz. Right: Resting after work.

brown coal mines of the former German Democratic Republic.

The landscape is still beautiful. A hike along the ridge from *Mała Kopa* to **Szrenica** ⓬ (1362 meters) will confirm this fact as a chair lift brings you comfortably down to **Szklarska Poręba** ⓯ (trail marked red: approximately 5½ hours.).

Alternative routes are offered on trail maps. Climb down from the mountain hut, *Schronisko pod Śnieżka (Silesian House)*, toward Karpacz Górny and take a rest at a small lake, such as *Mały Staw*, in one of the many other mountain huts.

OPOLE COUNTRY

The center of Opole country (Opolszczyzna) is the city of **Opole** ⓰. It has a population of 130,000. Most of its residents came from the east and settled here after the Second World War. The name Opole can be traced back to the Slavic word for settlement. The publication *Bavarian Geographer* mentioned that Opole, in the mid-9th century, was the center of the Slavic Opolanie tribe. From 1201 until 1532, the Piast princes resided here. The city was settled by Germans and given a city charter in 1217. In 1945, the heavily damaged city was given back to Poland.

All interesting highlights and tourist attractions are located in the **Old Town**, which has been partly preserved and partly reconstructed. The unsightly **City Hall**, built in 1936, is a gray, bulky imitation of Florence's Palazzo Vecchio. The **market houses** with their decorative Baroque façades look much nicer. Their foundations walls are Gothic or built during the Renaissance.

The Gothic **Cathedral of the Holy Cross** (*Kościół Św. Krzyża*) located north of the market is also interesting. The last prince of Opole, Jan II (the Good), who died in 1532, is entombed here. Near the market, toward the river Odra is a **Franciscan Church** (*Kościół Franciszkanów*) from the mid-14th century. In the St. Anna Chapel, seven Opole princes rest in beautiful late Gothic tombs.

An **open-air museum** (*skansen*) is located in a section outside the city center called Bierkowice, going toward Wrocław. There is also a collection of wooden buildings once typical of the Opole region, including a shingled church dating back to the 17th century. Seventy-five percent of the 600 churches built in Upper Silesia in the 18th century are a blend of the half-timbered style combined with the blockhouse construction common to the Carpathian mountain region.

Thirty kilometers south of Opole, is **Mt. Anna** ⓱ (*Góra Świętej Anny*), the more than 400-meter-high German-Polish "Mountain of Destiny") and the most important destination for pilgrims in Silesia. It gained its special importance in 1921 during the Third Silesian Uprising. The opponents to the annexation of Upper Silesia to Germany were not able to capture the mountain, which was being defended by a German volunteer corps.

UPPER SILESIAN COAL-MINING AREA

Since then, the mountain has served as the symbol of both sides' claim to Silesia.

A Baroque **Pilgrimage Church** on *Góra Świętej Anny* and the **Mount Calvary Church** with 30 Marian chapels (1700 to 1709) can be visited. To the west, an **amphitheater** was built into the mountainside. National Socialists held a number of their meetings here during the 1930's. After this region had changed hands again, the artist Xawery Dunikowski created an bombastic **Monument of the Silesian Uprisings** (1919-1921) in 1953, and the place was misused again for political gatherings. Grass now grows on the empty stage, and village interactions between Poles and the minority Germans seem peaceful. The new Wrocław-Katowice freeway will destroy the peace here. Polish Green Party members, who had protested by chaining themselves to nearby trees, were not able to stop this developmental plan.

UPPER SILESIAN COAL-MINING AREA

The **Upper Silesia Industrial Region** includes fourteen cities and three million people. In some cities, population density reaches 4400 persons per square kilometer. This region is home to 50 coal mines, 17 iron foundries, 8 non-ferrous metal foundries, 11 coke plants, 37 power plants, 80 metal processing and mechanical works, as well as 70 chemical factories. The first plants were established in the 18th century as a result of the supportive economic measures carried out by Frederick the Great, and the last ones during the era of Edward Gierek (1970-1980). Gierek, the Party's General Secretary and a former miner, paid great attention to this area. Upper Silesia is now a problem zone. The pollution is devastating. Many plants are losing money and the revamping required is too expensive.

For visitors there are few places of interest, unless there's a rock concert at the soccer stadium in **Chorzów** ⑱ (the Rolling Stones played here in 1998). Many of the factories and plants have been classified as worthy of preservation and fall under a preservation order, just as some of the residential buildings, which often border directly on the giant smokestacks and hoists of the coal mines; this is more for those interested in technology.

Between Katowice and Chorzów is a large **park**, the *Wojewódzki Park Kultury i Wypoczynku*, the green lung of the region. A cable car runs between the various attractions, which include a recreational park, a planetarium, a zoo, and an open-air museum featuring Upper Silesian wooden architecture.

The oldest mines, dating back to the 18th century, are located in **Tarnowskie Góry** ⑲, 15 kilometers north of Bytom and are worth viewing. In one lead-zinc mine, you can visit underground passageways 30 meters deep and 1700 meters long. Even more exciting is the Sztolnia Czarnego Pstrąga Mine, located outside of the city. Here you can ride in a boat lit only by a carbide lamp 30 meters underground through dark canals.

Recover from the hectic pace of Upper Silesia in the tongue twisting city of **Pszczyna** ⑳, a peaceful provincial town on the southern edge of the industrial region. Close to the quaint marketplace is the imposing **castle of the Promnitz family** (1743-1757). In 1847, the castle became the property of the Hochberg family and was soon remodeled in French Neo-Renaissance style.

This castle was the only Silesian castle (one of only five in Poland) not plundered in 1945, so the magnificent chambers can be visited. Most of the rooms, decorated with hundreds of antlers, date from the late 19th century and reflect past but not current tastes. In September, chamber music concerts honoring composer Georg Philipp Telemann (1681–1767) who spent three years of his life here, take place in the **Hall of Mirrors**.

SILESIA

SILESIA (ŚLĄSK)

WROCŁAW ☎ 071

Polska Agencja Promocji Turystyki, Rynek 14, Tel. 3443111, Fax 3442969, Mon-Fri 9:00 a.m. – 5:00 p.m., Sat 10:00 a.m. – 2:00 p.m. On the south side of the ring. Maps and current information on cultural programs in the city. **Księgarnia Turystyczna**, Świdnicka 19. The best selection of maps in all of Poland.

TRANSPORTATION: Two long distance train stations are located close to each other in Wrocław. The good trolley network makes traveling in the city easy (*bilety* at the kiosks, per ride 1.40 Zł/thirty cents). Only the Jewish Cemetery and the Centenary Hall are located outside the city and are not easily accessible on foot, unlike the other interesting sights. *TAXI:* Tel. 919.

Dwór Polski, ul. Kiełbaśnicza 2, Tel./Fax 3723415, 3723419, 3725829, www.wroclaw.com/dworpol.htm. Best location on the ring, but expensive. **Park Plaza Hotel,** ul. Drobnera 11, Te. 3721786, Fax 3721799. New luxury hotel situated on the northern bank of the Odra, opposite the University. **Maria Magdalena**, ul. św. Marii Magdaleny 2, Tel. 3410898, Fax 3410920, www.hotel-mm.com.pl. Newest hotel in the city. **Novotel Orbis Wrocław,** Wyscigowa 35 Tel. 3398051. **Wrocław**, ul. Powstańców Śląskich 7, Tel. 3614651, Fax 3616617, www.orbis.pl/hot_wro.html. The most expensive hotel in Wrocław, modern structure, though not central (S. of the train station on a large field). Swimming pool, handicapped access. **Zaułek**, ul. Odrzańska 18 a, Tel. 402945, Fax 402947. Near the University.

Monopol, ul. Modrzejewskiej 2, Tel. 3437041, Fax 3435103, www.orbis.pl/hot_mon.html. Located not far from the ring. As the only hotel in Wrocław with an atmosphere of the past, it has hosted many world celebrities; remodeled rooms (more expensive) and rooms not yet remodeled. **Art Hotel**, ul. Kiełbaśnicza 20, Tel. 3424249, Fax 3423929, www.arthotel.wroc.pl. Centrally located. Restaurant. **ODK**, ul. Kopernika 5, Tel. 3485027, Fax 3481706. Near the Centenary Hall in the so-called singles' hostel built by Hans Scharoun, interesting split-level rooms. Make reservations in advance since many conferences are held here. **Saigon**, Wita Stwosza 22/23, Tel. 344288-1 to -4, Fax 3433037. The hotel (good location) is better than its reputation: on the fourth floor there is supposedly a brothel, hotel guests are not bothered or disturbed. Socialist furnishings, good Vietnamese restaurant.

Youth Hostel, ul. Kołłątaja 20, Tel. 3438356. Often filled to capacity. **PTTK Hostel**, ul. Szajnochy 11, Tel. 443073. **Campgrounds**, Na Grobli 16, Tel. 3434442. Located on the banks of the Odra River.

Armine, ul. Bogusławskiego 83, Tel. 3671531. Small guesthouse where long distance trains literally roll over the heads of the guests. Quite a rarity with Armenian cuisine. **Casablanca**, ul. Włodkowica 8a, Tel. 3447817, 3448213. Exclusive restaurant/bar at the Market Square that fosters the cult of Humphrey Bogart. International cuisine, most beautiful summer garden around. **Królewska**, Rynek 5, Tel. 724896. Located at the Market Square, good selection of Polish cuisine (duck with apple is a good choice). **Lwowska**, Rynek 4, Tel. 3439887. Located at the Market Square. Is frequented by the eastern Poles longing for their lost homeland. Almost everything here is reminiscent of Lviv: decor, music and food. **Tequila**, Plac Solny 11, Tel. 3410114. Good, reasonable Mexican dishes (tamales, enchiladas, etc.). **Pod Kalamburen**, ul. Kuźnicza 29 a. Café that offers just small dishes, in (imitation) *fin-de-siècle* decor. **Saigon**, ul. Wita Stwosza 22/23, Tel. 442881. Located in the hotel of the same name; Far East cuisine with a Polish touch; the Vietnamese pancakes (*naleśniki po wietnamsku*) taste delicious. **Szwejk**, ul. Odrzańska 17, Tel. 3427071. Tasty Czech cuisine.

Rurka, ul. Łazienna 4, Tel. 442410. The legendary jazz club of the 1970's, just recently reopened. **Rag-Time**, Pl. Solny. New Orleans jazz.

Szuflada, ul. Świdnicka 13. Unconventional interior furnishings. **Klub Artystów**, ul. Jatki 6. Ear-splitting music, many extroverted art students, Tuesday is live jazz day.

Aula Leopoldina, pl. Uniwersytecki 1, Tel. 402271. Thurs-Tues 10:00 a.m. – 3:30 p.m. **Centenary Hall** (Hala Ludowa), ul. Zygmunta Wróblewskiego, can be reached from the train station by taking trolley 2 or buses 145 or 146. As long as there are no performances, the north entrance is open to visitors all day. In the foyer, there is a small exhibit on Max Berg. **Jewish Cemetery** (Cmentarz Żydowski), ul. Ślężna, Tel. 678236. During the summer open daily from 8:00 a.m. – 8:00 p.m. **Historical Museum** (Muzeum historyczne), in the City Hall, Sukiennice 14/15, Tel. 3441434. Mon-Fri 10:00 a.m. – 4:00 p.m., Sat 10:00 a.m. – 6:00 p.m., Sun 10:00 a.m. – 6:00 p.m. **National Museum** (Muzeum Narodowe), pl. Powstańców Warszawy 5, Tel. 3435643. Tues-Sun. 10:00 a.m. – 4:00 p.m. **Panarama of the Battle of Racławice** (Panorama Racławicka), ul. Purkyniego 11, Tel. 442344, Fax 343363. Tues-Sun 9:00 a.m. – 3:00 p.m. Reservations are recommended.

FESTIVALS: Two important festivals take place in Wrocław: **Jazz nad Odrą** (Jazz on the Odra; Tel. 3481821) in May with a variety of the best national and international jazz musicians, as well as the **Wratislavia Cantans** of classical music (often choirs) in September: Tel. 3427257, www.wratislavia.mtl.pl.

153

SILESIA

Unfortunately, the world-famous *Laboratorium*, the experimental theater of Jerzy Grotowski, is now part of history. However, the **Theater Center on the Ring** is continuing the tradition: Ośrodek Twórczości Jerzego Grotowskiego i Poszukiwań Teatralno-Kulturowych, Rynek-Ratusz 27, Tel. 445320.
A second famous theater, **Pantomima Henryk Tomaszewski**, can be seen with a bit of luck (in case it is showing in Wrocław between foreign tours). Appearances in Teatr Polski, ul. G. Zapolskiej 3, Tel./Fax 3438789, or in Teatr Pantomimy, Al. Dębowa 16, Tel. 675280.
For visits to the other Wrocław theaters, knowledge of the Polish language is necessary. One exception is the **Operetka Wrocławska**, where musicals are sometimes scheduled (for example *Anatevka*, Polish *Skrzypek na dachu*). Also study the programs of the **Opera** (Opera we Wrocławiu, ul. Świdnicka 35, Tel. 3438641) and the **Philharmonica**, ul. Piłsudskiego 19, Tel. 3422001 for musical presentations.

LEGNICA
LEGNICKIE POLE ☎ 076

PTTK Office, Legnica, Rynek 27, Tel. 8565163.
Cuprum, ul. Skarbowa 7, Tel. 8628041, Fax 8628544. Overpriced hotel downtown.
Youth Hostel, ul. Jordana 17, Tel. 8625412. Open year round. The hostel in Legnickie Pole is only open during the summer (Tel. 8682315).
Adria, Legnica, Rynek 9, Tel. 8523533. At the Market Square. Polish, Hungarian and Indian cuisine.
Museum of the Battle of Legnica (Muzeum Bitwy Legnickiej), Legnickie Pole, Wed-Sun 11:00 a.m. – 4:30 p.m.

BRZEG ☎ 077

ul. Piastowska 2, Tel. 4162100.
Piast, ul. Piastowska 12, Tel. 4162027. Located between the Old Town and the station for long-distance trains.
Ratuszowa is located in the cellar of the Town Hall. Nice atmosphere. Tel. 4165267. Old Polish specialties of the so-called Radziwiłł cuisine.
Museum Zamkowe in the castle: Thurs-Sun 10:00 a.m. – 4:00 p.m. and Wed 10:00 a.m. – 6:00 p.m.

KŁODZKO ☎ 074

PTTK Office, ul. Wita Stwosza 1, Tel. 673740.
Astoria, pl. Jedności 1, Tel. 673035. Centrally located near both train stations.

Youth Hostel: ul. Nadrzeczna 5, Tel. 672524.
Wilcza Jama, ul. Grottgera 5, and **Korona**, ul. Noworudzka 1, Tel. 673737, are the best choices in the city.
Chapel in Czermna near Kudowa: Open daily 10:00 a.m. – 1:00 p.m. and 2:00 p.m. – 4:00 p.m. **Fortress** (Twierdza Kłodzka): Open daily 9:00 a.m. – 6:00 p.m.

ŚWIDNICA ☎ 074

Piast Roman, ul. Kotlarska 11, Tel. 521393, 523477. A bit expensive, modest standard, but still the best choice in the city. **Youth Hostel** ul. Muzealna 4, Tel. 520480, Fax 533578. Open year round.
Hermes, ul. Grodzka 11, Tel. 535008.
Trinity Peace Church (Kościół protestancki Trójcy Świętej), Open daily 9:00 a.m. – 1:00 p.m. and 3:00 – 5:00 p.m.

KSIĄŻ / WAŁBRZYCH ☎ 074

Zamek Książ, ul. Piastów Śląskich 1, Tel. 8432618, Fax 8432679. Relatively reasonable accommodation in a fairy tale castle. Make reservations early. In May 1999, the complex was bought by Heritage International, a British chain, which wants to set up a luxury hotel on the spot. The days of inexpensive accommodation are now numbered.
Sudety, ul. Parkowa 15, Tel. 8477431, Fax 8476450. Located in downtown Wałbrzych; modern but by far no comparable alternative to Książ.
Youth Hostel, ul. Marconiego 1, Tel. 8477942.
Royal Prince, Wałbrzych, Plac Grunwaldzki 11, Tel. 8535008. Chinese specialties.
Książ Castle: May-Sept Tues-Fri 10:00 a.m. – 4:00 p.m., Sat-Sun 10:30 a.m. – 5:00 p.m.; Oct-April: closing times an hour earlier.

JELENIA GÓRA ☎ 075

ul. 1 Maja 42, Tel./Fax 7524054. Plac Ratuszowy, Tel. 7524506.
Orbis Jelenia Góra, ul. Sudecka 63, Tel. 7646480 to -89, Fax 7526269, www.orbis.pl/hot_jel .html. Four-star hotel built in the early 90's. It is a long walk to the Market Square.
Hotel Park, ul. Sudecka 42, Tel. 7526942, Fax 7526021. Thoroughly acceptable. **Youth Hostel,** ul. Bartka Zwycięzcy 10, Tel. 7525746. Open year round.
Karczma Grodzka, ul. Grodzka 5, Tel. 7646359. Country furnishings, country dumplings and pierogis. **Smok**, pl. Ratuszowy 15, Tel. 7525928. Specialities such as hare in cream sauce and vegetarian dishes.

SILESIA

Tokaj, ul. Pocztowa 6, Tel. 7524479. Hungarian specialties.

FESTIVALS: In June: Street Theater Festival, a second theater festival at the end of September.

AIR TOURS over the Karkonosze Mountains: **Aeroklub Jeleniogórski**, ul. Łomnicka 1, Tel. 7526020. Not exactly inexpensive but unforgettable.

KARPACZ, SZKLARSKA PORĘBA ☎ 075

😊😊😊 **Skalny**, Karpacz, ul. Obrońców Pokoju 5, Tel. 7619721 to -24, 7527000, Fax 7618721, www.orbis.pl/hot_sky.html. Expensive, frequented by countless German tour groups.

😊😊 **Sudety**, Szklarska Poręba, ul. Krasickiego 10, Tel. 7172736. The best address in town. **Pension Rezydent**, Szklarska Poręba, ul. Narciarska 6, Tel. 7172695. Neat and orderly.

😊 Reasonable alternatives in Karpacz: **Biały Jar**, ul. 1 Maja 79, Tel. 7619319. **Orlinek**, ul. Olimpijska 9, Tel. 7619548. Close to the chair lift. The town is full of workers' hostels, pensions, and private rooms to rent. In Szklarska Poręba: **Accommodation Service**, Tel. 7172393. **Youth Hostel**, ul. Gimnazjalna 9, Tel. 7619290. Open year round.

U Ducha Gór, Karpacz, ul. Olimpijska 5, Tel. 7618563. The interior as well as the cuisine originate from the Carpathian rather than the Sudeten Mountains, can still be recommended. **Agat**, Szklarska Poręba, ul. 1 Maja 11, Tel. 7173430. Specialty: pancakes Hungarian style (*placek po węgiersku*).

Vang Church, Karpacz Górny, www.sponsor.com.pl/wang/gb/str1.htm. Open daily 9:00 a.m. – 6:00 p.m. Tours every half hour.

CHAIR LIFTS: On **Mt. Mała Kopa**: from Karpacz, ul. Turystyczna, 8:30 a.m. – 5:30 p.m. The upper station is a starting point for the climb to Mt. Śnieżka.

On **Mt. Szrenica**: in Szklarska Poręba, ul.Turystyczna, 9:00 a.m. – 5:00 p.m. At the top is a mountain hut. The trail marked red is recommended for the climb down. The trail passes by the 27 meter high Kamieńczyk Waterfall. The recommended trail map "Karkonoski Park Narodowy" can be purchased in the bookstores in Jelenia Góra and elsewhere in the vicinity.

OPOLE ☎ 077

😊😊 **Opole**, ul. Krakowska 59, Tel. 4838651, Fax 536075, www.orbis.pl/hot_opo.html. Near the train station, a bit loud, but newly remodeled.

😊 **Youth Hostel**, ul. Struga 16, Tel. 4543352. Open only from July 2 to August 25. **Toropol**, ul. Barlickiego 13, Tel. 4536691. Can be reccommended as a reasonably-priced alternative.

Olimpijska, ul. Oleska 86, Tel. 4556011. Located in the hotel of the same name. Offers not only Polish but also Chinese specialties, also for vegetarians (for example, *kotlet Roquefort*).

Open Air Museum, Opole-Bierkowice, ul. Wrocławska 174: Tues-Sun 10:00 a.m. – 5:00 p.m. Located outside the city on the way to Wrocław. From October 15 to April 15: Only the grounds can be visited, the inside rooms are closed.

KATOWICE ☎ 032

😊😊😊 **Orbis Warszawa**, ul. Roździeńskiego 16, Tel. 2596011, to -15, Fax 2587066, www.polhotels.com/Katowice/Warszawa/. The best address in town. Make reservations in advance.

😊 **Sportowy**, ul. Ceglana 67, Tel. 51-0093/95. Among the numerous, inexpensive alternatives, well recommended. **Youth Hostel**, ul. Graniczna 27, Tel. 2555968, Open year round.

La France, ul. Mariacka 6, Tel. 2537737. French cuisine, as the name suggests.

TARNOWSKIE GÓRY ☎ 032

😊 **Sportowy**, ul. Korczaka 23, Tel. 1854524. Located somewhat out of town on a sports field.

Pod Sztolnią, ul. Janasa, Tel. 2853870.

Zinc and Lead Mine, ul. Szczęść Boże 52, Wed-Mon 9:00 a.m. – 2:00 p.m.

Black Trout Mine (Sztolnia Czarnego Pstraga). Reservations are necessary. PTTK Office, ul. Krakowska 12, Tel. 1854996. Ten persons per boat.

PSZCZYNA ☎ 032

😊 **PTTK Hostel**, ul. Kraszewskiego 90, Tel. 2103833, 2101847.

Karczma Stary Młyn, ul. Parkowa. Traditional dishes. Located next to a small open-air museum (skansen). **Bajadera**, ul. Korfantego 17, Tel. 2104944. Silesian specialties.

Castle: Tel. 2103037, www.muzeum.pszczyna.top.pl/str1_p.html. May to October Tues 9:00 a.m. – 3:00 p.m., Wed 9:00 a.m. – 4:00 p.m., Thurs-Fri 9:00 a.m. – 3:00 p.m., Sat 10:00 a.m. – 4:00 p.m., Sun 10:00 a.m. – 5:00 p.m. During the off-season, it is closed on Tuesdays and with shorter opening hours. Closed December and January.

Telemann Festival in September, information in Castle Museum, Tel. 2103037.

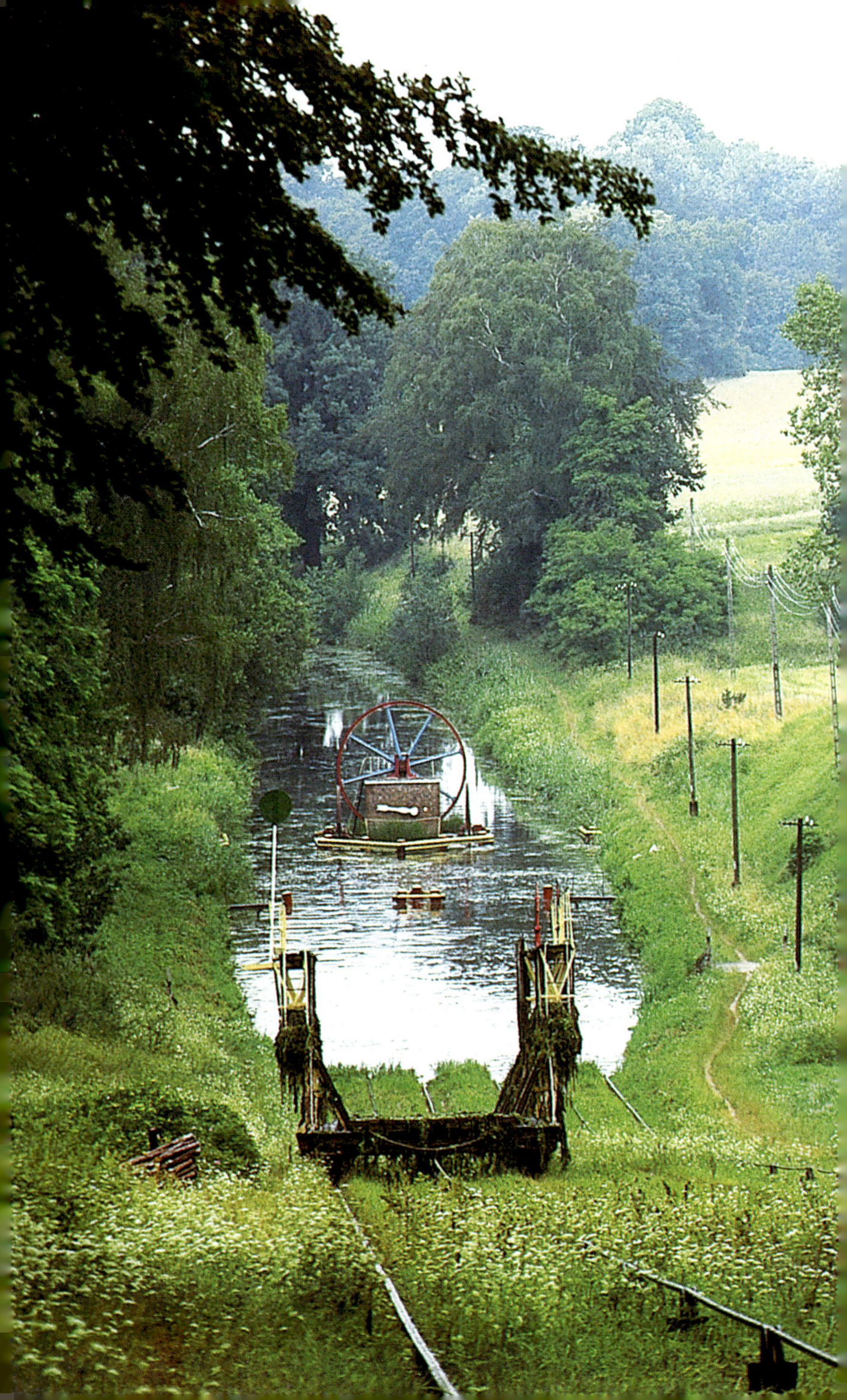

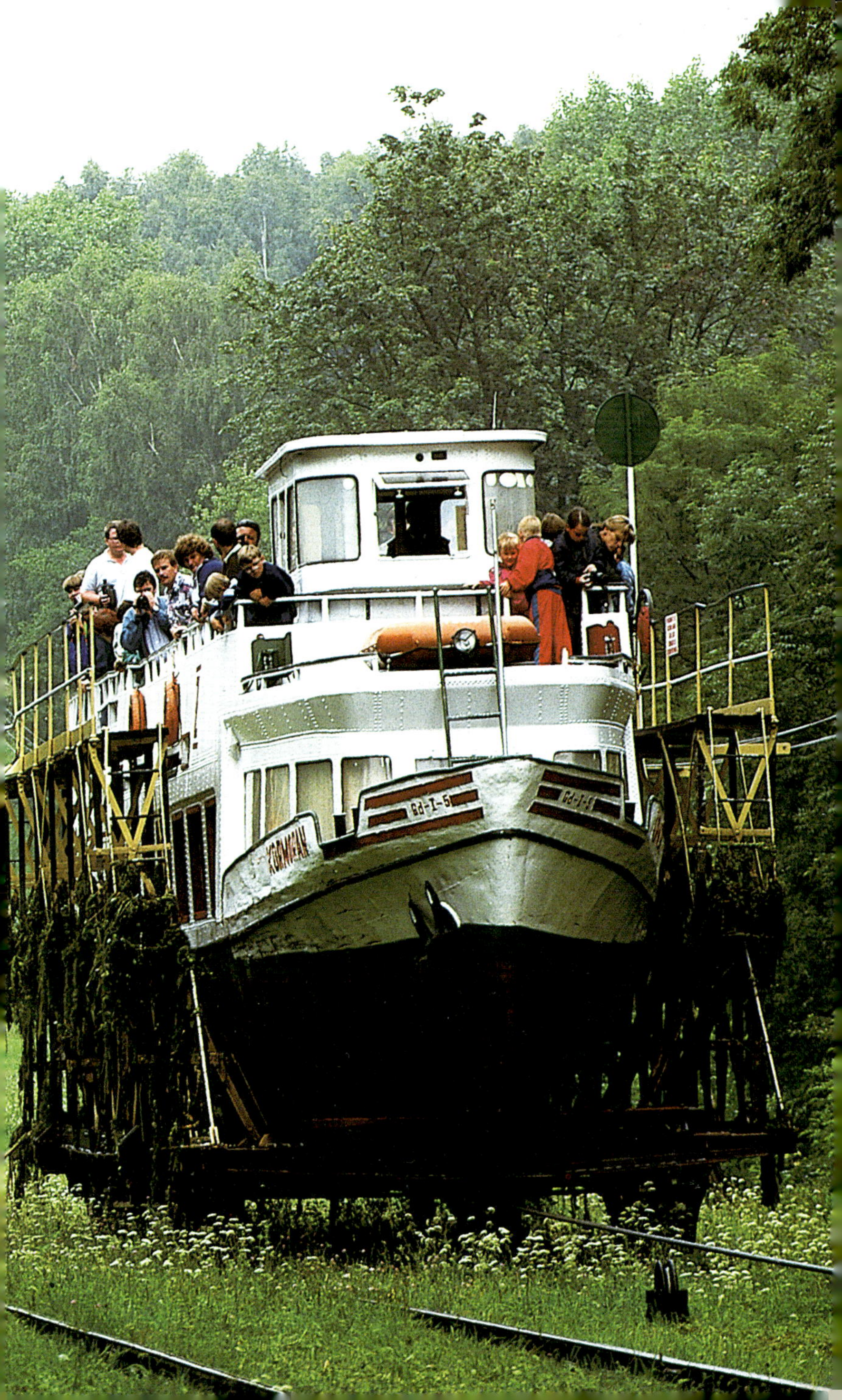
Gd-I-5
KORMORAN

FROM GDAŃSK TO TORUŃ

FROM GDAŃSK TO TORUŃ
Proud Hanseatic Cities, and Mighty Fortresses

GDAŃSK / KASHUBIA
MALBORK
VISTULA DELTA
ELBLĄG / KWIDZYN
CHEŁMNO COUNTRY / TORUŃ

The region around the lower reaches of the Vistula River offers the visitor three highlights not to be missed on a trip to Poland. First of all, there is the city of Gdańsk, once the proud home of the patricians. Its beautiful burghers' houses, city gates and churches have all been rebuilt or restored since the destruction of the city in the year 1945.

Further south along the Vistula River lies the second pearl of the region – maybe a bit dusty but in return a truly old place: the Hanseatic town of Toruń. Not too large, populated by students and with many cafés and bars, this is a spot where you might wish to linger. Furthermore, nearly every town in the region around Toruń has an impressive brick castle because this was home to the Knights of the Teutonic Order (Chełmno Country).

The powerful, medieval realm of the Teutonic Knights covered the province with a network of castles. One of the most impressive is the fascinating Marienburg Castle in the city of Malbork, the residence of the Grand Masters of the Teutonic Order. Lastly, this region is full of wonderful natural scenery and landscapes. The Kashubian region, for example, is scattered with lakes, and the countryside around the Vistula delta will probably remind you of scenes in Holland.

GDAŃSK

The historian N. Davies described the Hanseatic city of **Gdańsk** ❶ as "the German jewel in the Polish crown." The city is situated on the River Motława. "Gyddanzc" was first mentioned in the sacral legend of Saint Albrecht around the year 999 AD. In 1308, the city fell into the hands of the Teutonic Order. Davies' euphoric description refers to the three-hundred year existence of the free city of Gdańsk within the Polish-Lithuanian Kingdom, which began after the end of the city's 150 year old subordination to the Teutonic Order (1454) and lasted until the Second Partition of Poland in 1793.

Having a population of approximately 50,000 in 1600, Gdańsk was about double the size of Cracow and the most powerful city in the kingdom. More than seventy percent of the Polish export trade was handled here. The city coined its own money, had special jurisdictional power, and maintained its own militia.

Almost all Polish kings had resided here for longer periods of time, and they

Previous pages: On the Elbląg Canal, the elevation differences are surmounted by tracks and pulleys – not locks. Right: The massive Crane Gate in Gdańsk towers over the harbor quay.

GDAŃSK

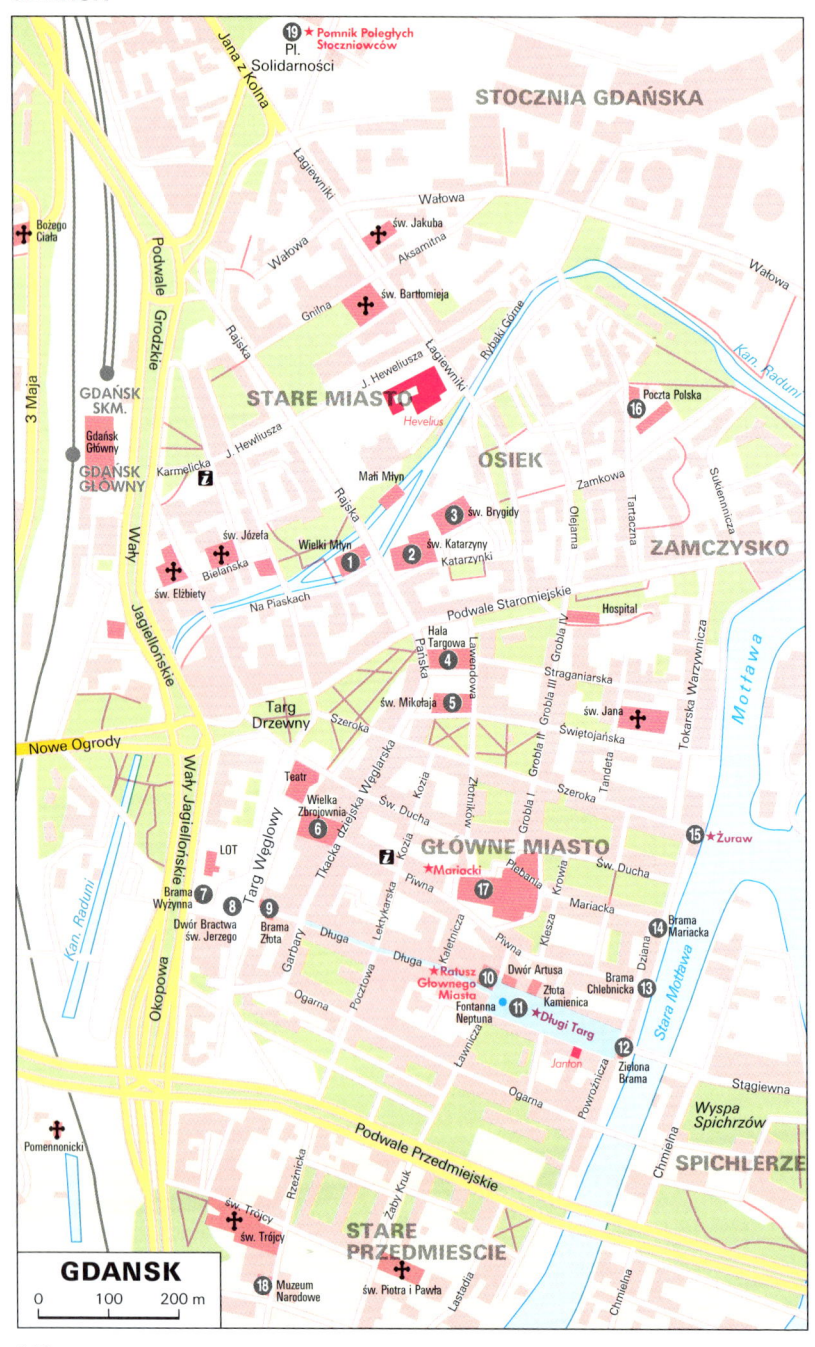

OLD TOWN

were paid great respect. In return, however, the city expected the recognition of its autonomy. In a crisis, the city was always loyal to the Polish state without much thought to its own national identity, that is, whether Gdańsk, (in German Danzig) was really a German or a Polish city.

A world view preoccupied with categories of "nationality" had gruesome consequences for this city in the twentieth century. In 1939, the shots fired from the German armored cruiser *Schleswig Holstein* at the island of Westerplatte signaled the onset of the Second World War. The end of this war would leave nothing but ruins in a city that was once a "jewel." The heavy bombing by American and British aircraft, the fierce and bitter battles for the city in March of 1945, and the pillaging and plundering by the Soviet troops left behind a picture of devastation. Ninety percent of the city had been reduced to rubble.

There is a difference of opinion today when the question is asked if Gdańsk represents a shining example of a city restored and reconstructed or if it is more of a superfluous Disneyland version of the once beautiful patrician city now surrounded by an inhospitable asphalt jungle. Probably Gdańsk is a little of both. However, at the same time, it is a proud city which many representatives of the political elite point to as their birthplace or childhood home.

If you stand on Gdańsk's magnificent Long Market (Długi Targ), looking at the town hall, the Artus Court and Neptune Fountain, you'll soon forget the city's turbulent history and the recent political unrest. You will also forget the question about the historical authenticity of the buildings because the splendor of their architecture will fill you with awe. It is the artistic expression, the architectural harmony and the unmistakable atmosphere of the city that really counts. Gdańsk – "a jewel in the Polish crown."

The Old Town (Stare Miasto)

A good place to start out on a tour of the city is at *Hotel Hevelius* located on the street with the same name (ul. Heweliusza). It is just a short walk from the main train station. Although you are in the **Old Town,** there is very little that will remind you of any historical reconstruction. Of the two most important city sections, Stare Miasto (Old Town) and Główne Miasto (Main Town), merely the latter was fortunate enough to be raised out of the ruins. In the Old Town, only the most important historical monuments have been restored.

Near the Hevelius Hotel you will find the **Great Mill** ❶ dating back to the year 1350 *(Wielki Młyn)*. It is considered the largest preserved medieval industrial enterprise in Europe. Up until 1945, there were 18 millstones in operation together with a giant oven. From 1308 until 1454 when the city belonged to the state of the Teutonic Order, the entire population of Gdańsk was supplied with bread from this one oven. Today, it is a business and shopping area.

Across from the mill is **St. Catherine's Church** ❷ (*Kościół św. Katarzyny*) dating back to the second half of the 14th century. Its prominent tower will strike your attention immediately. This is the last resting place of the famous astronomer and father of selenography (the study of the physical features of the moon), Johannes Hevelius (1611-1687). A plaque dedicated to him is located on the north column of the chancel and dates back to the year 1780.

In the shadow of St. Catherine's Church is the Gothic **St. Bridget's Church** ❸ (*Kościół św. Brygidy*). After its reconstruction in the 1970's, this church became the "parish church of Solidarność" (the Polish political party Solidarity). In the meantime, though, Father Jankowski has drifted off into the right fringe of political thinking. The

THE MAIN TOWN

modern interior furnishings impressively contrast with the Gothic stellar vault. Don't miss the naturalistically designed tomb of the priest Jerzy Popiełuszko, who was brutally murdered by the security police in the year 1984.

**The Main Town (Główne Miasto)

On the way to Główne Miasto, you will notice to the left the large **Market Halls** ❹ built in the 19th century. The place hums with activity all day, and a stroll around the booths and stands offers an enchanting diversion. Still to be found are the traditional selections of eel, the tasty, rich Cracow sausage, the famous Polish sour pickles and goose drippings in jars – specialties, which have often been replaced elsewhere with Western products in colorful packaging.

The Long Market featuring the Neptune Fountain in Gdańsk. Right: The Red Room of the old city hall in Gdańsk reflects the affluence of the aristocratic councilmen who met here.

The nearby **St. Nicholas' Church** ❺ (*Kościół św. Mikołaja*) is the only church in the city center which survived the war without damage. Since 1227, the church has belonged to the Dominican Order of Cracow, and was completely remodeled in the late Gothic period. The lavish gold altars, however, do not give any hint as to the original state of the interior rooms of other Gdańsk churches since this church was one of the very few Catholic places of worship in the city.

The **Great Arsenal** ❻ (*Wielka Zbrojownia*) is a prominent specimen of Dutch Mannerism and is often pictured in art lexicons. Erected sometime shortly after 1602, it is presumed to be the work of the Dutchman Anthonis van Opbergen, but no source has been found connecting his name to architecture in Gdańsk. The façade features sculptures and gables, framed with ornamental railings, and is simply captivating in its elegance.

To its rear side is the **Targ Węglowy** (coal market), where a series of city gates, one behind the other, served as a

City map page 160, Information pages 181-183

THE LONG MARKET

representative entrance to Główne Miasto. All Polish kings visiting Gdańsk entered through these gates. At the **Upland Gate** ❼ (*Brama Wyżynna*; 1574-1576), you will thus see, besides the crests of the Duchy of Prussia (the part of Prussia which belonged to Poland from 1445-1772) and of the city, the Polish eagle hung at the most prominent spot.

Two more structures follow, the **Prison Tower** and the **Torture House**, which constitute the **Foregate** ❽ . The small, elegant building of the **Fraternity of St. George** (*Dwór Bractwa św. Jerzego*), in which the patricians held their games and feasts, which imitated knights' tournaments, borders on the **Golden Gate** ❾ (*Złota Brama*; 1612-1614), which is similar to a decorative Roman triumphal arch.

From the Golden Gate you have direct access to **Long Street** (*ul. Długa*), the most beautiful street in Główne Miasto. It is lined with delightful town houses of all stylistic periods, which have been completely reconstructed since the war. A few of these houses are especially interesting, e.g. **Lion's Castle** (No. 35) and **Uphagen House** (No. 12), which reopened its doors in 1998 after decades of reconstruction work. It offers the visitor a one-time chance for a look at the private chambers of a patrician house in Gdańsk. The furnishings of the house, built in the 14th century but then altered to Baroque style in 1775/76, are authentic.

The ***Main Town's City Hall** ❿ (*Ratusz Głównego Miasta*) featuring an 80 m high tower (an wonderful lookout point) is the most famous secular piece of Gothic architecture in Gdańsk. It was built from 1379 to 1492 and magnificently furnished during the 16th and 17th centuries. Today it is the home of the **Historical Museum of the City of Gdańsk**. The tower apex (featuring a golden statue of the Polish-Lithuanian ruler Zygmunt II August), along with the inner rooms belongs to the Mannerism style imported from Holland. The wonderful furnishings of the **Red Room,** where the advisors held their meetings, surpass all else. You will find works of art not only on the walls but also on the ceiling. Twenty five large pictures connected to each other with fanciful frames decorate the room. There are scenes from the ancient world and the Bible depicting specific virtues.

The heart of the city is the ***Long Market** ⓫ (*Długi Targ*), with the **Neptune Fountain** in the middle. The market place is bordered by the Green Gate, the City Hall and a row of typical burghers' houses. It is a popular meeting place where tourists, musicians, peddlers and guests of the many street cafés mingle. Neptune, the heavenly ruler of the seas holding his trident, adorns the fountain, which dates from the first half of the 17th century. The symbolism here is obvious and corresponds with historical reality – Gdansk was truly the ruler of the Baltic.

Located behind the Neptune Fountain is the magnificent façade of the **Artus Court** (*Dwór Artusa*; built from 1478 to

From Gdańsk to Toruń

HARBOR QUAY

1481 and remodeled in 1617). Its name calls to mind King Arthur and his Knights of the Round Table. The city merchants must certainly have felt as such when they held their assemblies, business negotiations, and receptions here.

The neighboring **Golden House** (*Złota Kamienica*; Długi Targ 41) enchants the onlooker with its fascinating façade. This house is also called "Steffen's House" after a former owner. Gilded relief and ornamentation cover the walls, and on the gable of the four-story building, there are a number of classical figures: Cleopatra, Oedipus, Achilles and Antigone.

On the Waterfront

Gdańsk was oriented towards the water from its earliest beginnings. The most important streets, among them the Long

Above: The front entrances of the houses lining ul. Mariacka testify to the sociability of Gdańsk residents. Right: High-quality amber jewelry can be found on ul. Mariacka in Gdańsk.

Street, run perpendicular to the river and the harbor. There at the waterfront where the streets come together, magnificent gates were erected: the bombastic **Green Gate** ⑫ (*Zielona Brama*; 1564-68, at the end of Long Market); the **Bread Gate** ⑬ (*Brama Chlebnicka*; approx. 1454); and **St. Mary's Gate** ⑭ (*Brama Mariacka*; second half of the 15th century).

The waterfront has always been a busy, eventful place. In addition to numerous restaurants and street cafés, there are stands where everything under the sun is offered for sale. Mingling among the tourists, you will find gypsies who will tell your fortune, and pirates dressed in appropriate attire but without any recognizable function.

The symbol of the city is the ***Crane Gate** ⑮ (*Żuraw*) built in the years 1442-1444 and enlarged in the 17th century. The giant wooden crane hovering over the river had two large vertical wheel hoists. Heavy barrels could be loaded onto ships with the lower one, and the upper wheel was used to set up the ships'

164   *City map page 160, Information pages 181-183*

masts. Today the gate and the former granaries on the island in the Motława (can be reached by a small passenger ferry), is home to the **Maritime Museum.**

Excursion boats to the island **Westerplatte** depart from the pier. You can visit a small museum in a former guardhouse located next to a stately monument dedicated to the soldiers who died in the first days of the war. The attack on September 1, 1939 on the Polish ammunition depository, where 182 people were at the time, marked the beginning of the Second World War. The free city of Gdańsk had been under the control of the League of Nations as of 1919, with Poland having administrative governance. With the German share of the population being about 90 percent, this majority was against what they thought was an artifically created solution. When the Germans won a number of parliamentary seats in the elections of 1933 and 1935, the annexation (historically known as the "Anschluss") by Germany was Hitler's next objective for the year 1939. The defense of the Westerplatte soon became the symbol of the Polish resistance.

The Polish **Post Office** ⓰ was also defended at the beginning of the war. After a fourteen-hour clash with SS troops, its defenders were arrested and later executed, just like Jan Bronski in Günter Grass's novel *The Tin Drum* . Today it is a museum and can be reached from the northern end of the waterfront quay.

*St. Mary's Street and
*St. Mary's Church

From the waterfront passing through the **St. Mary's Gate** (⓮), it is recommended to turn into "***St. Mary's Street**", today called ul. Mariacka. This is the only street where a group of row houses with terraces have been preserved or completely restored. These small terraces were once a characteristic feature of this Baltic port. After they had lost their original function as the entrance to the storage cellars, they served as a place of neighborly contact and communication.

ST. MARY'S CHURCH

Nowadays you will find numerous small galleries and art shops nestled in the cellars and ground floors of these houses. Of course, amber, the "gold of the Baltic Sea," will not be missing from the showcases. Even the most discriminating buyer will find beautiful amber jewelry at this spot; there is less of a risk here than at one of the street stands of acquiring an expensive, more or less well-done plastic imitation.

Amber – actually nothing more than fossil resin from conifers during the Eocene epoch – comes in a variety of colors anywhere from clear yellow to dark brown. The value of amber is determined above all by its translucence and inclusions. Inclusions are defined as those primeval insects and plants, which have been condemned for all time by drowning in the resin 35 million years ago.

Above: Reconstructed town houses on the harbor quay in Gdańsk with St. Mary's Church in the background. Right: The astronomical clock in St. Mary's Church, Gdańsk.

The ul. Mariacka leads you directly to *St. Mary's Church 17 (Kościół Mariacki) built from 1342 to 1502. The church is hard to miss. This place of worship is 105 meters long and 68 meters wide. It is the fifth largest historical church in Europe and one of the largest brick churches in the world. It is not only impressive because of its size but because of the quality of its architectural construction, which features a combination of stellar, fan and cell vaulting.

After the Reformation, the church was white-washed and in 1945 heavily damaged, thus its interior – due to its immense size – appears rather sterile. Of the many art treasures found here, a few are worth mentioning: the astronomical clock in the north transept (1464-1470), the Renaissance tombstones (for example the freestanding tombstone of Simon and Edith Bahr) and an expressive late Gothic pietà.

In a chapel to the left of the foyer, close to the entrance to an apparently never-ending stairway to the church tower (excellent view), you will find a copy of

AROUND GDAŃSK

"The Last Judgment" by the Flemish painter, Hans Memling. The original painting dating back to 1471-1473 had ill fortune on its way to its owner in Italy. It was stolen from a Burgundian ship by Gdańsk pirates and then given as a votive offering to the Gdańsk church, where it was hung on the wall. As one of the most valuable paintings in Polish hands, it is kept today in the **National Museum** ⓲ in Gdańsk. The museum is located in a Franciscan Monastery south of the Main Town and is an important place of interest because it displays works of famous Gdańsk painters (Anton Möller, Daniel Chodowiecki, etc.) as well as works of well-known Dutch painters (Pieter Breughel the Younger, Jacob Jordaens, Jan van Goyen, etc.)

North of the historical city center and located on the grounds of the shipyard is the stirring ★**Memorial to the Shipyard Workers** ⓳ (Pl. Solidarności). Three giant crosses made out of unfinished steel plates covered with three anchors, the symbols of hope, make this memorial one of the most impressive of post-war Poland. Situated behind the memorial is the former Lenin Shipyard, the scene of the riots of 1970. In Gdańsk, Szczecin and Gdynia approximately 100 shipyard workers were killed by the militia. Ten years later, the strikes of the Gdańsk shipyard workers marked the beginning of the Solidarność Revolution of 1980/81. At this time the omnipotent State saw itself forced to sign an agreement on August 31, 1980 with the striking shipyard workers granting them civil rights and promising them the general democratization of the political system. The construction of the memorial was reluctantly approved by the representatives of the ruling party.

THE AREA AROUND GDAŃSK

A stay in the Hanseatic city is not complete without visits to Oliwa, Sopot and Gdynia. While Oliwa actually belongs to the greater city of Gdańsk, the other two locations make up the so-called "Tri-City" (*Trójmieście*), the metropolitan area of Gdańsk. The region has a population of 750,000.

Oliwa

Oliwa ❷ was originally established by Danish Cistercian monks in the year 1178. As was so often the case, the Cistercian monks chose an enchanting piece of land on which to carry out the rule of the order – *ora et labora* (pray and work). The name "Oliwa" is assumed to refer to the oil presses, which the monks had set up at a creek.

The Gothic ★**Cathedral,** of which the slender west façade was remodeled into Baroque style in 1688, has a length of 107 meters, making it the longest medieval church in Poland. There is a wonderful organ, constructed by a Cistercian monk named Johann Wulf from 1763 to 1788. Its beautiful sounds can be heard during recitals (cf page 181).

SOPOT / GDYNIA

The church's interior, burial place of the East Pomeranian dukes, is primarily Baroque because the original furnishings dating back to the 16th century were destroyed in a fire. In addition to the chancel with tombs and a beautiful stellar vault in the nave, the somewhat overdone Baroque altar is worth seeing. Smiling angel heads look down from cotton-like clouds painted on the ceiling.

Sopot

As early as the 16th century, the Gdańsk aristocrats had their summer retreats in **Sopot** ❸. In 1808, a physician from Napoleon's army, Jean George Haffner, recognized the health-enhancing advantages of the area's climate, and in 1824, he opened a bathhouse with six cabins and dressing rooms – the start of the most elegant swimming resort and

Above: Sopot was a well-known beach resort as early as 1900. Right: Hills, lakes, fields, forests – the Kashubian Switzerland.

spa on the Baltic Sea were established. Sopot works hard to maintain its image, and an evening stroll through the pedestrian zone or along the **mole,** a 512 meter long jetty, will invigorate you.

The **Grand Hotel,** dating back to the 1920's and located near the mole, has found its way onto the list of historical landmarks. For about US$ 100 per night, you as can enjoy sheer luxury in, for example, the General de Gaulle suite, decorated with antiques, though its former elegance is now somewhat faded. The hotel can boast an illustrious (if somewhat infamous) guest list including Adolf Hitler, Fidel Castro, the Shah of Iran together with his beautiful wife Soraya, and Omar Sharif. Incidentally, movie star Klaus Kinski was born as Nikolaus Nakszyński in Sopot in 1926. Recently, a plaque was put up in his honor at ul. Kościuszki 10.

Gdynia

Gdynia ❹ is a large city with a short history. At the end of the nineteenth century, only a small Kashubian village stood here. Between 1923 and 1927, a large seaport was built because Poland did not want to depend on the cooperation of the free city of Gdańsk for its overseas trade. As early as 1933, more goods were being loaded on ships in Gdynia than in any other Baltic seaport.

The most interesting part of the city is a wide jetty (Al. Zjednoczenia) which is open to traffic. On its quay, the **destroyer "Błyskawica"** from the Second World War (today a museum) as well as Poland's largest **sailing ship**, the *Dar Pomorza*, are moored. The sailing ship was built in 1909 in Hamburg as the "Prince Eitel Friedrich" and bought by Poland in 1929.

On the waterfront quay there is an interesting **aquarium** with piranhas, sharks and other sea monsters, as well as the **Joseph Conrad Monument**. Conrad, a great lover of the sea and author of such literary works as *Lord Jim* and *Nostromo*, is counted as an important English writer, but was actually Polish-born as Teodor Józef Korzeniowski (1857-1924), and first learned to speak English at age twenty.

KASHUBIA

The picturesque area northwest of Gdańsk is called **Szwajcaria Kaszubska** (Kashubian Switzerland). Its 300,000 residents, belong to the West Slavic tribe of the Kashubians. Their distinct language bears many similarities to Polish, and is often thought to be a dialect of Polish, but contains many old German and Old Slavonic words. In spite of efforts to preserve the language – recently a Kashubian studies program was set up at the University of Gdańsk – the number of native speakers is declining steadily. Standard Polish is taught in the schools, and many students are self-conscious about speaking a "hillbilly" dialect.

At the **Kashubian Open Air Museum** in Wdzydze Kiszewskie near Kościerzyna, and at the **Kashubian Museum** in Kartuzy, the unofficial capital of the

KASHUBIA / MALBORK

Kashubia, you can get a good first-hand look at Kashubian culture, architecture, fishing equipment, colorful textiles and musical instruments.

As the name suggests there is also a Carthusian **Monastery** in **Kartuzy** ❺. The unusual Baroque hipped roof of the church was supposedly modeled in the form of a casket and thus served as a reminder to the Carthusian Order's members, whose maxim was *memento mori* (remember that you must die). With regard to the interior furnishings, most of which date back to the 17th century, of special interest is the Flemish leather wall-covering (1685) at the chancel. The local ethnographic museum tells the story of the day-to-day life of the Kashubians. The open-air museum in **Wdzydze Kiszewskie** ❻, which is beautifully situated at Lake Wdzydze, the largest lake in the Kashubian region, provides an introduction through its twenty historical buildings to the traditional style of construction.

The original Kashubian culture is found, though, in the quaint villages in the countryside. Off the route between Kartuzy and Lębork lie the villages of **Chmielno**, **Brodnica** and **Mirachowo** nestled in a scenic landscape of lakes. The Kashubian people are very much attached to this beautiful but rather infertile and rugged region. They maintain that God forgot them when giving land to all of earth's tribes. A weeping angel then pointed out this omission to God, who took what was left in his box – clay and stones, small lakes and a piece of coastline, plains and rugged hills, making the Kashubian "Switzerland."

**MALBORK

On the banks of the Nogat River, a tributary of the Vistula River, you will find the largest brick castle in the world, the **Malbork Castle** ❼ (formerly known as Marienburg) in the city of Malbork. A tour of the castle can easily be planned as a day trip from Gdańsk. On the one-hour train ride from Gdańsk, you can see the Vistula Bridge at **Tczew**, which was opened for use in 1857. South of the modern railway bridge, this 890 meter bridge, was once the longest bridge in Europe.

Construction of the High Castle (the oldest section of the castle) was begun as early as the 13th century. When the Marienburg became the seat of the Grand Masters of the Teutonic Order in 1309, the castle with four wings was greatly extended; more sections were added to the north. The builders of this awe-inspiring castle were not Polish, indeed they were mortal enemies of the Polish state in the 14th and 15th centuries.

Teutonic Order – Fact and Fiction

The Teutonic Order was founded in Palestine in 1190 (Polish *krzyżacy* is of-

Above: Getting ready to dance – a Kashubian musician in traditional costume.

FROM GDAŃSK TO TORUŃ

ten incorrectly translated as *crusader*). The Polish Duke Konrad I of Mazovia asked the Knights of the Teutonic Order to help him fight against the pagan Prussians who were continually raiding his lands. The Duke granted the Order lands north of Toruń for their support. The Prussians were steadily conquered and subjugated, eventually eliminated entirely. The theocratic, centrally controlled state of the Teutonic Order took control of the lands of the Prussians and made its seat of government in Malbork until 1457.

With the brutal occupation of Gdańsk in 1308, the Teutonic Order made its former Polish benefactor its archenemy. Poland brought Christianity to Lithuania, joined forces with this state in 1386, and in 1410 defeated the Knights of the Teutonic Order in the Battle of Tannenberg. The Order's demise came 50 years later when its own vassals, who were tired of the strictly regulated economy, preferred to subordinate themselves to a less repressive lord, the Polish King in Cracow. The Teutonic Order's state in Prussia was divided in 1466, Poland receiving the western region including Gdańsk, Malbork, Toruń and the bishopric of Warmia, became known as Royal Prussia. In 1525, the Order's rule came to an end in the eastern region as well.

These are the historical facts, yet they are surrounded by a variety of opinions, and on a tour of Malbork Castle, you often hear other versions. The question most often asked is: "Was the Teutonic Order good or evil?" The Germans considered the Knights of the Teutonic Order to be honorable forerunners of the germanization of the East and heralds of their culture. When, in August 1914, Major General Hindenburg defeated the Russian troops under General Samsonow at Olsztynek, they called the victory the "Second Battle of Tannenberg" (an effective propaganda maneuver) and saw in this battle the revenge for the medieval defeat of 1410. That the German forces fought against Poland and Lithuania in those days and against Russia in 1914 was not considered significant.

For the Poles, on the other hand, the Teutonic Order personified a politically aggressive, expansionist German group. The novel *The Crusaders,* written by Henryk Sienkiewicz (1900), portrays the knights as a more or less arrogant band of thieves.

Attempts to understand medieval times within the framework of the contemporary nation-state will result in contradictions. Why did the German people of Gdańsk, stand up to the Teutonic Order and then, in 1454, seek protection of the Polish king? Currently, this is no longer an explosive subject. The Germans have generally forgotten who the Knights of the Teutonic Order were, and the Poles have learned a different version of history. Some local guides still tell rather gruesome stories about the castle, which convey outdated, incorrect information.

Tour of the Fortress

The three-hour tour of the castle grounds and complex (only possible on a guided tour) is best started at the west bank of the Nogat River. From there, you have a picture postcard view and and can see the individual sections of the fortress. The Front Castle is to the north. The Middle Castle, along with the protruding block of the Grand Master's Palace, faces the river and has an elaborate façade. The cubic High Castle can be clearly seen. To the south, the rather haphazardly reconstructed Old Town abuts the fortress wall. From the parking lot at the Front Castle, enter through a martial gate into the courtyard of the **Middle Castle** (*Zamek Średni*; dated after 1309). In the old guest

Above: Malbork Castle – symbol and relict of the former influence and power of the Knights of the Teutonic Order.

MALBORK

wing of the eastern section, is an impressive **amber collection**. Early Prussians recognized amber's value and exported it via four amber trade routes to Rome. The Teutonic Order later established a monopoly on amber trading, and inhabitants along the coast were forced to turn over all amber in exchange for salt. Any unauthorized collecting was punishable by hanging. The exhibits show beautiful, handmade items from the last centuries.

Connected to the west wing of the Middle Castle is the **Grand Master's Palace** (*Pałac Wielkich Mistrzów*), a boxy, compact building with battlements and a tent-like roof. Reopened to the public in 1991, after 17 years of renovations, it is considered one of the most beautiful and valuable parts of the castle, with **summer** and **winter refectories.**

Both refectory halls have magnificent radial vaults, supported by a single pillar, and have come to be referred to as "palm tree vaults," due to their shape. The Grand Master's Palace (1383-1399) was not built in the older, severe architectural style of a monastery fortress, but is an elegant building, flooded with daylight through large square windows, more reminiscent of late medieval times and their decadent festivities. Once the scene of such events, the **Great Refectory** is unfortunately closed for an indefinite period, due to danger of collapse.

The large square building south of the Grand Master's Palace, the **High Castle** (*Zamek Wysoki*), has quite a different character and features a **dansker** (toilet tower) attached to a wall. A well-preserved portal from the first fortress chapel, called the **Golden Gate** (*Złota Brama*), dates back to post-1280 when the Grand Masters still resided in Italy.

The castle was then the seat of the Order's regional commander, as were at least twenty-five similar castles spread throughout the country. Not until 1309, when the Grand Master Siegfried von Feuchtwangen moved his headquarters from Venice to Marienburg, did the real career of the castle begin, with extensive remodeling.

Map page 171, Information pages 181-183

VISTULA DELTA

The Middle Castle was built and the old fortress chapel to the northeast of the High Castle was enlarged and became the castle church. Its chancel juts out of a corner of the castle. Under the chancel, the **St. Anna Chapel** (*Kaplica św. Anny*) was erected. It was an burial chapel for the Grand Master, and its portal with carved figures is still very impressive. New rooms were built on the second and third floors of the High Castle and were connected by lavishly decorated arcades.

Despite the castle's impressive appearance, it is still true that not all that glisters is gold, that is, original. Much of Malbork Castle has been restored. The grounds were remodeled in the Baroque period when the fortress was home to Polish kings traveling to their northern territories. Later the castle became a Prussian military post and there were plans to tear it down around 1800. The castle was reconstructed and remodeled in the 19th century, guided largely by romantic notions and wild imagination. In 1882, Conrad Steinbrecht began a more accurate reconstruction. Polish restorers have been trying for years to undo the damage the castle endured in its bitter defense during World War II. The reconstruction of the castle church is still not complete.

THE VISTULA DELTA

The **Żuławy Wiślane**, a flat region east of Gdańsk, lies partly below sea level. With its numerous tributaries of the Vistula, small ferries and draw-bridges, the area gives you the impression of being quaint and quiet as if it were directly taken out of a picture painted by Vincent van Gogh. This is true especially of the areas near Tujsk, Marzęcino or Kępiny Wielkie. It was hard winning the fertile land from the sea, but those people who could do it best helped – the Dutch. As

Above: The Golden Gate of the High Castle in Malbork has been preserved through the years. Right: Fishermen on the beach near Stegny (Kąty Rybackie).

ELBLĄG

early as the 17th century, Dutch immigrants had been coming to Poland. Often these immigrants were members of religious communities unwelcome elsewhere, such as the Mennonites. In Vistula Delta they built canals, locks, floodgates, and windmills; and they transformed the countryside to benefit its inhabitants.

The Dutch also introduced their homes with typical **front arbor houses (*domy podcieniowe*)**. The house fronts jut out and are supported by large wooden pillars. They can be seen, for example, en route from Gdańsk to Elbląg in Koszwały. The most impressive examples of this architectural style are located in Trutnowy, Marynowy, and Lipce, a suburb of Gdańsk.

A wooded sand embankment divides the delta from the sea. Some popular beach resorts lie along the sandy beaches of the Amber Coast, e.g. **Stegny** ❽. Nearby, to the east on the sand bar is **Krynica Morska** ❾. Both cities were attractive vacation spots even before World War II.

Among the delights of the resorts, you will be confronted with the atrocities of the National Socialists. At the beginning of the sand bar in **Sztutowo** ❿ lies the **Stutthof Concentration Camp,** erected 1939. Members of the Polish elite from Gdańsk and former West Prussia were imprisoned here, and some were killed.

Later, Stutthof was converted to an extermination camp in which Greek and Hungarian Jews fell victim to the insanity of the Nazi regime in 1944. These Greeks and Hungarians represent about two-thirds of the 70,000 killed in this camp. The contrast between the camp, with gas chambers, and the carefree vacationers could not be more glaring.

ELBLĄG

From the appearance of the Old Town of **Elbląg** ⓫, one might imagine what Gdańsk might still look like today, if not for the destruction of war. The Teutonic Order granted Elbląg its charter in 1246, and the Hanseatic city experienced a pe-

FROMBORK

riod of cultural prosperity in the 16th century as a city-state. In the 20th century, the city developed into one of the greatest industrial centers of Western and Eastern Prussia. As a result of its industrial importance, it was almost completely destroyed in the Second World War.

In the succeeding years Elbląg was merely a green spot in the countryside, with only the reconstructed Gothic **St. Nicholas' Church** (*Kościół św. Mikołaja*) in its midst. The Gothic **St. Mary's Church of the Dominican Order** (today the Gallery *El*), a **City Gate** dating back to the 14th -15th century, and few remaining houses, were all that was left of one of the wealthiest cities in the Baltic region – once a rival to Gdańsk. By 1945 only twelve **house fronts** in the Old Town had not been destroyed (ul. Garbary, ul. Św. Ducha).

Reconstruction of the city began in the 1990's, with the erection of postmodern buildings on the original sites. Some critics maintain that the designers were given too much liberty, but everyone supports the objective of revitalizing the city.

The most compelling reason to visit Elbląg is an boat excursion on the *__Elbląg Canal__ (*Kanał Elbląski*), which begins here and leads to the inland port of Ostróda, gaining 99 meters in elevation using five slipways instead of locks. The experience of a boat with passengers on board being pulled up an incline with a rope is a highlight of this excursion. The most interesting portion of the journey is between Elbląg and Buczyniec (5-hour boat tour; return by bus (cf page 183).

FROMBORK

The city of **Frombork** ⑫ is located on the Vistula Lagoon (*Zalew Wiślany*) about 30 kilometers towards the east in Warmia, and can be visited on a day trip

Right: Frombork, famous for Copernicus and its massive fortified cathedral.

from Elbląg. The train ride passes through dense forests and, in part, right along the coast. Frombork is known as "the city of Copernicus," since the lay astronomer and cathedral clergyman, born in Toruń in 1473, spent more than 30 years of his life in Elbląg. In his book, *De Revolutionibus Orbium Coelestium*, he declared that the sun and not the earth was at the center of the universe. Apparently Copernicus received the first copy of his book, which had been printed in Nuremberg, on his deathbed.

Frombork is worth seeing not only because of Copernicus and his impact on the field of astronomy. It is also the location of what is probably the most beautiful sacral building of the Order's former state of Prussia. The massive ***Cathedral** built between 1329 and 1388 towers on a hill surrounded by fortification walls. Its gabled façade features two octagonal towers including stairwells. The towers will certainly catch your attention due to their unusual form.

The Baroque interior of the cathedral has one of the most beautiful sounding organs in northern Poland. In addition, there are no less than twenty altars and some admirable Renaissance tombstones. One of the oldest treasures is the late Gothic (1504) **winged altar**, located in the left aisle. The Madonna sits graciously in the center of the altar on a crescent moon.

After a tour of the cathedral, you should not be put off by the few flights of steps up the corner tower of the fortified wall to the **Radziejowski Bastion**. There is a picturesque view over the lagoon and the shingle bar, and it is said you can even see right to Kaliningrad.

KWIDZYN

An unusual view can be had from the Vistula Delta area in **Kwidzyn** ⑬. On the high riverbank, a bizarre structure can be seen – half church and half fortress. This is the impressive **Castle of the Pomesanian Cathedral Chapter** (a branch of the Teutonic Knights), where a large cathedral has in fact been integrated into the fortress. Both structures date back to the 14th century. The giant tower set in front of the fortress served as an toilet (dansker). It is adjoined to the actual fortress by means of a walkway supported by heavy pillars.

These outside toilets (danskers) generate many questions. Did the Knights of the Teutonic Order bring back this unusual (for the time) fixation on hygiene from the southern realm of Palestine? Were the towers also used for defense, or were they utilized solely as lavatories? Is the term "dansker" a satirical reference by the Knights of the Order to the citizens of Gdańsk, whom they disliked? Unfortunately, you will not find answers to these questions in the **Castle Museum**, which is nonetheless worth visiting.

Awaiting the visitor in the **Cathedral** are Gothic frescoes and the cubicle in which the blessed Dorothea of Montau, patron of Prussia, had herself walled in alive in the 14th century.

CHEŁMNO COUNTRY

The region called *Ziemia Chełmińska* stretches south of Kwidzyn and was the cradle of the Knights of the Teutonic Order in the principalities of Prussia. Three rivers mark the approximate boundaries of this region: to the west and south the Vistula River, to the north the Osa River and to the east the Drwęca River.

The beautiful city of **Chełmno** ⑭ situated on the banks of the Vistula River has given the region its name. The city has been able to maintain its medieval character up until this day. Evidence of this is seen in its **City Wall**, almost completely preserved, and in its numerous churches. Chełmno was granted a town charter in 1233. This charter was a model for a large majority of towns within the realm of the Teutonic Order. Besides the large **St. Mary's Church,** where late Gothic frescos (1400) were uncovered in 1925, the

TORUŃ

Above: Fresh vegetables at the market in Chełmno.

most popular attraction is the **City Hall** built in the Mannerist style. The City Hall is one of the few structures in northern Poland in which the influence of Italian architecture is apparent. Mannerism is displayed here in its purest, unadulterated form. The arrangement of the windows, that is, the higher the floor, the more windows there are, shows the playfulness of this architectural style. In fact, you could get the impression that the architect wanted to stand the building on its head. As on most Polish city halls, the high decorative attic is an obligatory feature.

If time allows, you should pass up the faster highway from Chełmno to Toruń and take the rather more roundabout way via **Radzyń Chełmiński ⓯**. The ***Ruins of the Teutonic Order Castle** along the road between Wąbrzeźno and Grudziądz will surely bring to mind the former medieval lords of the land. The structure dating back to the 14th century is a prime example of a fortress type described as castellated, meaning with battlements. It is easy to recognize the architectural structure of the cube-like building. It has four residential wings, grouped around an arcaded courtyard, four corner towers, and a keep (the strongest and securest part of the castle) in the northwest corner of the courtyard, of which only the foundations have been preserved. Especially impressive is the south façade of the structure, with black bricks in a repetitive diamond pattern.

Another castle belonging to the Teutonic Order can be found in **Golub-Dobrzyń ⓰**. This massive, square building features a decorative parapet, not usually found on the Order's castles, which indicates that an addition was made at the beginning of the 17th century. The Polish princess of Swedish ancestry, Anna Wasa (sister of Sigismund III. Wasa) had the castle rebuilt as it land had belonged to her since 1611. Every year the castle offers a fantastic backdrop for an impressive jousting contest of the knights in which they compete on horseback and on foot with sword, axe, and lance.

**TORUŃ

Toruń ⓱ is noteworthy not only for its architectural treasures. The city is also a lively, enjoyable place boasting an important university and plenty of cafés and restaurants. A stroll through the narrow streets and alleys of the Old Town, where the charm of the city unfolds, belongs to a visit here. A culinary specialty is Toruń gingerbread baked in various shapes and sizes – a true delight for the eyes and taste buds; however, a sure-fire way to ruin your teeth in the long run.

The earliest Knights of the Teutonic Order founded the city in 1233 and named it after a piece of land they had owned in Palestine, *Toron*. The new section of the city joined the Old Town (now city center) in 1264. These two sections

TORUŃ

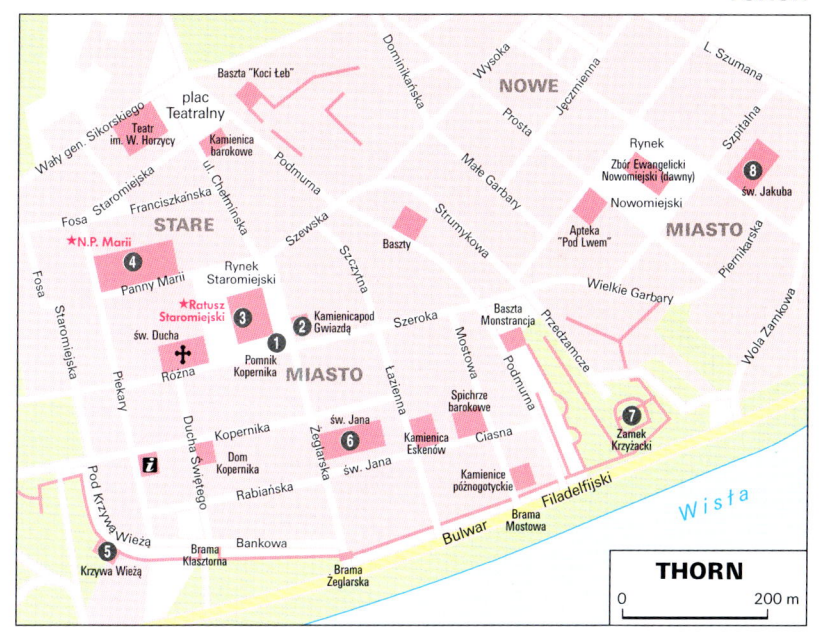

of Toruń, in German Thorn, were members in the Hanseatic League, soon to become the most important cities in the lands of the Teutonic Order in Prussia. In 1454, the Toruń patricians became disillusioned by the strict rule of the Teutonic Order. They stormed the castle and subordinated themselves to Polish protection. Supposedly only two bombs were dropped on Toruń during the Second World War, so the splendid medieval town, along with the somewhat provincial architecture of the onetime Prussian garrison, has been well preserved.

A tour of Toruń is best begun at the **Market Square**, near the **Copernicus Monument** ❶ (1853). The great Nicholas Copernicus was born in Toruń in 1473, and is claimed by both the Poles and the Germans as their own. A Latin inscription on the base of his memorial pays tribute to him as "the astronomer who moved the earth and brought the sun to a standstill." He was born on nearby St. Anna Street, now called ul. Kopernika. Two Gothic houses, partly reconstructed, make up a museum in which a large model of the medieval city is displayed. Around the Market Square, there are a number of delightful burghers' houses, but the most significant one has nothing to do with the Copernicus era; the **House of the Star** ❷ (*Kamienicapod Gwiazdą*) is built in Rococo style and features an authentic bourgeois entrance hall and Oriental pieces of art – providing a contrast to the previous sights.

The Market Square is dominated in the center by a massive brick structure, the **★City Hall** ❸. The four-winged building dating back to the end of the 14th century has a high tower. The City Hall embodies an architectural combination of the individual architectural structures preceding it. The interior was fashioned in Baroque style after fire damage in 1705.

The three Gothic brick churches in Toruń – among the most noteworthy in all of Poland – are impressive even to those not interested in architecture. The **★St. Mary's Church** ❹ (*Kościół Najświętszej Marii Panny*; 1343-1400), adja-

Information pages 181-183

TORUŃ

cent to the market, belonged to the Franciscan Order and has, according to the order's rules, no church tower since these were considered a symbol of power. The church nave is extremely narrow and thus appears to be very high. The large Gothic wall paintings feature slender, Italianate figures of saints. A chapel was erected in the presbytery for Anna Wasa, and houses her ornate sarcophagus (1636).

Of the rest of the city wall, the **Leaning Tower** ❺ (*Krzywa Wieża*; ul. Fosa Staromiejska), in the northwest corner of the Old Town, is the most interesting. The upper section of the rather low tower leans about two meters forward, giving it the appearance of having a precariously fragile stance. Many tourists, for fun, try to keep their balance while placing their feet directly at the base of the tower wall. Up until now no one has been able to accomplish this balancing act!

Above: Toruń belongs to the few Polish cities that were not destroyed in the war – an intact medieval atmosphere and a spirited city.

From a distance the massive tower of the **St. John's Church** ❻ (*Kościół św. Jana*) and its three characteristic roofs can be seen. The interior furnishings have been preserved for the most part, the exception being the church's most treasured work – the sculpture of a "beautiful Madonna." In an apse there is a copy of the original, which disappeared in 1944.

A short detour towards the Vistula River leads to the ruins of what once was a **Castle of the Teutonic Order** ❼ (*Zamek Krzyżacki*). The fortified structure, dating from the 13th century, was torn down bit by bit after it had been stormed by the citizens of Toruń. Curiously the only piece of the castle which has survived the years is the *dansker* (the lavatory tower).

Near the New Town Market (*Rynek Nowomiejski*) is lastly the **St. James Church** ❽ (*Kościół św. Jakuba* c. 1309 - 1340). This is a beautiful basilica with artistic buttress work. The interior has numerous Gothic frescoes and pictures and sculptures dating back to its origin.

FROM GDAŃSK TO TORUŃ

FROM GDAŃSK TO TORUŃ

GDAŃSK ☎ 058

Centralny Ośrodek Informacji Turystycznej, ul. Heweliusza 27, Tel. 3014355, 3016637. A good tourist office right across from the City Hall of the Main City, ul. Długa 45, Tel. 3019151. *Sopot:* ul. Dworcowa 4, Tel. 5512617.

Hevelius, ul. Heweliusza 22, Tel. 3015631, Fax 3011922, www.orbis.pl/hot_hev.html. Located centrally in the Old Town, this plush Orbis hotel still recalls the notorious drinking bouts of the Scandinavian guests in the 70's and 80's. **Hanza**, ul. Tokarska 6, Tel. 3053427, Fax 3053386, www.hanza-hotel.com.pl. The newest hotel in Gdańsk, located directly next to Crane Gate advertises that its professional service personnel can fulfil their guests' every wish. **Novotel**, ul. Pszenna 1, Tel. 3015611, Fax 3015619, www.orbis.pl/hot_novg.html. Typical of the hotel chain with American double beds. Ideal location on Granary Island. Good food.

Two hotels in *Jelitkowo*, relatively close to Sopot, are serenely located on the beach, but are only accessible by car or by trolley No. 2 and No. 6 (one hour from city center): **Posejdon**, ul. Kapliczna 30, Tel. 5531803, Fax 5530228, www.orbis.pl/hot_pos.html. **Marina**, ul. Jelitkowska 20, Tel. 5532079, Fax 5530460, www.orbis.pl/hot_mar.html. Outstanding house built by the British. **Grand Hotel**, Sopot, ul. Bohaterów Warszawy 12/14, Tel. 5510041, Fax 5516124, www.orbis.pl/hot_gras.html. Attractive even as a pale reflection of its former grandeur. Casino, sea view, good restaurant.

Some distance from city center: **Dal**, ul. Czarny Dwór 4, Tel. 5563944, Fax 5532951. **Nord**, ul. Hallera 245, Tel. 3435700, Fax 3435646. **Jantar**, ul. Długi Targ 19, Tel. 3019532, Fax 3013529. Very modest and not very clean. Best possible location on the Long Market.

Zaułek, ul. Ogarna 107/108, Tel. 3014169. Modest accommodation, directly located in the Main City on the same street where Daniel Fahrenheit lived.

Maryla, Sopot, Al. Sępia 22, Tel. 5516053. **Miramar**, Sopot, ul. Zamkowa Góra 25, Tel. 5518011, Fax 5510727.

Youth Hostels, at three addresses: ul. Wałowa 21, Tel. 3013461, next to the gate of the former Lenin Ship Yard; ul. Kartuska 245, Tel. 3024187. Sopot: Al. Niepodległości 751, Tel. 5511493.

Private rooms: Biuro Zakwaterowań Gdańsk-Tourist, ul. Heweliusza 8, Tel. 3012634.

Campgrounds: ul. Jelitkowska 23, Tel. 5532731 (in Jelitkowo near Sopot) and ul. Hallera 234, Tel. 3435531, Fax 3435547 (in Brzeźno), both near the beach.

In Sopot, there are two sites to choose from: ul. Zamkowa Góra 21/25, Tel. 5518011, and ul. Bitwy pod Płowcami 69/73, Tel. 5516523.

Pod Łososiem "the Salmon," ul. Szeroka 54, Tel. 3017652. The most renowned restaurant in the city is likewise expensive. It is located in the house in which "Danzig Gold Water" has been produced since the 17th century (a liqueur with gold leaf, also served here). Reservations recommended. **Tawerna**, ul. Powroźnicza 19/20, Tel. 3014114. Elegant, directly on the Long Market. The tasty duck is enough for the entire family. Many business people dine here. Reservations recommended.

Newly opened, sophisticated restaurants: **Major**, ul. Długa 18, Tel. 3011069. Specialities, such as salmon carpaccio and beafsteak Romanov with plums. **U Szkota**, Chlebnicka 9/12, Tel. 3014911, and **Gdańska**, ul. Św. Ducha 16, Tel. 3057672, fascinate guests with specialties such as wild boar, goose and flounder. **Euro**, ul. Długa 79/80, Tel. 3052383. Fine Polish and international cuisine in a refined Biedermeier atmosphere.

A bit more reasonable are: **Pod Wieżą**, ul. Piwna 51, Tel. 3013924, next to St. Mary's Church, good soups; and **Kubicki**, ul. Wartka 5, Tel. 3010050. On the former grounds of the Teutonic Knights' Castle.

Inexpensive: **Tan-Viet**, ul. Podmłyńska 1/5, and **Bar Smok**, ul. Grobla, Ecke ul. Szeroka. Asian cooking. For budget travelers: **Pod Złotym Kurem**, ul. Długa 4. **Bar mleczny**, Neptun, ul. Długa 33/34 or Szeroka 8/10.

Żak, Wały Jagiellońskie 1, Tel. 3014119. Student club in which good live jazz is played every night.

Uphagen House (Dom Uphagena), ul. Długa 12: Summer months, open daily 10:00 a.m. – 4:00 p.m.
Artus Court (Dwór Artusa): Tues-Thurs 10:00 a.m. – 5:00 p.m., Sun 11:00 a.m. – 4:00 p.m. (closes one hour earlier in off-season months). **Museum of City History** (Muzeum Historii Miasta Gdańska) in the Main City town hall, Tel. 3019721. Tues-Sat 10:00 a.m. – 5:00 p.m., Sun 11:00 a.m. – 3:00 p.m. Closes one hour earlier in off-season months. **Museum of the Polish Post Office** (Muzeum Poczty Polskiej), ul. Obrońców Poczty Polskiej 1/2, Tel. 3017611. Mon, Wed 10:00 a.m. – 4:00 p.m., Sat, Sun 10:30 a.m. – 2:00 p.m. **Westerplatte**, Guard house No. 1, Tel. 3436972. During the summer open daily 9:00 a.m. – 4:00 p.m. **National Museum** (Muzeum Narodowe), ul. Toruńska 1, Tel. 3016804: Wed-Fri, Sun 10:00 a.m. – 4:00 p.m., Tues, Sat 10:00 a.m. – 5:00 p.m. In off-season months: Wed, Fri, Sun 9:00 a.m. – 4:00 p.m., Tues, Sat 11:00 a.m. – 5:00 p.m.
Maritime Museum (Centralne Muzeum Morskie), ul. Szeroka 67/68. Tues-Sun 10:00 a.m. – 4:00 p.m., Thurs 12:00 – 6:00 p.m. In off-season months, shorter opening hours. **St. Mary's Church** observation platform: Mon-Sat 9:00 a.m. – 5:00 p.m., Sun 1:00 – 5:00 p.m.

FROM GDAŃSK TO TORUŃ

Oliwa: Organ recitals in the cathedral. Mon-Fri 11:00 a.m. – 4:00 p.m., Sat 11:00 a.m. – 3:00 p.m., Sun 3:00 – 5:00 p.m., beginning on the hour. **Gdynia**: Museum Ship Błyskawica: May to September, open daily 10:00 a.m. – 1:00 p.m. and 2:00 – 4:00 p.m. Muzeum Oceanograficzne i Akwarium Morskie: Tues-Sun 10:00 a.m. – 4:30 p.m.

LOCAL TRANSPORTATION: The Tricity (Gdańsk, Sopot, Gydnia) is served by a rapid transit systemn (regular departures from the central train station). You can also travel to Oliwa and Jelitkowo by trolley. Ferry excursions to the Westerplatte and to Hel depart from the pier at Zielona Brama (Green Gate; Tel. 3014926).

The **Opera House** is located in Gdańsk Wrzeszcz, Al. Zwycięstwa 15 (Tel. 3414644).

FESTIVALS: July: Northern Folklore Festival Days (Festiwal Folkloru Ludów Północy). Along with Scandinavian music groups, exotic guests such as the Yakuts or the Chukchis perform (Info Tel. 3011051).

July 31 to August 15: Jarmark Dominikanski: Since 1260, the largest fair honoring St. Dominic takes place with cultural presentations and programs. The streets are lively with vendors who sell everything under the sun. Watch out for pickpockets.

July: Festival of Song in Sopot in the woods, dating back to the year 1909. This is where the Swedish group *Abba* first drew crowds (Opera Leśna, ul. Moniuszki 12, Tel. 5511812).

July / August: Gdynia Summer Jazz Days in Teatr Muzyczny Gdynia and in the Opera Leśna Sopot. Progressive jazz music (Information Tel. 6200105).

Organ Festival in the Cathedral in Oliwa (watch for bulletins and posters or ask at the tourist information center). During this time, theater companies from all over Europe perform their best Shakespearean works (Shakespeare Festival) at the Teatr Wybrzeża on Targ Węglowy 1 (Tel. 3017021).

KASHUBIA ☎ 058

Pensjonat Hubertówka, PL-83315 Szymark-Wieżyca, Tel. 6843896. Near the highest peak in Kashubia, Mt. Wieżyca (328 m); Tennis court, sauna, ski lift, nightclub, etc. **Jezioranka**, Ostrzyce, Tel. 6841783. Nicely located pension.

Pomorski, Kościerzyna, ul. Gdańska 15, Tel. 6862290. **Rugan**, Kartuzy, ul. 3 Maja 36, Tel. 6811635, Fax 6811583. **Pod Niedźwiadkiem**, Wdzydze Kiszewskie, Tel. 6866080. **Campgrounds**: Dzierżążno, Tel. 6811000. Wdzydze Kiszewskie, Tel. 6861227.

Pizzeria Mammarosa, Kościerzyna, ul. Rynek 13, Tel. 6865530. Not much more than a pizza from the microwave oven awaits the hungry traveler. **Burczybas**, Dzierżążno (east of Kartuzy), ul. Gdańska 2, Tel. 6812656. Kashubian specialties. Folklore evenings take place regularly.

Kashubian Museum, Kartuzy, ul. Kościerska 1, Tel. 6811442. Tues-Fri 10:00 a.m. – 4:00 p.m., Sat 10:00 a.m. – 2:00 p.m. **Kashubian Open Air Museum** (Kaszubski Park Etnograficzny), Wdzydze Kiszewskie, Tel. 6863664. Tues-Sun 9:00 a.m. – 4:00 p.m., during the winter months open 10:00 a.m. – 3:00 p.m.

MALBORK ☎ 055

ul Piastowska 15, Tel. 2729246, Fax 2732892.

Zamek, ul. Starościńska 14, Tel. 2728400, Fax 2723367. Noble address in the Gothic building of the Front Castle.

Dedal, ul. Generała de Gaulla 5, Tel. 2726850, Tel./Fax 2723137. Far out of town, accessible only with a car.

Zbyszko, ul. Kościuszki 43, Tel. 2722640, Tel./Fax 2723394. Centrally located in the city center. Somewhat better since the remodeling.

Youth Hostel, ul. Żeromskiego 45, Tel. 2722408. Open July / August. **Campgrounds**, ul. Portowa 3, Tel. 2722413.

Zamkowa, in Hotel *Zamek*, ul. Starościńska 13, Tel. 2722738. The most elegant restaurant in the city. Good typical Polish dishes are served at the centrally located hotel restaurant **Zbyszko**, ul. Kościuszki 43, and at **Nad Nogatem**, Pl. Słowianski 5.

Castle Museum (Muzeum Zamkowe), ul. Starościńska 1, Tel. 2723364-211 (cashier's desk). May to September Tues-Sun 9:00 a.m. – 5:00 p.m. During the off-season open until 3:00 p.m. Only the castle grounds are open on Mondays. During the summer months, a *son-et-lumière* (sound and light show) is presented in the courtyard of the Middle Castle.

VISTULA DELTA ☎ 055

Among the numerous vacation spots along the "amber coast," Krynica Morska and Stegny are especially popular.

Pension Gallus, Krynica Morska, ul. Marynarzy 2, Tel. 2476126. A restaurant is located in the building. **Pension Karolina**, Stegny, ul. Grunwaldzka 37, Tel. 2478181.

Concentration Camp Stutthof, Sztutowo, Museum: Open daily 8:00 a.m. – 6:00 p.m.; (winter) 8:00 a.m. – 3:00 p.m.

ELBLĄG ☎ 055

Elbląg, ul. 1 Maja 30, Tel./Fax 2327373.

Elzam, pl. Słowiański 2, Tel. 2348111, Fax 2324083. Best hotel in town. The rooms vary greatly in size. It is recommended to take a look at the room first. **Kadyny Palace**, Kadyny, Tel. 2316120, 2316174, Fax

FROM GDAŃSK TO TORUŃ

2316200. Located at the lagoon between Elbląg and Frombork in a castle built by William II. Horseback riding is available at a neighboring stud farm.
Pensjonat Boss, ul. Św. Ducha 30, Tel. 2327973, Fax 2328366. Newly opened pension in beautifully restored old city town house. Highest standards. Friendly service. **Hotel Dworcowy**, ul. Grunwaldzka 49, Tel. 2337422. Near the train stations, recently renovated.
PTTK Hostel, ul. Krótka 5, Tel. 2324808. **Campgrounds**, ul. Panieńska 14, Tel. 2324307. Centrally located. **Kopernik**, Kościelna 2, Frombork, Tel. 2437285, Fax 2437300. Somewhat better than the **PTTK Hostel**, ul. Krasickiego 3, Tel. 2437252. **Youth Hostel**, ul. Elbląska 11, Frombork, Tel. 2437453. Open year round. **Campgrounds** on the road from Frombork to Braniewo, ul. Braniewska 14, Tel. 2437368.
Stara Gorzelnia, Kadyny, next to the hotel *Kadyny Palace* (see Accommodation) in an old distillery, Tel. 2316200. Polish, German and English cuisine.
At the foot of the cathedral hill in *Frombork* are two reasonably priced restaurants. **Akcent**, ul. Rybacka 4, Tel. 2437275. **Kopernik**, ul. Kościelna 2, Tel. 2437285. a true fossil of the socialist era is located on the hill in the **PTTK Hostel** with plastic flowers on the tables. Nonetheless, they serve tasty soups at the "horrendous" price of, for example, 0.97 ZŁ / US$ 0.20.
Galeria El, ul. Kuśnierska 6,Elbląg. **Cathedral** and **Bell Tower**, Frombork: Mon-Sat 9:30 a.m. – 5:00 p.m. **Museum of Old Medicine** (Muzeum Starej Medycyny), ul. Stara: Tues-Sun 10:00 a.m. – 6:00 p.m.
A boat ride on the **Elbląg Canal** (Kanal Elbląski), Departure time: 8:00 a.m. in Elbląg from Bulwar Zygmunta Augusta (behind St. Nicholas' Church, from May 1 – Sept. 15). Reservations: *Centrum Biznesu* in Hotel Elzam (Tel. 2325158, 2327373), and at the Campgrounds. Information available at *Żeluga Ostródzko-Elbląska*, ul. Panieńska 14, Tel./Fax 2324307.

ZIEMIA CHEŁMIŃSKA ☎ 056

Centralny, Chełmno, ul. Dworcowa 23, Tel. 6860212. The best house in this charming town. **Pod Jaszczurem**, Radzyń Chełmiński, ul. Grudziądzka 11, Tel./Fax 6886041. Located next to the castle ruins. Since the remodeling of its rooms, this small hotel can be well recommended. **PTTK Hostel**, in the castle at Golub. Tel. 6832455, Fax 6832666. Dirty and only to be recommended as a last resort.
The dining choices in *Chełmno* are modest. **Relaks**, ul. Powstańców Wielkopolskich 1. Plain and simple cooking. The **Hotel Pod Jaszczurem** in *Radzyń* offers good cooking. **U Karola** in nearby *Grudziądz* (ul. Toruńska 28) is also acceptable. A café located in the castle in Golub with the usual dishes such as tripe etc.

The restaurant **Kaprys** below in the town is best avoided.
Castle in Radzyń Chelmiński: Open June to September daily 9:00 a.m. – 9:00 p.m. **Castle** in Golub Dobrzyń: Open June to September Tues-Thurs 9:00 a.m. – 7:00 p.m.
FESTIVALS: Knights' Tournament in Golub Dobrzyń take place each year in the third week of July.

TORUŃ ☎ 056

Rynek Staromiejski 1, Tel. 6223746 (in the City Hall on the west side). Piekary 37/39, Tel. 6210931. **PTTK Office**, pl. Rapackiego 2, Tel. 6228228, 6224926.
Helios, ul. Kraszewskiego 1/3, Tel. 6225033 to 38, 6226244, Fax 6223565. A "luxury" hotel only in regard to its price. Built for Copernicus's 500th birthday (1973); had to be renovated since. Located near the Old Town.
Kosmos, ul. Ks. Jerzego Popiełuszki 2, Tel. 6228900, 6224320, Fax 6221341, www.orbis.pl/hot_kos.html. Could stand a little remodeling. Short walk to the Old Town. **Zajazd Staropolski**, ul. Żeglarska 10/14, Tel. 6226060, Fax 6225384. Next to St. John's Church. Somewhat modest, in the Old Town, worth your money.
Garnizonowy, ul. Wola Zamkowa 16, Tel. 6162883, 6522573. Next to St. James' Church. Former army hotel, the best in its category. **Trzy Korony**, ul. Rynek Staromiejska 21, Tel. 6226031 bis 2. The view of the City Hall makes up for other shortcomings. **Campgrounds**, ul. Kujawska 14, Tel. 6224187.
The best Polish cuisine is served by **Staropolska** (located in hotel of the same name), ul. Żeglarska 10/14, and the City Hall Cellar, **Ratusz**, Rynek Staromiejski 1, Tel. 6210292. **Hungaria**, ul. Prosta 19, Tel. 6224189. Reasonable Hungarian restaurant. **Pietrowskaja**, ul. Mostowa 6, Tel. 6210870. Russian cuisine. **Shao Lin**, ul. Królowej Jadwigi 9, Tel. 6210836. Chinese. **La Bella Italia**, at the Market Square. Italian. **Ristorante Italiano Staromiejska**, ul. Szczytna 4. Another Italian.
Night life is offered in the many bars and nightclubs. **Pod Aniołem** in the cellar of the City Hall (to find the entrance, look for an angel affixed to the wall). **Kaitachino** and **Azyl**, ul. Kopernika.
Regional Museum inside the City Hall building, Tel. 6227038: Open Tues–Sun 10:00 a.m. – 4:00 p.m. **Copernicus House** (Muzeum Dom Mikołaja Kopernika), ul. Kopernika 15/17, Tel. 6226748. Open Tues–Sun 10:00 a.m. – 4:00 p.m. **House Under the Star** (Kamienica pod Gwiazdą), Rynek Staromiejski 35: Open Tues–Sun 10:00 a.m. – 4:00 p.m.
Toruń Gingerbread. Especially fine gingerbread can be purchased in a shop on ul. Żeglarska between the market and St. John's Church.

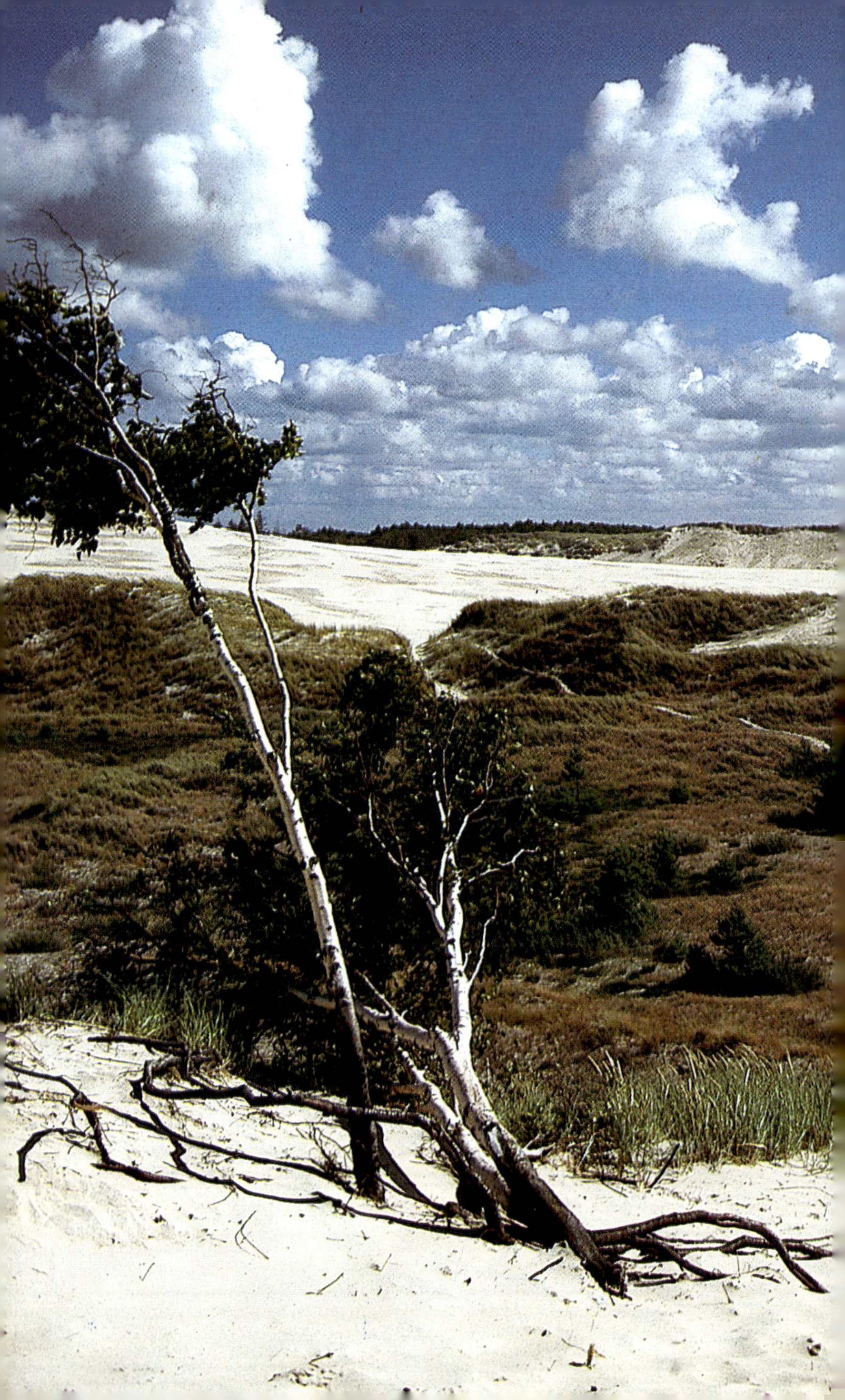

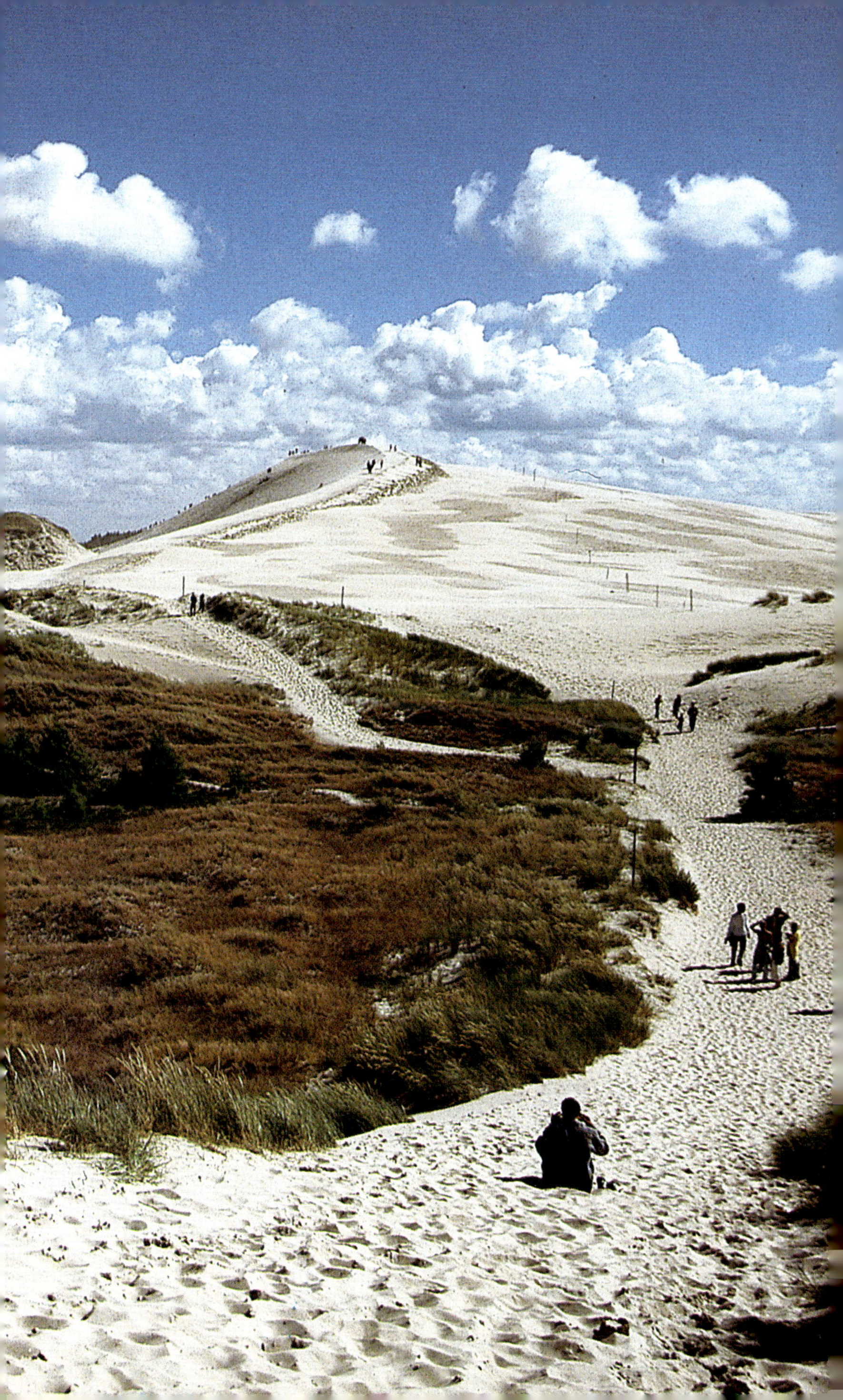

POMERANIA

POMERANIA
Sandy Beaches, Steep Coastlines and Shifting Dunes

SZCZECIN

THE ISLAND OF WOLIN

FROM KOŁOBRZEG TO SŁUPSK

ŁEBA AND THE SŁOWIŃSKI NATIONAL PARK

Hundreds of kilometers of white sandy beaches, which sometimes are as much as 100 meters wide, making them among the widest in Europe, draw hundreds of thousands of visitors to the Polish Baltic coast each and every year. The sea water, with the exception of the bay around Gdańsk, is clean enough to swim in. Onla the unpredictable climate and the relatively low water temperatures (seldom above 18°C) hold the region back from developing into a second Mediterranean. The exceptional beauty of the Pomeranian countryside cannot be denied. The steep coast of the island of Wolin is approximately 100 meters high and covered with primeval forests. Further eastward, the endless expanses of the sand dunes at Łeba await the eager explorer. Besides the natural wonders of the coastline, you will also find several historical and cultural attractions in the area.

The Land of the Gryfici Dukes

The coast and the bordering interior area belong to Pomerania – the wide region east of the Odra River. Today, it is also often called West Pomerania in reference to its Polish name *Pomorze Zachodnie*. This region was originally populated by Slavic tribes but was settled during the 13th century by the Germans, and therefore was almost entirely German speaking and Protestant in the early modern age. After the claims of Poland and Denmark had been warded off, the Gryfici (German: Greif) family clan ruled in Pomerania. The Gryficis were of Slavic origin, but became Germanized. When they died out in 1637, the Swedes, by the Treaty of Westphalia, seized the western part of Pomerania (West Pomerania and Szczecin), and the eastern section passed to the Brandenburg Electorate and was henceforth known as "East Pomerania." In 1720 West Pomerania and then in 1815 East Pomerania fell to Prussia, later becoming part of the "German Reich." Not until the upheavals of the Second World War did the region become Polish; its present day population comes primarily from eastern Poland.

The extensive moraine region is much more level than the hilly countryside of the Masurian Lakelands. Woods, meadows and endless potato fields, first planted under the rule of Frederick the Great, are characteristic of the region. The vast estates of the Prussian aristocracy (Bismark and von Blücher

Previous pages: The Lacka Góra (sand dunes) in Słowiński National Park shift two meters eastward every year. Left: Pomerania – ideal countryside for bikers.

SZCZECIN

both had homes here) were converted into agricultural production cooperatives after 1945. Most went bankrupt after the fall of the Iron Curtain, causing the unemployment rate to soar in this unindustrialized region.

SZCZECIN

Little is left of the beautiful pre-war city of **Szczecin** ❶ (formerly Stettin), once the third largest German city. After the war, the most important structures were carefully restored, but empty lots and socialist housing blocks still characterize the rest of the city. Until 1997, the castle, the old city hall, and the churches stood somewhat abandoned on a meadow. Today a "new old city" in the 17th century style is being rebuilt here.

The only parts that still retains their full splendor are is the Wały Chrobrzego boulevard on the banks of the Odra

Above: The former Berlin Gate – one of the few remains of pre-war Szczecin.

(Oder) River, and the somewhat dilapidated "extended city" surrounding Plac Grunwaldzki and Plac Odrodzenia (west of the city center). This section of the city was founded in 1873 after the fortress of Szczecin had been leveled to the ground. The wide avenues converging in a star-shaped fashion at centrally located squares conspicuously replicate the street network of Paris as conceived by George Eugène Haussmann.

The fate and fortune of the city began in the 12th century with the founding of a West Slavic fishing village named *Stitin*. The town was granted municipal autonomy in 1243, joined the Hanseatic League in 1278, and with numerous trading companies, it soon became the residence of the Duchy of West Pomerania. After a century of Swedish rule, Frederick William of Prussia bought the city from the Swedes "in legal contracts and for a justified price" – as the Latin inscription on the Harbor Gate (*Brama Portowa*, former **Berlin Gate**, pl. Zwycięstwa) proclaims.

AROUND SZCZECIN

The harbor city located closest to Berlin was lost by the Germans after the Second world War, when the city changed hands. Today, Szczecin has a large port complex and a flourishing shipping industry. It is also a leading city culturally, boasting a university, many places of higher education, several theaters and concert halls.

*Wały Chrobrego

A short walk through the town should start at its most beautiful spot: ***Wały Chrobrego**. Today this street is the main attraction of the city on the Odra River. The boulevard used to be called **Haken Terrace**, named after the city mayor Hermann Haken. The riverbank promenade was built in 1905 with the erection of three pompous buildings now placed under historical protection. The first of the buildings was the City Museum (today the **Maritime Museum**, a branch of the *Muzeum Narodowe*). The second building was the Parliament of Pomerania (now the provincial office); and the third, the State Insurance Company (today the Marine College). A terraced complex with two small lookout pavilions stretches out in front of the museum opening up a view of the harbor area. With a little luck, you may spot one of the huge sailing ships on the water.

The **St. Peter and St. Paul's Church** (*Kościół śś. Piotra i Pawła*), next to Trasa Zamkowa) is located towards the west. This is where the first church of Szczecin was supposed to have stood. The Polish Duke Bolesław III Krzywousty, the Wry-Mouthed, commissioned the church, built in 1124, and St. Otto von Bamberg preached in it. It is a fine example of a late Gothic brick structure featuring an interesting gabled façade. Colored brick and, above all, the terracotta busts of men and women (placed alternatingly) on the side walls decorate the building.

Near the Plac Hołdu Pruskiego is the former **King's Gate** (*Brama Hołdu Pruskiego*), one of the two best preserved city gates of modern times (completed in

Information pages 196-197

CASTLE OF THE POMERANIAN DUKES

1728). Close by, in a palace (ul. Farna) that is no longer standing, the most famous child of the city was born – Princess Sophie Friederike von Anhalt-Zerbst. She became the Empress of Russia (reigning 1762 – 1796) better known under the name of Catherine the Great. The admiration of the Poles for this woman is not particularly overwhelming since she was responsible for the partitioning of the country in the years 1771, 1792 and 1795.

In and Around the Castle

Located centrally on the banks of the Odra River is the **Castle of the Pomeranian Dukes** (*Zamek Książąt Pomorskich*). This castle was meticulously restored after the Second World War. Beginning in the 14th century it was continuously extended and remodeled, and thus

Above: St. Mary's Church in Stargard Szczecinski, an impressive example of a Gothic brick church. Right: Bisons in Wolinski National Park.

contains stylistic features from the Gothic, Renaissance and Baroque periods. The restoration was carried out based on a copperplate etching of the castle. Matthäus Merian the Younger from Switzerland created this etching dating from the 17th century and showing the castle with a fantastic Renaissance attic and a high tower. The tower has since been rebuilt and offers a beautiful view.

The Old Town stretches south of the castle. It suffered severe damage in a bombing raid by the Allies in 1944. Only a few of the buildings in this wealthy Hanseatic city were left standing after the attack. The **Seven Cloaks' Tower** (*Baszta Siedmiu Płaszczy*), a former watchtower, was left undamaged and now stands symbolically as part of the old Gothic city wall, like a relict from another world, next to a four-lane highway. Before the bombing of 1944, the tower was surrounded by houses, and so its presence was more or less forgotten. However, its four-meter thick walls are now the only structures left from the entire street.

Map page 189, Information pages 196-197

STARGARD SZCZECIŃSKI

The **Old City Hall** (*Stary Ratusz*; Museum of City History) immediately catches your eye with its almost too liberally reconstructed façade in a late Gothic style. This style is similar to that of the city halls in Stralsund or Lübeck. A wine bar (*U Wyszaka*) is located in its vaulted cellar. The **St. James' Church** (*Kościół św. Jakuba*) located on the Plac Orła Białego was extensively rebuilt in the 1970's. This late Gothic brick structure is the city's cathedral today. Very little has been preserved of its original interior furnishings. Although the church tower lost half its original height of 119 meters after the war, the 5.7 ton church bell could not yet be hung and the bell still rests on a provisional stand next to the church.

Trip to Stargard Szczeciński

Forty kilometers west of Szczecin is **Stargard Szczeciński** ❷, an old Hanseatic city. This place held equal rank with Szczecin in the Middle Ages. Trading disputes between the two cities even led to bloody conflicts (1454-1640).

Stargard was largely damaged in the war. Monotonous housing blocks border on the original buildings, which have been carefully restored, giving the city a somewhat chaotic appearance. Most of the original city wall with its unconventional **Mill Gate** (*Brama Młyńska*) was left undamaged by the war. The gate spans the Ihna River and is flanked by two towers allowing the city to be closed to ships by means of a portcullis.

For all art enthusiasts, a tour through Stargarder's ★**St. Mary's Church** (*Kościół Mariacki*) is a must. This church is considered the most precious historical structure in all of Pomerania. It was modeled after the "Marienkirche" (St. Mary's Church) in Lübeck around 1400. The impressive twin towered basilica with a chancel ambulatory and chapel cornice is one of the most captivating designs created by Hinrich Brunsberg. He is one of the few architects of the brick Gothic style known by name. The massive interior of the basilica is well proportioned. The distinctive glazed brick and the decorative ceramic masks make the outer walls an artistic masterpiece.

On the way back to Szczecin, a stop at **Lake Miedwie** is highly recommended. Small tasty white fish thrive in these waters and are grilled lakeside for hungry visitors. A Cistercian monastery dating back to 1173 is located at **Kołbacz**. Parts of the abbey church are late Romanesque – don't miss the rose window.

THE ISLAND OF WOLIN

Thereare two islands off the Polish coast, Wolin and Usedom (Uznam), but only small portion of the islands belongs to Poland. A trip there is a spectacular experience of nature, as well as great recreation; you can opt for a day at the beach or a hike in ★**Woliński National Park.**

Międzyzdroje, at the edge of the park, was a chic seaside resort early in the 20th

THE ISLAND OF WOLIN

century. The flamboyance and flair is still visible in the beautifully built villas dating back to the period of economic expansion of the 1870's, and the new hotels continue this tradition. This small town is trying to maintain tradition by building new hotels and with the restoration of the mole dating from 1907.

This place comes alive in the summer: the sun shines, the beaches are packed and boardwalks along the shore are crowded with strolling vacationers on the lookout for a grilled fish or ice cream. It's a continuous hustle and bustle between the beach and the city. Air mattresses and swimming rings bob back and forth, and the beach is covered in sand buckets, shovels, toys, and loud ghetto-blasters- the beach holiday basics.

It is much more peaceful in *Woliński National Park ❸. Within the park boundaries is the island's steep coastline, whose highest point lies 93 meters above sea level. The distinctive flora and fauna, e.g. sea eagles, spotted eagles, and eagle owls, are protected. With the assistance of the trail map "Woliński Park Narodowy," you can find a number of good hiking trails starting from Międzyzdroje. The green trail runs to the **bison preserve** in the middle of beautiful beech and oak stands. Here on a large piece of land the bison can live undisturbed as they once did when they ruled the forest. You will probably only be able to see them during the feeding times.

The red trail runs along the beach, leaving most vacationers behind. Here you can see waterfowl and, perhaps, seals. After seven kilometers you return to civilization at Wisełka. Buses run frequently run from here for the return trip. If you are fit, you can continue to hike along the picturesque Lake Czajce to a small train station in Warnowo (about five kilometers). The village of Wapnica, south of Międzyzdroje, is a good starting point for walks to **Turquoise Lake** (*Jezioro Tur-*

Above: Popular and populated – the beach at Międzyzdroje. Right: Vacation acquaintance in Kołobrzeg.

192 Map page 189, Information pages 196-197

KOŁOBRZEG

kusowe) and to the banks of the lagoon in Szczecin.

You can take a ferry to the island of Usedom where **Świnoujście** is located, or reach it by city bus from Międzyzdroje. This was and is a blend of Szczecin's outer harbor, with busy ferry traffic to Scandinavia, and a beach resort. In 1944 and 1945, the place was severely damaged and today has little to offer except a fishing museum and a few beautiful villas. The largest Polish market (so they say) is located on the border to Germany and offers the shopper everything from garden dwarf figurines to amphetamines (according to the police), Russian caviar, and supposedly authentic Levi jeans.

On the mainland, across from the east banks of Wolin, lies a gem of art history, the cathedral of **Kamień Pomorski** ❹. This cathedral is built partly in late Romanesque and partly in the Gothic style. The large, preserved building attests to the fact that Kamień Pomorski was once the bishopric of East Pomerania, from the 12th century for a period of 400 years.

In the summer international concerts are held on the famous 17th century cathedral organ. Frequent performances also make it possible at other times to enjoy the unusual timbre of this organ. The **City Hall,** built in the 14th and 15th centuries, and a few **half-timbered buildings** make the city, pleasantly located on the water, at least worth a detour.

KOŁOBRZEG TO SŁUPSK

Several vacations spots are located on the Pomeranian coast, the most popular being Mrzeżyno, Niechorze, Kołobrzeg, Ustronie Morskie, Mielno, Ustka and Łeba. They are all very similar– endless white sandy beaches and lots of activity, which is concentrated at former communist worker's vacation complexes, new hotels and the many camp grounds. There is more than beach life, however; several cities offer attractive cultural programs.

Kołobrzeg ❺ reveals its fascinating history just fragmentarily in its physical appearance. As early as the year 1000 AD, the later King Bolesław I, the Brave ("Chrobry"), established the first missionary bishopric for Pomerania at this location. Later on, Kołobrzeg became a member of the Hanseatic League, with a budding salt industry making the city prosperous. After 1800 the fortified Prussian city was often fought over and the scene of many battles. The fate of this city on the Baltic, which had become a very popular German swimming resort, was sealed when a ten-day siege in 1945 left ninety percent of it in ruins.

Kołobrzeg is once again a popular seaside resort. In the early 1990's, the old city was reconstructed according to the original plans, providing enough historic atmosphere so that a visitor will want to enjoy a cup of coffee here. The most impressive structure in Kołobrzeg is the massive **St. Mary's Cathedral** (*Katedra Najświętszej Marii Panny*) featuring five naves. As if a miracle had graciously

SŁUPSK

spared it, the cathedral was only slightly damaged in the 1945 fire. It was built over many decades, starting in 1301. The towers on the monumental west façade (15th century) were never completed. The interior holds a number of precious objects, for example, a bronze baptismal font (1355) supported at the base by four lions in a reclining position, a hanging chandelier in the nave, and a seven-armed candelabra (1327).

Darłowo 6, near the coast, is a sleepy hollow with country charm. Its buildings were not damaged during the last world war. Its **castle** dates back to the 14th century and is home to the collected works of the Regional Museum. It is in part dedicated to the castle's most prominent resident, Erik I, King of Denmark, Norway and Sweden, whose reign ran from 1397 to 1442. After losing the throne, he took up piracy, then, driven away by Visby in Gotland, he went into exile in the Pomeranian city until he died. Erik I lies buried in the nearby Gothic **St. Mary's Church** in a tomb commissioned by Emperor William II.

Passing by the sturdy **Stone Gate**, a remnant of the town fortification from the 14th century, you reach the city's most architecturally significant structure, **St. Gertrude's Chapel** (*Kaplica św. Gertrudy*) built in 1434. It is a small, twelve-sided cemetery chapel and was supposedly erected by King Eric I upon his return from a pilgrimage to Jerusalem. There is a similarity to the Anastasi Rotunda in Jerusalem.

Słupsk 7, much larger than Darłowo, was once known as the "Paris of East Pomerania." This title is no longer appropriate because the war left deep scares here, too. The city center now is rather monotonous collection of apartment buildings. It makes a well-kept, orderly impression and offers the visitor interesting nooks and crannies and several excellent restaurants.

Above: Poland's other face – a housing project in Słupsk. Right: Half-timbered architecture at the Open-Air Museum in Kluki.

During the Middle Ages the amber trade brought the city true riches. However, severe fires and blockage by silt of the shipping channels contributed to the city's collapse. In the 19th century, Słupsk recovered economically – as the new city hall on Plac Zwycięstwa candidly testifies.

On the edge of what was once the Old Town, is the **Castle of the Pomeranian Dukes**, home to the Regional Museum. Included in the exhibits are the noteworthy pastel drawings of Stanisław Ignacy Witkiewicz (1885-1939), known also as "Witkacy." Stanisław was a writer, artist, and Bohemian who always signed each of his works with a meticulously composed statement about the specific "stimulant" that contributed to its creation.

Near the castle is the **Castle Church** (*Kościół św. Jacka*). It has noteworthy tombs of the last Duchess and Duke of **Słupsk**, Anna de Croy and Ernst Boguslaw de Croy (1680-1682). A short detour leads you to the Market Square by way of the **Witches' Tower** (*Wieża Czarownic*). The tower, once a prison housing those sentenced to be burned at the stake, is now a modern art gallery. Also close by is **St. Mary's Church** (*Kościół Mariacki*). This is the parish church with a mighty tower dating back to the second half of the 14th century.

ŁEBA AND *SŁOWIŃSKI NATIONAL PARK

Łeba ❽ is a popular seaside resort without sightseeing attractions – and this for an obvious reason. The city was buried in quicksand and as a result was moved several hundred meters inland in the 16th century. Fast-food stands, several camp grounds and a sea of suntanned bodies greet you here in summer.

A 10 kilometer hike westward, on the spit between the Baltic Sea and Lake Łeba, the landscape changes to desert. Crescent moon shaped sand dunes reaching a height of up to 40 meters and reminiscent of those seen in pictures of the Sahara Desert, move eastward at a rate of up

SŁOWIŃSKI NATIONAL PARK

to two meters per year. The dunes are rapidly devouring the woods and years later, a bizarre cemetery of dead trees resurfaces as the sand moves on.

This area became *Słowiński National Park ❾ in 1967, not only because of the dunes, but also because of the more than 250 bird species, numerous rare mammals, and indigenous plants. UNESCO has placed the park on its list of World Heritage Sites for Biosphere Reserves. Germany's General Rommel took advantage of the desert conditions by training his Africa corps here. V-1 bombers were tested here, as the ruins of bunkers and several concrete runways testify.

The National Park is named after a Slavic people, the Slovincians, who were able to maintain two villages west of Lake Łeba – **Kluki** and **Smołdzino** – up into the 20th century. Kluki has a fine open-air museum featuring village architecture. In Smołdzino, a museum with exhibits on the National Park, offers more information on the four-legged and winged inhabitants of this region.

A few practical tips will make it easier for you to enter into a world wonder of nature. About three kilometers from Łeba is Rąbki, the farthest point visitors can take a motor vehicle. From Rąbki you can hike the remaining six kilometers to the largest dunes, *Łącka Góra*. You can also rent a bicycle or shorten the distance with an electric car.

In the summer, the noise of squealing children and rollicking teenagers fills the air. The earlier you arrive at the dunes, the longer you can enjoy the unique scenery undisturbed. From Łącka Góra, a short path leads to a quiet beach. You can go as far as a parking lot or back to Łeba along the shore. If you take the opposite direction (along the shore, then along the red trail), you will soon be almost alone, to enjoy the unforgettably beautiful landscape. You can also hike another 25 kilometers to the other end of the National Park at Rowy (return trip by taxi).

POMERANIA (POMORZE ZACHODNIE)

SZCZECIN ☎ 091

CIT, ul. Niepodległości 1, Tel. 4340440. Better yet: **Centrum Informacji**, Zamek Książąt Pomorskich (in the castle), Tel. 4891630, Fax 4340286, professional information kiosk.

Radisson, pl. Rodła 10, Tel. 4595595, Fax 4594594. American chain hotel, maintained by the Polish Shipping Company and the airline SAS. Probably the best hotel in northern Poland.
Neptun, ul. Matejki 18, Tel. 4883883, Fax 4884117, www.orbis.pl/hot_nep.html. Former number one hotel in the city. **Arkona**, ul. Panieńska 10, Tel. 4880261, Fax 4880260, www.orbis.pl/hot_ark.html.
Reda, ul. Cukrowa 2, Tel. 4822461, Fax 4826323, www.orbis.pl/hot_red.html. **Gryf**, al. Wojska Polskiego 49, Tel. 4334566, Fax 4334030. **Motel Malibu**, ul. Tczewska 61, Szczecin-Dąbie, Tel. 4600902. Good location on the road from Szczecin going east.
Garnizonowy, ul. Narutowicza 17 b, Tel. 4452413.
Youth Hostels (open July through August): ul. Monte Cassino 19 a, Tel. 224761. Ul. Grodzka 22, Tel. 4332924. The schools in which the youth hostels are located change frequently (for locations, ask at the tourist information center).
Campgrounds, ul. Przestrzenna 23, Tel. 4613264.
Chief, ul. Rayskiego 16, Tel. 4343765. Best restaurant in the city. Tasty fish dishes. **Admirał**, ul. Monte Cassino 37, Tel. 4342815. Good fish. At the **Radisson** Hotel there are several exclusive restaurants (Vivaldi, Renaissance).
Szczecin offers a good selection of Asian restaurants: **Hai Phong**, ul. Szarotki 16, Tel. 228910. **Wielki Mur**, pl. Stefana Batorego 4, Tel. 4339283. **China Town**, ul. Obrońców Stalingradu 24, Tel. 4882486. **Orientalna**, ul. Piastów 74, Tel. 4346805. **Balaton**, pl. Lotników 3, Tel. 4346873. Specialized in Hungarian cuisine, as the name indicates.
Maritime Museum (Department of the National Museum; Wały Chrobrego 3), **City Historical Museum** (Old City Hall, ul. Mściwoja 8) and. **National Museum**, ul. Staromłyńska 27, Tel. 4880249. Interesting collection of East Pomeranian art, for example Roman capitals from Kołbacz and precious items belonging to the Pomeranian dukes (burial objects). Tues, Thurs 10:00 a.m. – 5:00 p.m.; Wed, Fri 9:00 a.m. – 3:30 p.m.; Sat, Sun 10:00 a.m. – 4:00 p.m.
Szczecin **Philharmonic**, Armii Krajowej 1, Tel. 224723, 221252, is also an option for an evening. The **Puppet Theater** (Teatr Pleciuga), ul. Kaszubska 9,

Map page 189

POMERANIA

Tel. 4341002, Fax 4335804, is enjoyable for adults as well as children.

THE ISLAND OF WOLIN ☎ 091

CIT, Świnoujście, Pl. Słowiański 15, Tel./Fax 3224999. In Międzyzdroje: ul. Gryfa Pomorskiego 44, Tel 3280768, 3280209.

Amber Baltic, Międzyzdroje, ul. Promenada Gwiazd 1, Tel. 3281000, Fax 3281022. The best hotel around. Swimming pool, tennis courts and golf course (near Dziwnów), bowling and casino.
Slawia, Międzyzdroje, ul. Promenada Gwiazd 37, Tel. 3280098, Fax 3280764.
Rybak, ul. Turystyczna 1, Tel. 3280972, **Slavia**, Bohaterów Warszawy 38, Tel. 3280106, and **Merlin**, Bohaterów Warszawy 37, Tel. 3280728, in Międzyzdroje there are large complexes from the late communist era.
Polaris, Świnoujście, ul. Słowackiego 33, Tel. 3215412, Fax 3212437. Has a good restaurant.
Pod Muzami, Kamień Pomorski, ul. Gryfitów 1, Tel. 3822240. Comfortable hotel, newly remodeled, located at the Market Square. **Staromiejski**, Kamień Pomorski, Rybacka 3, Tel. 3822643, Fax 3822644.
Dom Rybaka, Świnoujście, Wybrzeże Władysława IV 22, Tel. 3212943. Near the passenger ferry from Wolin to Świnoujście. **Albatros**, Świnoujście, ul. Kasprowicza 2, Tel. 3212336.

Międzyzdroje: Many people prefer the fish stands on the beach promenade to the expensive restaurant in Hotel *Amber Baltic*. There are also two acceptable restaurants: **Marzanna**, ul. Gryfa Pomorskiego 4, Tel. 3280255 and **Piastowska**, ul. Kopernika 9, Tel. 3280657.
Świnoujście: **Chief**, ul. Armii Krajowej 3, Tel. 3212640. Restaurant in the **Polaris** hotel (see Accommodation).
Kamień Pomorski: **Magellan**, ul. P. Wysockiego 5, Tel. 3821454. Fish specialties.

Museum of Woliński National Park, Międzyzdroje, ul. Niepodległości 3: Tues-Sun 9:00 a.m. – 5:00 p.m. Bison compound: Tues-Sun 10:00 a.m. – 6:00 p.m.

FESTIVALS: Beginning of July: The Viking Festival with international guests brings to life the raw reality of the Middle Ages: medieval duels, rides with "real" Viking ships, etc. (information can be obtained under the number: 333068).

ORGAN CONCERTS in Kamień Pomorski: **June-Aug**, usually on Fridays at 7:00 p.m. Recitals on the organ from the 17th century take place daily during the summer at 11:00 a.m. and 4:00 p.m. (Reservations can be made under the number: 3821858).

A **narrow-gauge railway** connects Trzebiatów with Gryfice by way of Niechorze and Rewal (Information: Tel. 413363)

KOŁOBRZEG / DARŁOWO ☎ 094

ul. Duboisa 20, Tel. 3522311.
Solny, ul. Fredry 4, Tel. 3522401, 3545700, Fax 3525924. Close to the beach, similar to a Novotel.
New Skanpol, ul. Dworcowa 10, Tel. 3528211. Near the train station.
Dom Rybaka Bałtyk, ul. Bałtycka 7, Tel. 3525245. Centrally located. **Youth Hostel**, ul. Śliwińskiego 1, Tel. 3522769. Open July through August. **Campgrounds**, ul. IV Dywizji Wojska Polskiego 1, Tel. 3524569.
Albatros, Darłowo, ul. Wilków Morskich 2, Tel. 3143230.
Museum in the Castle, Darłowo, ul. Zamkowa 4: Tues-Sun 10:00 a.m. – 4:00 p.m. (in summer, Tues-Thurs to 6:00 p.m.).

SŁUPSK ☎ 059

ul. Jedności Narodowej 4, Tel. 424326.
Piast, ul. Jedności Narodowej 3, Tel. 425286, Fax 422741, and **Staromiejski**, ul. Jedności Narodowej 4, Tel. 428465, Fax 425019, are located next to each other in the center of town. **Rokowół**, ul. Ogrodowa 5, Tel./Fax 427211.
Zamkowy, ul. Zamkowa 2, Tel. 425294. Convenient location close to the castle.
Pod Kluką, ul. Kaszubska 22, Tel. 423469. On the arterial road to Łeba; one of the nicest restaurants on the coast, Kashubian touch to the interior. Try the walnut soup (*zupa orzechowa*) and pear Kashubian-style (*gruszka po kaszubsku*) for dessert. Also recommended: **Metro**, ul. 9 Marca 3, Tel. 422583, and **Franciszkańska**, ul. Jedności Narodowej 3, Tel. 422741.
Regional Museum (Muzeum Pomorza Środkowego), in the castle: Tues-Sun 10 a.m –4 p.m.
September: International Festival of Piano Music.

ŁEBA AND SŁOWIŃSKI NATIONAL PARK ☎ 059

Wodnik, ul. Nadmorska 10, Tel. 661366, 661960, Fax 661542. Former company housing, newly remodeled near the beach.
PTTK Hostels, ul. 1 Maja 6, Tel. 661324. **Campgrounds**: Przymorze, ul. Nadmorska 9, Tel. 661304. *Intercamp*, ul. Turystyczna 6, Tel. 661206.
Wodnik, in the hotel of the same name, recommends its eel in dill sauce. **Kowelin**, ul. Nad Ujściem 6, Tel. 661440 is also worth trying.
Kluki, Open Air Museum: Open May 15 to Sept. 15, Wed-Sat 9:00 a.m. – 4:00 p.m., Tues, Sun 9:00 a.m. – 6:00 p.m.

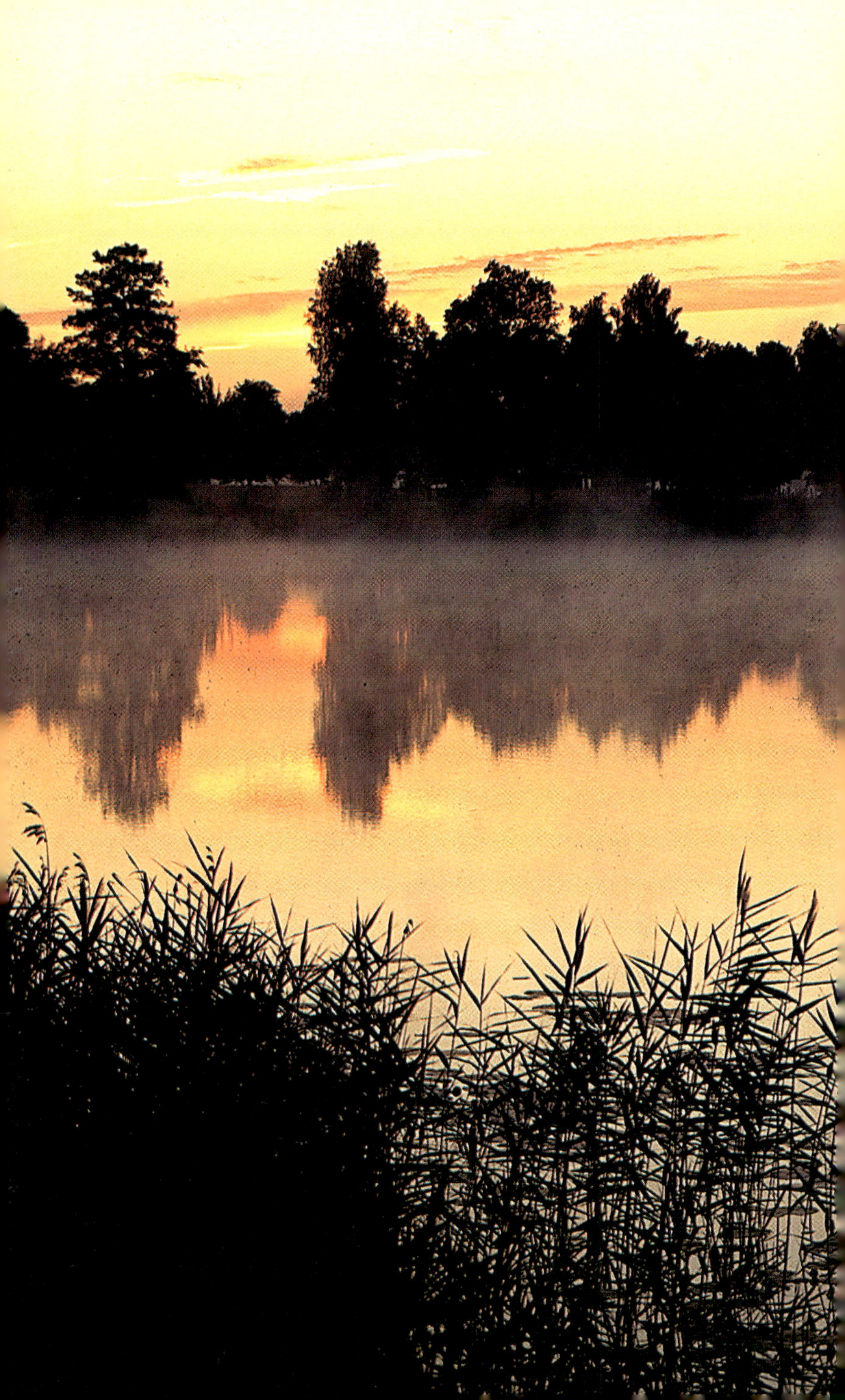

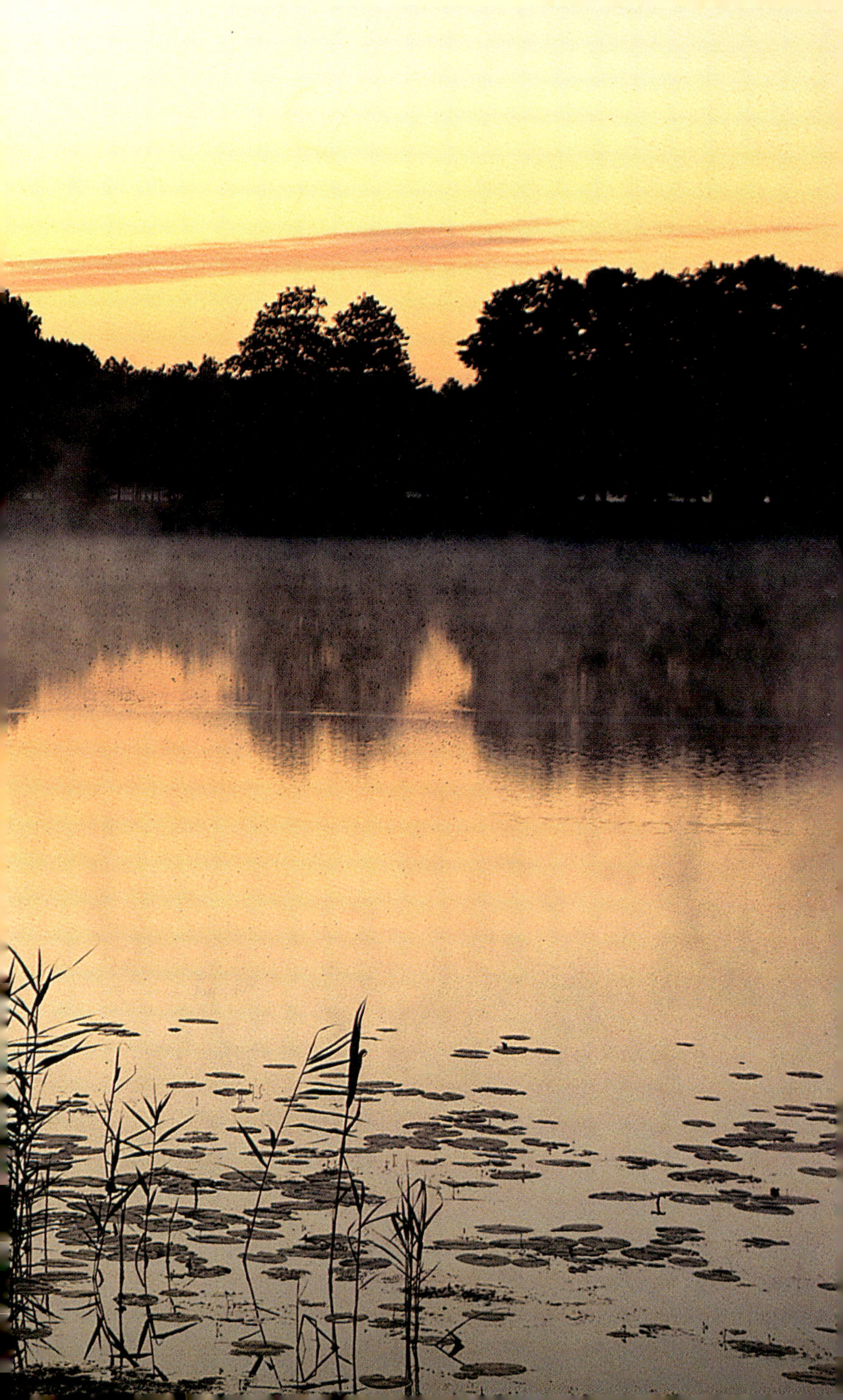

THE NORTHEAST

THE NORTHEAST

THE GREEN NORTHEAST
Rare Animals and Thousands of Lakes

OLSZTYN
MASURIA / SUWAŁKI,
BIEBRZAŃSKI NATIONAL PARK
BIAŁYSTOK
BIAŁOWIESKI NATIONAL PARK

Unspoiled forests, meadows and lakes, pristine nature – this is northeast Poland. You will search in vain for great historical monuments, and you will find neither large cities nor the blemish of industrial development. Village life seems to have stood still in the last hundred years. You will meet up with squawking geese, farmers on horse-drawn wagons, and storks circling in the blue sky. The landscape is soothing to the eye with chains of moraine hills and beautiful lakes shining in the bright sun. Attempts to count the individual lakes have remained unsuccessful, but there must be thousands of them in any case.

The countryside is divided into different topographical regions. The first of these regions is Warmia, which takes on the form of a triangle widening towards the southeast. Its northwestern point touches on the Vistula Lagoon at Frombork. Within this area lies the city of Olsztyn, the center of northeast Poland. Masuria, the most attractive section bordering to the east has been drawing tourists by the thousands for some time now. This area is an El Dorado for sailboats and canoes with the lakes stretching for 70 kilometers as the crow flies. It is also a paradise with hills all around for hikers and bikers. Due to the significance of this region's natural environment, a proposal was put forth in 1992 to declare all of northeast Poland – 15 percent of the entire area of Poland – a nature reserve.

Until the plan is put into effect, four national parks, several nature reserves, and other smaller preserved areas await the eager traveler. You will discover and experience an enchanting region – in a class of its own in all of Europe.

OLSZTYN

The largest city in the area is **Olsztyn ❶**, with a population of 167,000. At first glance it doesn't reveal its attractions since an endless number of unsightly concrete housing blocks dominate the scene around the city center. However, a pleasant surprise awaits you in the small Old Town section of the city.

Coming from the main train station, for example, you can enter the Old Town through the Gothic **High Gate**. A cobblestone street leads you past beautifully restored town houses up to the first street crossing, where you can turn left towards **St. James' Church** (*Kościół św. Jakuba*). From the outside, this brick structure's prominent tower is very impres-

Previous pages: Evening setting at Wigry Lake (Wigierski National Park). Left: Geese and their keeper – a typical sight in Masuria.

OLSZTYN

sive. Inside, a rare fan vault will catch your attention. If you turn right at the aforementioned street crossing, you will pass by the picturesque **Town Hall Market** and a small Protestant church before you reach the **Castle of the Warmia Cathedral Chapter**. This castle houses an interesting Regional Museum, *Muzeum Warmii i Mazur.*

In the courtyard of the castle you will first notice large sculptures – roughly carved stone figures of the medieval inhabitants of the country, the early Prussians. These figures are supposedly connected with their native religion and sacrificial offerings. A tribe of the Prussians, the Warmians, gave the region its name, Warmia.

As one of the four bishoprics in the Teutonic Order's realm in Prussia, Warmia enjoyed an autonomous status as early as the 14th century. This autonomy was also maintained during the Polish reign from 1466 to 1772. Due to the influence of the Catholic prince-bishops and the heavy Polish immigration to the southern part of Warmia, the region remained Catholic all through the years, in contrast to the other areas of eastern Prussia, which became Protestant in 1525.

The history of the region is told in the castle museum. Furthermore, you will also find information on the folklore and flora and fauna of the area. One section of the museum is even dedicated to the most prominent resident of the castle, Nicholas Copernicus (Mikołaj Kopernik: 1473-1543). He had studied in Cracow and in Italy and was a subject of the Polish King. As a Warmia city official, Copernicus corresponded with the king, and in 1519, he requested that financial support be sent for the fortification of the castle at Olsztyn because it was being threatened by the Knights of the Teutonic Order.

Copernicus left his signature above the entrance to his living quarters in the form of secretive scribbling – his attempts to calculate the equinoxes. Today his living

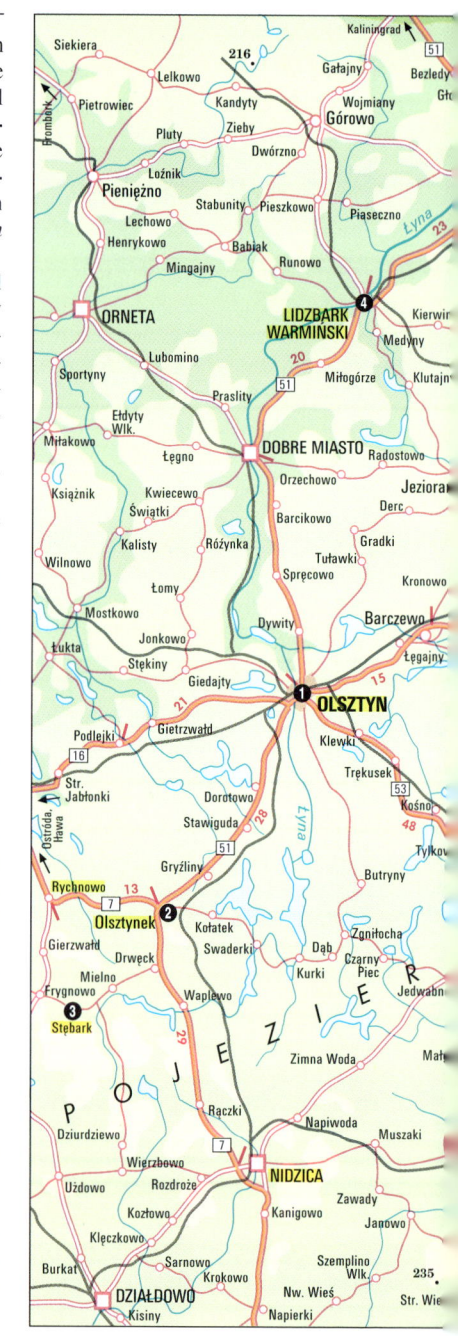

202 *Information pages 221-223*

MASURIA

OLSZTYNEK

quarters exhibit, among other things, historical equipment relating to astronomy.

Olsztynek

South of Olsztyn lies the ***Open Air Museum for Folk Architecture** in **Olsztynek ❷**. Besides the museums of the south Polish cities of Zubrzyca Górna and Sanok, this is the most noteworthy museum in the country. It was first established in Kaliningrad (now Russian, formerly Königsberg) and exhibited merely copies of significant architectural objects.

In the year 1940, the museum was transfered to Olsztynek, where it was an additional attraction to the Tannenberg Monument. The colossal monument, known as the "Teutonic Stonehenge," commemorated the victory of Germany over Russia in 1914, and was blown up in 1944 before the retreat of the Germany army. The rubble was later used, among other purposes, to build new houses, so the only parts of the monument that are left are the entrance arcade, now located near the restaurant *Zajazd Mazurski,* and a stone lion placed at the market place of the small town.

On the other hand the open-air museum was widely extended by the Poles after the Second World War. Unique architectural specimens were dismantled at their original sites in Warmia, Masuria and Powiśle, the region on the eastern shore of the Lower Vistula River. The buildings were then reconstructed in Olsztynek. One of the most eye-catching of the forty exhibits is a beautiful eight-sided wooden church dating back to the founding of the museum. It is covered with a thatched roof and decorated with frescos (the original is in Rychnowo on the way to Ostróda). There is also a small house with a covered entrance from the area of Pasłęk, as well as several wind-

Above: The castle of the Warmia Cathedral Chapter in Olsztyn houses an excellent Regional Museum. Right: The Open-Air Museum in Olsztynek.

LIDZBARK WARMÍNSKI

mills, and a Lithuanian farm from the area of Klaipeda from the founding era of Königsberg.

The location of one of the most significant medieval battles, the Battle of Tannenberg, lies some 20 kilometers southwest of Olsztynek, near **Stębark ❸**. It is believed that about 60,000 men fought a battle of life and death on a hot summer day in July of 1410. The defeat of the Knights of the Teutonic Order and the death of their Grand Master, Ulrich of Jungingen, set the stage for the Polish-Lithuanian State of the Jagiellon dynasty to become a European power. In 1960, a huge **monument** commemorating the occasion was set up on the former battlefield. Noisy school classes crowd the **Battle Museum,** in which a modest collection is exhibited.

On the return trip to Olsztyn a detour through **Niedzica** is worthwhile. On a hill in town stands a well-preserved **Castle of the Teutonic Order**. This castle was built to protect the border to the southern lowlands of Mazovia. The castle was built rather late, at the end of the 14th century and was less a monastery for the brother members of the Order but rather a functional military structure to accommodate mercenaries. Today the café in the renovated courtyard is a nice place to take a break from sightseeing.

Lidzbark Warmiński

Second to the cathedral in Frombark, the most interesting historical building in all of Northeast Poland is the residence of the bishops of Warmia in **Lidzbark Warmiński ❹**. Apart from Malbork Castle, there is no castle in the realm of the former Teutonic Order that is as well preserved as this **★Bishop's Castle**. It was erected in the 14th century and largely remodeled in the 19th century. This castle is comparatively small, but in parts is actually more sophisticated than the one in Malbork. Unlike Malbork, where little was preserved, the original substance of the castle can be seen throughout the building.

KĘTRZYN

Especially well preserved is the unique two-story **arcade cloister** circling the courtyard. Medieval sculptures and mementos of Ignacy Krasicki (1735-1801), the last archbishop of Warmia and great Polish philosopher of the Enlightenment, are displayed in the **inside rooms**. Krasicki's high sacred orders did not prevent him from severely condemning the injustices and abuses of the Catholic Church, as in his poem "Monachomachia" (War of the Monks).

The **castle chapel** is also worth visiting. Baroque stonemasons have set decorative accents on its Gothic stellar vault. On every intersection of the vault, they have placed chubby-cheeked cherubs – a curious sight. The **Great Refectory** has remained unchanged. It is considered (next to the one in Malbork Castle of the same name) the second largest secular room in the entire country dating back to the Middle Ages. To conclude the tour, the Gallery of Modern Painting with several notable pieces of work can be seen, as well as the icon collection originally from the town of Wojnowo in Masuria. Both constitute an artistic contrast to the collection of medieval sculptures from various churches in Warmia.

KĘTRZYN AND SURROUNDINGS

Kętrzyn ❺ is the largest city east of Warmia and north of Masuria. It has a small **castle** built by the Teutonic Order, in which a library and a town museum are maintained. The neighboring **fortified church** has rare late Gothic cell vaulting. Evidently, the church was to have been connected to the defence wall – as its chancel, adjoining at an angle, suggests.

Twenty kilometers towards the Soviet border lies the city of **Drogosze** (formerly Dönhoffstädt). You can reach it by traveling through Garbno or through Barciany. This city was the largest resi-

Above and right: The Baroque pilgrimage church of Święta Lipka enchants the visitor with organ music.

WOLF'S LAIR / ŚWIĘTA LIPKA

dence of the East Prussian royalty. The neo-classical **Manor House** was built by the well-known family Dönhoff. The house was later passed on to another aristocratic family (Stolberg-Wernigerode) so that the Countess Marion Dönhoff, the well-nown journalist, did not spend her childhood here.

In contrast to these lesser tourist attractions, the **Wolf's Lair** ❻ (German: Wolfsschanze), approximately eight kilometers east of Kętrzyn, receives a great deal more attention (*Wilczy Szaniec* near Gierłoż). Crowded parking lots, soft-drink vendors, amber merchants and souvenir stands generate a picnic atmosphere, which does not really suit the grim past associated with this complex.

The Wolf's Lair is an enormous complex of 2.5 square kilometers, including several concrete bunkers with walls measuring up to 6 meters thick and served as the **Main Headquarters of Adolf Hitler** between September 1941 to the fall of 1944. Hitler spent most of that time here, except for short stays in Berchtesgaden and Berlin. It was constructed in the fall of 1940 by the Todt Organization. On January 20, 1945, the retreating Germans destroyed all the buildings, so now only ruins remain.

A ten minute walk through dense woods (well camouflaged with netting so that the quarters could not be identified from the air) leads you to bunker number 13 belonging to the "Führer." On the way to this bunker, you will pass the spot where Hitler was to have been assassinated. A plaque, in Polish and German, commemorates the unsuccessful assassination attempt, stating: "Here stood the barracks in which Claus Count Schenk von Stauffenberg attempted to assassinate Adolf Hitler on July 20, 1944. He and many others who had conspired against the National Socialist dictatorship paid with their lives." Only rubble remains of the barracks. The building was constructed only partially of reinforced concrete, so that the pressure of the explosives was diffused and Hitler survived.

*Święta Lipka

A completely different atmosphere surrounds the famous ***Pilgrimage Church** in **Święta Lipka** ❼ (Holy Lime Tree) located south of Kętrzyn. Architect Georg Ertly of Vilnius, who was originally from South Tyrol, designed this church, erected between 1687 and 1730. According to a legend, the Virgin Mary once appeared in the night to a prisoner, who was to be executed the following day, and ordered him to carve her likeness in wood. The judges, after seeing this piece of work, were so convinced of the prisoner's remorse and forgiveness from heaven that they reversed the conviction. The man hung the sculpture on a linden (lime) tree and soon tales of its miraculous powers spread throughout the land. The church was built on exactly this spot. So much for the legend.

MASURIA

What is true, however, is that a center of pilgrimage grew up here in the 15th century. However, after the conversion of Duke Albert of Brandenburg to Protestantism in 1525, the center was torn down, true to the maxim *cuius regio, eius religio* (the faith of the ruler is the faith of the ruled). The construction of the second church in the 17th century was greatly supported by the Polish King Sigismund III Wasa. He wanted to promote and encourage the return of Catholicism to Prussia, whose duke was his vassal.

The church, the third on this site, was built in Baroque style and painted yellow. Although local artists participated in its construction, this grandiose structure doesn't quite fit into the architectural world of northern Poland, which widely favored brick. Enter the church and let yourself be swept away by the illusionistic paintings while listening to organ music (hourly presentations). When the well-known Ogiński Polonaise (the last piece of music in the presentation) starts, the organ seems to take off on its own – Maria bows her head and waves graciously; angels blow their trumpets and the stars spin and twinkle.

Near Święta Lipka lies the small town of **Reszel**, ❽ the site of a well-preserved **Bishop's Castle** dating back to the second half of the 14th century. The castle houses artists, who frequently exhibit their works here. If rooms are vacant, tourists can stay overnight. The courtyard is a pleasant place to relax with a fresh cup of coffee.

MASURIA

Around Mikołajki

Since the name East Prussia is often associated in Poland with the unpopular State of Prussia, the designation *Warmia i*

Right: Feeding swans – children having fun at one of the 5000 Masurian lakes.

Mazury (Warmia and Masuria) was introduced in 1945. Now the average Pole regards the land between Suwałki and Iława as "Mazury" (the name "Warmia" is frequently omitted). This region is considered to take in land where lakes, forests and hills are in abundance. Historically, Masuria was a much smaller area. It encompassed the Great Masurian Lakelands, bordering eastern Warmia.

The early Baltic Prussians lived in this region until the Middle Ages. After the Knights of the Teutonic Order decimated the Prussian population, the area remained uninhabited until settlers from the Polish Mazovia region moved into the area, starting in the 15th century and named it Mazury. They cleared the forests, fished and farmed, and built villages with the characteristic wooden houses.

These people spoke a Polish dialect but were Protestant and without any attachment to their old homeland. Although they had been germanized since the 18th century, their descendents were allowed to stay in the country after 1945. However, a majority did emigrate from Masuria to Germany. Today, the descendents of those forced out of former east Poland and settlers from central Poland live in Masuria. City dwellers are moving here to seek peace and quiet and nature's unique beauty.

The special appeal of Masuria is its fantastic scenery and landscape. Huge ice masses covered this countryside about 500,000 years ago, and finally melted only 30,000 years ago. The region carved out by the ice sheets filled with melting snow and ice from the retreating glaciers and, thus, the famous thousand lakes were born (actually the lake count is about 5000). There are long deep piedmont lakes, large shallow lakes, cirque lakes, and kettle lakes scattered like little pearls in the landscape. The terminal moraine, the ground moraine, and lateral moraine have built mountain ridges up to a height of 300 meters. The

MRĄGOWO / MIKOŁAJKI

mountain ridges in Dylewska Góra in places reach a height of 312 meters.

Leaving Olsztyn, the first Masurian city reached is **Mrągowo** ❾. This is a good home base for excursions into the region. The old part of the city was lightly damaged in the war and still has many buildings and houses dating back to the 19th century. On the last weekend in July, this quaint, sleepy city bursts with life: the big Country Music Festival takes place. Strange figures wrapped in American flags and driving powerful Harleys and jeeps dominate the scene. However, everything remains quite peaceful. The concerts take place in the city's large amphitheater on the shore of Lake Czos. Nearby is the luxurious hotel *Mrongovia*: an overnight stay there is another reason to remain and explore the area from here.

It seems the most popular vacation spot in the Great Masurian Lakelands is **Mikołajki** ❿. This town lies on the long Lake Mikołajskie, which to the south spills into Lake Bełdany. Mikołajki is much smaller than Mrągowo, and therefore, only offers the visitor the sights of a large yacht harbor and a cobblestone shopping lane (ul. 3 Maja) ending up at the market square (Pl. Wolności). After a pleasant stroll on the harbor quay, the market square is a nice place to take a break and get some refreshments.

Mikołajki is the home of the "Smelt King." This particular "fish king" has been immortalized here three times over (twice in concrete at the quay and market square and once as a tin model swimming under the railroad bridge). According to legend, he was a terrible nuisance because he destroyed the fishermen's nets and caused boats to capsize. When the fishermen finally captured the smelt, he promised to fulfill all their wishes if they put him back into the water. This rather imprecise request was promptly carried out. The clever fishermen put the smelt king back into the water as he had wished, but chained him to the shore so that he could do no more harm.

Tour boats leave here: northward to Giżycko (cf page 211) and southward to

LAKE ŚNIARDWY / LAKE ŁUKNAJNO

Ruciane-Nida, which is an excellent area for water sports. On the trip to Ruciane-Nida, the boat makes a loop on **Lake Śniardwy**, often called the "Masurian Ocean." This lake has an area of 110 square kilometers and is the largest lake in Poland. The boat also has to go through a water lock, making the tour even more exciting.

The shortest outing from Mikołajki leads you four kilometers toward the southeast. At the end of the market square turn left, then take a right turn at the fork in the road going away from the city. After traveling a while on the beautiful tree-lined country road past fields and meadows, you will arrive at the canal that connects the Śniardwy with Lake Łuknajno. At this point, you can proceed on foot along the path to the left, which leads to the observation tower, from where a spectacular view of the area can be enjoyed.

The shallow **Lake Łuknajno** sometimes appears to be covered with a coat of white paint because hundreds of swans are swimming on its surface. This is the largest wild mute swan colony in the world, numbering about 1300 during the breeding season. In recognition of the uniqueness of this lake, the UNESCO bestowed upon the natural preserve the title World Heritage Biosphere Reserve, an honor that only three other national parks in Poland enjoy – Słowiński, Białowieski and Babiogórski Park Narodowy.

The vehicle ferry, running hourly from Wierzba (five kilometers south of Mikołajki), will bring you to the shore of Śniardwy Lake, near the village of **Popielno** ⓫. The zoological research institute here experiments with the selective breeding of animals that have become extinct (for tours, cf page 222). A herd of tarpans, a European wild horse, has already been released into the wild in a large forested area south of the city.

South of Popielno in the forest west of the city of Pisz lies the village of **Wojnowo** ⓬. It is populated by Russians of the confession Raskolnikis or "Old Believers." This group refused to accept the liturgical reform imposed on them by the Russian Orthodox Church and broke away from it in the 17th century and were severely persecuted. They fled from Russia to and came to Poland. Later, in the first half of the 19th century, they settled in Prussia. It is rather thought-provoking to hear that the reasons for their brutal persecution in Czarist Russia were over the trivial questions of whether you should cross yourself with two or three fingers or if processions should go with or against the path of the sun in the sky.

Many of the Old Believers' descendents have emigrated in the meantime from here to Germany; but they left behind a brick church and a convent (founded in the mid-1800's) just outside

Above: Many marshy areas are home to the numerous storks. Right: Punting comfortably along the Krutynia – an enchanting outing for nature lovers.

the village. The picturesque convent grounds situated at the lake are home to two nuns and an older gentleman, who shows visitors the church with its the impressive icon collection on the wall.

A nature experience of a special kind is a paddle tour on the ***Krutynia**, a small river, inits natural state, with countless bends as it meanders through the countryside. You will feel like you are sliding through a green tunnel with the closely set trees hanging over the crystal-clear water. The natural backdrop and the incredible calm will contribute to the unforgettable fascination and charming appeal of this outing. As long as you are not following a group of tourists, you will probably be able to spot some animals in the trees and in the shoreline reeds.

You will need ten days to cover the entire distance from Sorkwity to Mikołajki (110 kilometers). A two-day excursion can be taken from Spychowo to Krutyń. Finally, a (half) day tour is possible from Krutyń (cf page 222). A wonderful impression of the countryside is also given to you when you join a two-hour ride in flat boats just punting along on the river.

Around Giżycko

Giżycko ⓭, is located on the spit of land between the lakes Niegocin and Mamry (actually Lake Kisajno), and competes with Mikołajki as the unofficial capital of Masuria. Countless tour groups crowd the city's hotels and guesthouses as well as those of the neighboring towns. Boaters congregate at the marina because from this spot there are more than 70 km of uninterrupted waterways. Canals and chain lakes connect the entire distance between Węgorzewo to the north and Lake Nidzkie to the south.

Although you might occasionally wonder how the combination of a Prussian provincial city and an authentic socialistic concrete housing project could have ever contributed to this place becoming a tourist attraction, Giżycko nonetheless has nice nooks and crannies to be proud of. The first of these is the small, former

PUSZCZA BORECKA

Castle of the Knights of the Teutonic Order. It has just one wing and a Renaissance gable, which was added later on. The castle is located next to the Motel *Zamek*. Secondly, there is the **Boyen Fortress** built from 1847-1853 and situated in a lovely wooded area. Thirdly, the **Protestant Church** (1826-1827), constructed with the help of Karl Friedrich Schinkel, a famous German architect, is worth seeing. During the summer months, interesting organ concerts take place at the church (for information, watch for posters or ask at the desk of Hotel *Wodnik*).

An outing into the unspoiled countryside, far away from the usual tourist trails, leads northeast through Kruklanki to **Puszcza Borecka** (Borecka Forest). In 1956, bison from Białowieski National Park were released into the wild in the vicinity of Wolikso, where a small ranger's station situated on a serene lake is surrounded by an extensive forest of dense coniferous and deciduous trees. In the meantime, the herd has grown to about 70 in count. Since the bison are extremely shy, you will probably only be able to observe them in the early morning hours, e.g. at the break of dawn, or in winter when they search for food in the open fields. To be able to catch a glimpse of this earthy yet awesome animal in its natural habitat is an experience you won't easily forget.

Puszcza Borecka is, fortunately, far from any tourist commercialization. The marshy area can be reached only by means of a paved trail. Nothing more than forest paths guide you further through the natural preserve. If you keep a sharp eye open, you may spot such animals as elk, lynx, wolves, and even the extremely rare golden eagle. It is best to travel on foot or by bike, although there are no official hiking trails.

North of Giżycko lies **Sztynort** ⓴. Here there is a rather dilapidated **palace** belonging to the Lehndorff family. The

Above: If you are lucky, you might spot one of the rare golden eagles in the Puszcza Borecka.

SUWAŁKI / BIEBRZAŃSKI NATIONAL PARK

inside rooms cannot be visited. Many of the potential buyers of the castle have been discouraged by the extremely high costs involved in a renovation. The renovation costs of other castles in the area are likewise exorbitant. However, the location and setting of the castle on the peninsula would be ideal for a hotel. The beautiful countryside with its age-old oak woods is a wonderful vacation destination, and the town of Sztynort is a popular place to moor sailboats.

Leading onto the town there is a **bridge**, built after the war at the narrowest part of Lake Mamry (exactly between the partial basin of Lake Dargin and Lake Kirsajty, which actually spills over into Mamry Lake). From the bridge, you have a wonderful view, and with any luck, the paradise-like settings will not be disturbed by motorboats.

Sailboats share this area with cormorants, red-necked grebes and swans. High in the air soar hawks (kites), spotted eagles and sometimes even sea eagles. The serene beauty of the region is simply breathtaking, as in many other parts of the Masurian Lakelands.

SUWAŁKI

Suwałki country (Suwalszczyzna) has – similar to the Masurian Lakelands – wonderful lakes and beautiful woods. The villages are more interesting than those in Masuria since they are populated by families who had become established here many centuries ago (Poles, Lithuanians, Russians and Old Believers). The colorful wooden houses in Lithuanian style bear witness to this fact. Besides the two beautiful convents in Sejny (on the Lithuanian border) and Wigry (cf page 214), most visitors come here primarily to enjoy the beautiful scenery. The countryside has been left pretty much in its natural state – no hotels, less tourist activity, and no Germans coming back to their homeland. If you can slightly lower your western comfort requirements when traveling, you will be richly rewarded with the unspoiled quality of pristine nature.

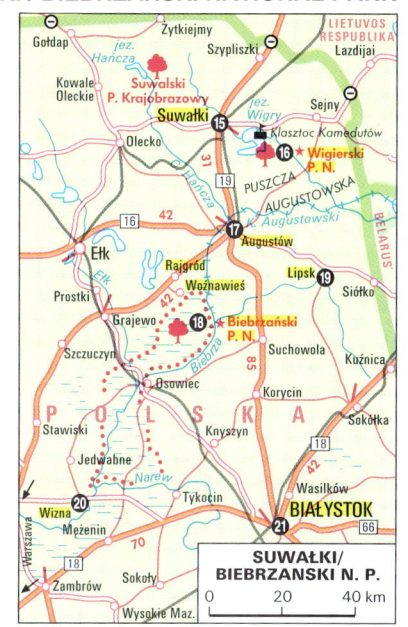

The varied moraine landscape begins about 20 kilometers north of **Suwałki** ⑮, a quiet, sleepy town. This is the starting point for excursions into the **Suwalski Landscape Park.** The park is full of lakes and hills, with elevations of up to about 300 meters. The shorelines of the lakes are rough and rugged, and therefore remind you of typical mountain lakes. The deepest of all lakes in the lakelands south of the Baltic Sea is called Lake Hańcza. According to the most recent measurements, the lake has a depth of 105 meters.

*Wigierski National Park

Proceeding eastward from Suwałki, you will soon arrive at the scenic Lake Wigry whose surrounding area was declared ***Wigierski National Park** ⑯ in 1989. The beaver is the symbol of this park. Once almost extinct, then in the

AUGUSTÓW

Above: Wigry Monastery – today an artists' residence with overnight accommodations for tourists.

1960's released to the wild from the breeding stations, this delightful mammal has reproduced itself so successfully that the regional farmers want to have it removed from the list of protected animals. The dams that the beavers build on the rivers flood the fields, causing the farmers considerable damage.

On a canoe trip down the **Czarna Hańcza River** (for example, starting in Wigry), you can see for yourself what the beavers are doing. This 140 kilometer long arm of the Nieman River is a true paradise for paddlers. You will not only see beavers, there are wolves, lynx, elk, badgers, spotted eagles and sea eagles living on and around the banks of the river.

The best way to become acquainted with the these residents of the National Park is to follow the 50 kilometer trail marked green, which circles around the entire 22 square kilometer lake. The trail also takes you over the Wigry peninsula to a former Camaldolese hermitage towering high above the lake's surface. King Johann Casimir established this monastery in 1667, and in 1785 it was secularized. Today it serves as a residence for artists, but travelers can also stay overnight in the interesting rooms of the hermitage.

Augustów

To the south, the National Park directly borders on the **Puszcza Augustowska** (Augustów Forest). Regarded as Poland's largest single forest region, it measures a total area of 1000 square kilometers. In the pine and fir woods, you will also encounter much wildlife, such as elk, deer, wild boars and wolves. The forest was named after the nearest city, **Augustów** ⓱. Augustów in turn received its name from the Jagiellon King Zygmunt II August, who founded the city as a sign of the reaffirmed peace with the Duchy of Prussia in the year 1558.

Map page 213, Information pages 221-223

BIEBRZAŃSKI NATIONAL PARK

The **Hotel Hetman**, in Augustów, is warmly recommended. Formerly a PTTK hostel, it is the only structure in Poland built by the well-known architect Matthew Nowicki in the year 1938. He was one of the pioneers of modern architecture and later designed the famous Paraboleum in Raleigh, North Carolina, USA. He also worked with the internationally renowned architect, Le Corbusier, building the Indian city Chandighar in Punjab and the United Nations building in New York. In 1951, Nowicki was killed in an airplane crash at the age of 40.

Above all, Augustów is the perfect spot for sailing. It is also the best place to begin paddle tours on the Czarna Hańcza River and trips over the **Augustów Canal**. This canal was built between 1824 to 1839, according to plans of General Ignacy Prądzyński, who was the hero of the Polish November Revolution against the Russians in 1830-1831. The canal is 102 kilometers long and connects, via Narew and Biebrza, the Vistula River with the Nieman River. It was one of the most challenging and ambitious engineering projects of its time. The use of new techniques, such as making concrete with water-resistant limestone, and the size, were only surpassed 50 years later with the construction of the French Canal du Midi. There are 14 historical **locks** located on the river on Polish soil. Some of them were damaged in the war and then to somewhat inaccurately restored. The rest have been under historical protection since the 1970's. In the summer, tour boats travel from Augustów on various routes. The one-day trip to Lake Paniewo is the most interesting (cf page 223).

*BIEBRZAŃSKI NATIONAL PARK

This park is a true paradise, and not only for ornithologists. Being the most extensive marshland in Europe, it stretches south from Augustów along the 164 kilometer long Biebrza River. The Biebrza is one of the last rivers on the European continent to have been left in its natural state for its entire length. Here 253 of the 280 species of birds in Europe nest. Many birds extinct or rare elsewhere can be found here. There are bittern, little bittern (type of heron), northern shovelers (duck family), serpent eagles, sea eagles, booted eagles, black grouse, cranes, white-backed woodpeckers, double snipes, ruffs, and reeves. It is a sight to behold when colorful ruffs perform their courtship display in the springtime. No two male ruffs with the same feathering have been found. Many mammals also make their homes in the Biebrza marshlands. The largest herd of elk in Central Europe (next to that in Kampinowski National Park near Warsaw) can be found here: they number 350 and are counted each year from helicopters.

Rajgród is the gateway to the ***Biebrzański Park Narodowy*** ⑱. The area was declared a national park in 1992. Overnight accommodation is available. From Rajgród, you can drive to the village of Woźnawieś and plunge for a few hours into the heartland of the Red Marsh (*Czerwone Bagno*), named after a characteristic moss growing there. You may be lucky enough to see a deer, wolf or beaver in the moors and wet aspen woods. The round trip is 18 kilometers long, on the red trail. The map "Biebrzański Park Narodowy (1: 20,000") is useful.

A canoe trip on the **Biebrza River** is just as exciting. The trip should begin at **Lipsk** ⑲ to **Wizna** ⑳ located on the Narew (135 kilometers). An alternative is a trip on the Ełk and the Jegrznia (65 kilometers from Jezioro Rajgródzkie to Goniądz). The river is perfect for kayaking, but you need stamina, a keen desire for adventure, and a pass from the National Park Service (cf page 223) because the shoreline is inaccessible and the countryside very rugged.

BIAŁYSTOK

The largest city in this region is **Białystok** ⓴ (population: 280,000). It was established in the Middle Ages but first flourished in the 1800's as a center of textile industry and trade and was a strong rival of Łódź. The city did not belong to the Polish puppet state under Russian rule called the Congress Kingdom of Poland (as had been stipulated in the Congress of Vienna in 1815), but belonged directly to the Russian Empire. Between 1939 and 1941, Białystok fell to the Soviet Union, and was the only land acquisition of the Stalin empire according to the Hitler-Stalin pact of 1939 that had to be given back after 1945.

Several Orthodox churches give testimony to the Russian influence and control. The classical **St. Nicholas' Church** (*Cerkiew św. Mikołaja*) dating from 1846 has frescos modeled after those found at the St. Sophie Cathedral in Kiev. About 200,000 Orthodox Belorussians (White Russians) live near Białystok, and the sheer size of the sacral building leads you to believe that both nations are involved in religious competition. In Białystok you first see the huge Neogothic **Cathedral of the Assumption of the Virgin Mary** (*Kościół Wniebowzięcia Najświętszej Marii Panny*; Rynek Kościuszki) onto which a small Baroque church seems literally to be stuck. Since the czarist authorities only grudgingly gave permission for the construction of Catholic churches (cf Ojców, page 112), a trick was employed, and the new cathedral was deemed simply an "extension" to the small Baroque place of worship.

A second symbol of the triumph of Catholicism is **St. Roch's Church** (*Kościół św. Rocha*; ul. Dąbrowskiego). This impressive church is 80 meters high and was built on a hill accentuating its grandeur even more. Alfred Sosnowski designed this house of worship in 1927 in an unconventional expressionistic style.

The retaliation – a huge **Orthodox church** (*Cerkiew św. Ducha*; ul. Antoniuk Fabryczny) – was completed in 1998. Representing the twelve apostles, twelve crosses on the gables or domes surround the central onion-topped tower, which is topped by a cross weighing 1500 kilograms.

The ***Palace of the Branicki Family**, also known as the "Polish Versailles," is characterized by its overwhelming enormity. The original complex built built in the late 17th century by Tilman van Gameren, a Dutch architect, was extensively remodeled in the 18th century. Two flanking towers, characteristic of the Polish palaces and state seats in the Baroque period, developed out of the tradition common to fortification style architecture. The large *Cour d'honneur (Honor Court)* is very reminisent of Versailles.

The small balcony in the center front section is commonly called *"Balcony Dzierżyńskiego"* after the notorious Polish executioner, Feliks Dzierżyński. He was the right hand of Lenin and founder of the Soviet Security Apparatus (Cheka and other police security groups, later the KGB). He called out the "Polish Soviet Republic" during the Polish-Soviet War from this balcony in 1920. Fortunately, the republic was only short-lived.

Białystok was 70 percent Jewish until 1941. The Jewish physician Ludwik Zamenhof (1859-1917) lived here. He was created the artificial language Esperanto (meaning "hope") in 1887 because he hoped and believed that the peoples of the earth would someday live in harmony. Of course, this was not true of the Poles, Russian and Jews in Białystok at the turn of the century.

By 1944 the world of the Polish Jews in Białystok had been annihilated. The Jewish population had been driven to the gas

Above: A ruff in courtship display. Often seen in the spring at Narew National Park.

TYKOCIN / SUPRAŚL

chambers; and countless historical monuments had been destroyed, such as the wooden synagogue from the 17th and 18th centuries and a true masterpiece of carpentry. Just a small **monument**, in ul. Żabia, commemorates the uprising in the city's ghetto on September 16, 1943 and testifies to the fact that the majority of the residents in Białystok were Jewish.

A Day Trip to Tykocin

You can get a good idea of what a typical Jewish village or town in eastern Poland once looked like by visiting the town of **Tykocin** ㉒, approximately 25 kilometers west of Białystok. Small wooden houses frame the large market square of this quiet town. It also has a Catholic church, the ruins of a castle, and a historical monument from the 17th century honoring Stefan Czarniecki, the hero of the wars with Sweden. The main attraction is a recently restored **Synagogue** built in 1642, now a museum. A massive *Bimah* (podium or platform for sacred readings) and the *aron ha-qodesh* (a decorated ark for the Torah scrolls) will certainly catch your eye. Nature lovers will be drawn toward **Narew National Park** ㉓ south of Tykocin.

East of Białystok

This sparsely populated region in the middle of nowhere offers the visitor astounding sights. Your first stop will be in the town of **Supraśl** ㉔. Its orthodox monastery and seminary are among the most important ones in Poland. The wings of the monastery enclose a spacious courtyard, where until 1990 only its foundation had been left exposed. In the meantime, the famous fortified Orthodox church has been rebuilt and has regained its former splendor. Originally built in 1503 to 1511, it combined elements of Gothic and Renaissance with those of Byzantine style. The church was obviously an offence to the German army, and was blown up in 1944. A large number of the frescos were salvaged from the rub-

GRABARKA

The descendents of the Tatar warriors still live in Kruszyniany and in the town of **Bohoniki** near Sokółka, where a second wooden mosque can been visited. The cemeteries are also very interesting: "normal" looking tombstones have inscriptions carved in Arabic. The number of believers has rapidly declined in the course of the last years. It is estimated that approximately 3000 descendents of the Tatars still live in Poland, particularly in Białystok, Warsaw and Gdańsk, where they recently erected a modern mosque on ul. Polanki.

Grabarka

Try to imagine a journey back to the Middle Ages. In the night from August 18th to August 19th, an extraordinary mystical medieval spectacle, unlike any other in Central Europe, takes place in **Grabarka** ㉖, a village near Siemiatycze south of Białystok. During the night of the Orthodox Festival of the Transfiguration, believers carry heavy crosses up the hill to the monastery while humming monotone melodies. The bigger the sins committed in the previous year, the bigger the cross must be. About 17,000 crosses have been put up on the hill so far. Vigil is kept the entire night. The human figures appear mysteriously eerie as they sit in the cemetery by candlelight and tolling bells. The spectacle may remind you of the "Forefathers' Eve" of Adam Mickiewicz, the greatest romantic poet of Poland. This ceremony eternalized the ancient heathen Lithuanian custom in which the deceased souls are tempted out of the hereafter for a short moment by offerings of food and drink.

Back into the present, and down the hill, the surreal, disquieting night atmosphere suddenly changes to carnival life – sausages are being fried, loud music in undefined East Slavic languages is being played, and tired folks are lying down on the dusty ground beside their cars for a

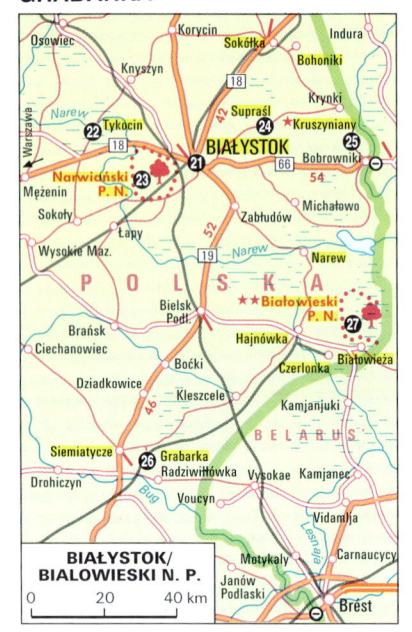

ble, and are exhibited in the Regional Museum in Białystok. The frescos will eventually be viewable at their original location.

Travelling to the impassable Belorussian border, there are many impressive sights. In the town of ★**Kruszyniany** ㉕, there is a building with a roof similar to that of a wooden parish church from the 1800's but it is decorated with a shiny half-moon. This is the region of the legendary villages of the Tatars with their **wooden mosques**.

The Tatars' history dates back to the 17th century. The Tatar Major Murza-Krzeczowski fought with King Jan III Sobieski against the Turks in the 1600's. Murza-Krzeczowski won the king's gratitude in the battle at Parkany in Hungary in 1638, where he saved the king's life. The king consequently rewarded Murza-Krzeczowski and the other loyal Tatars with three villages.

Right: Carrying crosses as repentance for sins, a yearly Orthodox ritual in Grabarka.

Information pages 221-223

short rest. The next morning, when the Orthodox bishops arrive, everyone attends church. The pilgrims go to nearby sacred springs and soak various textiles, especially scarves and towels, so that they absorb the "miraculous powers."

The origin of this "Orthodox Czestochowa" event is based on a true incident. In 1710, believers were saved from the plague epidemic by escaping up the hill in Grabarka. Later, the existing convent and a church were erected here. The church burned down in 1990 but was rebuilt. On the Orthodox holidays, thousands make pilgrimages to this place, proving that the minority of Ukrainians and Belorussians in Poland are stronger than the communists, propagandizing a united, secular, nationalistic empire wanted them to be.

**BIAŁOWIESKI NATIONAL PARK

Many European forests have mistakenly been designated primeval forests, meaning that they have never been altered by human hands. However, in most of the national parks there are no true primeval forests to be found. In all of Europe, there is only one impressive exception – Białowieża Forest. This forest has an area of 270 square kilometers on the Polish side and one-fifth of it can actually be specified as primeval. On the other side of the border in Belarus (formerly White Russia), the 1000 square kilometer forest also has primeval woods. The primeval woodlands were the private hunting grounds of the Polish kings. Only the king could hunt the bison, aurochs, tarpan, sloth and brown bear here. In the 19th century, the Russian czars enjoyed the hunting privilege.

In *Białowieski National Park ㉗ (*Białowieski Park Narodowy*) you will find lynx, wolves, brown bears, elk and even tarpans living today that have been selectively bred and reintroduced to the wild. In 1914, there were some 700 bison (related to the North American species). By the end of the First World War, the

BIAŁOWIESKI NATIONAL PARK

mighty bison had nearly died out in Białowieża, the viction of the German army, who lacked provisions, and who also completely cleared the forests of five million cubic meters of wood. Illegal hunting by poachers also played a part.

When the last wild bison died in 1925, it seemed as if these mighty animals would share the same fate as the aurochs (a type of wild ox), of which the last specimen worldwide was killed near Warsaw in 1627. Fortunately, zoologists have built up a new population of bison from Białowieża with the few specimens which had been living in the zoological gardens. Today the bison is no longer acutely endangered. There are 230 animals living here presently with another 210 on the Belorussian side.

The National Park, designated a strictly protected area in 1929, originally encompassed only a section (500 square kilometers) of the forest on both sides of the border. After an intense dispute, going on for years about the extension of the National Park since the lobby for the timber industry was very much against such plans, the entire forest was in the year 2000 incorporated into the national park.

In the strictly protected area, there is just one trail, which can only be hiked with a guide. The chance of spotting a bison in the wild is rather slim, though some can be seen in a compound on the road between Białowieża and Hajnówka, or in the museum in Białowieża. Unfortunately, only mounted bison remain.

Several tourist trails lead through the wooded preserve in the vicinity of the National Park, e.g. the trail marked green from Hajnówka to Białowieża, the one marked red from Hajnówka to Narewka (each more than 20 kilometers) and finally the trail marked blue from Białowieża to a small train station in Czerlonka (approximately nine kilometers). The return trip is best done by train.

Above: A Tarpan wild horse in snowy Białowieski National Park – rebred and reintroduced to the wild.

Map page 218

THE NORTHEAST

NORTHEAST POLAND

OLSZTYN ☎ 089

i Księgarnia "Press Info Tour," Pl. Wolności 2/3, Tel. 5272738, 5273090. **PTTK Office**, ul. Kopernika 45, Tel. 5274087.

😊😊😊 **Park Hotel**, ul. Warszawska 119, Tel. 5236604, Fax 5276077. Far from the center on the main route to Warsaw. **Novotel**, ul. Sielska 4 a, Tel. 5274081, Fax 5275403. On the road to Ostróda; swimming at a nearby hotel. **Centrum**, ul. Okopowa 25, Tel. 5340780, Fax 5276933. Directly below the castle. The German-Polish Youth Center, which opened in 1993, has turned into a luxury hotel, where you will more than likely meet business people rather than youth groups. Very high standards. Attended parking in front of the building.
😊😊 **Warmiński**, ul. Głowackiego 8, Tel. 5335353, Fax 5336763. A little run down. **Relaks**, ul. Żołnierska 13a, Tel. 5277534. **Nad Łyną**, Al. Wojska Polskiego 14, Tel. 5267166.
😊 **Garnizonowy**, ul. Artyleryjska 15, Tel. 5269211. **PTTK Hostel**, ul. Staromiejska 1, Tel. 5273675. In the High Gate. **Youth Hostel**, ul. Kopernika 45, Tel. 5276650. Located in the city center. Accommodation in **private rooms** can be found through the Information Office.

✘ The better hotels have good restaurants, especially **Centrum** and **Warmiński**. **Francuska**, ul. Dąbrowszczaków 39, Tel. 5275301. French haute cuisine. **Eridu**, ul. Prosta 3-4. Inexpensive Syrian cuisine, located in the Old Town. **SARP**, ul. Kołątaja 15. Nice café in an old granary. **Staromiejska**, ul. Stare Miasto 4/6. café / restaurant downtown, delicious pancakes.

🏛 **Regional Museum** (Muzeum Warmii i Mazur), ul. Zamkowa 2, Tel. 527-95-96. Open Tues-Sun 9:00 a.m. – 5:00 p.m. (Sept. 15 – June 15 open until 4:00 p.m.).

AIR TOURS over Masuria: **Aeroklub Warmińsko Mazurski**, ul. Sielska 34, Tel. 5273827, 5275240.
HORSEBACK RIDING: inquire at **Janusz Kojrys**, Tel. 5238802.

OLSZTYNEK ☎ 089

😊 **Zajazd Mazurski**, Park 1, Tel. 5192885. Located in the forest near the Tannenberg Monument (at the crossing with the highway leading to Gdańsk, then immediately turn left).

🏛 **Open Air Museum** (skansen), ul. Sportowa 21, Tel. 5192164. From April 15-30 and throughout October: Tues-Sun 9:00 a.m. – 3:00 p.m. May through August: Tues-Sat 9:00 a.m. – 5:00 p.m., Sun 9:00 a.m. – 6:00 p.m. September: Tues-Sun 9:00 a.m. – 4:00 p.m. At all other times, only the grounds are open from 9:00 a.m. – 3:00 p.m.

Museum in Grunwald (Muzeum Bitwy Grunwaldzkiej w Stębarku), Tel. 6472227. During the summer open daily 8:00 a.m. – 6:00 p.m.

LIDZBARK WARMIŃSKI ☎ 089

😊😊 **Zajazd pod Kłobukiem**, ul. Olsztyńska 4, Tel. 7672521. Two kilometers south of the city center on the road to Olsztyn. This restaurant is better than the ominous sounding *Happy End* in the city center.
🏛 **Castle Museum** (Muzeum Zamkowe), Tel. 7672111. Open Tues-Sun 9:00 a.m. – 5:00 p.m. (Sept. 15 – June 15 open until 4:00 p.m.).

KĘTRZYN ☎ 089

😊😊 **Pod Zamkiem**, (**U Szwagzów**) ul. Struga 3, Tel. 7523117. Next to the castle.
😊 **Agros**, ul. Kasztanowa 1, Tel. 7515240, 7515241. Late communist flair. **Pensjonat U Krystyny**, ul. Świerkowa 118, Tel./Fax 7514564. **Youth Hostel**, ul. Kopernika 12, Tel. 7515276. Open May to October. **Hotel Wilcze Gniazdo**, Gierłoż, Tel. 7524429. For fans of the Wolf's Lair (see below). **Zamek, Dom Pracy Twórczej**, Reszel, ul. Podzamcze 3, Tel. 7550216. Romantic accommodation in the castle.

✘ **Agros**, ul. Kasztanowa 1, Tel. 7515240. In the hotel of the same name. **Belje**, Stara Różanka (5 km north of Kętrzyn), Tel. 7511370. In an old windmill.

⚔ **Wolf's Lair** (Główna kwatera Hitlera), Gierłoż, Tel. 7524429. Open daily from dawn until dusk (foreign language tours available).
Święta Lipka (Holy Lime Tree): Basilica open daily 8:00 a.m. – 6:00 p.m. No sightseeing permitted during Sunday masses at 7:00, 8:45, and 11:00 a.m., 2:00 and 5:00 p.m. Organ recitals in Święta Lipka: Mon-Sat 9:30, 10:30 and 11:30 a.m., and at 1:30, 2:30, 3:30 4:30 and 5:30 p.m., on Sundays at 10:30 a.m.and 12:30, 1:30, 3:30 and 4:30 p.m. In July and August, evening organ concerts take place Fridays at 8:00 p.m. (advance reservations: Tel. 7551481).
Galeria "Zamek," Reszel. Castle tower can be climbed Tues-Sun 10:00 a.m. – 4:00 p.m.

MRĄGOWO ☎ 089

i ul. Ratuszowa 5, Tel. 7418331, Tel./Fax 7418151. The reception desk of the Mrongovia Hotel is also a good source of information.

😊😊😊 **Mrongovia**, ul. Giżycka 6, Tel. 7413221, Fax 7413220. The best hotel in the area, Skandinavian architecture. Situated directly on the edge of the lake. Swimming pool, sauna and riding stable, etc. 😊😊 **Pension Jakubowo**, Tel. 7424333, Fax 7424344. In the countryside near Kosewo; ideal for relaxation, outstanding cuisine (also vegetarian dishes).

221

THE NORTHEAST

ⓘ **Youth Hostel**, ul. Wojska Polskiego 2, Tel. 7412712.
Campgrounds, ul. Jaszczurcza Góra 3, Tel. 7412533. Also cabins.
✗ **Krutynianka**, Krutyń, Tel. 7421219. Caters especially for German tour groups; somewhat overpriced (risk of being fleeced). Good cuisine; nettle soup recommended. Specialty: small white fish. Beautiful terrace above the river.
⚑ Equipment for water sports can be rented on the bank of Czos Lake next to Hotel Mrongovia.
⚑ **Country Picnic Festival**, on the last weekend in July in the amphitheater at Czos Lake. Internationally famed country music festival (information: Tel. 022/6465333). **Kresy Festival**, in July: Music from the former Polish regions to the east.

MIKOŁAJKI ☎ 087

ⓘ **Informacja Turystyczna**, Pl. Wolności 3, Tel. 4216850.
▬ ☺☺☺ **Gołębiewski**, ul. Mrągowska 34, Tel. 4216517, 4216120, Fax 4216010. The giant concrete cube looks out of place in the Masurian countryside. Swimming pool with slide, etc., bowling, fitness studio, riding course, tennis courts. Bike and boat rental. Balloon and helicopter tours.
☺☺ **Mazur**, Pl. Wolności 6, Tel. 4216941. Newly opened in the former city hall. **Wałkuski**, ul. 3 Maja 13, Tel./Fax 4216628. In the center of town.
☺ Large choice of pensions: **As**, ul. Na Górce 7, Tel./Fax 4216889. **Na Skarpie**, ul. Kajki 96, Tel. 4216418. **Wodnik**, ul. Kajki 130, Tel. 4216141. **Król Sielaw**. ul. Kajki 5, Tel. 4216323. **Mikołajki**, ul. Kajki 18, Tel. 4216325. **Youth Hostel**, ul. Łabędzia 1, Tel. 4216434 (open July and August). **Campgrounds**: Wagabunda, ul. Leśna 2, Tel. 4216018. A second campsite is in Kosewo, Tel. 089/7424521, 14 km to the west.
✗ **Król Sielaw**, ul. Kajtki 5, Tel. 4216323. The best restaurant in the city. Tasty dishes, fast service, Polish cuisine including venison. Heads and antlers stare down on the guests from the dining room walls.
🏛 **Zoological Research Station** (Stacja badawcza PAN), Popielno, Tel. 4231519. Guided tours only with advanced reservations); at 9:00 a.m., 11:00 a.m. and 1:00 p.m. during the busy season.
⛴ *FERRIES* in Wierzba (Mikołajki – Popielno): To Mikołajki: Mon-Sat hourly (on the hour) 6:00 a.m. – 4:00 p.m. and 5:15 p.m. Sundays and holidays hourly (on the hour) 7:00 a.m. – 1:00 p.m. and 2:15 p.m. Return trip to Popielno every twenty minutes later, no charge.
BOAT TOURS depart from Ruciane Nida (10:00 a.m., 2:40 p.m.), Giżycko (10:30 a.m.; 2:40 p.m.), also a round trip across Śniardwy (1.5 hours) from the boat dock (Przystań Żeglugi Mazurskiej, Tel. 4216102).

⚑ *SAIL BOATS* can be rented at **Wioska Żeglarska PZŻ**, ul. Kowalska 3, Tel. 4216720.
BIKE RENTAL: **Sagit**, ul. 3 Maja 13, Tel. 4216470.
HORSEBACK RIDING: **Hotel Gołębiewski**, Tel. 4216517, and in the neighboring village **Zełwągi**, Tel. 4213083.
PADDLING: Kayak (and bike) rentals at the office of the Masurian Landscape Park (Siedziba Zarządu Mazurskiego Parku Krajobrazowego), Krutyń 66, Tel. 089/7421405. Guided tours into the nature preserves are organized from this spot. Punting down the river is possible (about 20 Zł / US$ 4.25 for 1.5 hours); inquire in the Krutynianka restaurant.
Half-day and day tours on the Krutynia are organized by **Andrzej Nosek**, Krutyń 42, Tel. 089/7421218.

GIŻYCKO ☎ 087

ⓘ **Centrum Informacji Turystycznej**, ul. Warszawska 7, Tel./Fax 4285760.
▬ ☺☺ **Wodnik**, ul. 3 Maja 2, Tel. 4283871 to 76, 4282098, Fax 4283958. Centrally located. **Mazury**, ul. Wojska Polskiego 56, Tel. 4285956. Has its own dock, water sports equipment rental. ☺ **Motel Zamek**, ul. Moniuszki 1, Tel. 4282419, Fax 4283958. **Youth Hostel**, ul. Turystyczna 1, Tel. 4282959. Open May through October. Attractively located in the Boyen Fortress. **Campgrounds**: Zamek, ul. Moniuszki 1, Tel. 4283410. Open May through October.
✗ **Pod Złotą Rybką**, ul. Olsztyńska 15, Tel. 4285510. Fish specialties. **Pod Kominkiem**, ul. Olsztyńska 11, Tel. 4284081. Basic cuisine, e.g. onion soup and salad with fresh oyster mushrooms. **Mazurska**, ul. Warszawska 2. **Wodnik** (see: Hotels). **Pizzeria Nicola**, ul. Warszawska 14, Tel. 4282685.
⛴ Boats to Mikołajki (9:00 a.m., 3:00 p.m.), Węgorzewo (11:00 a.m., 2:30 p.m.), departures once a day to Cormorant Island (10:30 a.m., sometimes 6:00 p.m.) and every second day to Sztynort (12:00 noon, from the boat dock, Przystań Żeglugi Mazurskiej, ul. Jeziorna 14, Tel. 4282578).
⚑ *DIVING*: **Klub Działalności Podwodnej**, Tel. 4282905.
HORSEBACK RIDING: e.g. in Pozedrze, Tel. 4279017, or in Przykop, Tel. 4211086; Information also available at the tourist office. *WATER SPORTS*: Equipment rental at the campgrounds Zamek, at the Baza LOK, ul. Lotnicza 4, Tel. 4282530, and at the Water Sports Centers (Centralny Ośrodek Sportu), ul. Moniuszki 22, Tel. 4282335, on Lake Kisajno, in Wilkasy also at the PTTK office. *SAILING*: **Mazury Incoming Bureau**, ul. Dąbrowskiego 3.
BALLOON TOURS: Tel. 090/545083 and at the Hotel Mazury.

THE NORTHEAST

SUWAŁKI ☎ 087

ℹ️ ul. Kościuszki 45, Tel. 5665872, 5665494, **PTTK Office**, ul. Kościuszki 37, Tel. 5665961.

🛏️ 😊😊 **Dom Nauczyciela**, ul. Kościuszki 120, Tel. 5666900, 5666908, Fax 5666028,
http://www.domnauczyciela.suwalki.pl. **Dom Pracy Twórczej**, Wigry Peninsula, Tel. 5164249. Situated in the former Camaldolese monastery.

⛺ **Campgrounds** at Stary Folwark, Tel. 5661227, 5661223.

❌ **Hotel Hańcza** and **Dom Nauczyciela** have good restaurants (wild boar). Pizzerias: **Rozmarino**, ul. Kościuszki 75, Tel. 5665904, **Tivoli**, ul. Mickiewicza 3, Tel. 5677655. **Shanghai**, ul. Kościuszki 82, Tel. 5651460: New, recommended Chinese restaurant.

🚣 Canoe tours on the Czarna Hańcza; information, organizers, etc., from the tourist information center.

AUGUSTÓW ☎ 087

ℹ️ **Orbis Office**, Rynek Zygmunta Augusta 12, Tel. 6433850, 6432319. **PTTK Office**, ul. Nadrzeczna 70a, Tel. 6433850.

🛏️ 😊😊 **Hotel Hetman**, ul. Sportowa 1, Tel. 6445345. Newly remodeled, former PTTK hostel is located somewhat outside city center on Lake Necko.

😊 **Motel Turmot**, ul. Mazurska 4, Tel. 6432867, 6432868, Fax 6432057. **Campgrounds**, ul. Sportowa 1, Tel. 6433455. Next to Hotel Hetman.

🚣 *PADDLING:* Canoe and kayak rentals: **Hotel Hetman** (Tel. 6433455) and **Dom Nauczyciela**, ul. 29 Listopada 9 (Tel. 6432021).

SAILING: **Ośrodek Żeglarski**, ul. Nadrzeczna 70a, Tel. 6433850. Sail boat rental (also with captain).

🎵 **Summer Blues Meeting** in Augustów. Jazz musicians perform in July and August on the beach of Necko Lake (Tel. 6433659).

⛴️ Boat tours on the Augustów Canal depart from the dock at ul. 29 Listopada 7; tickets can be purchased on the same day.

BIEBRZAŃSKI NATIONAL PARK

Visitors still find themselves in tourist "terra incognito," though this situation should change sometime soon.

ℹ️ Administrative Office of the National Park: Osowiec 3, Tel./Fax 085/7163266, 7163311. Goniądz, ul. Wojska Polskiego 72, Tel. 086/2723001.

🛏️ 😊 **Knieja**, Rajgród, ul. Leśna 21, Tel. 086/721468, Fax 721407.

😊 **Raj**, Rajgród, ul. 1 Maja 22, Tel. 086/721616. **Gród**, Rajgród, Pl. 1000-lecia, Tel.086/721528.

Youth Hostel (open July and August): Grajewo, Goniądz. **Campgrounds**: Lipsk, Goniądz, Osowiec, Wizna, etc.

🚤 *WATER SPORTS:* Equipment rental at **Ośrodek Wypoczynkowy Sum**, Goniądz.

Bird Service Tours, Maciej Zimowski, Białystok, ul. Popiełuszki 105, Tel. 085/6616768. Bird watching.

Natur Travel, Marek Czerny, Białystok, ul. Wyszyńskiego 2/1, lok. 204. Tel. 085/7444562, Fax 7444534. Specializing in kayak and bike tours.

BIAŁYSTOK ☎ 085

ℹ️ **Centrum Informacji Turystycznej**, ul. Piękna 3, Tel. 4454600. **PTTK Office**, ul. Lipowa 18, Tel. 6223005.

🛏️ 😊😊😊 **Gołębiowski**, ul. Pałacowa 7, Tel. 7435435, Fax 6537399. A huge complex with a Tropicana swimming center, like to the one in Mikołajki.

😊 **Dom Nauczyciela**, ul. Warszawska 8, Tel. 7435949.

Youth Hostel, al. Piłsudskiego 7b, Tel. 6524250.

❌ In addition to the hotel restaurants in **Cristal** and in **Leśny**, the restaurant in **Astoria** can be recommended (ul. Sienkiewicza 2, Tel. 7435221). Speciality: *kotlet Branickich*.

Grodno, ul. Sienkiewicza 28, Tel. 7435240. Belorussian cuisine. **Kaunas**, ul. Wesoła 18.Lithuanian specialties, e.g. good Chłodnik. **Arsenał**, ul. Mickiewicza 2, Tel. 7428565. Excellent fish (pike) filled with pistachios. **Pastel**, ul. Waszyngtona 24a, Tel. 7442744. Among the highlights of the menu are honey cooked pork knuckle and wild boar in porcino sauce.

🏛️ Museum in the **Synagogue**, Tykocin, ul. Kozia: Open daily 10:00 a.m. – 5:00 p.m. (in winter Tues-Sun 10:00 a.m. – 5:00 p.m.).

BIAŁOWIEŻA NATIONAL PARK
☎ 085

ℹ️ **PTTK Office**, at the entrance to the castle park grounds. Tel. 6812295. **Teresa**, Tel. 6812291. Private travel agency next to the PTTK Office.

🛏️ 😊 **Iwa**, in the Park Pałacowy, Tel. 6812260, 6812385. Popular address. **PTTK Hostel**, Park Pałacowy 10, Tel. 6812505. Close by *Iwa*. Located somewhat further away are the **Youth Hostel** (ul. Waszkiewicza 6, Tel. 6812560) and **Żubrówka** (ul. Olgi Gabiec 3, Tel. 6812303, Fax 6812624).

❌ The selection at the restaurant in Hotel **Iwa** ranges from venison to wild boar to elk and sometimes even to bison. Other restaurants are located in hotels **Unikat** (you should certainly try the dumplings filled with sauerkraut) and **Żubrówka**.

🏛️ **Natural History Museum of the National Park** (Muzeum Przyrodniczo-Leśne BPN), Park Pałacowy 39, Tel. 6812275. Open Tues-Sun 9:00 a.m. – 3:30 p.m. (June to September until 4:00 p.m.). The museum offers information on tours into the national park.

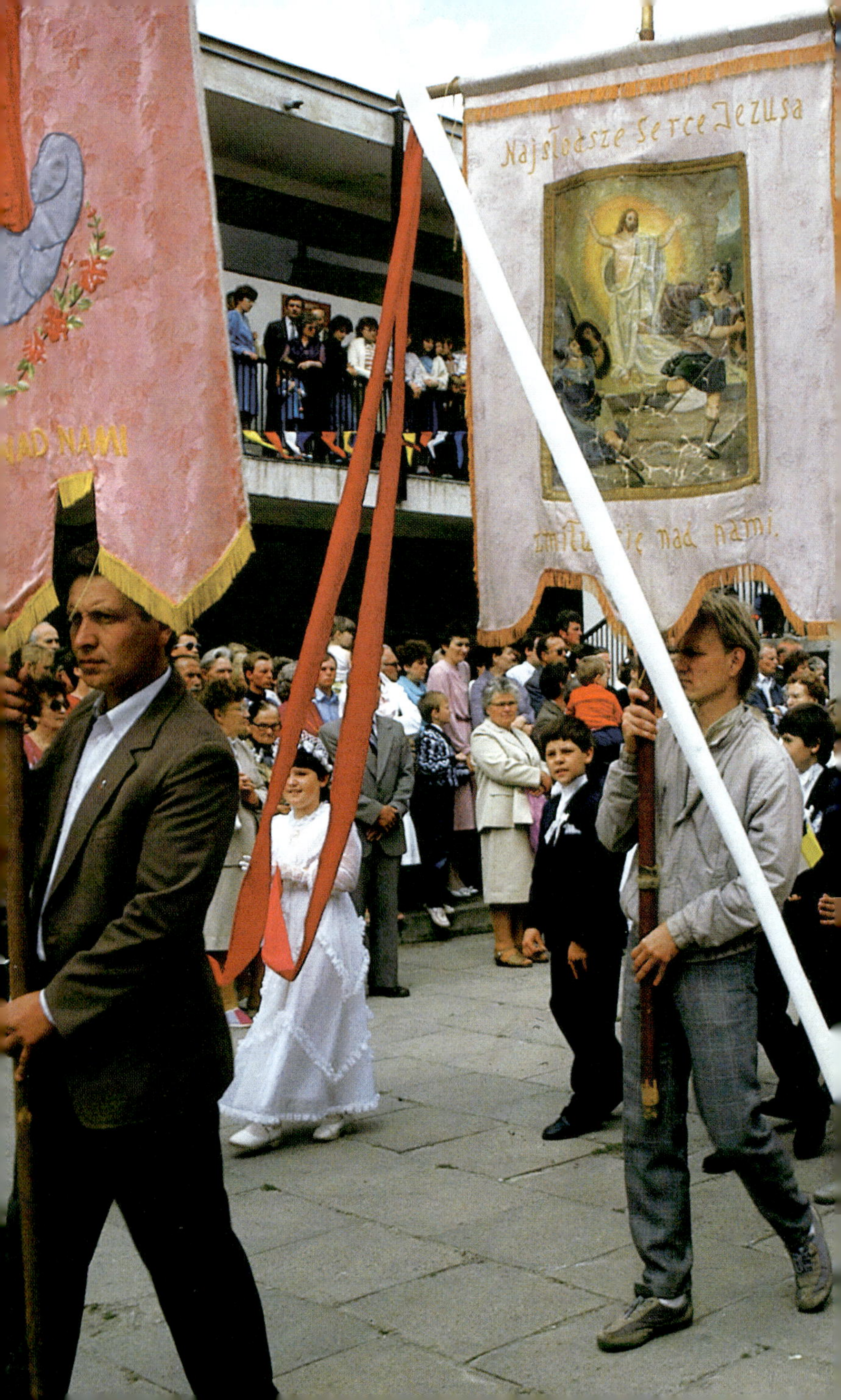
NAD NAMI
Najsłodsze Serce Jezusa
nad nami

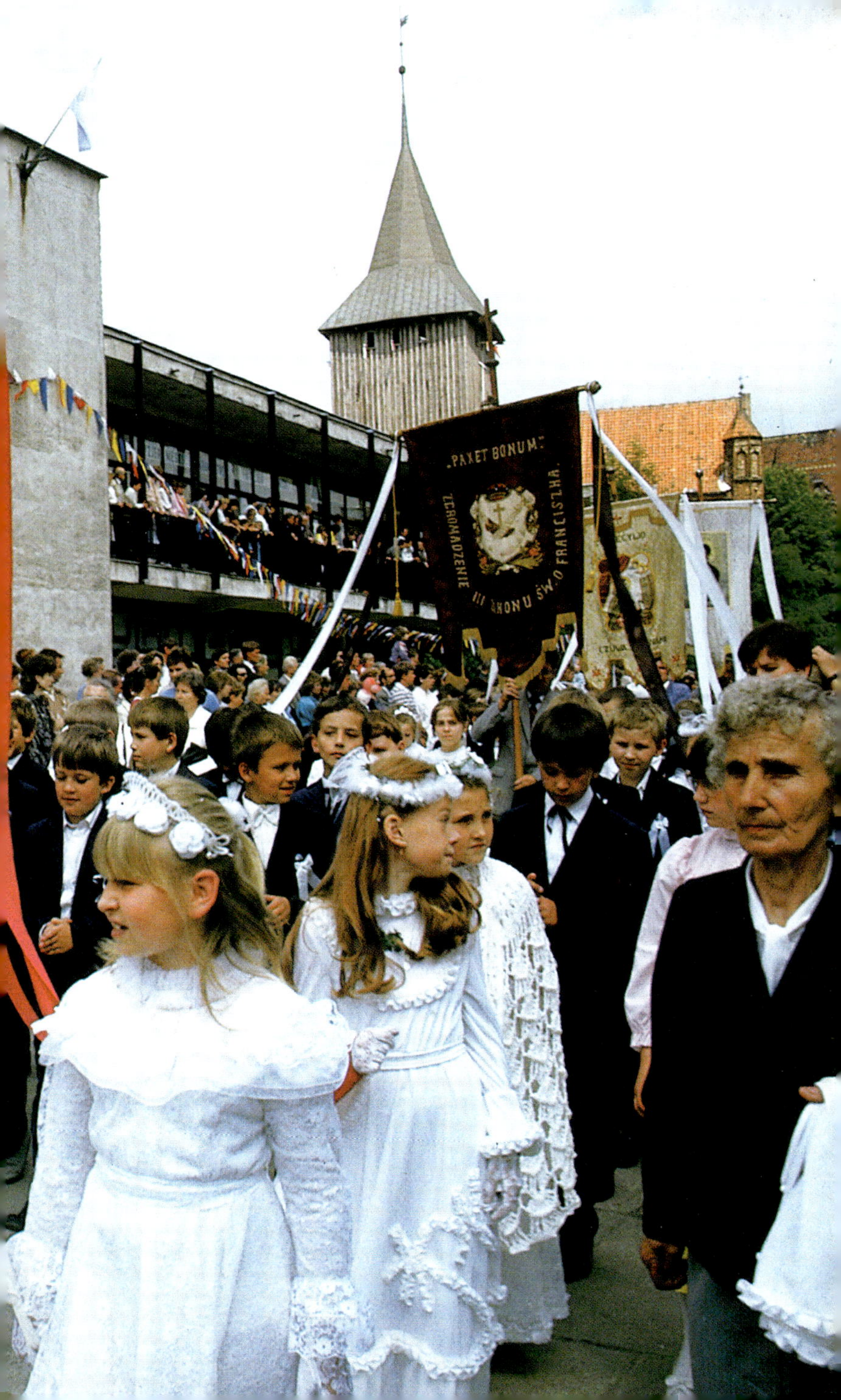
„PAX ET BONUM"
ZGROMADZENIE III ZAKONU ŚW. O FRANCISZKA

THE DIFFICULT RELATIONSHIP BETWEEN JEWS AND POLES

There are some 5,000 Jews living in Poland today, the tiny vestige of a community of 3.5 million before 1939. From the 16th century to the Second World War Poland was, second to the United States, the country where more Jews lived than anywhere else in the world. In Poland Jewish culture blossomed, it was the birthplace of such movements as the Chassidism, and the place the Germans chose to erect their gas chambers, snuffing out this world forever. Jewish heritage is inseparable from Poland and its history and strong emotions can still be aroused. Since 1988/89, a Carmelite convent, directly adjacent to the concentration camp of Auschwitz has been making international headlines. Since it is generally known that the majority of the victims of the Auschwitz-Birkenau extermination camp were Jews, the presence of the convent was interpreted as an attempt to claim the Jewish victims for Christianity. Followers of the Orthodox Rabbi Weiss from New York tried to occupy the grounds in protest, but were driven off by workers. Although the Jewish community and the Catholic Church agreed to move the convent (which has been done), the incident has not been forgotten.

Again, in 1998, a dispute arose over crosses that had been erected in a gravel pit next to the concentration camp, where Poles had been executed. This action contradicted the understanding in the Jewish community that in and around the concentration camp no religious symbols should be erected. The other side argued that no one should be allowed to dictate where Poles could or could not erect their crosses, and the conflict escalated: in 1999 a memorial sites law was introduced and three hundred crosses were removed, under heavy police protection.

Previous pages: Corpus Christi in Malbork. Above: The old synagogue in Kazimierz (Kraków). Symbol of the successful coexistence of Poles and Jews in the 16th century.

The leaseholder of the gravel pit, a confessed anti-Semitic and former member of Parliament, had previously threatened to blow himself up, should the police enter his property.

Poland – Paradise on Earth?

Why such incidents cause great turmoil can be explained by the history of Jews and Ploes living side by side. The Jews first constituted a considerable percentage of the total population during the rule of Kazimier III Wielki (1333-1370). Persecuted in Germany, the Jews streamed into Poland by the thousands in the 14th century. The King encouraged the Jews to settle and remain in Poland by granting them special rights. He recognized their potential as settlers within the framework of his policy of founding and maintaining new cities within his empire.

The Jews made up about 10 percent of the entire population of the Polish-Lithuanian Empire until the end of the 18th century, and constituted the largest Jewish community in the world, with approximately one million members. An active cultural life blossomed, with Talmud schools, for example the one in Kazimierz, today a part of Cracow, where the great educator Moses Isserles Remuh taught. An saying from the 16th century maintaining that Poland was a "paradise on earth" for the Jews was, of course, exaggerated. If the country had ever been heaven on earth to anyone, then it had been heaven for the aristocracy. However, it is true that the Jews did not have to fear anyone in this empire.

The situation in East Ukraine was very different. The members of the numerous Jewish communities were used as instruments by the Polish high aristocracy against the Ukrainian peasants in order to promote their repressive policies and politics. Jews were employed as tax collectors and leaseholders. During the Cossack uprisings against the Polish state, more animosity was directed towards the Jews than towards the aristocracy, and during the Chmielnicki revolt in 1648, thousands of Jews were brutally slaughtered.

Hardening of Positions

The partitioning of Central Poland ended the relatively conflict-free coexistence of Jews and Poles. After the assassination of Czar Alexander II in 1881 and the subsequent malicious campaigns aimed at the Jews, a wave of Jewish immigrants flooded the Vistula region. Life was found to be more secure and economically more attractive than in Russia.

The Poles reacted with a certain economically motivated anti-Semitism,but mostly, they feared the socialistic tendencies among the new arrivals. The new arrivals, in turn, had little interest in the sole objective of the Polish aristocracy, which was to win back its independence. The Second Republic of Poland, the interim period between the World Wars, was a time of economic hardship as well as, from 1935, escalating discrimination against the Jews. Concurrently, this was the period in which the Jews were represented in all walks of public life just short of the highest administrative circles. They were newspaper and book publishers; they ran thousands of Jewish athletic clubs; they held parliamentary office in the Sejm and Senate; they had their own school system; all this testifying to the active political and social life of the Jews in Poland during the 1920's and 1930's.

The Jewish population in 1939 numbered about 3.3 million and was even larger than it had been in 1918 despite immigration to the United States and to Palestine. Some 740,000 Jews considered themselves Poles of Mosaic belief, the remaining numbers considered themselves Jewish in nationality, especially since they spoke Yiddish and had very little command of the Polish language.

JEWS AND POLES

German Occupation

The Polish–Jewish relationship took on a new, macabre dimension with the invasion of Poland by the Germans in 1939. The Jewish population was systematically put to death in the extermination camps specially built for this purpose.

Opportunities for the Poles to help their fellow Jewish countrymen were rare. However, the Council for Aid to Jews (Żegota), a section of the Home Army (the Polish underground organization), was active. This organization found hiding places for Jews, financially supported those in hiding, and carried out death sentences on informers. If a Jew in hiding was betrayed or discovered by the Gestapo, not only were the direct helpers executed, but all residents of the house.

Some 100,000 Jews survived the German atrocities, aided by the Home Army and individuals. Of the 13,618 people awarded the Israeli commendation, "The Righteous Among the Nations," for the rescue of persecuted Jews, there are 4688 Poles – the largest group represented.

Polish people, however, were sometimes also perpetrators, as in the atrocity at Jedwabno in July 1941. The book, "Neighbors: the Destruction of the Jewish Community at Jedwabne, Poland," by Jan Tomasz Gross, published in 2000, records the horrific massacre of 1600 Jews and hascaused a wide-ranging media debate, regarding a new evaluation of the role that Poland played in the events of the Holocaust.

However, in the memory of the Jews the great agony persists, which was caused by the apathy and indifference of the masses – the people on the other side of the ghetto wall who abandoned the Jews to this unspeakable fate. Outside the ghetto wall, there was enough to eat and people led a seemingly normal life. A fair was even held close to the Warsaw ghetto at the time, which in a gruesome way made clear the thin line between life and death (cf. the poem "Campo di Fiori" by Czesław Miłosz).

Survivors after 1945

About 370,000 Polish Jews survived the Nazi occupation, the majority of them in the Soviet Union. Around 200,000 returned to Poland; however, many returned only to then emigrate to other places, especially to Palestine. Those remaining in Poland often became officials or representatives in the newly established state, which was supposed to bring about a better and more just system. The overrepresentation of Jews within the Polish security organizations in the years 1944-1956 can be attributed, without doubt, to the fact that the Jews were the most dependable group of people for the Soviet Union. They had socialist ideals and had had a more extensive schooling in the "home of the world proletariats."

The resulting anti-Semitism exploded on July 4, 1946 in a pogrom in Kielce. A mob murdered more than 40 Jews, as the police and the church looked on passively. It is assumed that this attack was a purposeful provocation by the Soviet security forces. The previous week, the falsified outcome of a referendum legitimized the establishment of the Soviet political model in Poland. This massacre was supposed to ruin Poland's reputation to such an extent that protests from the West against the Soviet takeover of the country would be mild in comparison.

Whatever motives played a role in this incident, the pogrom at Kielce and the ease with which people became murderers has become a nightmare of Polish post-war history. Taboo for decades, the court case, in which some death sentences were imposed shortly after the incident, was hesitantly reopened in 1992.

Right: Many Jews died of typhoid fever and starvation in the confined quarters of the Warsaw ghetto set up by the German army.

JEWS AND POLES

The 1967 Israeli–Arab War (in which the Soviet Union supported the Arabs) and the struggle for power within the Polish politburo led to a malicious campaign against the Zionists. Consequently, the Jews left the country of their own accord or were forced to leave due to constant harassment. The conditions and background of the infamous events of March 1968 have only been partially reappraised. In general, this anti-Semitic (and anti-intellectual) media campaign is seen as a – unsuccessful – attempt of the chauvinistic Minister of the Interior, Mieczysław Moczar, to gain power.

Anti-Semitism without Jews

The Jews left, the anti-Semitism remained. Largely, Judaism and the State of Israel are given positive coverage in the media, leading to counter reactions by the demagogic or extreme right wings of the political spectrum. On the streets, the heritage of prominent politicians – Jewish or not Jewish – is subject of speculation. Sometimes a rule of thumb is visible in this absurd routine. It seems that everyone in Poland who has made something of him or herself, be it of political, financial or intellectual nature, has been a Jew.

Polish anti-Semitism is the result of a – not always pleasant – coexistence of two peoples that was destroyed from outside. Now that there is no longer a significant Jewish population in Poland, verbal anti-Semitism from contemporary arm-chair politicians and the opposite extreme, fascination for the Yiddish culture (which recently seems to be on the rise in student and intellectual circles) are nothing more than the aftershocks of the common legacy of Jews and Poles.

What is left is a feeling of emptiness and the realization that a mutual cultural enrichment has come to an end. The death of Polish-born American author Isaac Bashevis Singer (born 1904 in Radzymin near Warsaw, died 1991 in Florida), who best described the decline of the Jewish-Polish world in his writings, symbolizes the finality of this division.

FOLK ART IN POLAND

Among the earliest examples of Polish folk art are figurines for Christmas mangers, children's toys, wayside shrines, and carved beehives. Polish peasants liked to hang long rows of pictures in their homes, and so the simple but very impressive works of art by folk painters were quite popular. The *verre églomisé* (glass engraved on the back with unfired painting or gold or silver leaf) was widely distributed. This type of artwork was first produced around the end of the 18th century in Silesia and the High Tatra, in the vicinity of the glass factories. Less expensive woodcarvings were an alternative for the peasants who could not afford the more expensive picture paintings.

The colorfully painted dowry chests, displaying the talent of many folk artists, originally sought to imitate the Renaissance furniture belonging to the patricians and royalty. This was also true of the famous silhouette cutters from Łowicz and Kurpie. The elegant paper cuts in the form of birds or flowers served as an alternative to the exorbitantly costly lace being sold.

Wood Sculptures

Polish folk art is at its most unique in its wood sculpture. Adorning innumerable village churches, wayside shrines and crosses throughout the country is the figure of Christ, his bowed head in his hands, his face expressing timeless grief. Polish folk artists have carved this "Suffering Christ" *(Chrystus Frasobliwy)* many times over, as if this so human portrait of God symbolizes their own wearisome lives.

Wood carvers most frequently chose religious themes for their work. In addition to carved figures of Christ, you will find scenes from the Easter and Christmas stories. Angels and devils are also often portrayed, as well as numerous regional saints. The works of art are usually painted in an array of colors. However, in northern Poland and in the region around Zakopane you will discover unpainted or merely stained carvings. The carvers usually use wood from the linden tree. Sometimes poplar, aspen, or willow is chosen but seldom hard woods or stone. Figures carved out of hard coal are typical of the Upper Silesian coal mining area.

It was often the artists' own hardships which they sought to express, e.g. loneliness, isolation, or illness. The folk artist Szczepan Mucha (1908-1983) avoided all contact with the people in his village and surrounded his house with a high fence made out of imaginative figures, which were supposed to protect him from the hostile world.

Painting

Teofil Ociepka (1892-1978), one of the most famous "naive" painters of the country, fought in the Balkans in the First World War. His experiences of war, coupled with a prolific fantasy and readings from cheap novels and pseudo-scientific literature, were transposed by the artist into surrealistic pictures in which he used bright, gaudy colors. He painted incredibly extraordinary animals from a foreign planet as if through them he could flee his Upper Silesian homeland with its dismal everyday life and its all-pervading filth.

The most important non-professional Polish painter is known only by his first name: Nikifor (1895-1968). Examples of his works can be seen in the Ethnographic Museum in Warsaw and in the resort Krynica Górska, where his father was a guest at the health spa and his handicapped Ukranian mother was a waterbearer. Nikifor's name has been associated for decades with the local scene of

Right: Wayside shrines testify to the devoutness and great craftsmanship of Polish woodcarvers.

this Carpathian Mountain health resort. The deaf-mute beggar began painting his aquarelles in old school notebooks of the village children. He intuitively applied the perspective of "importance" as used in icon paintings, i.e. the most important persons are painted larger even when in the background. In his pictures, Nikifor painted himself as an archbishop or a professor at a lectern. He often signed his pictures "Jan Matejko," the name of a historical painter from the 19th century and synonymous in Poland with great painting. From 1959, Nikifor no longer had to beg. At a Paris exhibition, his work was discovered and he was acclaimed one of the greatest naive painters of Europe.

Architecture

The creatively decorated characteristic wooden architecture – churches, inns, granaries and cabins – can be found in Mazovia, in Upper Silesia, around the High Tatra and in eastern Little Poland. Be sure to plan a visit to some of the 30 open-air museums, such as: Sanok (two Orthodox churches); Olsztynek, (excellent collection of folk architecture from East Prussia); Nowy Sącz, (gypsy hamlet); Zubrzyca Górna, (with a manor house built without a chimney, so that smoke had to escape through the windows).

Arts and Crafts

Polish folk art is also colorfully painted Easter eggs and leather goods made by the highlanders (Górales). Handbags, belts and *kierpce* (leather shoes) are all decorated and adorned with brass buckles and clasps. Specialties of northeast Poland (Suwałki) are the woven tapestry and wall hangings decorated with floral and figurative designs, as well as a large selection of pottery. In central Poland, pottery is often ochre or left unglazed. In the south, ceramic goods are tastefully painted, and earthenware from Kashubia is famous for its tulip and arabesque designs coated with a light blue glaze.

POLISH CUISINE

The Poles have always had a hearty appetite and have always liked to eat well. In the year 1364, a contemporary source bravely reported that at a gathering of a number of crowned heads in Cracow, all types of fowl, fish and meats were being served for days on end. Among the sumptuous delicacies were bear claws, beaver tails and elk nostrils. These luxurious treats were then downed with a warm or cold fermented beverage made of water, honey, malt and yeast, called mead. This honey beverage can be enjoyed even today (*miód pitny*).

The Poles are still highly fond of game – for example, roasted hare in a cream sauce, duck served with blueberries or stuffed partridge and pheasant roasted to perfection. These dishes are culinary remnants of the aristocratic cuisine in the 16th and 17th centuries. Polish cuisine today is complemented with the specialties of simple cooking – such as *pierogi*, (a dough pocket similar to a ravioli, filled with meat, cabbage, mushrooms or curd cheese, also called *piroggen*; *naleśniki* (thin pancakes filled with meat or curd cheese), and buckwheat porridge, along with foreign contributions introduced by the countries whose people settled the Polish-Lithuanian monarchy. The final product is a charming blend, as is much of the Polish culture.

The ingredients used to make the small meat ravioli (*kołduny*) put into soup are Lithuanian, and the borscht dishes *(barszcz)* are Ukrainian. Jews, Hungarians, Armenians and Italians brought their own recipes with them when they came to Poland, and these recipes have remained in the country. Many meat dishes with thick sauces and gravies are of German origin. In general, Polish cuisine has a strong similarity to the Southern German – Bohemian cooking tradition – at least before this way of cooking fell victim to the calorie and cholesterol watchers.

Soups

Soups open this chapter on cooking for the simple reason that the Poles are European champions in this field. Not only does Polish soup consumption break world records (78 liters per capita annually); moreover, the Polish people can make soups out of almost anything – literally even out of a nail (*zupa z gwoździa*) or out of nothing (*zupa nic* – milk with egg-whites cooked in a special way)!

Getting back to the more serious types of soup, the many varieties of borscht are not only appealing to the eye but especially to the taste buds. *Barszcz,* which is red beet soup, is often enjoyed as a clear broth, but sometimes *vol-au-vents* (*barszcz z pasztecikiem*) or croquettes with a meat filling (*barszcz z krokietem*) are added. In *barszcz z uszkami* you will find dumplings with meat filling; and in *barszcz ukraiński* lots of red beet greens float in the soup, and it is rounded off with a large spoonful of cream. On Christmas Eve *barszcz z fasolą* is served with green beans. On hot days, *chłodnik* is an excellent sweet cold soup with a base of red beets and sour cream, with ham, egg, cucumber and more added to taste.

To realize the varieties and array of Polish soups, you need just take a quick glance at the following list: cucumber, tomato, sorrel soup (*zupa szczawiowa*); broths and bouillons with meat ravioli (*rosół z kołdunami*), nettle soup (*zupa pokrzywowa*), beer soup (*piwna*), pea soup (*grochówka*), soup made from sauerkraut (*kapuśniak*), mushroom soup (*grzybowa*) and onion soup (*cebulowa*). The proper translation of a few soup names is almost impossible because there is no close equivalent outside of the coun-

Right: Cracow sausages are excellent for roasting over a campfire – a popular way for Poles to have a good time.

POLISH CUISINE

try for some of these liquid specialties, e.g. *żurek,* (a sour flour soup containing bacon and cubed and chopped sausage along with egg) which is absolutely an Upper Silesia favorite. There is also *czernina,* goose blood soup. This soup is served to ward off an unwelcome suitor asking for the hand of the daughter of the house. The suitor should quickly get the idea that any further efforts will be in vain.

The Classics: Flaki and Bigos

It may take a while to get used to *flaki* – tripe served in a fiery hot broth. To reduce the spiciness, you eat flaki with bread. This dish belongs to the omnipresent specialties in Poland, and the honor it deserves as the national specialty is shared with *bigos.* Bigos is distantly related to an Alsatian cabbage dish, *choucroute garnie.* Here we have a stew of sauerkraut and fresh cabbage, which is cooked for hours with different types of meat and sausages.

There are as many recipes for the "true bigos" as there are homemakers in Poland. It is dished up in the most modest of hostels and at hot food stands, but it is also offered at the most elegant restaurants in the country, prepared and served with venison, red wine and porcino mushrooms. As an old game dish, bigos can be warmed up again and again; and according to unanimous opinion, it's even better on the second day.

The Polish Menu

The culinary schedule for the day begins with an opulent breakfast. Hard cheese (*ser żółty,* yellow cheese) and a soft, quark-like, usually homemade cheese (*ser biały,* literally white cheese), eggs, and frequently hot sausages belong to this meal. Families have lunch between 2:00 p.m. and 4:00 p.m. due to school and working hours. Homemade aspic and smoked fish are popular as starters. Until recently, you could marvel at the selection of appetizers behind the glass counter in restaurants: tartar with egg yolk in the center or herring in a cream sauce. But the custom of ordering an appetizer is dying out, and the trend is toward pizzas, nasi goreng and gyros – just as the European mainstream dictates.

Naturally, the next course is soup, and then comes the main dish, which is usually meat (*schabowy,* the Polish version of the Austrian wiener schnitzel, is one of the favorites), with vegetables and potatoes (also noodles or ground meal).

The Poles like to eat fish: trout, pikeperch, perch, eel, tench and carp, a Masurian specialty. Small whitefish (*sielawa*) and, on the Baltic coast, flounder and herring are also favored. A specialty not found in every restaurant is enjoyed in Germany as "carp, Polish style" and in Poland as "carp, Jewish style" (*karp po żydowsku*). This type of carp is often served as a Christmas dish and is prepared with a sweet jelly, almonds and raisins. In late summer, mushrooms are added to the menu. Porcino, chanterelle, butter mushrooms and fried parasol mushrooms (*kanie*) are either dishes in themselves or an excellent side dish. For dessert, you will frequently be offered a stewed fruit, ice-cream, or wonderful cakes, whose recipes originated in the Austrian Empire.

And last but not least, there is the evening meal which is served around 7:00 p.m. This meal is seldom a hot dish and usually consists of a plate of widely assorted cold cuts, not just the world-famous Cracow sausage. Sausages and cold cuts are often a mixture of beef and pork and are frequently spicier than their Western European equivalent.

A Sumptuous Christmas Dinner

The most celebrated meal in Poland is served on Christmas Eve. There are a

Right: Na zdrowie! – a shot of vodka cannot be refused.

number of dishes especially reserved for this particular occasion. You dine with a twelve-course meal at a table traditionally set with an extra plate and silverware for a homeless wanderer, who may unexpectedly ask for entrance to your home. The meal starts out with a wafer (*opłatek*), a very thin, unleavened biscuit, similar to those served at Holy Communion. One after the other, each person breaks off a piece of the other person's wafer and, at the same time, everyone exchanges Christmas wishes.

A soup is then served (often *barszcz z fasolą* or a cepe mushroom soup) followed by a fish dish (for example breaded carp), *pierogi* with sauerkraut and mushrooms, as well as a special kind of *bigos*. Despite the abundance and magnificent display of food, this is a day of fasting and meat-filled bigos are frowned upon. Sweets round off the festive meal. Stewed fruit made of dried fruit, *makiełki* (poppy seed with honey, raisins and figs) or – more of an eastern Polish custom – *kutia* (wheat meal with poppy seeds and raisins), and finally gingerbread, honey bread and poppy seed roll.

Beverages – From Tea to Vodka

Tea (*herbata*) and "coffee Turkish style" (*kawa po turecku*), with the coffee grounds swimming in the cup, are enjoyed everywhere – frequently served in a cup or glass hot enough to burn your fingers. This pitiful circumstance has supposedly motivated many young Poles to emigrate. In the meantime, filtered coffee and standardized serving manners have become established.

With regard to alcoholic beverages, more and more beer is being consumed by the Poles each year. This trend cannot be explained simply by the assumption that more people are switching from vodka to beer, but is attributable to strong competition and a merciless campaign among the large breweries. Polish beer is less bitter than German beer, but is stronger – *Żywiec, Okocim, EB, Tyskie* and *Lech* are the most popular brands.

Wine-drinking culture culture in Poland is still rather undeveloped. Wine, such as the well-known *Sofia*, is nonetheless imported from the former socialistic brother countries of Bulgaria and Hungary. The western brands found in the shops and served often lukewarm in pubs, bars and restaurants are frequently of poor quality and horribly overpriced.

Finally, we come to the inevitable discussions of vodka, simultaneously the joy and the sorrow of the country. Literally, *vodka* means quite innocently "little water" but this beverage is a main source of the country's social problems, not apparent from pure statistics. With an estimated consumption of pure alcohol at 9 liters per person per year (including estimates on alcohol smuggled and self-distilled), Poland ranks well behind Russia and even Germany (12.1 liters) in alcohol consumed. However, because consumption is limited almost entirely to vodka and is consumed quickly and in large quantities, the social consequences are alarming, contributing to the desolate condition of state-owned agricultural concerns. Despite this less pleasant aspect of the drink, the most reputable vodka brands are very good. The clear vodka*s Wyborowa* or *Grasowka* (in Poland *Żubrówka*), with a blade of grass in the bottle, are considered the best. Various companies also produce kosher vodka, which is distilled according to the requirements of the Jewish faith. A liqueur *Jarzębiak*, made from the berries of the mountain ash, is popular.

A perfect souvenir is a bottle of Chopin vodka. It comes in a decorative bottle on which the composer's portrait shines through the glass from the back of the label. It is milder and smoother than other brands. Regardless of the type of vodka you choose or are served, it will come in a small glass of 50 grams, you will toast saying *"na zdrowie"* (to your health), then you take a deep breath and – bottoms up – drink it down in one swallow.

GUIDELINES

METRIC CONVERSION

Metric Unit	US Equivalent
Meter (m)	39.37 in.
Kilometer (km)	0.6241 mi.
Square Meter (sq m)	10.76 sq. ft.
Hectare (ha)	2.471 acres
Square Kilometer (sq km)	0.386 sq. mi.
Kilogram (kg)	2.2 lbs.
Liter (l)	1.05 qt.

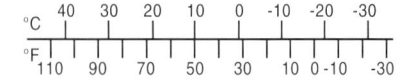

°C 40 30 20 10 0 -10 -20 -30
°F 110 90 70 50 30 10 0 -10 -30

TRAVEL PREPARATIONS

Climate and Best Travel Times

Poland is situated in the transitional zone between the oceanic climate of West Europe and the continental climate of East Europe, causing great weather variations during the year. The weather is nevertheless a bit more stable than in Northern Germany, for example. The winters are relatively mild (seldom under -10°C) with heavy snowfalls restricted to the mountains (great winter sports conditions). An exception to this is Suwałki in the northeastern region of the country, where heavy snow can fall and the temperatures may drop down to -30°C.

A good time to travel is late spring. May is usually sunny and warm. It is almost impossible to forecast the summer weather. One year it can be scorching hot under blue skies, then in the following year, it can be very rainy and relatively cool. You must always be prepared for rain and even heavy thunderstorms. According to travel experts, early fall is the best time to visit Poland. It is not yet foggy and wet, the children are back in school, the days are still mild, and the countryside is enchantingly beautiful with fields and shimmering trees displaying all the colors of the rainbow.

Entry Regulations

Citizens of the United States, EU nations, Japan, and Israel need no visa for visits up to 90 days (UK six months); your passport, which will be stamped on entry, must be valid for at least six months. Citizens of Canada, Australia and New Zealand do need visas.

There are several other nations from which a citizen can visit for up to 30 days or 90 days visa-free; since the rules are so country-specific it is best to check with the nearest Polish consulate. Visa costs vary according to type (single-entry up to 3 months, multiple-entry up to 6 months, transit) age of visitor (reduced for students and children), and the nationality of the applicant. If you need a visa, your passport must be valid for 12 months from date of issuing the visa. A recent ruling (1999) requires visitors to show means of support (approx. $25 for each day you plan to stay).Pets need a inoculation pass with proof of a rabies vaccination given at least 3 weeks in advance of entry but not more than one year old. In addition, you need an official health certificate for the pet from a veterinarian.

Health Precautions

If you wish to spend your vacation in wooded or forested areas (for example, Masuria), a vaccination against tick-born encephalitis is recommended before your departure. For details, contact your physician. It is advisable to take out private travel health insurance coverage.

Information

The **Polish National Tourist Office** offers information through its offices abroad and over the Internet. Serving USA and Canada: 275 Madison Avenue, Suite 1171, New York, NY 10016, Tel (212) 338-9412, Fax (212) 338-9283, www.polandtour.org, pntonyc@poland

GUIDELINES

tour.org. UK address: First Floor, Remo House, 310-312 Regent Street, London W1N 5AJ, Tel. (020) 7580 8811, Fax (020) 7580 8866, pnto.dial.pipex.com, pnto@dia.pipex.com.

Staying Safe

A serious risk of theft is present at train stations and in long-distance trains. The risk of becoming a victim is greatest in the rush of boarding and leaving the train. Automobile theft is not uncommon. In most cases, the driver will be tricked into stopping the car due to faked accidents or breakdowns. The car is then forcibly taken away. On the transit freeway between Wrocław and Görlitz or Cottbus, there have been cases where tires have been damaged without the driver realizing it. A few kilometers down the road, as soon as the tire has just been changed, the thieves jump into the car, drive away, and the owner is left standing with the jack in his hand. Newer automobile models from VW, Audi, Mercedes, and BMW are prime targets.

In general, foreign license plates are attractive to thieves because a foreigner will probably need more time to contact the police. The time factor is an important consideration in thefts because stolen automobiles must be immediately smuggled over the border into the former Soviet states. Having a Polish newspaper visible on the seat of your car can be a good deterrent. A few precautionary measures: Never leave your car unattended overnight in large cities. Never leave valuables (even the radio) or bags in your car. These items could tempt potential thieves. Attended parking is available almost everywhere now.

Customs Regulations

Personal items may be brought into the country in unlimited amounts; however, it is important that goods entering the country are not meant for resale or trade. Gifts should not exceed a value of $100. You are allowed to bring in two cameras, one video camera and an unlimited amount of Western currency. It is not permitted to bring in or take out large sums of Polish currency. The import of weapons is forbidden.

The export of antiques requires permission from the respective office for historical protection and preservation (*wojewódzki konserwator zabytków*). In the European Union you are allowed 1 liter of alcohol and 2 liters of wine, as well as one carton of cigarettes or 250 grams of tobacco duty-free.

ARRIVAL

By Air

Warsaw's airport Warszawa Okęcie is served from several North American airports including New York/Newark, Chicago, and Toronto, and from many European airports including Frankfurt/Main, Berlin, Vienna, Zurich and Geneva. International connections to other Polish airports are increasing. If you fly through Warsaw, you must change terminals for inland connections. A shuttle bus will take you from international flights in Terminal 1 to domestic flights in Terminal 2.

The Polish airline LOT (www.lot.com) maintains offices internationally. For information and flight reservations contact:
USA: Reservation Center in New York, Tel. 1-800-223-0593
500 Fifth Ave., Suite 408, New York, NY 10110, Tel. (212) 869-1704.
6033 West Century Blvd., Suite 1107, Los Angeles, CA 90045, Tel. (310) 645-7690.
CANADA: 1-800-668-5928.
3300 Bloor St. West, Suite 3080, Etobicoke, Ont. M8X 2X3, Tel. (416) 236-02-86 for ticketing.

Other airlines flying into Warsaw include Delta, British Air, British Mid-

GUIDELINES

lands, Lufthansa, Austrian Airlines and Swissair.

By Car

Despite the rumors and horror stories regarding frequent vehicle thefts, millions of tourists drive to Poland each year with their own vehicle (cf page 236). You need a valid home state / national driver's license and vehicle registration, the international driver's license, as well as proof of insurance coverage. There are several border crossings from Germany, the Czech Republic and Slovakia. Passage through the border crossings usually goes quickly, except on important religious holidays and at the start of school vacation. Of course, weekends are busier than weekdays since many Poles drive over the border to Germany, where they have a second home.

By Rail

The fastest train connections between Germany and Warsaw are the Eurocity trains from Berlin. They take approximately 6 hours (twice a day from the station "Zoo"). There is also a Eurocity connection with Vienna (*Südbahnhof*, e.g. South Train Station, 8.5 hours):

From Frankfurt/Main there is a direct connection to Wrocław and Cracow (stopping at Leipzig and Dresden); these Polish cities also have a direct connection from Berlin. In the north there are also three daily trains from Berlin (Lichtenberg) to Gdańsk (ca. 7.5 hours). Information on schedules from German Rail (*Deutsche Bahn*): Tel. 01805-99 66 33.

By Bus

From within Europe, the most inexpensive way to reach Poland is by long-distance buses, which run regularly from many major German cities. Many Poles who live in Germany use these buses for regular visits home. The three most popular routes are Wrocław – Katowice – Cracow, Poznań – Warszawa (sometimes just Bydgoszcz – Toruń) and Szczecin – Gdańsk. The cost one way is approximately $50 (U.S.)

By Ferry

The following ferry connections are maintained by the Polish company "Polferries" (www.polferries.com.pl).

Gdańsk – Nynäshamn (twice weekly; during the peak season: daily); Gdańsk – Oxelösund (once a week); Świnoujście – Malmö (daily.); and Świnoujście – Copenhagen (five days a week). During the months of July and August, there is also a ferry connection from Świnoujście to Bornholm (twice weekly). Representing the Polish Baltic Sea Shipping Company are the travel agencies (in Germany) DARPOL GmbH, Kaiser-Friedrich-Str. 19, D-10585 Berlin, Tel. 0 30/3 42 00 74, Fax 3 42 24 72; and (in Austria) Universal Reisen Ges. mbH, Schubertring 9, A-1015 Vienna, Tel. 01/71 36 34 80, Fax 7 13 34 07.

TRAVELING IN POLAND

By Air

Domestic routes are served by the Polish airlines LOT. There are flights from Warsaw to Poznań, Wrocław, Cracow, Katowice, Rzeszów, Gdańsk and Szczecin, however, there are no plane connections between these latter cities. You can ask for information in the numerous LOT offices (telephone information for the entire country: Tel. 952, 953).

Warsaw, Al. Jerozolimskie 65-79 (in the *Marriott* Hotel), Tel. 022/6305009, 0800-25959; at the airport: 6504220, 6503943, 8461803.

Gdańsk, ul. Wały Jagiellońskie 2/4, Tel. 058/3013666, 3012821.

GUIDELINES

Cracow, ul. Basztowa 15, Tel. 012/4224215, 4117451.
Poznań, ul. Piekary 6 Tel. 061/8529668.
Szczecin, Al. Wyzwolenia 17, Tel. 091/4335058.
Wrocław, ul. Piłsudskiego 36, Tel. 071/3439032.

By Car

In addition to your locally issued (state, etc.) driver's license, it is required to have a proof of insurance card. The road conditions are generally good. Exceptions are the freeways built during the Third Reich (such as at Szczecin), some side roads, and some city streets, where you might want to watch out for potholes (Wrocław seems to be about the worst in this respect). The prescribed speed of 60 km/h inside city limits should be respected – not only because of the many radar controls. Should you be stopped by a police officer, remain friendly and wait to see if you are ticketed (the fine will be expensive) or offered the option of a "lesser" fine. In the latter case, the money will certainly not be used for building and repairing freeways or for the fight against organized car theft. On country roads, the speed limit is 90 km/h, and on highways a speed of 110 km/h is allowed. However, this is a regulation that no one seems to respect. Caution is required: the common driving style is extremely fast and, more often than not, the driving techniques leave much to be desired. Mothers with baby carriages, horse-drawn wagons without lights, and intoxicated persons also use the streets and have to be reckoned with at all times. The number of vehicles in Poland has increased 10-fold within the last years, which means the streets are very crowded (especially in Southern Poland). There are few stretches of expressways, such as Wrocław to the German border and Katowice to Cracow. A network of some 2600 kilometers is in the planning stage, with completion projected for the year 2015. Until then, the average speed on long stretches of road is 60 – 70 km/h. The legal blood alcohol limit is 0.02%. A seat belt regulation is in force; warning triangles must be carried. From October 1 to April 1, dimmed headlights must be turned on. Vehicles in traffic circles, and also all trams, have the right-of-way. A green arrow at traffic lights permits a driver to turn right on a red light (watch for pedestrians!). The police must be notified in case of an accident.

CAR RENTAL AGENCIES:
Warsaw: *Orbis-Hertz*, ul. Nowogrodzka 27 (Tel. 022/6211360, Airport 6502896), *Avis*, Al. Jerozolimskie 65/79 (in *Marriott* Hotel, Tel. 630 73 10, Airport: 6504872) and *Europcar*, ul. Moliera 4/6 (Tel. 8263344, 6248566, Airport: 6504454).
Gdańsk: ul. Heveliusza 22, Tel. 058/3014045.
Cracow: al. Focha 1, Tel. 012/6371120.
Wrocław: Rynek 29, Tel. 071/3433371.
Vehicle Breakdown Assistance: Tel. 981 (PZM) or 954 (Polmozbyt).

By Rail

Trains serve almost every city. They are slow and often overcrowded. Only express trains travel at an average speed of about 90 km/h. Local lines reach the breathtaking speed of 50 km/h (*pociąg osobowy*) Rail schedules are posted in yellow at the railway stations (railway station: *dworzec kolejowy,* main railway station: *dworzec centralny* or. *główny.* You can also purchase a schedule (*rozkład jazdy*). Tickets, very reasonably priced, can be purchased at the counter in the station. Seat reservations are recommended (can be made at the station or at the Orbis offices); we also recommend first class tickets, which cost 50% more. A "Polrailpass" allows unlimited travel (valid for 7, 15, 21, or 31 days; price US$65 to US$110. The junior tariff is

GUIDELINES

available to travelers under the age of 26, upon presentation of passport; this pass is non-transferable, and surcharges are to be paid extra. Baggage checking is available in the train schedules; since insurance is included, the fee is based on the declared value of the luggage checked in.

The Polish State Railway (PKP) maintains a website at www.pkp.com.pl.

Rail schedule information: Tel. 022/ 6200361 (national), 6204512 (international); Reservations: Tel. 365720 (national), 8256600 (international).

By Long Distance Buses

The PKS buses (*Państwowa Komunikacja Samochodowa*) serve most cities and towns in Poland. Express bus schedules are marked red on the departure tables. There are also slower buses serving almost every village in the country. In the mountains and along short stretches, the bus is a better means of transportation than the train.

The bus stations (*dworzec PKS)* are often located next to the train stations. Tickets can be purchased at the counter; or if the bus is just passing through, directly from the driver or conductor. Sometimes on transit buses, you may be unable to board due to overcrowding.

PKS Information: Tel. 022/8236394.

Local Transportation

In every larger city there are buses, trolleys or trolley buses (*trolejbus*). They run from 5.30 am to 11 pm. Tickets (*bilety*) can be purchased at newspaper kiosks (*ruch*). Tickets must be canceled immediately upon boarding. At the time of going to press, a one-way ticket in Warsaw costs about 2 Zł/ US$ 0.40. At night, bus ticket prices double.

The public transportation system in Gdańsk is somewhat complicated since the ticket price depends on the time required to complete the ride. Increasingly popular are the day passes (*bilet jednodniowy*), which are, once validated, good for all types of public transportation. Should you not find them at the kiosks, you can buy them in the ticket office of the local transportation company MZK, Senatorska 37, next to the bank square. In other cities, for example, Cracow, Gdańsk and Wrocław, the day passes are increasingly available at kiosks. You can see in certain areas in Warsaw, which are devastated, as if they had been hit by an earthquake, that the subway is being widely extended (this has been going on with interruptions, since 1926). Line 1 travels from the Palace of Culture southwards (Ursynów to Natolin). The tickets for buses and trains are also valid for the subway.

Taxi

The basic price per kilometer is considerably lower than in western European cities (about 2 Zł/ US$ 0.40). In the evening, as well as on weekends and holidays, a five percent surcharge is added.

The taxi meter will show the correct amount to be paid, as long as it has been turned on. The fare per kilometer often fluctuates; and there are enough opportunists who lie in wait for people not knowing their way around. This "taxi mafia" is mainly active in Warsaw and can often be recognized by their brand new Mercedes or BMW's (cf page 56). At the main station in Gdańsk, there are also such types to watch out for.

The best way to go is to order a radio taxi. These drivers work honestly and usually without extra charge for the pickup service. There are numerous companies, and in every big city *"radiotaxi"* is represented (Tel. 919)

Hitchhiking

Poland was probably the only country in the world in which hitchhiking became an institution. At the PTTK offices, at the *Autostop* Association, at the tourist information or in some youth hostels, you could, for a small fee obtain a "hitchhiker package" that included insurance, but this arrangement has been discontinued since the end of the Iron Curtain days. Hitchhikers today either wave or hold out an upraised thumb as in western Europe and North America. Many drivers like to pick up hitchhikers. Occasionally you may be expected to pay a share of the cost of gasoline.

PRACTICAL TIPS FROM A TO Z

Accommodation

The hotels in Poland range from a rating of four and five star luxury hotels, in which a single room can run from about $100 to $250 U.S., to the cheaper one star hotels, motels (*gościniec* on the national roads), sport hotels (*hotele sportowe*), vacation houses, and workers' resorts that now gratefully welcome all visitors in the competitive struggle to stay in business.

There are also more than 200 youth hostels, most of which are open only in July and August (list of hostels at PTSME, ul. Chocimska 28, 00-791 Warsaw, Tel./Fax 022/8498128), as well as a comparable chain of hostels belonging to the Polish Hiking Club (PTTK: cf "Information," page 236 and related information boxes) .

About 250 camping sites are generally open from June 15 (some even open in May) until the end of September. They are rated in three categories, however, the price per person is in all cases under US$ 10. The sites in category I and the majority of sites in category II are suitable for trailers (electricity hook-ups, etc.). There are also a large number of unattended camping sites (*pola namiotowe*). A list can be obtained at the Polska Federacja Campingu i Caravaningu, ul. Grochowska 331, PL-03-838 Warsaw, Tel./Fax 022/8106050).

It is easy to make reservations for private accommodation through the Orbis office or special accommodation services, and even easier when the rooms offered are posted (*noclegi* oder *pokoje*). Taxi drivers are also a good information source. Orbis offices also help vacationers find summer homes to rent in charming areas throughout Poland.

The Polish hotel rating system is somewhat confusing. In the information boxes in the travel guide, you will find the listed hotels divided into three categories (the prices for a double room are given below):
❸❸❸ above $50
❸❸ about $50
❸ about $25

Addresses: Diplomatic Representation in Poland

USA: (Embassy) Aleje Ujazdowskie 29/31, 00-540 Warsaw, Tel. (22) 628 3041, Tax (22) 628 8298, www.usaemb.pl. (Consulate entrance around the corner) Ulica Piekna 12, Tel. (22) 628 3041, Fax (22) 625 0289, after hours Tel. (22) 625 0055. Consulate in Cracow: ul. Stolarska 9, Tel. (12) 429 6655, Fax (12) 421 8292.
CANADA: (Embassy) Reform Plaza, 10th Floor, Al. Jerozolimskie 123, 02-017 Warsaw, Tel. (22) 629 8051, Fax (22) 629 6457. www.dfait-maeci.gc.ca/dfait/missions/menu-e.asp
UK: (Embassy) Aleje Róz 1, 00-556 Warsaw, Tel. (22) 628 1001-5, Fax (22) 621 7161, www.britishembassy.pl.

Should your passport be lost or stolen, a replacement will be issued. You need two passport pictures and a missing passport report filed at the local police station. U.S. citizens will find the process easier if you have (kept separately!) a copy of your birth certificate or a photocopy of the stolen passport (or, at the least, the passport number).

GUIDELINES

Addresses of Polish Embassies Abroad:

USA: 2640 16th Street, NW, Washington, DC 20009, Tel. (202) 234-3800, Fax (202) 328-6271,
www.polishworld.com/polemb.
CANADA: 443 Daly Avenue, Ottowa, Ontario K1N 6H3, Tel. (613) 789 0468, Fax (613) 789 1218,
www.polonianet.com/eng/embassy.
UK: Ambasada RP, 47 Portland Place, London W1N 4JH, Tel. (0171) 580 43 24, 580 29 69, www.poland-embassy.org.uk.
IRELAND: Ambasada RP, 5, Ailesbury Rd, Dublin 4, Tel. (3531) 2830-855, 2837-562.

Addresses of Polish Consulates:

USA: Consular Section of the Embassy of the Republic of Poland, 2224 Wyoming Ave. NW, Washington, DC 20008, Tel. (202) 232-4517, 232-4528; Consulate General of the Republic of Poland, 233 Madison Avenue, New York, NY, Tel. (212) 889-8360, Fax (212) 779-3062. There are also consulates in Chicago, Los Angeles, New York, Boston, Miami, Honolulu, and San Juan PR. E-mail: polconsul.dc@ioip.com.
CANADA: 1500 Pine Ave. West, Montreal QC H3G 1B4, Tel. (514) 937-9481, Fax (514) 937-7271; 1177 West Hastings Street, Suite 1600, Vancouver BC V6E 2K3, Tel. (604) 688-3530, 688-3537; 2603 Lakeshore Blvd., Toronto N8Z 1G5, Tel. (416) 252-5471.
UK: 73 New Cavendish Street, London W1M 8LS, Tel. (020) 7580 0476, Fax (020) 7323 2320; (*Scotland*): Konsulat RP, 2 Kinnear Rd, Edinburgh E3H 5PE, Tel. (0131) 552-0301.

Biking

Poland can be wonderfully explored by bike (take along a repair kit and spare parts). The narrow tree-lined roads in Masuria are a paradise for bikers. Bikes can be transported by train except in the Eurocity and in several express trains. The bike can be placed in the corridor or on longer rides in the baggage car (sometimes a fee is charged). Take along a good bike lock because bicycles are frequently stolen. Take bikes up into your hotel room or ask at the reception desk for a place to put your bike for safekeeping.

Business Hours

There are no official closing hours in Poland. Every city has at least one store open 24 hours a day. However, store selections can be limited to the bare essentials: bread and vodka.

Usual business hours from Monday through Friday are: grocery stores: 6 am – 7 pm (some are also open on Sundays and late evening), other stores: 11 am – 6 pm (no midday breaks); banks: 8 am – 6 pm; money exchange offices: 9 am – 6 pm, several without midday breaks, for example at the main train station in Warsaw. Official offices and authorities open at 8 am and close at 3 pm. Shortly before closing hour and on Fridays, it may be difficult to take care of official business.

Dangers

The drastically increasing crime rate is one of the biggest problems in Poland since the change in the political system. However, the probability of being personally assaulted is still minimal. The robbery and murder statistics lie far behind those of Western Europe. You should observe certain precautions, though.

If you leave a good hotel in the evening (be it the Novotel in Gdańsk or the Mrongovia in Mragowo) for a walk, it is best to leave your valuables, even handbag, in the hotel safe.

The **police** can be reached countrywide under the telephone number: 997

GUIDELINES

Electricity

Electricity in Poland operates with 220 volts AC/H2. Visitors from North America may consider bringing small dual-voltage appliances such as travel irons and hair dryers with adaptor plugs. Use of 110 or 115-volt appliances without transformers poses a risk of blowout and fire.

Emergency Telephone Numbers

Police: 997
Fire Department: 998
Ambulance: 999
Vehicle Breakdown Assistance: 981

Entertainment

Many operas and theater performances, especially the musical variety, can be enjoyed even by those who do not understand the language (The opera "Halka," by Moniuszko, in Warsaw is a must), (Teatr Dramatyczny Warszawa, Teatr Muzyczny Gdynia, Operetka Wrocławska).

The cinemas show films almost always in their original version with Polish subtitles – a nice alternative for a free evening or rainy afternoon. Warsaw offers the monthly English *Warsaw Insider*, which gives a good rundown on all cultural programs.

Large hotels have discos and bars, many of which once served more or less as places to meet prostitutes. Since the women have moved to the *agencje towarzyskie*, the atmosphere has improved. There are casinos, e.g. in the Marriott Hotel in Warsaw or in the Grand Hotel in Sopot.

If you are looking for a normal disco, ask a student or teenager. In Warsaw there are *Remont, Park, Stodoła, Hybrydy*; in Cracow *Pod Jaszczurami, Karlik* and *Forum*; in Gdańsk *Rudy Kot*; and in Posnan *Eskulap* and *Blue Note*. The Warsaw jazz club *Akwarium* (ul. Emilii Plater 49, Tel. 6205072) offers entertainment for more discriminating tastes.

Fishing and Hunting

A fishing license valid for 7, 14 or 21 days for a certain fishing area can be obtained at the nearest fisheries office (*Państwowe Gospodarstwo Rybne*) or at the nearest police station (two-week license: approx. $13 U.S.). They can be most easily obtained from the Polish Fisheries Organization (PZW), ul. Twarda 42, PL-00-105 Warsaw, Tel. 022/6205196, 6208966; sometimes also from local travel agencies.

Holidays

The Catholic holidays (Christmas, Easter Monday, Corpus Christi, Ascension Day, and All Saints Day) are legal holidays. November 11 (Independence Day 1918) and May 3 (Constitution Day 1791) are also legal holidays.

Information

In all larger cities there are now tourist information offices which are often designated "IT" (*Informacja Turystyczna*, see Guideposts). These offices differ greatly among themselves in the quality of information available, the degree of desire to inform, and the ability to speak foreign languages. Tourist information can also be obtained at the Orbis Offices, the reception desk of good hotels and the Office of the Polish Hiking Association (PTTK), which usually has good information material (Main office in Warsaw: ul. Świętokrzyska 36, Tel. 6208244).

Before departure, you can obtain information at the Polish Tourist Information Office (cf Travel Preparations, page 236). The Internet websites printed in this section are also good sources(cf page 236).

GUIDELINES

Maps

The days are thankfully over when you could only obtain a street map of Gdańsk in Cracow, and of Cracow only in Gdańsk. Every bookstore has a wide selection of reasonably priced city and regional maps (large scale), as well as maps of the National Parks and hiking trails.

A wide selection of maps of Poland is available through Omni Resources; catalog available from 1004 South Melbane St., P.O. Box 2096, Burlington NC 27216 USA, Tel. (336) 227-8300, also online at www.omnimap.com. For genealogical research, maps showing the old German place names can be useful; these are easily available in Poland.

Money Exchange / Currency

The Polish currency is the Złoty (literally guilder or florin) which is made up of 100 Groszy. The conversion rate for US dollars is $1 = 4.2 Zł. Since the financial reform of 1990, the Złoty can be freely converted. You can exchange cash at private exchange offices all over the country. At the border and in finer hotels you will receive a slightly less advantageous exchange rate. Never exchange money on the street! As long as the Złoty is stable, these people whispering "change money" can only be cons, who will leave you with worthless slips of paper or counterfeit bills. Old bills with a million Złoty value (as in circulation before 1995) are no longer accepted in the shops and department stores but can be exchanged at Polish banks until the year 2002.

The currency exchange offices (*Kantor*) will exchange travelers' checks but it is better to go to a bank. Cash machines are still relatively rare. Finer hotels, restaurants and shops (also gas stations) will accept credit cards (mainly American Express, VISA, EuroCard/MasterCard). Foreign currencies can be imported and exported in unlimited amounts. If the sum imported exceeds 5000 US$, filling out a currency declaration is mandatory. You will have to present this at departure; undeclared cash can be confiscated.

Photography

You can usually take pictures of locals without any problems. However, the more picturesque someone is, the less likely he or she will agree to have a picture taken. The question "*Czy mogę zrobić zdjęcie?* (May I take your picture?) will prevent misunderstandings.

Western brands of film can be purchased everywhere. However, always check the expiration date, especially in souvenir shops. The prices for film can be fairly expensive. Film for slides can only be purchased in larger cities. Less common battery types should be brought with you.

Physicians and Pharmacies

In emergencies, you will be treated in a hospital. The treatment is to be paid in cash. However, the catastrophically overburdened Polish clinics are no source of pleasure. We strongly recommend taking out a travelers' health insurance policy that will reimburse you for expenses incurred while traveling in Poland.

You can purchase medication in the state-owned and private pharmacies (*apteka*; 8 am to 7 pm). In all larger cities, there is at least one emergency pharmacy open twenty-four hours (information in the daily newspapers and signs posted at all pharmacies).

Emergency assistance is available in all of Poland by dialing: 999.

Post Offices / Telephone

Post offices are generally open from Monday to Friday 8 am to 7 pm. Some offices are open all night (Warsaw: ul.

GUIDELINES

Świętokrzyska, Cracow: ul. Wielopole, Wrocław: main train station). Stamps can be purchased at the post offices or at the larger hotels. A postcard within the EU costs 1 Złoty, a letter within the EU 1.40 Złoty. Your mail should arrive home within a week.

Although trying to telephone was a nightmare up until recently, it is no longer a problem to call in or out of Poland. To call the USA and Canada dial 00 1 before the area code; the U.K. 00 44, Ireland 00353, Australia 00 61, New Zealand 00 64, South Africa 00 27, Japan 00 81.

The country code for calling into Poland is 48, preceded by the international access code. Phone calls placed from hotel rooms are expensive. It is recommended to use the new blue card telephones. Telephone cards can be purchased at the post offices and sometimes at kiosks and hotel reception desks (*karta telefoniczna*) for 50 or 100 units. Important: Tear off perforated corner before use!

Restaurants

Poles go to dinner earlier than many other Europeans and many restaurants close as early as 10 pm.

There are a number of fast food restaurants – from McDonalds to small stands, where you can purchase hot dogs or *Zapiekanki* (bread with cheese and mushrooms). Popular among student travelers and backpackers, and increasingly for the less well-to-do (and subsidized by the government) are the *Bary Mleczne* (milk bars) that sell tasty traditional specialties but also vegetarian dishes. The milk bars in Warsaw next to the university and near the Barbican now cater to the young traveler with English menus.

Restrooms

The Polish Minister of the Interior, Sławoj-Składkowski, had outhouses erected in the villages long before the war. They are still popularly known as *sławojki,* named after the minister. In the meantime, capitalism has celebrated its greatest success in this field – the scent of coconut is prevalent and the lavatory attendant pleasantly smiles at each guest. To help ward off the unemployment problems, the employment of lavatory "grandmothers" (*babcia klozetowa*) has been maintained. They request a usage fee (usually 0.5 Zł), and this charge applies even when you are a guest using the restrooms in a restaurant.

Just a short translation of the restrooms' secretive symbols. The small circle stands for "Women," the triangle stands for "Men." An explanation of these signs is nowhere to be found; moreover, the triangle sometimes points down and sometimes up. In some places, you may find the less ambiguous terms of *Damski* and *Męski.*

Shopping

The most popular gifts and souvenirs are items of Polish folk art. Such items can be purchased in the state-owned *Cepelia* shops. The best shop is located in Warsaw in the Old Town at the Market Square (*Dom Sztuki Ludowej*, Rynek Starego Miasta 10). You can purchase works of art – woodcarvings, glass paintings, printed textiles, pillow lace, carpets, tapestry and national costumes – sometimes directly from renowned artists.

In Gdańsk you can purchase the traditional amber jewelry. The best places to do so are the small shops on ul. Mariacka. You can frequently find interesting antiques at the various flea markets (*pchli targ;* in Gdańsk *Targ Dominikański*, only in August) or at the *Desa shops.*

The antique boom, however, is over. Antiques have become very expensive and are not of the best quality. Many items, especially those from the former Soviet Union (samovars, icons, etc.), are

GUIDELINES

imitations. In any case, the export of items made before 1945 is prohibited without a permit according to Polish law (cf Custom Regulations, page 237).

On the other hand, the large selection of high-quality modern art is a treasure trove. Books (art volumes in English and German), music cassettes, and CDs (from Chopin to the famous Polish jazz of Urbaniak or Namysłowski) are nice souvenirs. Among foodstuffs, good choices are the great tasting *krówki* (a hard candy with a cow on it; different flavors), chocolate-coated plums (*śliwki w czekoladzie*), sesame crackers (*sezamki*), and the "Chopin vodka."

Tourists from outside Poland can request reimbursement of the value added tax paid when purchasing goods.

Sports

Water sports enthusiasts – canoeing and sailing – are at the right spot in the lake region of Northern Poland. All tourist towns have rental offices for sports equipment. Sailing over the 70 kilometer-long stretch of connected lakes in the Masurian Lakelands between Węgorzew in the north and Ruciane or Pisz to the south is inviting. Before starting out on your boat tour, it is a good idea to purchase a quality map to avoid shallow water and hidden rocks. The idyllic weather conditions can be deceiving, especially on the Śniardwy, where sudden weather changes and high waves can be treacherous. There are interesting canoe routes in Masuria, Suwałki (Czarna Hańcza), and in Pomerania (for example, along the rivers Parsęta or Brda). For exact route suggestions, contact the office of the Polish Canoe Association (*Polski Związek Kajakowy*), e.g. at ul. Księcia Józefa 24, 30-205 Cracow, Tel./Fax 012/4271081.

Winter sports take place primarily in the south, even though Gołdap on the Russian border has a ski lift and slope with artificial snow and Olsztyn is the center of cross-country skiing. The best spots to ski are in the High and West Tatra (Zakopane), in Szczyrk south of Upper Silesia or in the Giant Mountains (Szklarska Poręba / Karpacz).

Horseback riding is well organized in Poland, and there are numerous stables that organize vacations on horseback. Information can be obtained at the Warsaw Tourist Information Center (cf page 236). For detailed information, contact the Polish Riding Association (*Polski Związek Jeździecki*), ul. Cegłowska 68/70, PL-01-809 Warsaw, Tel. 022/8347321, 8342683, Fax 834 52 28. There are two stables connected to the two largest hotels in Masuria (*Mrongovia* in Mrągowo and *Gołębiewski* in Mikołajki) that offer the vacationer horseback and carriage rides. The following towns are also recommended: Biały Bór, Kadyny, Łobez, Racot, Sieraków Wielkopolski, and Czerniejewo (bei Gniezno), where you can stay in a stylish castle as well.

Supplementary Reading

Ash, Timothy Garton: The Polish Revolution. Solidarity 1980-1982. London 1983. Davies, Norman: God's Playground: a History of Poland. Oxford 1981 and New York 1982.

Grass, Günter: The Tin Drum. 1959. Available from various publishers.

Singer, Isaac Bashevis: A Day of Pleasure – Stories of a Boy Growing Up in Warsaw. 1969. Available from various publishers.

LANGUAGE GUIDE

English has now replaced Russian as the most prevalent foreign language. German is understood in many regions (especially Silesia and Masuria). But it is important to know a few words in Polish.

The West Slavic language is not easy. It is closely related to the Slovakian and Czech languages and has seven cases.

GUIDELINES

When sentences, such as *chrząszcz brzmi w trzcinie w Szczebrzeszynie strząsając ze skrzydeł źdźbła* (a tongue twister for foreigners about a noisy little bug) can be shocking, the pronunciation follows strict rules and the majority of the seemingly unusual sibilants do occur in other languages, with other spellings.

Some pronunciation rules: all Polish vowels are pronounced short and open. The consonants sz = sh (shoe), cz = ch (champion), szcz = shch (fresh cheese), ż and rz = like the s in *measure* or the j in the French *bonjour*), dz = ds (voiced), dż = j (as in *jungle*) etc. A diacritical mark above the consonant changes or softens it, so that ń = the gn sound in *cognac* and *España*, ć = tsh. The often encountered Ł (*Łódź, Wałęsa*) is like the w in *what* or *water*. Ó is close to long u, or the oo in *food*. The nasal sound (ą, ę) is also heard in French, for example, in *teint, vin* (ę) or in *bon, Caen* (ą).

In Polish, the stressed syllable is just about always the second-last syllable.

General Terms

Yes. . . . . *tak*
No . . . . *nie*
Thank you . . . . *dziękuje bardzo*
Please . . . . *proszę*
Good morning . . . . *dzień dobry*
Good evening . . . . . . *dobry wieczór*
Goodbye . . . . *do widzenia*
Good night . . . . *dobranoc*
Hi or bye . . . . *cześć*
How are you? . . . . *Jak się Panu* (m)/ *Pani* (f) *powodzi?*
Fine, ok. . . . . *dobrze*
I don't want.... . . . . *Nie chcę.*
I don't understand. . . . *Nie rozumiem.*
Please repeat it. . . . . *Proszę powtórzy*
What does it mean? . . . *Co to znaczy?*
again . . . . *jeszcze raz*
How do you say ... in Polish?
. . . . . *Jak się nazywa po polsku ... ?*
Mr. / Mrs., Ms or Miss . . . *Pan / Pani*
I am (an) American (man / woman). . .
. . *Jestem Amerykaninem / Amerykanką*

I, you, ... *ja, ty*
he, she, we. . . . . *, on, ona, my*
Entrance / Exit . . . . *wejście / wyjście*
Open . . . . *otwarte*
Closed . . . . *zamknięte*
Prohibited . . *wzbronione / zabronione*
free / occupied . . . . . *wolny / zajęty*
Caution! . . . . *Uwaga!*
End. . . . . *koniec*

Terms of Time
Hour . . . . *godzina*
Today . . . . *dzisiaj*
Yesterday. . . . . *wczoraj*
Tomorrow . . . . *jutro*
Week . . . . *tydzień*
Month. . . . . *miesiąc*
Year . . . . *rok*

Question words
who, what . . . . *kto, co*
where, where (to), where (from)
. . . . *gdzie, dokąd, skąd*
how, how much . . . . *jak, ile*
when, why . . . . *kiedy, dlaczego*

On the go
Airplane . . . . *samolot*
Airport . . . . *lotnisko*
Train . . . . *pociąg*
Long distance train station
. . . . *dworzec kolejowy*
Bus . . . . *autobus*
(bus) stop . . . . *przystanek*
Car . . . . *samochód*
Taxi . . . . *taksówka*
(attended) Parking . *(strzeżony) parking*
Ticket. . . . . *bilet*
Normal, reduced . . *normalny, ulgowy*
First/second class . . . .
. . . . *pierwsza / druga klasa*
Reserved seat. . . . . *miejscówka*
Couchette car . . . . *kuszetka*
Luggage storage
. . . . *przechowalnia bagażu*
Departure . . . . *odjazd*
Arrival . . . . *przyjazd*
Where is the tourist information? . . .
. . . *Gdzie jest informacja turystyczna?*
How do I get to ...? . *Jak dojadę do ...?*

247

GUIDELINES

Museum . . . . *muzeum*
Exhibit . . . . *wystawa*
Castle / Fortress . . . . . *zamek / pałac*
Church . . . . *kościół*
Street / Square . . . . *ulica / plac*
Beach . . . . *plaża*
Border . . . . *granica*
Post office . . . . *poczta*
Stamp for America
. . . . *znaczek do Ameryki*
Letter . . . . *list*

Accommodation
Hotel . . . . *hotel*
Youth hostel . . . . *schronisko młodzieżowe*
Mountain hut . . . . *schronisko górskie*
Do you have a room available? . . . . .
. . . *Czy ma Pan / Pani wolne pokoje?*
I would like... . . . . *Chciałbym* (m) ... / *Chciałabym* (f) ...
Single-/double room . . . . *pokój jednoosobowy / dwuosobowy*
with / without a bathroom . *z łazienką / bez łazienki*
May I see the room? . . . .
. . . . . . *Czy mogę zobaczyć pokój?*
Shower . . . . *prysznic*
Restroom . . . . *toaleta, WC*
(pronounced Voo Say)
How much does it cost (the room per night)? . . . .
. . . *Ile kosztuje (pokój na jedną dobę)?*
Inexpensive . . . . *tanio*
Expensive . . . . *drogo*
The check / bill please! . . . . *Proszę o rachunek!*
Tent . . . . *namiot*
Key . . . . *klucz*

Food and Beverages
Eat . . . . *jeść*
Drink . . . . *pić*
Breakfast . . . . *śniadanie*
Lunch . . . . *obiad*
Dinner . . . . *kolacja*
The check / bill please! . . . . . *Proszę o rachunek.*
Appetizer . . . . *przekąska*
Main course . . . . *drugie danie*
Dessert . . . . *deser*
Soup . . . . *zupa*
Ice cream . . . . *lody*
Beverages . . . . *napoje*
Water . . . . *woda*
Coffee / Tea . . . . . . *kawa / herbata*
Wine (white, red) *wino (białe, czerwone)*
Beer . . . . *piwo*
Shop . . . . *sklep*
Restaurant . . . . *restauracja*
Cheers! . . . . *Na zdrowie!*

Money
Where is a bank (money exchange?) . .
. . . . *Gdzie jest bank (kantor)?*
I would like to exchange money . . . . .
. . . . *Chciałbym* (m) / *Chciałabym* (f) *wymienić pieniądze.*
Do you accept credit cards? . . . .
Czy honorowane są karty kredytowe?
What is the exchange rate?
. . . . *Jaki jest kurs wymiany?*

In Emergencies
I feel ill . . . . *źle się czuję.*
I need a doctor . . . . *Potrzebuję lekarza.*
Please help me! . . . *Proszę mi pomóc!*
May I use the telephone?
. . . . *Czy mogę skorzystać z telefonu?*
Dentist . . . . *dentysta*
Hospital . . . . *szpital*
Where is the pharmacy? . . . *Gdzie jest apteka?*
Medicine . . . . *lekarstwo*
We had an accident .. . . *Mieliśmy wypadek.*
My car has been broken into / has been stolen
. . . . *Mój samochód został okradziony / ukradziony.*
I've been robbed . . . . . *Zostałem okradziony* (m) / *zostałam okradziona.* (f)
Thief . . . . *złodziej*
Please call the police . . . . . . *Proszę wezwać policję.*
American / Canadian Embassy . . . . .
ambasada Amerykańska, Kanadyjska

AUTHOR

Tomasz Torbus was born in 1961. He studied art history and cultural anthropology in Warsaw and Hamburg, where he received his PhD. in 1998 with a thesis on the Castles of the Teutonic Order. As an art historian, he has focused much of his research on Eastern/Central Europe. In addition, he is a study tour guide and freelance author in Poland and Germany.

Note of Thanks

The author kindly thanks Ms. Dörte Muß-Gorazd, who carefully read the manuscript, and Mr. Janusz Tycner, who contributed the chapter "Poland After the Change of Power" (pages 30 - 33).

PHOTOGRAPHERS

Archiv für Kunst und Geschichte, Berlin   12, 18, 23, 25, 26, 29, 38, 40, 60, 92/93, 229
Bauer, Rudolf (Silvestris)   125
East News (transparent)   31, 32
Fischer, Berndt (Silvestris)   17, 80, 220
Galikowski, Elisabeth   44, 94, 96, 100, 104, 105, 106, 118/119, 209, 224/225, 233
Hackenberg, Rainer   53, 54, 55, 188, 194, 200, 205, 207, 235
Häusler, Nicole (Archiv Häusler)   19, 168, 184/185, 192
Irsch, Wilhelm (Silvestris)   129
Janicke, Volkmar E.   71, 72, 87, 88, 131
Joerissen, Heinz   39, 226
Korall, Wolfgang (Silvestris)   163, 166, 167, 204, 206
Legler, Peter (Silvestris)   cover
Müller, Kai Ulrich   10/11, 49, 51, 111, 113, 130
Pollmann, Bernhard (Montanus)   150
Probst, Manfred   33, 98, 101, 107
Quaukies, Claudia   63, 165, 175
Reinhard, Hans (Tierbildarchiv Angermayer)   15, 89
Schmidt, Rudolf (Tierbildarchiv Angermayer)   14
Scholten, Jo   134/135, 141, 145, 151
Stankiewicz, Thomas   8/9, 16, 36, 66/67, 68, 74, 75, 136, 143, 147, 148, 156/157, 162, 164, 169, 173, 178, 180, 186, 193, 195, 198/199, 210, 211
Tierbildarchiv Angermayer   212
Torbus, Tomasz   21, 30, 35, 37, 41, 42/43, 58, 62, 64, 84, 85, 86, 99, 103, 110, 114, 124, 142, 158, 170, 174, 177, 190, 191, 214, 219, 231
Wengel, Tassilo (Montanus)   120, 126
Ziesler, Günter (Tierbildarchiv Angermayer)   78/79, 217.

INDEX

A

Amber 166, 173
Śnieżka, Mountain 16, 137
Anjou Dynasty 20
Anna, Mountain 151
Antonin 75
Arkadia 62
Asam, Cosmas Damian 38, 146
August II (the Strong) 22
Augustów 214
Augustów Canal 215
Auschwitz 111, 226
 Birkenau 111, 112
 Main Camp 111
Świdnica, Mountain 127

B

Balcerowicz, Leszek 30, 32
Baranów Sandomierski 37, 84
Batory, Stefan 22
Bellotto, Bernardo (Canaletto) 39, 41, 50
Bernini, Gian Lorenzo 144
Berrecci, Bartolommeo 36, 106
Białowieski National Park 219
Białystok 216
 Cathedral of the Assumption of the Virgin Mary 216
 Orthodox church 216
 Palace of the Branicki Family 216
 St. Nicholas' Church 216
 St. Roch's Church 216
Biebrza National Park 215
Biebrza River 215
Bieszczady 131
Bieszczadzki National Park 132
Biskupin 34
 Lusatian Culture Settlement 34
Black Madonna of Częstochowa 22, 114, 115
Błędowska Pustynia 113
Bobolice 113
Bohoniki 218
Bolesław I Chrobry (the Brave) 19
Bolesław II Śmiały (the Bold) 108
Bolesław III Krzywousty (Wry-Mouthed) 19, 61, 189
Brama Morawska 16
Brzeg 146
Buzek, Jerzy, President 19
Bydgoszcz 75

C

Casimir the Great (see Kaszimierz III Wielki) 19
Catherine the Great 22, 190
Chełmno 177
 City Hall 178
 City Wall 177
 St. Mary's Church 177
Chełmno nad Nerem 63
Chmielnicki, Bohdan 22, 227
Chochołów 125
Chochołowska Valley 127
Chopin, Frédéric 24, 52
Chorzów 152
Communism 28
Conrad, Joseph 13, 122, 169
Copernicus, Nicholas 39, 103, 176, 179, 202
Cracow 20, 24, 34, 35, 36, 38, 95
 Barbican 102
 Center of Jewish Culture 108
 Church of St. Peter & St. Paul 104
 Church of the Holy Cross 102
 Cloth Hall 99
 Collegium Maius 103
 Coronation Cathedral 105
 Dominican Church 103
 Dragon's cave 105
 Florian Gate 102
 Franciscan Church 104
 Isaac Synagogue 108
 Jagiellonian University 103
 Jama Michalikowa 102
 Kazimierz 107, 110
 Kolekcja Czartoryskich 102
 Main Market Square 98
 Mickiewicz Monument 102
 National Museum 102
 Old Synagogue 108
 Old Town 98
 Planty 98, 103
 Remuh Synagogue 108
 Royal Castle 106
 Shrine of St. Stanislaus 105
 Sigismund Chapel 106
 St. Adalbert's Church 101
 St. Andrew's Church 34, 104
 St. Anne's Church 103
 St. Mary's Church 100
 Szołayski House 102
 Town Hall Tower 102
 ul. Floriańska 102
 ul. Kanonicza 105
 ul. Szeroka 108
 Wawel 105, 106, 107
Cracow Gorge 112

Cracow-Częstochowa Jura 16, 105, 112
Curie, Marie 13, 51
Częstochowa 22, 114
 Chapel of the Birth of Mary 115
 Jasna Góra (Bright Mountain) 115
 Knight's Hall 115
 Monastery Church 115
Czarna Hańcza 214, 215
Czarny Staw 128
Czartoryska, Izabella 74, 102
Czerwony Wierchy (Tatra) 127
Czorsztyn, Castle 128

D

Dębno 124
Darłowo 194
 St. Gertrude's Chapel 194
Dientzenhofer, Kilian Ignaz 38, 146
Drogosze 206
Dunajec Gorge 129
Dürer, Hans 34, 106
Duszniki Zdrój 147
Dzierżyński, Feliks 216

E

Elbląg 142
 City Gate 176
 St. Mary's Church of the Dominican Order 176
 St. Nicholas' Church 176
Elbląg Canal 176

F

Fischer von Erlach, Johann Bernhard 144
Frombork 36, 176

G

Galicia 24, 121, 122
Gameren, Tilman van 38, 51, 54, 62, 103, 216
Gąsawa 76
Gąsiennicowa Valley 128
Gdańsk 25, 29, 34, 36, 159, 161
 Artus Court 163
 Bread Gate 164
 Crane Gate 164
 Foregate 163
 Golden Gate 163
 Golden House 164
 Great Arsenal 162

250

INDEX

Great Mill 161
Green Gate 164
Long Market 163
Long Street 163
Main Town 162
Maritime Museum 165
Market Halls 162
Memorial to the Shipyard Workers 167
National Museum 167
Old Town 161
Oliwa monastery 167
Oliwa Monastery 34
Post Office 165
Sopot 168
St. Bridget's Church 161
St. Catherine's Church 161
St. Mary's Church 165
St. Mary's Gate 164, 165
St. Mary's Church 36, 166
St. Nicholas' Church 162
Targ Węglowy 162
Uphagen House 163
Upland Gate 163
Westerplatte 26, 161, 165
Gdynia 168
Gerlach Peak (High Tatra) 125
Giant Mountains (see Karkonosze) 149
Gierek, Edward 28, 152
Giewont, Mountain 126, 127
Giżycko 211
Gniezno 19, 75
Cathedral 75
Golub Dobrzyń 178
Gołuchów 74, 75
Gomułka, Władysław 28
Góra Świętej Anny 151
Górale 123
Gorbachev, Mikhail 29
Góry Stołowe, Mountains 147
Góry Świętokrzyskie 16, 81, 82
Gothic brick architecture 35
Grabarka 218, 219
Great Poland 20, 25, 69, 73
Great Poland National Park 69, 73

H

Hasior, Władysław 41
Hevelius, Johannes 161
High Tatra Mountains 121, 123, 124, 125, 230
Hitler-Stalin pact 26, 122, 216
Holy Cross Mountains 16

I

Isserles, Rabbi Moses (Remuh) 108, 227

J

Jadwiga, Queen 20, 103
Jagiellonian Dynasty 20, 37, 96, 104, 106, 205
Jan III Sobieski 18, 22, 55, 107
Jaruzelski, Wojciech 29
Jaszczurówka 125
Jedwabne 228
Jelenia Góra 149
John Paul II, Pope 13, 18, 103, 122

K

Kamień Pomorski 193
Kampinowski National Park 59
Karkonosze Mountains 14, 16, 149
Karpacz 149
Kartuzy 169
Kashubia 169, 170, 231
Kasprowy Wierch, Mountain, West Tatra 127
Katowice 138, 152
Katyń 27
Kazimierz Dolny 84
Górski House 85
House of Bartłomiej Celej 85
Przybyło Houses 85
White House 85
Kazimierz III Wielki 19, 20, 35, 105, 107, 112, 227
Kętrzyn 206
Kielce 81, 228
Cracow Bishops' Palace 81
Pogrom 228
Kinski, Klaus 168
Kłodzko 146
Kościeliska Valley 127
Kościuszko, Tadeusz 23
Kołbacz 191
Kołobrzeg 193
Kórnik 73
Krasicki, Ignacy 206
Krasiczyn 37, 131
Kruszyniany 218
Krutyń 211
Krynica Morska 175
Krzeszów 38, 148
Krzyżne Pass (Tatra) 128
Krzyżtopór Castle 37, 83
Książ 148

Kudowa Zdrój 147
Kujawy 75, 76
Kwidzyn 176

L

Lake Śniardwy 210
Lake Bełdany 209
Lake Czajce 192
Lake Czos 209
Lake Górecki 73
Lake Hańcza 213
Lake Kisajno 211
Lake Kociołek 73
Lake Mamry 211
Lake Mamry 213
Lake Miedwie 191
Lake Mikołajskie 209
Lake Morskie Oko 128
Lake Nidzkie 211
Lake Niegocin 211
Lake Łeba 195
Lake Łuknajno 210
Lake Paniewo 215
Lake Wdzydze 170
Lake Wigry 213
Łańcut
castle 130
Museum of Interior Design 130
Synagogue 130
Lassalle, Ferdinand 144
Łeba 187, 193, 195
Legnickie Pole 38, 146
Lem, Stanisław 13, 95
Lesko 132
Liczyrzepa, Mountain Spirit, see Rubezahl 149
Lidzbark Warmiński 36, 205
Lipsk 215
Little Poland 20, 83, 121, 122
Łódź 59, 62, 64
Jewish Cemetery 63
Kindermann Family Villa 64
Museum of Modern Art 64
Palace of the Herbst Family 64
Poznański Factory 64
ul. Piotrkowska 64
Łokietek Cave 112
Łowicz 61
Lublin 85
Café Pod Czarcią Łapą 88
Castle 86
Cathedral 87
Cracow Gate 87
Dominican Church 87
Holy Trinity Chapel 86
Majdanek Concentration Camp 88

251

INDEX

Market Square 87
Old Town 87
Luxemburg, Rosa 90

M

Małopolska 69, 121
Malbork 34, 36, 159, 170, 172, 174
  Front Castle 172
  Golden Gate 173
  Grand Master's Palace 172, 173
  High Castle 173
  High Castle 170
  Middle Castle 172
  St. Anna's Chapel 174
Mała Kopa 149, 151
Marienburg (see also **Malbork**) 170
Masuria 25, 201, 208
Masurian Lakelands 209
Matejko, Jan 39, 100
May Constitution 23
Mazovia 59, 60
Mazowiecki, Tadeusz 30
Międzyzdroje 191
Michałowicz, Jan 37, 72
Michałowski, Piotr 40, 100
Mickiewicz, Adam 24, 101, 106
Mieszko I 19, 69, 72
Mikołajki 208, 209
Mining 152
Miłosz, Czesław 13, 228
Mirów 113
Mosina 73
Mrągowo 209
Mrożek, Sławomir 13, 95
Mt. Śnieżka 149
Mucha, Szczpan 230

N

Narew National Park 217
NATO (Polish membership) 13, 33
Nazis 26, 88, 90, 175, 228
Nieborów 61
Niedzica Castle 128
Nikifor 230
Nordic War, First 22
Nowy Świat 53
Nowy Sącz 123, 231
Nowy Targ 123

O

Ociepka, Teofil 230
Łańcut 130

Ogrodzieniec 113
Ojców 112
Ojców Valley 112
Olsztyn 201, 202
  Castle of the Warmia Chapter 202
  High Gate 201
  St. James' Church 201
  Town Hall Market 202
Olsztyn Castle 113
Opatów 34, 82
Opole 138, 151
  Cathedral of the Holy Cross 151
  City Hall 151
  Franciscan Church 151
  open-air museum 151
Osowa Góra 73
Ostrów Wielkopolski 75
Oświęcim (Auschwitz) 111
  Brzezinka (Birkenau) 111

P

Partition of Poland, First 22, 23, 121
Partition of Poland, Second 23, 69, 159
Partition of Poland, Third 23, 96
Pięciu Stawów Polskich Valley 128
Piast Dynasty 19, 146, 151
Pieniny Mountains 128, 129
Pieniny National Park 129
  Dunajec Gorge 129
Pieskowa Skała 113
Piłsudski, Józef 25, 106
Podhale 123, 124
Płock 60
  Cathedral 60
  Mazovian Museum 60
Polański, Roman 63
Polish United Workers' Party (PZPR) 28
Pomorze Zachodnie (Pomerania) 187
Poniatowski, Józef 39
Poniatowski, Stanisław August 22, 38, 54
Popielno 210
Popiełuszko, Jerzy 162
Pöppelmann, Matthäus Daniel 52
Poster Art 41
Poznań 19, 69, 70, 71, 72
  Adam Mickiewicz University 71
  Cathedral 72
  Historical Museum 71
  Monument to the Victims of June 1956 72
  National Museum 71
  Old Town Square 70
  Palace of Culture 71
  Parish Church 71
  Raczyński Library 71
  Town Hall 70
  Ulica św. Marcina 71
  Wielkopolska National Park 73
Prussia 20, 23, 69, 163, 172, 177, 202, 208
Przemyśl 130, 131
Pszczyna 152
Puszczykowo 73

R

Radzyń Chełmiński 178
Reszel 208
Reymont, Władysław 64
Rogalin 74
Roztoczański National Park 90
Rubezahl 149
Rubinstein, Arthur 63
Ruciane-Nida 210
Rydzyna 75
Rysy, Mountain 16, 126, 128

S

Sandomierz 83
  Benedictine convent 83
  Cathedral 83
  Opatów Gate 83
  St James' Church 83
  Town Hall 83
  Wine and Grain Cellars 84
Sanok 132, 231
Schindler, Oskar 108
Schinkel, Karl Friedrich 39, 73, 75, 212
Schlüter the Younger, Andreas 34, 51
Schultz, Bruno 122
Sienkiewicz, Henryk 22, 50, 172
Silesia 35, 137, 140, 145, 147
Singer, Isaac Bashevis 88, 229
Slovincians 196
Słowacki, Juliusz 24, 106
Słowiński National Park 196
Słupsk 194
  Castle Church 195
  Pomeranian Dukes' Castle 195
  St. Mary's Church 195
  Witches' Tower 195
Solidarność (Solidarity) 13, 29, 30, 161, 167
St. Adalbert 75

INDEX

St. Hedwig 145
St. Stanislaus 105, 108
Stargard Szczeciński 191
  Mill Gate 191
  St. Mary's Church 191
Stauffenberg, Claus, Count Schenk von 207
Stave Church from Vang, Norway 150
Stębark 205
Stegny 175
Stęszew 73
Stoss, Veit 34, 36, 75, 96, 101, 105
Strążyska Valley 126
Strzelno 34, 76
  Church of the Holy Trinity 76
  St. Procopius' Church 76
Supraśl 217
Suwałki 213, 231
Świdnica 147
  Trinity Peace Church 147
Święta Katarzyna 82
Święty Krzyż 82
Święta Lipka
  Pilgrimage Church 207
Święta Lipka 207
Świnoujście 193
Szczecin 188, 189
  Berlin Gate 188
  Castle of the Pomeranian Dukes 190
  King's Gate 189
  Old City Hall 191
  Seven Cloaks' Tower 190
  St. James' Church 191
  St. Peter and St. Paul's Church 189
  Wały Chrobrego 189
Szklarska Poręba 149, 151
Sztutowo 175
Sztynort 212
Szymborska, Wisława 13, 95

T

Tarnowskie Góry 152
Tatars 218
Tatra - see High Tatra Mountains 121
Tczew 170
Telemann, Georg Philipp 152
Teutonic Knights 20, 159, 177
Thorvaldsen, Bertel 39, 52, 105
Toruń 36, 149, 172, 178
  City Hall 179
  Copernicus Monument 179
  House of the Star 179

Leaning Tower 180
Market Square 179
St. James Church 180
St. John's Church 180
St. Mary's Church 179
Teutonic Knights' Castle 180
Treaty of Versailles 24
Trzebnica 35, 145
Trzy Korony, Mountain 129
Tykocin 217

U

Ujazd 83
Uznam Island 191

V

Vang Stave Church 150
Vistula Delta 174

W

Wajda, Andrzej 13, 64
Wałbrzych 148
  Książ 148
  St. Stanislaausand St.Wenzel's Church 147
Wałęsa, Lech 13, 30, 31
Wang, see Vang 150
Warmia 25, 176, 201, 202, 205
Warsaw 24, 27, 39, 41, 45, 47
  Academy of Fine Arts 52
  Aleje Ujazdowskie 53
  Barbican 50
  Birthplace of Marie Curie (Maria Skłodowska) 51
  Castle Square 49
  Center of Modern Art 53
  Chopin Monument 54
  Church of the Nuns of the Holy Sacrament 51
  Church of the Nuns of the Visitation 52
  Column of Zygmunt III Waza 49
  Equestrian Statue of Prince Poniatowski 52
  Historical Museum of Warsaw 50
  Holy Cross Church 52
  Jewish Cemetery 49
  Jewish Historical Institute 48
  Krakowskie Przedmieście 51
  Krasiński Palace 51
  Łazienki Park 54
  MDM district 48
  Monument to Adam Mickiewicz 52

Monument to Copernicus 52
Monument to the Heroes of the Ghetto 49
Monument to the Warsaw Uprising 51
National Museum 53
New Town 51
New Town Square 51
Nowy Świat 53
Nożyk Synagogue 48
Old Orangery 55
Old Town 49
Old Town Hall 53
Old Town Market 50
Open Air Theater 54
Opera House 52
Palace of Culture and Science 48
Palace upon the Water 54
Plac Konstytucji 48
Plac Trzech Krzyży 53
Poster Museum 55
Radziwiłł Palace 52
Royal Castle 49
Royal Way 51
Saxon Gardens 52
St. Anne's Church 52
St. John's Cathedral 50
Staszic Palace 52
Tomb of the Unknown Soldier 52
Ujazdowski Castle 53
ul. Marszałkowska 48
Umschlagplatz Monument 49
University 52
White Cottage 54
White House 53
Wilanów Palace 55
Warsaw uprising 47
Warsaw Uprising 27
Wasa style 38
Wdzydze Kiszewskie 170
West Tatra 125, 127
Wieliczka 110
Wielkopolska 69
Wierzchowska Górna Cave 113
Wigierski National Park 213
Wigry Peninsula 214
Wilczy Szaniec 207
Witkiewicz, Stanisław Ignacy 125, 195
Wizna 215
Władysław II Jagiełło 20, 86, 103, 104, 105
Władysław II Łokietek 20, 96, 112
Wojnowo 206
Wolf's Lair (Wilczy Szaniec) 207

253

INDEX

Woliński National Park 191, 192
Wolin Island 187, 191
Wooden Mosques 218
World War I 24
World War II 26, 27, 161
Wrocław 34, 35, 137, 138, 139, 140, 142
  Aula Leopoldina 143
  Battle of Racławice (Painting) 143
  Cathedral Island 144
  Cathedral of John the Baptist 144
  City Hall 141
  Hala Ludowa 145
  Holy Cross Church 35, 144
  Jesuit Church 143
  Jewish Cemetery 144
  Market Hall 143
  Market Square 141
  National Museum 144
  St. Elizabeth's Church 142
  St. Mary Magdalene Church 34, 142
  St. Mary on the Sand, Church 35
  St. Mary on the Sand, church of 144
  St. Vincent's Church 143
  University 143
Wyspiański, Stanisław 40

Z

Zakopane 123, 124, 125
  Krupówki Boulevard 124
  Tatra Museum 124
  Władysław Hasior Art Gallery 124
Zamenhof, Ludwik 49, 216
Zamość 88
  Armenian Merchants' Houses 89
  Collegiate Church 90
  Market Square 89
  Orthodox Uniate Church 90
  Synagogue 90
  Town Hall 89
Zawrat, Mountain 126
Żelazowa Wola 60
  Birthplace of Frédéric Chopin 60
Ziemia Chełmińska 177
Żnin 76
Żuławy Wiślane 174
Zygmunt II August 20, 21, 38, 107, 163, 214
Zygmunt III Waza 22, 47, 49, 96

Explore the World

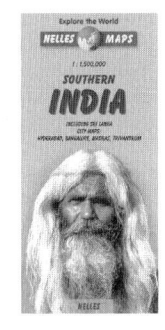

NELLES MAPS

AVAILABLE TITLES

Afghanistan 1 : 1 500 000
Argentina *(Northern),* **Uruguay**
 1 : 2 500 000
Argentina *(Southern),* **Uruguay**
 1 : 2 500 000
Australia 1 : 4 000 000
Bangkok - *and Greater Bangkok*
 1 : 75 000 / 1 : 15 000
Bolivia - **Paraguay** 1 : 2 500 000
Burma → *Myanmar*
Caribbean - **Bermuda, Bahamas, Greater Antilles** 1 : 2 500 000
Caribbean - **Lesser Antilles**
 1 : 2 500 000
Central America 1 : 1 750 000
Central Asia 1 : 1 750 000
Chile 1 : 2 500 000
China - *Northeastern*
 1 : 1 500 000
China - *Northern* 1 : 1 500 000
China - *Central* 1 : 1 500 000
China - *Southern* 1 : 1 500 000
Colombia - **Ecuador** 1 : 2 500 000
Crete - Kreta 1 : 200 000
Cuba 1 : 775 000
Dominican Republic - **Haiti**
 1 : 600 000
Egypt 1 : 2 500 000 / 1 : 750 000
Hawaiian Islands
 1 : 330 000 / 1 : 125 000

Hawaiian Islands – **Kauaʻi**
 1 : 150 000 / 1 : 35 000
Hawaiian Islands – **Honolulu**
 - Oʻahu 1 : 35 000 / 1 : 150 000
Hawaiian Islands – **Maui - Molokaʻi**
 - Lānaʻi 1 : 150 000 / 1 : 35 000
Hawaiian Islands – **Hawaiʻi, The Big Island** 1 : 330 000 / 1 : 125 000
Himalaya 1 : 1 500 000
Hong Kong 1 : 22 500
Indian Subcontinent 1 : 4 000 000
India - *Northern* 1 : 1 500 000
India - *Western* 1 : 1 500 000
India - *Eastern* 1 : 1 500 000
India - *Southern* 1 : 1 500 000
India - *Northeastern -* **Bangladesh**
 1 : 1 500 000
Indonesia 1 : 4 000 000
Indonesia **Sumatra** 1 : 1 500 000
Indonesia **Java - Nusa Tenggara**
 1 : 1 500 000
Indonesia **Bali - Lombok**
 1 : 180 000
Indonesia **Kalimantan**
 1 : 1 500 000
Indonesia **Java - Bali** 1 : 650 000
Indonesia **Sulawesi** 1 : 1 500 000
Indonesia **Irian Jaya - Maluku**
 1 : 1 500 000
Jakarta 1 : 22 500
Japan 1 : 1 500 000
Kenya 1 : 1 100 000

Korea 1 : 1 500 000
Malaysia 1 : 1 500 000
West Malaysia 1 : 650 000
Manila 1 : 17 500
Mexico 1 : 2 500 000
Myanmar (Burma) 1 : 1 500 000
Nepal 1 : 500 000 / 1 : 1 500 000
Nepal Trekking **Khumbu Himal - Solu Khumbu** 1 : 75 000
New Zealand 1 : 1 250 000
Pakistan 1 : 1 500 000
Peru - **Ecuador** 1 : 2 500 000
Philippines 1 : 1 500 000
Singapore 1 : 22 500
Southeast Asia 1 : 4 000 000
South Pacific Islands 1 : 13 000 000
Sri Lanka 1 : 450 000
Taiwan 1 : 400 000
Tanzania - Rwanda, Burundi
 1 : 1 500 000
Thailand 1 : 1 500 000
Uganda 1 : 700 000
Venezuela - Guyana, Suriname,
 French Guiana 1 : 2 500 000
Vietnam - Laos - Cambodia
 1 : 1 500 000

IN PREPARATION

South America - The Andes
 1 : 4 500 000

Nelles Maps are top quality cartography!
Relief mapping, kilometer charts and tourist attractions.
Always up-to-date!

Explore the World

NELLES GUIDES

AVAILABLE TITLES

Australia
Bali / Lombok
Berlin and Potsdam
Brazil
Brittany
Burma → Myanmar
California
  Las Vegas, Reno,
  Baja California
Cambodia / Laos
Canada
  Ontario, Québec,
  Atlantic Provinces
Canada
  Pacific Coast, the Rockies,
  Prairie Provinces, and
  the Territories
Canary Islands
Caribbean
  The Greater Antilles,
  Bermuda, Bahamas
Caribbean
  The Lesser Antilles
China – Hong Kong
Corsica
Costa Rica
Crete
Croatia – Adriatic Coast
Cyprus
Egypt
Florida

Greece – The Mainland -
  Peloponnese
Greek Islands
Hawai'i
Hungary
India
  Northern, Northeastern
  and Central India
India – Southern India
Indonesia
  Sumatra, Java, Bali,
  Lombok, Sulawesi
Ireland
Israel - West Bank,
  Excursions to Jordan
Kenya
London, England and
  Wales
Malaysia - Singapore
  - Brunei
Maldives
Mexico
Morocco
Moscow / St. Petersburg
Munich
  Excursions to Castles,
  Lakes & Mountains
Myanmar (Burma)
Nepal
New York – City and State
New Zealand
Norway
Paris

Peru
Philippines
Poland
Portugal
Prague / Czech Republic
Provence
Rome
Scotland
South Africa
South Pacific Islands
Spain – Pyrenees, Atlantic
  Coast, Central Spain
Spain
  Mediterranean Coast,
  Southern Spain,
  Balearic Islands
Sri Lanka
Sweden
Syria – Lebanon
Tanzania
Thailand
Turkey
Tuscany
U.S.A.
  The East, Midwest and South
U.S.A.
  The West, Rockies and Texas
Vietnam

Nelles Guides – authoritative, informed and informative.
Always up-to-date, extensively illustrated, and with first-rate relief maps.
256 pages, approx. 150 color photos, approx. 25 maps.